V

Edited by:

Mike Davis, Fred Pfeil, and Michael Sprinker

Verso

THE YEAR LEFT

An American Socialist Yearbook
1985

Verso is the imprint of **New Left Books**

The Year Left is an annual publication.

British Library Cataloguing in Publication Data

The Year left: an American socialist year book.
 1985–
 1. Socialism—United States
 335'.00973   HX86

 ISBN 0–86091–114–4
 ISBN 0–86091–821–1 Pbk

Verso
15 Greek Street, London W1
Distributed in North America by Schocken Books, 62 Cooper Square, New York, NY 10003

Editorial correspondence should be directed to:

The Year Left
c/o English Department
SUNY–Stony Brook
Stony Brook, NY 11794

Contents

Statement of Purpose

Arguably the single most important and disastrous political event in the Americas during the year just past has been the solidification of national support for U.S. President Ronald Reagan which culminated in his massive electoral victory in November 1984. In the wake of this triumph, and of the concomitant defeat of an imploding, rightward-drifting Democratic Party and its tepid 'back-to-basics' strategy (so ominously similar to that adopted by the British Labour Party at the last national elections — with equally catastrophic results), it seems imperative to rethink and redirect the organizational and electoral possibilities among progressive forces in America. We are launching this first installment of *The Year Left: An American Socialist Yearbook* with a sense of the overriding and immediate necessity for new analyses by and for the American left — analyses and initiatives shaped by the specificity of the historical moment which North America has now definitively entered. That moment, in our view, contains significant opportunities for political renewal on the left (along with the more obvious danger of revanchism from the right), but only if the left is truly determined to 'see its way clear.'

A word at the outset about the purview of the term 'American' in our subtitle. We believe that a genuinely strategic discussion of socialism in the U.S. must henceforward be increasingly and self-consciously pan-American in scope and inspiration; that the next phase of political growth among the Marxist left in the U.S. will only be possible through a combined development of new levels of solidarity and interdependence with the Canadian, Mexican, and Caribbean lefts. The current revolutionary crisis in Central America (addressed in a preliminary way in Section II of this issue, though open in future issues to more extended discussion) underlines the urgency of adopting such an orientation without exhausting its possible contexts and dimensions. Thus, we aim to make this and future volumes of *The Year Left* genuinely 'North American' in both a geographical and a conceptual sense, by assuring that its contributors and contents address both the specific differences characteristic of politics, economy, and culture in Canada, the U.S., Mexico, and the countries of Central America and the Caribbean Basin individually, and their present and future integration within this latest, American-led phase of multinational capitalism.

That said, we frankly admit that in this first volume we have focused significant attention on the 1984 U.S. elections. Since the new turn in American politics and economy during the 1970s seems for the moment to have reached a kind of symptomatic terminus with the advent of Reaganism, and since, as a Salvadoran once said to one of us, 'Your President is our President, too,' any attempt to understand where the North American left might be headed must necessarily begin with sober, in-depth reflection on the causes and possible outcomes of the most recent electoral triumph of a revived, militant right in the U.S. At the same time, we wish to urge the continuing importance to left strategy of both longer-range historical problems and issues that may seem less immediately political, at least in the narrow sense of the term. Consequently, we have included a group of essays on culture and ideology and one review essay on recent historiography of the CPUSA; both sections are to become regular, ongoing features of *The Year Left*. The purpose of the former is to develop and maintain an informed political perspective on the specific conjunctural relationships between socially constructed modes of consciousness and the forms of cultural production which they project, from 'postmodernism' (high and low) and the 'professional-managerial class' in the U.S., to the place and function of culture and ideology in the political space opened up by the revolutionary movements in Central America. The review section offers extended consideration of significant recent work in historiography, political science, and economics, emphasizing the importance to current left thinking and strategy of scholarly work in these disciplines, and providing a reasoned valuation of its general intellectual contribution from the perspective of historical materialism.

Future numbers of *The Year Left* are currently planned; some pieces have already been commissioned, while other essays and topics are yet to be assigned. Readers are encouraged to submit proposals for topics, essays, and replies to pieces published in the yearbook. The editors are eager to stimulate debate among the broadest possible constituency on the left, and therefore welcome any and all suggestions for future volumes of the yearbook. Among the topics we ourselves have projected, the following seem of particular moment:

— the new political economy of U.S. imperialism
— the contemporary working class(es)
— the functional specificities of white racism, and the political articulations and disarticulations among racial minorities
— the history of American Marxism
— ideological apparatuses in American societies
— relationships and conflicts between American feminism(s) and Marxism(s)
— components of the national culture(s)
— the political system of U.S. capitalism
— the present state of American socialism

We encourage our readers to submit completed essays as well as prospectuses for pieces in all of these areas. Our aim is to promote non-sectarian dialogue among the different strata and segments of the U.S. left, as well as to achieve a measure of integration between political movements in the U.S. and throughout the Americas. Our hope is that such dialogue will lead ultimately to new, mass-based political alignments and organizations whose programs combine the best aspects of existing socialist parties and groups with innovative strategies for the medium range future. We are convinced, most of all, that the present moment in the history of American capitalism demands a combination of sober self-criticism and loyal solidarity among American leftists. In this spirit, we have launched *The Year Left* on what we hope will be a long and successful career within a fully American socialist movement.

SECTION ONE

Right Turn: The 1984 U.S. Elections

1. Race and Realignment in American Politics

Manning Marable

I

The reelection of President Ronald Reagan in 1984 was not a watershed in American electoral history, but it did accelerate deep trends in popular political culture which could produce an authoritarian social order in the very near future. This is an examination of various political currents and social blocs competing for power within the bourgeois state apparatus. Although there is a brief overview of the political dynamics of the Democratic Party primaries, the emergence of the Rainbow Coalition of Jesse Jackson, and the general election, my principal concern here is to examine the increased racial polarization within elements of both the American left and right as part of a broader process of electoral political realignment of the party system. Most Marxists seriously underestimate the presence of racism as an ideological and social factor of major significance in the shape of both American conservative and liberal centrist politics; in the pursuit of U.S. foreign policies, particularly in the Caribbean and Africa; and as an impediment in developing a mass left alternative to the Democratic and Republican parties. Although class prefigures all social relations, the burden of race is a powerful and omnipresent element that has helped to dictate the directions of contemporary politics.

An explicitly racist aspect of the Reagan agenda manifested itself domestically and internationally. Black workers suffered disproportionately from both unemployment and social service reductions. In 1983, for example, 19.8 percent of all white men and 16.7 percent of white women were unemployed at some point; for Blacks, the figures were 32.2 percent for men, and 26.1 percent for women workers.[1] Between 1980 and 1983, the median Black family income dropped 5.3 percent; an additional 1.3 million Blacks became poor, and nearly 36 percent of all Afro-

1

Americans lived in poverty in 1983, the highest rate since 1966.[2] The Reagan Adminstration slashed aid to historically Black universities and reduced student loans, forcing thousands of Black youth out of schools.[3] The U.S. Commission on Civil Rights and Office of Federal Contracts Compliance Programs were transformed into bulwarks for racial and sexual discrimination. In its foreign affairs, the Reagan administration authorized a policy of 'constructive engagement' with apartheid South Africa. In 1981, Reagan asked Congress to repeal the Clark amendment prohibiting covert military aid to Angolan terrorists; authorized the U.S. training of South Africa's Coast Guard; and vetoed a UN Security Council resolution condemning South Africa's illegal invasion of Angola. In 1982, the Reagan administration rescinded controls on 'non-lethal' exports to apartheid's military and police; voted for a $1.1 billion loan from the International Monetary Fund to South Africa; sent 2,500 electric shock batons to the South African police; and appointed a pro-apartheid U.S. executive, Herman Nickel, ambassador to Pretoria. The next year, the administration established offices in downtown Johannesburg to promote accelerated U.S. investment in the regime, and granted a license for U.S. firms to service South Africa's Koeberg nuclear power plant.[4] By 1984, about 6,350 U.S. corporations held direct subsidiaries or did some form of business inside the racist regime. U.S. firms supplied 15 percent of the state's imports, and absorbed 8 percent of its exports, amounting to $4 billion.[5]

Given the unambiguously racist, sexist, and anti-labor character of the Reagan offensive, oppositional social movements were inevitable. In September 1981, the AFL-CIO broke with tradition to stage a massive 'Solidarity' march against the administration. On 12 June 1982, over one million Americans demonstrated in favor of a freeze on the production and deployment of nuclear weapons. Black middle-class formations such as the NAACP and Operation PUSH, combined with Black nationalist, left and peace forces, held a March on Washington, DC on 27 August 1983, bringing more than 300,000 demonstrators to the capital. Unfortunately, the Democratic Party was ill prepared to accommodate the new militancy of women, national minorities and trade unionists, and that for several reasons. For nearly half a century, the Democrats had controlled Congress, a majority of state legislatures, and most major municipal governments. Unlike the Republicans, the Democratic

Party consciously had attempted to bring together a broad spectrum of social forces and classes – trade unions, small farmers, national minorities, eastern financial and industrial capitalists, Southern whites, the unemployed. It was a capitalist party, in that its governing ideology of Keynesian economics and Cold War liberalism benefited sectors of the ruling class. But in the absence of a mass labor or social democratic party, it also functioned as a vehicle for minorities' and workers' interests to be represented, if in a limited manner. This governing coalition was first seriously weakened by democratic social movements of Afro-Americans in the late 1950s and 1960s, which forced the destruction of legal segregation and increased the number of Black elected officials from 100 in 1964, to over 5,000 in 1980. The Black freedom movement combined with the anti-Vietnam war movement to contribute to the defection from the party of millions of Southern segregationists and conservatives. By the late 1960s, a political backlash against social reforms developed among many white ethnic, blue collar workers, who had long been Democrats. Although the economic recession of 1973-75 and the Watergate scandal temporarily set back the Republicans and contributed to Carter's narrow electoral victory in 1976, the general trend among whites to the right in national political culture continued. This was most evident in an analysis of the racial polarization in presidential elections between 1952 and 1976. During this period, the average level of electoral support for Democratic presidential candidates among Blacks was 83.4 percent, vs. 43.7 percent among white voters. The results in 1980 were even more striking: 85 percent of all Blacks and 59 percent of Hispanics voted for Carter, while only 36 percent of all white voters supported his reelection. Not since 1948 had a majority of white Americans voted for a Democratic presidential candidate.[6]

The defections of major electoral groups from the Democrats had reduced the party to four overlapping social blocs. The first tendency, which was clearly subordinated within the coalition, was the democratic left: Afro-Americans, Latinos (except Cuban-Americans), feminists, peace activists, liberal trade unionists, environmentalists, welfare rights and low income groups, and ideological liberals. In national electoral politics, they were best represented by the Congressional Black Caucus, and a small group of white liberals in the House and Senate. To their right was the rump of the old New Deal coalition, the liberal centrists: the AFL-CIO, white ethnics in urban machines, some consumer goods industrialists and liberal investment bankers, Jewish organizations. This tendency's chief representative in national politics was Minnesota Senator and former Vice President Hubert Humphrey. Following Humphrey's death in 1977, his protégé, Walter Mondale, assumed leadership of this bloc. A third tendency, which exhibited the most independent posture toward partisan politics, was comprised of what some have called the 'professional managerial class' and sectors of the white, salaried middle income strata. These white 'neoliberals' tended to oppose U.S. militarism abroad and large defense expenditures. But on economic policies, they tended toward fiscal conservatism and a reduction of social welfare programs. They were critical of nuclear power, and favored federal regulations to protect the environment; but they also opposed 'special interests' such as organized labor. This constituency was behind the unsuccessful presidential campaigns of Morris Udall in 1976, and John Anderson in 1980. Its principal spokesman in the 1984 Democratic primaries was Colorado Senator Gary Hart, who as early as 1973 had proclaimed that 'American liberalism was near bankruptcy.'[7] At the extreme right of the party were those moderate-to-conservative Southern Democrats who had not yet defected from the party, and a smaller number of Midwestern and 'Sunbelt' governors and legislators who had ties to small regional capitalists, energy interests, and middle income white constituencies. The most prominent stars of this tendency in the 1970s were Carter, Florida governor Reuben Askew, millionaire Texas Senator Lloyd Bentsen, and Ohio Senator John Glenn. All of these groups, in varying degrees, opposed the general agenda of the Reagan administration. But only the democratic left, and most specifically the Afro-American community, mounted a sustained series of social protests against literally every initiative of the Republican president.

In the Democratic presidential primaries of 1984, each of these tendencies was represented by one or more candidates. Conservative Democrats Glenn, Askew, and former segregationist Ernest Hollings, currently Senator from South Carolina, were in the race; the 'yuppies' and white neoliberals gravitated to Hart; Mondale drew the early endorsement of the AFL-CIO, and most of the party apparatus. Three candidates split the forces of the democratic left. California Senator Alan Cranston, a strong advocate of the peace movement, received support from many

freeze candidates and western liberals. Former Senator George
McGovern drew backing from traditional liberals, some
feminists and peace activists. The Reverend Jesse Jackson,
president of Operation PUSH and the central political leader
within the Black community, was the last candidate to
announce. The Jackson and Hart campaigns were far more significant than the others, including Mondale's. Jackson's decision
to run was made against the advice of most of the Black petit
bourgeois leadership, the NAACP and the Urban League, who
had already committed themselves to Mondale. Even the
Coalition of Black Trade Unionists, which on economic matters
was a good deal to the left of the NAACP elite, supported
Mondale. The Jackson campaign's core constituency, which was
absolutely vital to its subsequent success, was the Black Church.
Nearly 90 percent of the Afro-American clergy had endorsed
Jackson by the end of 1983. Church leaders and members were
active in every aspect of the campaign, from distributing
literature to bringing Black voters to the polls. The failure of most
civil rights leaders and Black elected officials to get involved in
the early stages of the effort permitted several thousand Black
nationalists, Marxists, peace activists, and feminists to gain
positions in local and statewide campaign mobilizations. Thus
Jackson, who previously had been an advocate of 'Black
Capitalism' and had a history of political opportunism, was
influenced by his campaign workers, aides and policy advisers
to articulate an essentially 'left social democratic' program. By
mid-spring, the Jackson campaign's foreign and domestic policy
positions were clearly to the left of any Democratic candidate for
national office in U.S. history. Jackson called for a 20 to 25
percent reduction in the defense budget; a bilateral nuclear
weapons freeze, with billions of dollars reallocated from defense
programs to human needs; the normalization of U.S. relations
with Cuba, and an end to American armed intervention in
Central America, the Mideast and the Caribbean. Despite
limited funds and the absence of virtually any television
advertising, Jackson received 19 percent of all total Democratic
primary votes, about 80 percent of all Afro-Americans' votes. He
won primary victories in the District of Columbia, Louisiana,
South Carolina, Mississippi and Virginia. Most significantly,
Jackson forced the national Democratic leaders to recognize the
centrality of the Black electorate within the party. The dynamic

race by Jackson motivated hundreds of thousands among the nation's poor and minorities to register and to participate in the political process.[8]

Jackson's success among Afro-American voters denied Mondale approximately 15 to 17 percent of the total Democratic primary votes.[9] Hart was thereby enabled to maintain a credible campaign against Mondale as well. The Colorado Democrat received 36 percent of the national Democratic vote, winning victories in New England, Florida, California, Ohio and Indiana. But unlike Jackson, who attempted to create a multiracial, progressive coalition on the left, Hart ran simultaneously on the left and right against Mondale. On foreign affairs, Hart was more critical of U.S. military intervention in Central America than Mondale. But on domestic economic matters, Hart had previously opposed the federal loan program to the nearly-bankrupt Chrysler corporation on fiscal grounds; he supported a 'cost-effective' nuclear arsenal and annual increases of 4 to 5 percent in military expenditures. Pointedly condemning Mondale as the 'candidate of special interests,' Hart implied that he would not be subject to the mandates of organized labor. Although he did not receive his party's presidential nomination, Hart's critique was extremely effective, and it established the basis for the Reagan-Bush attack on Mondale during the general election.[10]

On balance, Mondale should have been denied the Democratic nomination in 1984. Despite the endorsements of more than 107 Senators and Representatives, the AFL-CIO, and the vast majority of Democratic mayors, the Minnesota centrist received only 38.7 percent of the national primary votes. He received 45 percent of the labor union members' votes, 31 percent from Democratic college graduates, and only 28 percent of all Democratic voters between 18 and 34 years old.[11] But Mondale had several distinct advantages over Jackson and Hart. By the end of May, Mondale had received over $18 million in campaign contributions, vs. $9 million for Hart and $1.7 million for Jackson. Such spending ratios were roughly similar to the final percentage of delegates each candidate received at the Democratic National Convention in San Francisco: Mondale, 56.8 percent; Hart 31.1 percent; and Jackson, 12.1 percent. A large bloc of convention delegates were directly selected by the party apparatus, virtually guaranteeing Mondale's nomination. In many states, the selection of convention delegates had little to do with the actual primary vote. For example, in Pennsylvania's primary, Jackson received 17 percent of the statewide popular vote to Mondale's 45 percent. On the convention floor, however, Mondale received 117 delegate votes to Jackson's 18.[12] As a 'minority' candidate, Mondale should have recognized that he had to make credible, programatic overtures to both Hart and Jackson's constituencies in order to build an electoral coalition to defeat the incumbent president. But throughout the long primary season, Mondale learned nothing new. Mondale delegates were in no mood to compromise. Jackson minority platform proposals calling for major reductions in defense expenditures and for placing the party 'on record as unconditionally opposed to any first use of nuclear weapons' were soundly defeated. The selection of Congresswoman Geraldine Ferraro as the ticket's vice presidential running mate was a positive concession to the women's movement, although Ferraro's politics were only slightly more progressive than Mondale's, if at all. In general, Afro-Americans and the liberal-left supporters of Jackson left the convention without receiving even token concessions, beyond the appearance of their candidate on prime-time television for one evening. The only real factor that would later motivate these forces to support Mondale in the general election was the real fear of the ignorant demagogue in the White House.

Given Mondale's forensic ineptitude and dull demeanor, the Republican strategy was all too easy. First, the administration defended Reagan's aggressive foreign policies, including the destabilization of Nicaragua and the illegal invasion of Grenada, while making new overtures to the Soviet Union for a resumption of arms negotiations. The administration pressured the Federal Reserve System to ease the amount of currency in circulation, which helped to extend the economic recovery through the election. The 1983-1984 recovery also permitted the President falsely to claim his program of tax cuts and deregulation for corporations as the key to prosperity. More than in any previous administration, Reaganites followed the lead of Ayn Rand: they wore the name ' "Capitalism" printed on (their) foreheads boldly, as a badge of nobility.'[13] On domestic social programs, the President hinted at even deeper budget reductions ahead, but solemnly vowed never to diminish Social Security benefits to the elderly, a major voting bloc. Like Hart, Reagan rhetorically projected himself 'as a candidate of all the people, and Walter Mondale as the weak puppet of "interest groups" and "special interests" '. As the 'special interests' accused of manipulating

Mondale included women, trade unionists, Blacks, Hispanics, gays, and environmentalists — that is, seventy to eighty percent of the population — this is a rather peculiar accusation, and its success demonstrates the extent to which political life has been degraded by right-wing populism. Mondale repeatedly defended himself against such rhetoric, but 'too often it was as if no one was listening.'[14]

In retrospect, it almost seems that the Democrats deliberately threw the election to Reagan. Two basic themes which could have united nearly all of the factions inside the Democratic Party were social 'fairness' and 'peace.' The overwhelming majority of white low-to-middle income families had not been touched by the 1983-84 economic recovery. Millions of white workers were unemployed or underemployed. Yet throughout his campaign, Mondale focused narrowly on the issue of federal budget deficits, and the necessity to hike income taxes on all families earning more than $25,000 annually. Instead of demanding massive federal initiatives to reduce joblessness and poverty, the Democratic candidate proposed another $29 billion cut in social expenditures to diminish the federal deficit. Instead of supporting a halt to the rate of massive defense spending, Mondale called for annual military increases of 3 to 4 percent over the inflation rate — only slightly less than Reagan's budgetary projections.[15] Mondale's central fallacy, however, was his erroneous belief that the further to the ideological right his campaign projected its image, the greater his ability to undercut Reagan's base, especially among white ethnic, blue collar voters and white collar professionals. The reverse proved the case. Mondale probably lost a section of the Hart antiwar constituency by proposing a 'military quarantine' against Nicaragua and by attacking Reagan's failure to 'retaliate' against 'terrorists.' Mondale applauded the invasion of Grenada, reversing his previous position, and he promised that he would be even 'tougher' in negotiations with the Soviets than Reagan. Afro-Americans were outraged that the Democratic candidate was virtually silent on the Reagan administration's détente with apartheid. In short, Mondale took the Black vote absolutely for granted, and devoted nearly his entire campaign to courting fractions of the white electorate which historically had voted for Republican presidential candidates.[16]

II

Several striking parallels exist between Reaganism and classical fascism. Most obvious is the truculently anticommunist foreign policy of the present administration. The invasion of Grenada, the deployment of U.S. troops in Lebanon, and the covert war against Nicaragua were all projected as part of an anticommunist offensive. As Sweezy and Magdoff observed in late 1983, such aggression was not 'a literal copy of what went on in the 1930s; but, given the different circumstances of the two periods, it was about as close as you could get . . . Nothing could have been more reminiscent of Hitler than the Big Lies and phony excuses Reagan came up with to justify the occupation of Grenada.'[17] Usually the term 'fascism' is employed as a rhetorical device by leftists to condemn the actions of U.S. conservatives or the state, and lacks any serious analytical meaning. But let us examine this issue more closely.

If we begin with Dimitrov's definition of fascism as 'the open terrorist dictatorship of the most reactionary, most chauvinistic, most imperialist elements of finance capital,' the Reagan administration clearly falls short. Since the early 1970s, however, there has been a marked degeneration of bourgeois democratic political culture, characterized, in part, by the breakdown of the New Deal party system, and the hegemony of the far right within the leadership of the Republican party. In the last five years, a new element has been added — a popular ideology of extreme national chauvinism, described by the media as the 'new patriotism.' The 1984 Republican National Convention in Dallas was eerily reminiscent of the Nazi Party Convention in Munich in 1935. The Republicans called themselves 'America's Party,' implying that Democrats were somehow less than patriotic. Congressman Jack Kemp charged that Democrats were 'not just soft on communism — they're soft on democracy.' United Nations ambassador Jeanne Kirkpatrick, resurrecting her Cold War liberal past, placed the anti-communism of Reagan firmly in the political tradition of Harry Truman and Scoop Jackson, and argued that Mondale had betrayed this heritage. Barry Goldwater, the party's 1964 presidential nominee and 'old warrior' of the ultra-right, also told the convention: 'And let me remind you, extremism in the defense of liberty is no vice.' Nor were the racial dimensions of the convention far to seek. Only 3.1 percent of the delegates were Black. In the platform adopted by the convention, one-half page specifically mentioned national minority affairs. The only strong statement pertaining to Blacks in the party's manifesto was an explicit rejection of racial and gender quotas in hiring policies.[18] Foreign press observers were repulsed by the spectacle. The British *Guardian* correspondent noted:

> There was something distasteful, almost sinister, in the closing scenes. When the President observed that 'not one inch of soil has fallen to the Communists since he took office,' he provoked the first of a number of demonstrations which may have set the pulse racing of those who remember the Berlin Olympics in 1936. Clean-cut youths in grey slacks, white shirts and red bandanas lifted their arms with salutes reminiscent of fascism, mindlessly chanting 'four more years, four more years.' They waved the large American flags on wooden poles in a kind of mesmerized unison. This was not the fresh and encouraging patriotism of the Olympic torch as it traveled across the country, but an uglier, more menacing version.[19]

None of this is fully developed fascism. But if a road toward an American form of facism exists, it will be predicated on the conjunction of several ideological and political factors currently visible. The 'new patriotism,' like fascism, is a 'vehement nationalist ideology.' As Togliatti commented, 'fascist ideology contains a series of heterogeneous ingredients' that serve to 'solder together various factions in the struggle for dictatorship over the working masses and to create a vast movement for this scope.' Fascism is a *'romantic* ideology revealing the petty bourgeoisie's effort to make the world, which is moving forward toward socialism, turn back.'[20] Also pivotal in both fascist ideology and the 'new patriotism' is racism. In *Friendly Fascism*, Bertram Gross observes that racism 'invigorated' the political dynamics of classical fascism, by serving 'as a substitute for class struggle and a justification of any and all brutalities committed by members of the Master Race against "inferior" beings.'[21] Ideologically, there is the need not simply to identify a public scapegoat — Jews in Hitler's Germany, and national minorities in the U.S. — but to cultivate sharply divergent racial perceptions and conceived racial interests that reinforce the drive to the right. An August 1984 national survey of the Washington, DC-based Joint Center for Political Studies presents a disturbing racial polarization in contemporary American political attitudes. The vast majority of Blacks, 82 percent, disapproved of 'Reagan's job performance,' compared to only 32 percent of whites. Few whites described Reagan as being racially 'prejudiced,' while 72 percent of all Blacks defined him as a racist. In general, the poll found that 'Blacks and whites assess the state of the nation very differently': 48 percent of whites but only 14 percent of Blacks were 'satisfied with the way things are going in the country'; 38 percent of all Blacks but only 6 percent of the whites 'think civil rights is one of the most important issues' in the 1984 presidential campaign; and 40 percent of all Blacks and 15 percent of whites agree with the statement that 'white people want to keep Blacks down.'[22]

Classical fascism developed only when the internal contradictions of a society reached a point when 'the bourgeoisie [were] compelled to liquidate the democratic forms.' To accomplish this end, Togliatti adds, the 'mobilization of the petty bourgeoisie' was imperative.[23] In the U.S., the 'old' Right of the late 1950s was comprised almost solely of conservative intellectuals, such as Russell Kirk and William F.Buckley, and a small tendency of extreme anticommunists in groups like the John Birch Society. What truly distinguishes the New Right from these older formations is its commitment and capacity to build mass movement-style organizations within the American middle classes. The most prominent of these is the Reverend Jerry Falwell's Moral Majority, which has several million evangelical conservative members and supporters. The Moral Majority was instrumental in lobbying against the nuclear freeze movement, which Falwell describes as being led by 'the freeze-niks, ultra-libs and unilateral disarmers.' State affiliates of the Moral Majority have also been active in selecting school texts and library books, screening instructors to eliminate 'subversives' and homosexuals, and lobbying to introduce evangelical training inside public classrooms. In Alabama, Moral Majority members clashed with school officials over a textbook which 'failed to express adequately the merits of capitalism.' In North Carolina, members created an 'Index Prohibitorium' of all books 'unfit for young leaders . . . anti-family, anti-God, (and) anti-Bible.' One particularly objectionable text was Aldous Huxley's *Brave New World*, which Moral Majoritarians characterized as 'continued degradation of youth,' adding for good measure, 'it would make a nice bonfire.'[24]

Nor can this phenomenon be dismissed as a lunatic fringe. In 1980, the Moral Majority spent $2.5 million and registered one million working-class and middle-class Christians on behalf of Reagan. In 1984, its political expenditures exceeded $12.5 million. Phyllis Schlafly's 'Eagle Forum' mobilized thousands of middle-class whites to help defeat the ratification of the Equal Rights Amendment. The Conservative Caucus, directed by Howard Phillips, claims a membership of 600,000. Richard Viguerie, the 'ideological godfather' of the New Right, owns six communications companies, is syndicated in 550 newspapers in a weekly political column, and runs a political commentary show on more than 3,400 radio stations. After Reagan's election in 1980, new formations were created. Viguerie, Phillips, Terry Dolan (chairman of the National Conservative Political Action Committee), and Ron Godwin of the Moral Majority formed the 'Conservative Populist Tax Coalition' (CPTC). The goals of the CPTC are to 'attract new constituencies of disaffected Americans including blue collar Democrats and minorities' by advocating a 10 percent flat federal income tax rate, and emphasizing themes 'on patriotism, a "bootstraps" economy and strong family and traditional values.' Millionaire Lew Lehrman, a conservative Republican narrowly defeated by Mario Cuomo in New York's 1982 gubernatorial race, has created the 'Citizens for America (CFA).' The CFA recruits 'leaders' from the small business sector to mobilize rightists in Congressional races; recently it has also initiated a campaign to station the National Guard in 'high crime areas' of major cities. Both the CPTC and the CFA, like previous fascist groups, 'use an appeal to themes stressing the alienation of the "common man".' Both groups are projecting Lehrman 'as a national leader and possible successor to Reagan.'[25]

In Congress, rightwing Republicans led by Georgia Representative Newt Gingrich established the 'Conservative Opportunity Society' (COS) in 1983, with the expressed purpose of leading an 'intellectual-populist revolution' against the Democrats and 'moderate' Republicans. Pivotal members of COS include Representatives Jerry Lewis of California, chair of the House Republican Research Committee, Trent Lott of Mississippi, and Vin Weber of Minnesota.[26] Providing research for these forces are several well-funded centers, chiefly the ultra-right Heritage Foundation, formed by brewer Joseph Coors and Paul Weyrich, head of the 'Committee for the Survival of a Free Congress.' What all of these tendencies have in common, despite their nominal allegiance to the Republican party, is an absolute contempt for the present two-party system, and a ruthless commitment to build a multiclass, conservative order. For Gingrich, the challenge of the right is to shape 'a movement, a party and western civilization' impelled by the 'driving force of an ideological vision.' Weyrich adds: 'We are no longer working to preserve the status quo. We are radicals, working to overturn the present power structure of this country.'[27]

The growth of a mass radical Right in the 1980s has also permitted the renaissance of even more extreme racist formations, such as the Ku Klux Klan, and the coalition of various racist political factions under more 'acceptable' labels. A prime example is the development of the 'Populist Party' in 1983-1984. The impetus for the new Populists came from a merger of the old American Independent Party, formed in 1968 around presidential candidate George Wallace, and the Liberty Lobby, whose weekly tabloid *The Spotlight* has a circulation of one-half million. The guiding force behind the merger was a notorious racist Willis Carto, founder of the Liberty Lobby. Like Gingrich's COS, Carto has long been critical of eastern monopoly capitalism, which he defines as 'the means of production, money banking, and the political process . . . controlled by a small group of oligopolist/monopolist capitalists for their personal gain,' and which 'inevitably degenerates to crisis and Marxism.' Carto advocates the development of an authoritarian state apparatus to ensure 'the primacy of nation, culture, family, people and race' and to 'protect America's racial integrity.'[28] Under the Liberty Lobby's leadership, over 600 delegates from every state attended the founding convention of the Populist Party in Nashville, Tennessee on 19 August 1984. The party's charismatic candidates were selected to appeal to low to moderate income whites, farmers, and small businessmen who had not benefited significantly from Reagan's economic policies, and who were disaffected from both major parties. For president, the choice was celebrity Bob Richards, an Olympic gold medalist at the 1956 and 1960 games. Best known for his breakfast cereal commercials, Richards has traveled across the nation for two decades as an 'inspirational lecturer' for the Chamber of Commerce and civic clubs. Vice presidential nominee Maureen Kennedy Salaman is also a dynamic public speaker and self-described 'freedom fighter.' Her political base is the 100,000-member 'American Health Federation,' which she serves as president. Richards and Salaman project a wholesome, middle-class image — ideal for Carto.[29]

Again as in classical fascism, the Populist Party's public agenda is eclectic. As the anti-racist journal, *The Hammer*, comments: 'Populist literature takes a four-square stance against feminism, women's equality, civil rights for homosexuals, and racial equality . . . The Party is extremely right-wing but it is not conservative. It emphasizes free enterprise, but it is not anti-union.'[30] In its initial party documents, the Populists denounced 'international parasitic capitalism,' and called for tariffs to protect Americans' jobs, parity for small family farmers, and federal spending to expand public transportation facilities. It also advocated the repeal of the federal income tax, and a non-interventionist foreign policy. But the heart of the Populist program was its demand that 'every race' should pursue 'its destiny free from interference by another race.' Populist members promised to oppose 'social programs which would radically modify another race's behaviour, [and] demands by one race to subsidize it financially or politically as long as it remains on American soil . . . The Populist Party will not permit any racial minority, through control of the media, culture distortion or revolutionary political activity, to divide or factionalize the majority of the society . . . '[31] With this program, party organizers initiated local clubs in 49 states within six months. By mid-September 1984, *The Spotlight* announced that the party's major candidates would be on the ballot under the Populist label in only nine states. However, in Alabama, Tennessee, Louisiana and Mississippi, Richards and Salaman obtained ballot access as 'Independents'; in Kansas, they were listed as the national candidates of the state's 'Conservative Party'; and in California, they were the candidates of the American Independent Party.[32]

The actual 'cadre' of the new Populist Party is nothing but a rogue's gallery of racists and anti-Semites like Carto. The first national chairman of the party was Robert Weems. In the late 1970s, Weems was Mississippi chaplain of the 'Invisible Empire' Knights of the Ku Klux Klan. Other party leaders have similar histories. Dale Crowley, national party treasurer and 1984 Senatorial candidate in Virginia, was a major promoter of the anti-Semitic tract, *For Fear of Jews*. Wisconsin State Populist chairman Joseph Birkenstock is also a state leader of Posse Comitatus, a rural, right-wing vigilante organization. Retired U.S. Colonel Jack Mohr, a member of the Populists' national speakers bureau, is also leader of the paramilitary 'Citizens Emergency Defense System,' a subgroup of the 'Christian Patriots' Defense League.'

Mohr's major contributions to the Populists are his extensive contacts in the extreme right 'Christian Identity' network, groups of evangelical whites who teach that 'Jews are the children of the devil' and that Afro-Americans are 'pre-Adamic' — that is, 'false starts before God achieved perfection and made a white Adam.' Kansas Populist leader Keith Shive, who was also nominated for vice president at the Nashville convention, is also leader of the right-wing 'Farmer's Liberation Army' and has connections with Posse Comitatus. Shive's speeches to low income farm communities throughout the Midwest have blamed Jews 'as the source of all the world's ills.' Two prominent North Carolina Populists are state party vice chairman A.J.Barker and chairman Hal Beck. Barker is the leader of the racist 'National Association for the Advancement of White People'; Beck is a member of the policy board of the Liberty Lobby, and has openly called for a coalition between the new party and the KKK. In Kentucky, state party chairman Jerrold Pope is also a member of the neo-Nazi National States Rights Party, founded in 1958. The major Klansman besides Weems in the Populist Party is Arkansas leader Ralph Forbes, who in 1982 was a featured speaker at a Klan rally in Washington, DC. As *The Hammer* observes: 'the new Populist Party operation, combining the spirit of rural revolt, anti-capitalist rhetoric, and the party's slogan of "Power to the People," is a cleverly packaged job to help Carto consolidate a much larger constituency of people who would be repelled by an open appeal to Nazism under other circumstances.' But the phenomenon of U.S. Populism has rough parallels in Western European politics on the far right: the British National Front, Spain's Fuerzas Nuevas, the National Political Union in Greece, and especially the French National Front led by Jean-Marie Le Pen, which won 11 percent of the vote in the European Parliament elections in June 1984. Carto's *Spotlight* has praised Le Pen's National Front as 'France's Populist Party,' and U.S. rightists would like to duplicate the French neofascists' electoral successes.[33]

I am not suggesting that the Populists have any realistic prospects for becoming a major electoral force. But I am claiming that Reaganism has permitted and encouraged the involvement of blatantly racist and anti-Semitic forces in the electoral arena to an unprecedented degree; that the ideological 'glue' in the appeals of these formations to low-to-middle income whites is racism; and that the inevitable social byproduct of the ultra-right's mass political mobilization is terrorism and increased violence. Throughout 1984, literally hundreds of incidents of racially-motivated, random violence erupted across the U.S., directly and indirectly provoked by these forces. Klansmen and racist vigilantes had an especially busy year. On 8 April, several hooded and robed Klansmen, passing out leaflets in Cedartown, Georgia, beat an eighteen year old Black youth with brass knuckles; on 19 June, racists leaving the message, 'KKK: Nigger go home,' burned the home of an Indianapolis Black woman; on 11 August, a Black family residing in a predominantly white neighbourhood of Daytona Beach, Florida had a cross burned in their front yard; on 27 August, racist vandals leaving the mark 'KKK' attacked a Black church in a predominantly white Milwaukee suburb; on 7 October three racist whites, in an unprovoked public assault, left a twenty year old Black male a quadriplegic in Fontana, California.[34] Chicago probably experienced the greatest upsurge of racist violence, especially in the aftermath of the election of Harold Washington as the city's first Black mayor. The Chicago Police Department recorded 127 separate 'racial incidents' in 1984, an increase of 24 or 23.3 percent over 1983. The most dramatic were the firebombings of the parsonage of a Black minister in suburban Hickory Hills on 26 August, and a six hour-long stoning attack of the home of a Black family by dozens of whites, who were said to be celebrating Reagan's reelection.[35] Racial brutality in the U.S. is hardly new. What is ominous is that such groups have openly entered the electoral arena in many states, working vigorously for independent rightists and/or conservatives in the major parties. In North Carolina, Klansmen organized white registration drives, and state leader Glenn Miller ran in the Democratic primary for governor 'on an open Klan and white supremacy platform.' Klansmen in Georgia and Alabama succeeded in being named county deputy voter registrars. Although some Klansmen gravitated to the Populist Party, most worked aggressively for Reagan's reelection. The national leader of the Invisible Empire KKK, Bill Wilkinson, publicly endorsed the President.[36]

Reagan has created the social space or political environment for fascist and terrorist groups to operate with comparative impunity. One example was the emergence of Taiwan-backed death squads, which since 1981 have assassinated eight prominent critics of the regime inside the U.S.[37] In the northwestern states, the Idaho-based 'Church of the Aryan Nations' has committed public beatings, robberies and several murders. Federal authorities investigating the formation state that the 'Aryan Nations' maintains a computerized 'hit list' that targets for assassination major figures in Black, labor, Jewish, and Marxist organizations.[38]

The latest innovation in the Right's vigilante forces is the series of bombings, threats and assaults on abortion and family planning clinics. There were no bomb threats on such clinics from 1977-1980, and only four incidents during 1983. The following year, 27 abortion clinics in seven states were firebombed by evangelical anti-abortionists and rightwing groups, frequently identifying themselves as the 'Army of God.' A total of 157 'violent incidents' were reported last year, including assault and battery, kidnapping, vandalism, death threats, and attempted arson. A few neofascist groups have been formed in part to halt women's legal rights to abortion, such as the southern California-based 'White American Resistance' (WAR). WAR leader Tom Metzger, who ran openly as a Klansman for Congress in 1980, and for the Senate in 1982, has publicly attributed abortions to 'Jewish doctors' and 'perverted lesbian nurses' who 'must be punished for this holocaust and murder of white children.'[39] The Reagan administration's 'response' to these bombings was revealing. A national campaign by the National Organization of Women began on 2 March 1984, demanding that the U.S. Justice Department investigate anti-abortion terrorism. On 1 August, federal authorities finally agreed to begin to monitor the violence. Federal Bureau of Investigation director William Webster, however, declared that he saw no evidence of 'terrorism.'[40] Only on 3 January 1985, in a pro forma statement, did the President criticize the series of bombings as 'violent anarchistic acts,' but he still refused to term them 'terrorism.' Reagan deferred to Moral Majoritarian Jerry Falwell's latest campaign — to have 15 million Americans wear 'armbands' on 22 January 1985, 'one for every legal abortion' since 1973. Falwell's anti-abortion outburst epitomized Reaganism's orientation: 'We can no longer passively and quietly wait for the Supreme Court to change their mind or for Congress to pass a law'.[41] Extremism on the right was no vice, moderation no virtue. Or, as Hitler explained in *Mein Kampf:* 'The very first essential for success is a perpetually constant and regular employment of violence.'[42]

III

A preliminary anatomy of the 6 November 1984 election results seemed to give Reagan a resounding mandate. The President received 59 percent of the popular vote, and carried popular majorities in 49 states. Predictably, Reagan did best in constituencies controlled by the far right, or among those who had benefited most from the administration's economic policies. The incumbent received strong support from voters identifying themselves as ideological conservatives (81 percent), white 'born-again' Christians (80 percent), voters with annual personal incomes above $50,000 (68 percent), and those with incomes between $35,000 and $50,000 (67 percent). Mondale's core support came from Afro-Americans (90 percent), Jewish Americans (66 to 70 percent), Hispanics (65 percent), unemployed workers (68 percent), lesbians and gay men (60 to 80 percent). Reagan's reelection can be attributed to the continued erosion of partisan loyalties among the various segments of the Democratic coalition. One-third of the voters who supported Hart in the Democratic primaries switched to Reagan in the general election. Voters between the ages of 18-29, who had given Reagan only 43 percent of their votes in 1980, produced 58 percent for the Republican in 1984. About 49 percent of all Catholic voters, 26 percent of the total electorate, had supported Reagan in 1980; their 1984 vote for the President increased to 55 percent, despite the presence of Catholic Ferraro on the Democratic ticket.[43] One of Mondale's greatest disappointments was the inability of organized labor leaders to produce a substantial majority for the Democrats. After exerting 'maximum energy' to guarantee a level of support of 65 percent or more, only 57 percent of all union members backed Mondale. Among all blue collar workers, union and nonunion, Reagan received 53 percent of the vote.[44]

The most striking characteristic of the election was the racial polarization of the electorate. Nationally, Reagan obtained 66 percent of the white vote, and an unprecedented 73 percent from white Protestants. The feminists' 'gender gap' — the recent trend for women to support liberal centrist candidates more so than males — was largely irrelevant, as white women supported the incumbent by a 64-36 margin. Electoral support for Reagan among white women in 1980 had been only 52 percent.[45] Racial stratification in the electorate was particularly sharp in the

South, where Reagan, the Moral Majority and other conservative forces nearly succeeded in creating a 'white united front.' Reagan's campaign speeches during the fall repeatedly reminded whites of his firm opposition to affirmative action and civil rights. In Charlotte, North Carolina, the President attacked 'forced busing' for school desegregation; in Macon, Georgia, Reagan invoked the racist motto of regional segregationists by declaring, 'The South will rise again!'[46] On election day, 72 percent of all white Southerners voted for Reagan.[47] Although the Black voter turnout was up by 750,000 over 1980, 'most goals set by Black politicians went unfulfilled,' noted the *Washington Post*. In the Democratic primaries, Black Democratic Congresswoman Katie Hall of Indiana was defeated by a white candidate. In the November elections, the number of Black state legislators rose by only three, to 376 nationally. The most painful defeat occurred in Mississippi, where Black Democrat Robert Clark, in a well-financed campaign, lost by over four thousand votes to conservative Republican Congressman Webb Franklin. The contested Congressional district had 53 percent Black voters, but a massive voter registration drive among rural whites and selective intimidation of poor Black voters produced a Republican victory.[48] Most of the white democratic left, feminists and progressive trade unionists refused to acknowledge or even to discuss critically the obviously racial composition of Reagan's conservative electoral bloc; Blacks, on the other hand, had no choice except to face reality. Chicago Congressman Gus Savage observed that 'white Americans [had] voted en masse to accept the Reagan philosophy of narrow individualism, me-tooism and greed.' NAACP organizer Joseph Madison viewed the election as a 'white backlash.' White Americans of nearly all social classes were 'probably fearful of Blacks getting too big for their political breaches. They responded in a manner that reflected a fear of Black political power.'[49]

On closer examination, however, the Reagan 'mandate' was not as definitive as it may at first appear. A few media commentators drew parallels between Reagan's victory and that of Lyndon Johnson twenty years earlier, when the Texas Democrat received a popular vote of 61.3 percent and 486 electoral votes. Actually, the 1984 results were much closer to Dwight Eisenhower's 1956 reelection 'mandate' of 57.6 percent than to the Johnson victory. Johnson's triumph produced two-thirds Democratic majorities in both houses of Congress, while in 1956 the

Democrats had retained small Congressional majorities despite the Republican presidential sweep. Similar to the latter, in 1984 the Republicans gained only 14 seats in the House, and lost two Senate seats. Eight of the fourteen House seats lost had been held by Southern 'Boll Weevils' or conservative Democrats who were already backers of Reagan, including Representatives Jack Hightower of Texas and Elliott H. Levitas of Georgia. Afro-American voters provided the critical margin of support to elect three white Senators and at least eight Democratic representatives. Liberal populist Tom Harkin defeated ultra-right Republican Senator Rogert W. Jepsen in Iowa; liberal Democrat Paul Simon received only 43 percent of the white vote in Illinois, but with 87 percent of the vote from Blacks, defeated powerful Republican Senator Charles Percy. In gubernatorial elections, the Republicans gained four states vs. three for Democrats.[50]

There were other anomalies as well. Reagan carried Los Angeles County by 55 percent, but a 'Jobs With Peace' referendum on the same ballot, calling for cuts in the military budget to fund jobs programs and human services, passed with 61 percent.[51] In a few states, Communist Party candidates received their highest margins in several decades. In Arizona, a Communist candidate for state representative received 5 percent; in Massachusetts, Communist Congressional candidate Laura Ross received 15,668 votes against Democratic House speaker 'Tip' O'Neill, Jr., roughly 8 percent of the district's electorate.[52]

Odds are that the Democrats will take back the Senate in 1986, since nearly twice as many incumbents seeking reelection that year will be Republicans. Representative Tony Coelho, chairman of the Democratic Congressional Campaign Committee, emphasized his colleagues' defiance to the reelected president: 'As of today, you are a lame duck. Accept it. Elected officials do not have you to contend with any more.'[53] New Right leader Richard Viguerie agreed, predicting that 'Reagan faces two years with a hostile Congress — and the likelihood of an electoral disaster in the 1986 congressional elections.'[54]

For the Republicans, Reagan's reelection simply meant that the struggle for power between the moderate conservatives vs. the radical Right would now be fought without quarter. Both tendencies had benefited from Reagan's electoral white united front, but traditional Republican conservatives sought to break the leverage of radical reactionaries inside Congress. Veteran

Senator Robert Dole of Kansas, denounced by Gingrich as the 'tax collector for the welfare state,' handily defeated New Right candidate James McClure for the post of Senate Majority Leader. Liberal Republican John Chafee of Rhode Island defeated ultra-rightist Jake Garn of Utah to become chairman of their party's Senate Conference Committee. Pennsylvania moderate John Heinz also overcame a challenge by another Reaganite, Malcolm Wallop of Wyoming, to be appointed chairman of the 1986 Republican Senate campaign committee. Dole and other traditional conservatives promptly indicated they would seek to reduce federal budget deficits and Reagan's defense expenditures to a rate of five percent at most. The New Right sustained other blows as well. The removal of presidential adviser Edwin Meese to the post of Attorney General reduced the rightists' immediate access to Reagan. The resignation of Kirkpatrick from the UN, lamented Viguerie, was 'a loss from which Reagan's foreign policy will never recover.'[55] The battle to succeed Reagan is now on, and its resolution may well determine the future of the Republican Party. Currently, the best known Republican aspirants are traditional conservatives: Dole, former Senate Majority Leader Howard Baker of Tennessee, and Vice President George Bush, who is so vehemently hated on the far right that he has been popularly described as having 'put his manhood in a blind trust.' If Reagan remains 'neutral' in the 1988 campaign, the Republican presidential nomination will probably be won by an ultra-rightist. The two leading candidates are Jack Kemp and Lew Lehrman. In 1984 Kemp campaigned personally for nearly one hundred Congressional Republican candidates, and raised $220,000 on their behalf. Kemp is a favourite of the Moral Majority, is the 'mentor' of Gingrich's COS, and has the powerful backing of reactionary academic and financial institutions, including the Heritage Foundation, the American Enterprise Institute, and the Smith Richardson Foundation. As of late 1984, Lehrman's CFA was established in over 225 congressional districts, and although he has never held public office, political observers note that his private wealth is such that 'there's no limit to what he can spend.'[56] Closely behind these candidates and even further to the radical right is Gingrich, who may ultimately become the Right's spearhead for bringing its quasi-fascist agenda into state power.[57]

As the Republican leadership has degenerated into a series of fractious squabbles, the Democrats have turned their post-election blues into a thinly veiled condemnation of Blacks and other progressive currents inside the party. Georgia Democratic chairman Bert Lance argued that Mondale's loss was due to the party's inability 'to move in the direction the voters are moving in,' especially 'in the South.'[58] But which voters? Most leaders focused on Mondale's abysmal totals among white professionals, managers, and white collar employees. Carter's domestic policy adviser Stuart Eizenstat declared: 'We must win back the middle class that has drifted from our ranks . . .'[59] It was 'not enough just to hand the middle class a bill for new taxes,' concurred party consultant Bob Squier. The moment had arrived to 'unchain the ghost of Roosevelt' and to find 'new solutions to old problems.'[60] What is to be done? The first step proposed was to reduce democratic access of Blacks, feminists, and other insurgent social forces inside the party's governing apparatus, the Democratic National Committee, by giving state chairmen and moderate governors greater authority. Second, the party's 'welfare state' image had to be scrapped. Neoliberal *New Republic* editor Morton Kondracke suggested that the party give 'maximum sway for free market competition and individual initiative.'[61] Oklahoma Representative James R. Jones advanced the 'slogan of passionate conservatism.'[62] But most emphatically, the Democrats should 'insure' that the Rainbow Coalition and Jackson do 'not drive the party further left,' according to Kondracke. 'A minority of activists . . . coalition[s] of underprivileged racial, ethnic and other groups and single-issue advocates' had for too long dominated 'the national party's affairs,' advised Peter Rosenblatt, head of the centrist Coalition for a Democratic Majority. 'These groups do not add up to a majority of the voting population.'[63] Other white Democrats unwilling to go on public record were more blunt, charging that the party was 'pandering' to Black voters at whites' expense, and that 'they shouldn't have given Jesse Jackson everything he wanted' — ignoring that the Rainbow Coalition had received virtually nothing at the San Francisco convention.[64]

The Black Movement was suddenly forced to confront a victorious Reagan, and, at the same time, a Democratic leadership who blamed Mondale's loss partially on the active presence of Afro-Americans inside the party. Instead of capitulating to the pressure, Black leaders struck back in a bold and imaginative manner. Two early activists within the Rainbow Coalition campaign, U.S. Civil Rights Commissioner Mary Frances Berry and Randall Robinson, executive director of TransAfrica, along with Congressman Walter Fauntroy, coordinator of the 27 August 1983 march on Washington, decided to initiate a series of anti-apartheid demonstrations outside of the South African Embassy in Washington, DC. Throughout 1984, there had been an outbreak of demonstrations inside South Africa, similar to the 1960 Sharpeville uprisings and the 1976 Soweto revolts. On 5-6 November almost one million people participated in a nation-wide strike against the regime; in September and October alone, over 150 demonstrators were murdered by police, and an unknown number were detained without charges. Despite Reagan's recent 'mandate,' activists recognized that the administration's flagrant policies favorable to apartheid made it vulnerable to domestic criticism. In a small demonstration on 21 November, Berry, Fauntroy and Robinson were arrested. With in days, other members of the Congressional Black Caucus staged non-violent protests and were also detained, including Parren Mitchell, Ronald Dellums and Charles Hayes. Civil rights leader Joseph Lowery, head of the Southern Christian Leadership Conference, and Rosa Parks, the initiator of the 1955 Montgomery bus boycott movement, soon followed. In two weeks, a new national campaign had begun, the 'Free South Africa Movement.' Every constituency in the Rainbow Coalition, plus national figures in the more moderate centrist bloc of the Democratic Party, began to volunteer to be arrested next. Leaders of the American Jewish Congress and the Union of American Hebrew Congregations organized pickets; Black nationalists, most prominently the National Black United Front led by Rev. Herbert Daughtry of Brooklyn, staged major protests; feminists, socialists and trade unionists all joined the demonstrations. Bill Lucy, secretary-treasurer of the American Federation of State, County and Municipal Employees, AFL-CIO secretary-treasurer Thomas Donahue, Steelworkers vice president Leon Lynch, and Newspaper Guild president Charles Perlik, Jr., were arrested in Washington protests. Even AFL-CIO leader Lane Kirkland, who had been mute on the question of apartheid and was a bitter opponent of the Rainbow Coalition, saw the light. In a well-publicized meeting with Secretary of State George Shultz on 29 November, Kirkland advocated a 'progressively selective ban on the importation of South African products and . . . if necessary, a full boycott, barring of new investment, complete disinvestment and severance of all social, cultural and diplomatic ties.'[65]

A national 'Free South Africa Movement' steering committee quickly formed, which included Jesse Jackson, Berry, Fauntroy, Robinson, Lowery and NAACP leader Benjamin Hooks. The strategy had been refined by early December to encourage local mobilizations with a deliberate anti-Reagan emphasis, drawing the obvious connections between domestic and international racism. Demonstrations in December and January 1985 assumed different forms across the country. In New York, South Africa's consulate was picketed daily at 3:00 in the afternoon, religious groups on Tuesdays, Black nationalists on Mondays, youth and student groups on Wednesdays, and so forth. In San Francisco, longshoremen refused to unload South African cargo. In Mobile, Alabama, Fauntroy and Lowery led a 'pray-in' protest at the house of South Africa's honorary consul on December 6. The next day, in Berkeley, California, one thousand students held an anti-apartheid rally, blockading the administration building for three hours, resulting in 38 arrests. In Cleveland, more than 200 trade unionists, religious leaders and civil rights activists organized a public demonstration. On 9 December, four hundred protesters in Seattle picketed the home of the honorary consul; 23 were arrested. FSAM proponents in electoral politics introduced divestment legislation in 44 states; the National Conference of Black Mayors agreed to pressure all mayors and city councils to withdraw public funds from banks with apartheid connections. Reagan desperately tried to stem mounting criticisms of his policies, as administration officials announced that the demonstrations would have absolutely 'no impact' on government policy. 'The real losers in this are the Black community,' explained one aide. Such denials were immediately undercut by a group of 35 New Right Congressional leaders, led by Gingrich, Vin Weber and Robert Walker of Pennsylvania. In an open letter to South African Ambassador Bernardus Fourie, they warned that they would 'seek sanctions' against the regime unless it moved immediately to end racial violence and 'demonstrated a sense of urgency about ending segregation laws.'[66]

Despite the achievement of a new level of unity among Black, progressive, and centrist political forces in combatting apartheid and Reagan, larger questions remain unanswered regarding the future of the Democratic Party and the necessity to build a permanent coalition of social groups capable of defeating the Right. The classical strategy of developing fascism is to splinter the working class, winning over the bulk of the discontented lower petit bourgeoisie, then enact a series of authoritarian laws constricting bourgeois democratic liberties. Appeals to the 'race consciousness' of white workers were a decisive factor in Reagan's 1984 victory, especially in the South. And the administration has already prepared plans to initiate a series of 'Palmer Raids' against democratic and progressive forces when the opportunity presents itself. On 4 April 1984, the President signed Executive Order 12472, which gives the Secretary of Defense the authority to seize all 'telecommunications resources' in the event of a vaguely-defined 'national emergency,' without prior Congressional approval.[67] Reagan has authorized the use of 'lie detectors, wiretapping, blacklisting and censoring'; has forbidden liberal critics like Coretta Scott King from speaking on the Voice of America; and has attempted to void the Freedom of Information Act.[68] During the next three years, Reagan may have the opportunity to place three to four more judges on the Supreme Court, thus guaranteeing a conservative majority for the next quarter century.[69] On 12 October, Reagan signed into law a series of 'anti-terrorism' bills, mandating stiff penalties for the taking of hostages and airline sabotage, and providing cash rewards for information leading to the arrest and conviction of individuals who commit 'terrorist' acts. Six days later, the new laws permitted four hundred FBI agents and New York City police to seize nine activists on the grounds that they were planning to commit jail breakouts and robberies.[70] But the Ku Klux Klan, which committed at least six hundred documented acts of racist violence between 1978 and 1984, is 'not regarded as terrorist by FBI guidelines.'[71] Racism, institutional and vigilante, is the essential ideological approach for the ultra-right's efforts to divide workers and to build a permanent white united front. Authoritarian legal measures are the means to ensure that the left and national minorities will be unable to fight back.

Reagan's reelection was not inevitable, and despite the financial and organizational power of the New Right, a future authoritarian order in America remains only a possibility. However, the bulk of the Democratic Party's leaders, with their eyes fixed upon the white upper middle class, are looking in the wrong direction if they seriously intend to regain power. It is true that more than 67 percent of all Americans earning more than $35,000 annually voted for Reagan, and that this sector comprises 31 percent of the electorate. But they also total only 16.3 percent of the voting age population. They are over-represented in national elections because they are ideologically motivated to affirm their social class interests at the polls. Workers who earn less than $12,500 annually supported Mondale by 53 percent, and comprise 28 percent of the adult population, but only 15 percent of the active electorate. Unemployed workers, who supported the Democrat by 68 to 32 percent, stand for 3 percent of the electorate, but 8 percent of all adults. Had Puerto Ricans, Mexican-Americans, Afro-Americans, the unemployed, low-income workers and people with less than a high school education participated in the election at identical rates of those earning above $35,000, Mondale would have won. The weakness in this scenario is that, had these constituencies actually voted in these numbers, the Democratic Party would now no longer be the 'Democratic Party,' but would be forced programmatically toward a Western European labor party model. Hence the refusal of Mondale, Glenn, Hart and company to support demands for massive voter registration and education made by the Rainbow Coalition of Jackson. Given the domination of sections of capital, Southern moderates and the trade union bureaucracy within the party's internal apparatus, it is highly unlikely that the left and its liberal allies, led by Blacks' demands, will be able to reverse the Democrats' stampede toward 'passionate conservatism.'

These democratic left forces will only sustain themselves if they coalesce as an independent political entity, which may operate for a time inside the Democratic Party, but run 'independent candidates' against the two major parties in local and statewide races. To do so will take the same panache displayed in Jackson's primary campaign and the FSAM demonstrations in late 1984. Fundraising and the recruitment of personnel are important factors, but not crucial to the development of this strategy, pace David Gordon (see 'Up from the Ashes II: Getting Our Act Together,' *The Nation* [9 February 1985] pp.138-43). The real challenge is the creation of a realistic social program that can actively unify blue collar employees, semi-skilled workers, the unemployed, and other disadvantaged sectors across the color line. In March 1985, the principal organizers of the Rainbow Coalition met in Gary, Indiana to create a permanent national formation. Jackson's new thirteeen point program, which includes demands for 'fair immigration policies, revitalization of cities, aid to small farmers, and revamping the tax structure,' has the potential for reaching oppressed whites and Latinos who resisted participation in the 1984 primary campaign.[72] The paradox of American social history is that the activism of people of color has been the decisive component in moving the boundaries of politics further to left for the entire society; yet 'race politics' is also the central component for the far Right to discipline the entire working class. Whether the Rainbow's progressive utilization of race is able to transcend the conservative racist social movement and the white working class's tendency to affirm their racial identity rather than material interests at the polls is a political question of such decisive importance for the future of democratic politics in the U.S. that progressives of all races and classes can ignore it only at their peril.

Notes

1.   Victor Perlo, 'Unemployment and racism,' *Daily World* (30 August 1984).

2.   'Reagan Bad News for Blacks,' *Buffalo Challenger* (17 October 1984).

3.   See Vivian Aplin-Brownlee, 'Black Colleges: On Razor's Edge,' *Washington Post* (19 November 1984); and Manning Marable, 'The Quiet Death of Black Colleges,' *Southern Exposure* 12 (March-April 1984), pp. 31-39.

4.   See *Washington Notes on Africa* (Winter 1984), published by the Washington Office on Africa.

5.   Anna DeCormis, 'Trading with enslavers: How U.S. companies keep apartheid going,' *Guardian* (26 December 1984).

6.   Dianne M.Pinderhughes, 'The Black Vote — The Sleeping Giant,' in James D.Williams, ed., *The State of Black America, 1984* (Washington, DC, 1984), p. 92; and 'Portrait of the Electorate,' *New York Times* (8 November 1984).

7.   William G.Mayer, 'Running on New: The Hart Choices,' in Anne Doyle Kenney, ed., *Institute of Politics* (Cambridge, 1984), pp. 19-20.

8.   See Manning Marable, 'The Rainbow Coalition: Jesse Jackson and the Politics of Ethnicity,' *Crosscurrents*, 34 (Spring 1984), pp. 21-42; Gerald M. Boyd, 'Black Churches a Mainspring of Jackson's Efforts,' *New York Times* (February 14, 1984); and Benjamin F.Chavis, Jr., 'Theology Under the Rainbow,' *The Witness* 67 (May 1984), pp. 6-9.

9.   Afro-American voters comprised 21 percent of the total Democratic primary vote. Mondale received less than one-fifth of the national Black vote, the remainder going to Jackson. Had Jackson not been in the race, Black voter turnout rates would have fallen, but at least 75 percent of those Afro-Americans who voted would have selected Mondale. Thus Mondale probably would have won the nomination with little difficulty had Jackson decided not to run.

10.   David Plotke, 'Reaganism and the Problem of Special Interests,' *Socialist Review* 15 (January-February 1985), p. 21.

11.   'Mondale and the Voters,' *New York Times* (19 July 1984).

12.   Marable, 'The Rainbow Coalition,' pp. 30-32.

13.   See Ayn Rand, *Capitalism: The Unknown Ideal* (New York, 1967).

14.   Dennis Altman, 'A New Barbarism,' *Socialist Review* 15 (January-February 1985), p.10.

28

15. Anna De Cormis, 'Why is Mondale so obsessed with the budget deficit?' *Guardian* (17 October 1984).

16. Jack Colhoun, 'Mondale-Ferraro: Peace candidates or cold warriors?' *Guardian* (3 October 1984); and Jack Colhoun, 'How do You Debate When You Don't Really Disagree?' *Guardian* (31 October 1984).

17. Paul M.Sweezy and Harry Magdoff, 'Where Are We Going?' *Monthly Review* 35 (December 1983), pp. 1-2.

18. Lorn S.Foster, 'On the Scene in Dallas,' *Focus* 12 (September 1984), p. 3.

19. Quoted in Tristram Coffin, 'The Radical Right: From Paranoia to Power,' *Washington Spectator* 10 (1 December 1984), p. 2.

20. Palmiro Togliatti, *Lectures on Fascism* (New York, 1976), p. 9.

21. Bertram Gross, *Friendly Fascism: The New Face of Power in America* (Boston, 1980), p. 21.

22. 'JCPS Survey of Political Attitudes,' *Focus* 12 (September 1984), p. 8.

23. Togliatti, *Lectures on Fascism*, p. 3.

24. Coffin, 'The Radical Right,' p. 3.

25. 'Beyond the Reagan Revolution: New Strategies on the Right,' *Interchange Report* 5 (Summer 1984), pp. 1, 5.

26. Kris Jacobs, 'The Life of the Party: GOP Moving to the "Nouveau-Right," ' *Interchange Report* 5 (Fall 1984), pp. 11-12.

27. Coffin, 'The Radical Right,' p. 1

28. A brief note on Carto: Expelled from the John Birch Society for his 'extreme anti-Semitism,' Carto founded the Liberty Lobby in 1956. In 1968, Carto coordinated the national 'Youth for Wallace,' and in the 1970s he created two political action committees, United Republicans and United Congressional Appeal, which raised funds to defeat liberal Democrats. Carto also directs the California-based Institute for Historical Review, which has asserted that the Nazi holocaust was 'a myth made up by Jews to further their interests.' Carto has stated that 'if Satan himself had tried to create a permanent disintegration and force for the destruction of nations, he could do no better than invent the Jews.' Kristine Jacobs, 'The Populist Party,' *Interchange Report* 5 (Fall 1984), p. 2

29. *Ibid.*, pp. 1-2.

30. 'It's Not Populism, America's New Populist Party: A Fraud by Racists and Anti-Semites,' *The Hammer* 8 (Fall 1984), p.20.

31. 'When is a 'Populist' Really a Klansman?' *The Hammer* 7 (Summer 1984), pp. 14-15.

32. 'It's Not Populism, America's New Populist Party,' p. 21.

33. *Ibid.*, pp. 22-23, 27; and 'Populists: Racists Under Cover,' *National Anti-Klan Network Newsletter* (Fall 1984), pp. 1, 7.

34. 'Klan, Nazi and Other Incidents From Across the Nation,' *Klanwatch Intelligence Report* (July 1984), pp. 2, 6; and *Klanwatch Intelligence Report* (December 1984), pp. 2-3.

35. Kevin B. Blackistone, 'Racial Violence and Harassment Escalate in Chicago Area,' *Chicago Reporter* 14 (January 1985), pp. 1, 6.

36. 'Klan Holds White Voter Registration Drives, Backs Candidates,' *Klanwatch Intelligence Report*, p. 4.

37. Leach Nordson, 'Death squads still stalk U.S. Asian community,' *Guardian* (12 December 1984).

38. John Wojcik, 'Expose racist plans of terror,' *Daily World* (8 January 1985).

39. 'Anti-Abortion Violence Increases,' *The Hammer* 8 (Fall 1984), pp. 10-12; Anne Finger, 'Activists urge fightback against the bombers,' *Guardian* (23

January, 1985); Tim Wheeler, 'NOW vigils to protest bombings,' *Daily World* (19 January, 1985).

40. Editorial, 'What the FBI won't probe,' *Guardian* (12 December, 1984).

41. Finger, 'Activists urge fightback against the bombers.'

42. Quoted in Gross, *Friendly Fascism*, p. 294.

43. 'Portrait of the Electorate,' *New York Times* (8 November 1984); and Christine R.Riddiough, 'What Happened to the Gender Gap (and Other Gaps) in the 1984 Elections?' *Socialist Review* 15 (January-February 1985), p. 24.

44. 'Portrait of the Electorate'; and Bill Keller, 'Unionists Reassess Mondale Support,' *New York Times* (9 November 1984). The voting trends of these traditional Democratic constituencies become more apparent when viewed historically. During the five presidential elections between 1952 and 1968, the Democrats received approximately 64 percent of the Catholic vote, 57 percent of the blue collar vote, 55 percent of the votes of Americans with less than a high school education, and 52 percent from voters under 30 years old. Carter's 1980 totals in these groups were generally lower: Catholics (42 percent), blue collar (46 percent), less than high school education (51 percent), and voters under 30 (44 percent). Mondale did marginally better than Carter among Catholics, fell short among youth, and received roughly the same totals in the other groups. See Kevin P. Phillips, *The Emerging Republican Majority* (Garden City, New York, 1970), p. 30.

45. Hanna Lessinger, 'Shot Down at the Gender Gap,' *Guardian* (5 December, 1984).

46. Akinshiju C. Ola, 'Racism won big in the elections,' *Guardian* (28 November 1984).

47. Studies by the Joint Center for Political Studies indicate that race was a decisive factor in Southern whites' voting behaviour. Polls indicated that 73 percent of all Southern whites 'considered Reagan a strong leader'; most approved of his overall 'performance' as President (62 percent), his economic policies (57 percent), and his opposition to 'preferential treatment for Black job applicants' (77 percent). Only 26 percent of all whites in the South were critical of 'Reagan's civil rights policies.' Conversely, 87 percent of all Black Southerners polled strongly 'disapprove of Reagan's economic performance,' and 89 percent of the Black electorate in the region voted for Mondale. See Thomas E. Cavanaugh, 'Election Round-Up,' *Focus* 12 (November-December 1984), p. 5.

48. Ola, 'Racism won big in the elections'; Juan Williams and Paul Taylor, 'Blacks: They Lost With Mondale and Made No Gains in Congress,' *Washington Post* (19 November 1984); and Tom Wicker, 'Fighting White Drift,' *New York Times* (26 October 1984).

49. Ola, 'Racism won big in the elections.' Considerations of space preclude a fuller discussion for the reasons that the white left, with few exceptions, was unwilling or unable to come to terms with the racist behaviour of the bulk of white Americans. As Anne Braden, leader of the Southern Organizing Committee for Economic and Social Justice [SOC] observed: 'Most of them voted squarely against their own best interests. There is no way to explain this except to acknowledge that they did it for racist reasons, subtle or otherwise. As one of SOC's staff said, "Reagan is calling white America back to order." ' Braden, 'Today's Crisis: A Pledge to Struggle,' *Southern Fight-back* 10 (January 1985), p. 1.

50. Romulo Fajardo, 'Black voters reject Reagan,' *Daily World* (8 November 1984); David S. Broder and George Lardner, Jr., 'Did Anybody See a Conservative Mandate Go By?' *Washington Post* (19 November 1984); and Cavanaugh,

'Election Round-Up.'

51.   Emily De Nitto, 'People's groups: no mandate,' *Daily World* (8 November 1984).

52.   Nora Bonosky, 'Communist Candidates make gains,' *Daily World* (8 November 1984).

53.   Broder and Lardner, 'Did Anybody See a Conservative Mandate Go By?'

54.   Tim Wheeler, 'Short coattails frustrate the ultra-right,' *Daily World* (17 January 1985).

55.   Kevin J. Kelley, ' "Revenge of the Moderates" has New Right Reeling,' *Guardian* (26 December 1984).

56.   James Dickenson, 'After Reagan,' *Washington Post* (19 November 1984); and Jacobs, 'The Life of the Party: GOP Moving to the "Nouveau-Right," ' p. 12.

57.   Gingrich is clearly the most dangerous national figure on the Right for the next decade. He not only has called for the complete 'dismantling of the liberal welfare state,' but has even suggested that all federally-funded public housing should be 'converted into condominium apartments.' Additional 'prisons should be built for hardcore criminals,' and inmates 'must work to pay for their keep.' People accused of crimes should 'bear the primary burden' of proof in courts, and defense attorneys 'who are particularly disruptive or exploitative of the system should suffer economically and, ultimately, professional penalties for having failed to behave in a manner beneficial to society.' Gingrich argues that teenagers should be enrolled into 'the workforce as apprentices laboring for a modest wage.' For youngsters, 'a $500 bonus' should be rewarded 'for any child who enters the first grade reading at a fourth grade level.' These authoritarian prescriptions may become mainstream views inside the Republican Party by the mid-1990s. See 'The Gospel According to Gingrich,' *Interchange Report* 5 (Fall 1984), pp. 13-14; and Kevin J. Kelley, 'But GOP's future may belong to its Newts,' *Guardian* (26 December 1984).

58.   James R. Dickenson, 'It Seems the Democrats Can Win Anything but the White House,' *Washington Post* (19 November 1984).

59.   Kevin J. Kelley, 'After the deluge, how do the Democrats rebuild?' *Guardian* (5 December 1984).

60.   Bob Squier, 'F.D.R., the Ghost of Democrats Past,' *New York Times* (5 December 1984). None of these centrist Democrats or neoliberals produced data to illustrate that the 'white middle class' had abandoned the Democrats only in the past decade. Mondale's 40 percent vote from white collar workers was only slightly less than the average total received by other Democratic presidential candidates from 1952-80 (43 percent). His share of votes from all college graduates (40 percent) was somewhat higher than the 1952-80 average (38 percent), and his vote from managers and professionals was identical (37 percent). The Democrats never *lost* the white, upper middle-class vote; they never had it — *especially* under Roosevelt. See Phillips, *The Emerging Republican Majority*, p. 30; and 'Portrait of the Electorate.'

61.   Kelley, 'After the deluge.'

62.   John Herbers, 'Party Looks Inward for Ways to Regain Majority,' *New York Times* (8 November 1984).

63.   Peter R. Rosenblatt, 'Centrism is Crucial,' *New York Times* (19 November 1984).

64.   Tom Wicker, 'A Party of Access?' *New York Times* (25 November 1984).

65.   Sue Dorfman, 'Struggle scorches South Africa,' *Guardian* (12 September 1984); Heinz Klug, 'Bigger Than Soweto,' *Guardian* (21 November 1984); Jack

Colhoun, 'Wider protests, mounting pressures,' *Guardian* (19 December 1984); and Gerald Horne, 'Movement mounts to free South Africa,' *Daily World* (4 January 1985).

66.   Jack Colhoun, 'South Africa's apologists: A vanishing breed,' *Guardian* (26 December 1984); Denise Winebrenner, 'Cleveland labor protests apartheid,' *Daily World* (15 December 1984); Horne, 'Movement mounts to free South Africa'; and Colhoun, 'Wider protests, mounting pressures.'

67.   *Interchange Report* 5 (Summer 1984), pp. 6-7.

68.   Joan Claybrook, 'Reagan Ballooned "Big Government," ' *New York Times* (1 November 1984).

69.   See Howard Levine and Tim Keefe, 'A Supreme election issue,' *Guardian* (24 October 1984).

70.   Akinshiju Ola, 'FBI raids: A prelude to another witchhunt?' and Eleanor Stein, 'Some Bills Did Pass,' *Guardian* (31 October 1984).

71.   According to an FBI spokesman, the Ku Klux Klan has not committed 'any act of terrorism in the last few years.' See Evelyn Newman, 'Terrorism, Reagan and the Klan,' *National Anti-Klan Network Newsletter* (Fall 1984), p. 5.

72.   'The Rainbow will continue as Independent "Third Force," ' *Southern Fight-Back* 10 (January 1985), p. 5.

2.   The Paradox of Social Democracy:

The American Case

Robert Brenner

I   A New Social Democracy?

A very long time ago — in the Paleolithic days of the new left
of the later 1960s — few red-blooded radicals would have been
caught dead inside the Democratic Party. This was the era of the
student and anti-imperialist movements, of SDS; of the militant
Black movements, of SNCC, the Black Panther Party, and the
League of Revolutionary Black Workers; and of the nascent rank
and file movements among industrial and public service workers. In those days, it was strictly the politics of the streets and of
mass direct action. 'Power to the people' definitely did not mean
'part of the way with RFK.' The Democratic Party was recognized
as firmly wedded to American imperialism, as expressed in LBJ's
Vietnam War, not to mention Harry Truman's A-Bomb over
Hiroshima or his Cold War or Kennedy's Bay of Pigs. Moreover,
despite the fact that workers, Blacks, and the poor did vote, in
their majority, for the Democratic Party, that Party was viewed
as clearly pro-capitalist, anti-working class, and anti-Black.
Neither workers nor Blacks controlled, nor even much participated in the Democratic Party. So, it was hardly surprising to the
60s radicals that the Party never tried to repeal the viciously
anti-labor Taft-Hartley Act, that it refused to seat the Mississippi
Freedom Democratic Party at its 1964 convention in place of the
arch-segretationist official delegation, and that the Kennedy
presidency failed to achieve a single significant piece of social
legislation.

Indeed, the one lesson that the new left absorbed, at least
superficially, through its rather vague notions of corporate liberalism and participatory democracy, was that the labor bureacratic, party politico, service professional, and Black petty
bourgois elements which constituted the core of official reformism could never be counted on to put into effect even their own

programs. Left to their own devices, they would find a way to compromise with 'the powers that be.' The first generation of the new left grew up on the rather crude slogan of 'never trust a liberal,' and their successors did not foresake that credo. The accepted premises, therefore, for an effective new left politics were understood to be an organizational and political independence from the forces of official reformism, a reliance on militant direct action to impose reforms from the outside, and the sort of direct democracy inside the movements which was anathema to the party, labor, and Black bureaucratic forces that dominated the Democratic Party and the official institutions of liberalism.

Today, in the Democratic Party, nothing fundamental has changed since the 60s. But in most other respects, we live in a different political world. Above all, the mass direct action movements which made reforms possible and which provided the material basis, so to speak, for the rise of radical organizations and ideas have suffered more than a decade of disastrous decline. In connection with the deepening crisis of the international economy, the secular decline of American manufacturing, and the accelerating offensive by employers against all sections of the working class and the poor, the decline of the movements is *the* overriding factor determining the political universe of the left. The militant mass movements which motivated hundreds of thousands of people to strike, to demonstrate, to sit-in and to sit-down in the 60s and 70s — these were, and are, the only real sources of power for the left. These movements provide the *indispensable* basis for actually winning reforms and imposing policies on the government — above all in periods like this one of economic contraction. In consequence, they provide the critical condition for making left perspectives realistic and, in this way, the necessary basis for winning people to a left worldview. For, as a rule, people will not maintain a political perspective — no matter how empirically and logically compelling — unless they can see a more or less immediate possibility of putting it into practice. The decline of mass direct action movements over many years, and especially the collapse of rank and file working-class organizations, is thus the overriding reason for the disarray of the left, as well as of liberalism, and it has opened the way for massive confusion.

Unable to suck mass movements out of their thumbs, the majority of leftists in the U.S. for more than a decade have relentlessly searched for *substitutes*, new social agencies and new political strategies. By the late 70s and early 80s, there had issued inside the left — though nowhere else in society — a broad commitment to move in the direction of a 'new social democracy.' In late 1978, Doug Fraser, president of the United Auto Workers (UAW) and a self-styled socialist, revealed that there was a 'one-sided class war' going on against the American working class. He subsequently withdrew from Secretary of Labor John T. Dunlop's Labor Management Advisory Group (whose explicit function was indeed to manage labor) and convened the 'Progressive Alliance,' a new multi-constituency organization ostensibly designed to 'revive the spirit of Selma and the sit-downs,' support grass roots organizing efforts, and bring the disparate movements together. The Progressive Alliance drew large numbers of liberal and social democratic officials from the women's, Black, environmental, and consumer groups, as well as from the unions, to its first meeting.[1] A short time later, the New American Movement (NAM), the last surviving organization of the new left, merged with the Democratic Socialist Organizing Committee (DSOC), the official social democratic organization in the U.S. and a member of the Second International, to form the Democratic Socialists of America (DSA). In the meantime, since the early 70s, the overwhelming majority of those who had survived from the Black movements of the 60s had immersed themselves in a single-minded electoralism, aiming to capture key offices in the cities both north and south. By 1984, Manning Marable, a well-known Black writer and a national officer of DSA, was hailing this tendency, too, as a new (Black) 'social democracy.'[2] Indeed by 1984, all wings of this new social democracy had found their fore-ordained home inside the Democratic Party. Almost the entirety of the American left, in one incarnation or another, participated in the 1984 election in support of the Democratic Party candidates. The campaign of Jesse Jackson for president constituted the near-exclusive focus of the left's organizing efforts throughout the election year.

Not surprisingly, the proponents of this new social democratic strategy have justified their approach in terms of a return to realism. 'We were ultra-left,' say the ex-Maoists, who have foresaken the 'New Communist Movement' in order to invade the Harold Washington and Jesse Jackson campaigns. 'We have to get out of the sandbox into the real world,' say the ex-CP *realpolitikers* who have joined DSA in order more effectively to implement the old popular front line inside the Democratic

Party. What all this means, in brief, is that to be practical you have to relate to the Democratic Party, since that's where the action is.

Proponents of working in and for the Democratic Party argue, then, that because the Party has been historically and is today *the* party of the mass movements and *the* party of reform, it must be the central vehicle for left struggle. These progressives point to the fact that a majority of working people, Blacks, and other oppressed groups, even now, generally vote Democratic. But they fail to distinguish between the passive, private, and individualist act of voting and the active, collective, power-creating act of organizing to confront the employers or the government. The pro-Democratic Party progressives also notice, quite properly, that the unions, the official Black organizations, and the offical women's organizations constitute the backbone of the Democratic Party. But they fail to distinguish between the interests of bureaucratic and middle-class elements which dominate these organizations and which represent them inside the Democratic Party and the very different interests of the rank and file and working-class elements which constitute the membership of these organizations but play essentially no active role inside the Democratic Party. The new social democrats point out further that the stated programs of the 'left' Democratic Party officials, Black politicos, and trade union leaders are generally at the left extreme of the political spectrum in the U.S. today, and that, if implemented, these programs would amount to a giant step forward for the American people. But they fail to distinguish between talk and action, what's on paper and what's implemented. They simply ignore the near-total incapacity not only of Democratic Party Congressional majorities, but also of fully fledged social democratic governments around the world, to impose reforms upon capital throughout the period of crisis which began in the early 70s. Nor do they recognize how totally committed these parties have been in power to austerity and attacks on the working class. Finally, those who would rebuild social democracy in the U.S. point out that social democracy in general, and the Democratic Party in particular, has appeared as the 'vehicle' of those great waves of reform which have, periodically, shaken the advanced capitalist countries. But they fail to distinguish between the immediate legislators of reforms and the creators of the mass political offensives which actually made reform legislation possible. They characteristically, and disas-

trously, neglect the tumultuous mass movements which transformed, willy-nilly, what hitherto had been do-nothing
reformist politicans into agents of social and political change.

II   The Paradox of Social Democracy

The point is that most of the U.S. left, like most of the left
throughout the world, still remains transfixed by social democracy's passive mass base, its left paper programs, and its
historic association with reform. They refuse, therefore, to take
social democracy seriously as a distinct social and historical
phenomenon — one which represents distinctive social forces
and, as a result, advances specific political theories and strategies, and, in turn, manifests a recognizable political dynamic
within capitalism. Since the end of the nineteenth century, the
evolution of social democracy has been marked by a characteristic paradox. On the one hand, its rise has depended upon
tumultuous mass working-class struggles, the same struggles
which have provided the muscle to win major reforms and also
the basis for the emergence of far left political organizations and
ideology. The expansion of working-class self-organization,
power, and political consciousness, dependent in turn upon
working-class mass action, has provided *the* critical condition
for the success of reformism as well as of the far left. On the other
hand, to the extent that social democracy has been able to consolidate itself organizationally, its core representatives —drawn
from the ranks of the trade union officials, the parliamentary
politicians, and the petty bourgeois leaderships of the mass
organizations of the oppressed — have invariably sought to
implement policies reflecting *their own* distinctive social positions and interest — positions which are *separate from* and
interests which are, in fundamental ways, *opposed to* those of the
working class. Specifically, they have sought to establish and
maintain a secure place for themselves and their organizations
within capitalist society. To achieve this security, the official
representatives of social democratic and reformist organizations
have found themselves obliged to seek, at a minimum, the implicit toleration, and, ideally, the explicit recognition of capital.
As a result, they have been driven, systematically and universally, not only to relinquish socialism as a goal and revolution as
a means, but, beyond that, to contain, and at times, actually to

crush those upsurges of mass working-class action whose very dynamics lead, in tendency, to broader forms of working-class organization and solidarity, to deepening attacks on capital and the capitalist state, to the constitution of working people as a self-conscious class, and, in some instances, to the adoption of socialist and revolutionary perspectives on a mass scale. They have done this, despite the fact that it is precisely these movements which have given them their birth and sustained their power, and which have been the only possible guarantee of their continued existence in class-divided, crisis-prone capitalism. The paradoxical consequence has been that, to the extent that the official representatives of reformism in general and social democratic parties in particular have been freed to implement their characteristic worldviews, strategies, and tactics, they have systematically undermined the basis for their own continuing existence, paving the way for their own dissolution.

For these reasons, even those most intent on calling into existence a new reformism have before them an ironic prospect. To the extent they wish to create a viable social democracy, they will have to maintain their political and organizational *independence from*, and indeed systematically to *oppose*, those who represent actually-existing social democracy. To the extent, on the other hand, they end up, as they have until now, merging themselves with the offical forces of reformism, they will be disabled for carrying out what is clearly the cardinal (if enormously imposing) task facing those who wish to implement *any* left perspective: to rebuild the fighting capacity, organization, and left political consciousness of the working class and oppressed people. Indeed, to the degree that the proponents of a new social democracy bind themselves to already-existing reformism — its distinctive organizations, leaderships, strategies, and ideas — they will contribute, if unwittingly, to the further erosion of collective and class-based forms for pursuing workers' interests, and thereby encourage the adoption of those individualistic and class-collaborationist forms of achieving workers' interests which literally pave the way for the right.

None of this is mere logic, nor is it ancient history. Remarkably, the American left has crystallized its own trend toward social democratic politics immediately in the wake of an extended series of experiments in social democracy in Europe, experiments that have proven catastrophic for the entire left. By the mid-70s, through most of Europe, the social democratic and

Communist parties had succeeded in channelling the energies of the mass worker and student movements of the previous decade into the parliamentary/electoral arena and, on this basis, had achieved for themselves practically unprecedented positions of political authority. At the same time, the near totality of those leftists who had, during the late 60s and early 70s, constructed a small but significant extra-parliamentary left out of those same mass movements also moved *en masse* into the ostensibly revitalized and reconstructed Eurocommunist and Eurosocialist parties. Their justification for this turn? Precisely the same one invoked by America's new social democrats: entering into these organizations appeared to them the best way to hook up with the workers, to fight effectively for reforms, and to rebuild the mass movements.

The results are now plain for all to see. The Communist Parties outside Italy have suffered massive, probably irreversible decline, as the European working classes have seen no need for two mass reformist parties and have preferred to back the official ones. Much more importantly, labor and socialist parties in Portugal, Spain, and above all France have won smashing electoral/parliamentary victories and ascended to 'power.' In every case, these electoral campaigns and electoral victories took place in the wake of alarming *declines* in working-class organization — indeed as more or less explicit *substitutes* for working-class action nevertheless, most of the left insisted on interpreting them as in themselves mass movements and, therefore, as working-class triumphs. What has been the outcome? In every case, with no independent mass movements to 'keep them honest,' the labor and socialist governments have used their newly-won authority to 'restructure' their national capitalisms in the interests of international competitiveness. In the process, they have imposed upon the working class policies of austerity even more vicious and thoroughgoing than those of their conservative predecessors, and have undermined further the workers' main defensive organizations, especially the trade unions. The consequence of social democratic hegemony has been neither a new period of reform, nor an opening to the left. On the contrary, capitalist restructuring under social democracy has brought about the most massive political demoralization of the working class and the most devastating discrediting of socialist and Marxist ideas within memory. Not surprisingly, the medium term consequence has been to breathe vibrant new life into long-discredited right wing political perspectives, to prepare not only the revival of the most virulent forms of free enterprise ideology, but also the emergence of a dynamic crypto-fascism — above all, and not accidentally, in Socialist France. So, once again, the paradoxical but predictable dynamic: in the absence of mass movements to supply their own, independent material force for reform and for the rise of left ideas, the most decisive victories of social democracy have issued, in the end, in the most decisive undermining of social democratic perspectives, organizations, and movements in Europe since the 1950s. This despite a deepening long term capitalist economic crisis which has brought the highest levels of unemployment and the most severe suffering for the working class since the 1930s.

III   The Dynamics of Reformism

Activity, Power, Consciousness

It should be a commonplace within the left that the indispensable condition for beginning to reconstruct working-class organization, power, and political consciousness is the rise of mass direct action by working people against the employers and the government, in the factories and the offices, as well as in the streets. This is because, as a rule, it is only where working people have *in fact* broken through their own passivity, created new forms of solidarity, and, on that basis, amassed the power needed to confront capital, that the goals of reform and revolution *premissed upon* collective, class-based action can appear at all relevant and practical. In the absence of class solidarity and collective power, working people are reduced to the 'other side' of 'what they really are' under capitalism, viz. sellers of commodities, notably their own labor power. If people cannot, *in fact*, struggle for their interests by means of class-based organizations and class-based strategies, they will find that it only makes sense to treat the social world, its institutions and balances of power, as *given*, and to pursue their interests by devising the individualist and class collaborationist strategies which will allow them best to pursue the competitive struggle among commodity sellers.

Because of the profound interdependence of collective action, social power, political effectiveness, and political consciousness, abrupt, large scale changes in the level of working-class struggle have tended to be the condition for significant political trans- formations — the onset of broad waves of reform, the transition from craft to industrial unionism, the rise of mass social demo- cratic parties and the like. At the same time, because class-based strategies tend to *depend on* collective mobilization of social power, working people and oppressed groups normally confront a classic double-bind: without a significant level of organization and power, it seems suicidal to initiate collective action; yet, without a significant level of collective action, it is impossible to amass organization and power, and to develop consciousness. Understandably, even the ideological and organizational inter- vention of socialists is often useless for actually breaking this bind. Historically, then, as Rosa Luxemburg clearly saw, 'the unconscious movement tends to precede the conscious move- ment.' Her classic account of the mass strike phenomenon captures the psychological dynamics of mass working-class movements in general: 'The first direct action reacted *inward* . . . as it for the first time awakened class feeling and class consciousness . . . This awakening of class feeling expressed itself forthwith in the circumstances that the proletarian mass . . . quite suddenly and sharply came to realize how in- tolerable was the social and economic existence which they had endured for decades.' Thus, 'the moment that the real, earnest periods of mass strike begin, all those calculations of "cost" [which previously had discouraged working class initiatives] become merely projects for exhausting the ocean with a tum- bler.'[3] The result, in potential, as Luxemburg goes on to explain, is not only the emergence of unprecedented forms of organiz- ation, involving previously disorganized layers, around novel demands, but the politically self-conscious confrontations of workers with capital and the state, and the placing of socialism itself once more on the agenda.

Once in struggle, people can find meaning in hitherto irrele- vant strategies requiring working-class collective action and hitherto utopian goals requiring working-class power. As winning becomes conceivable, it is reasonable to try to do what is required to win: to break the law and confront the state, as well as to develop new forms of social connections with 'outside' social forces — between organized and unorganized, between employed and unemployed, between Black and white. Correlat- ively, as collective action leads to collective power, it makes sense to consider broad programs of reform which hitherto were incapable of inspiring action. In other words, it is in the process of actually constituting themselves as a class in order to struggle that workers come to conceive the interconnected notions of a class-divided society, of a strategy of class struggle, and of social-ism as a goal as constituting a reasonable perspective.

Reformism as an Ideology of the Working Class

Naturally, periods of mass activity are temporally limited. Although trade unions, social democratic parties, and revo-lutionary groups, as well as mass organizations of oppressed people, tend to establish themselves at high points of struggle, they must operate for significant periods in an environment shaped by relatively low levels of working-class activity. Indeed, in 'normal' times, working-class activity takes on a character the reverse of that in periods of mass upsurge. By its very nature, it is sharply limited in scope: mass political parties tone down their rhetoric of class; trade unions organize workers from only a particular firm, craft, or industry; shopfloor militants can attract only a small proportion of their fellow workers. Attempts to spread struggles beyond a narrow sphere do not as a rule meet with success.

In such periods of downturn, the minoritarian and restricted character of working-class activity appears to be its natural and permanent character. It therefore tends to form the material basis, the starting point, for the formation of working-class political consciousness. Class-wide attacks upon the preroga-tives of the capitalists, let alone the transition to socialism, are off the agenda. A majority of working people conclude, therefore, that they must accept as given the basic ground rules of the capitalist system — especially the requirement for capitalist profitability as the basis for the operation of the system. It is the apparent unchallengeability of capitalist property and the capit-alist state which forms the necessary, although *insufficient*, con-dition for the widespread acceptance within the working class of reformism — viz., the worldview and strategy for action which takes the capitalist property system as given, but asserts the special interest of the working class within it, above all, the working class's 'right' to appropriate a 'fair share' of the total product. In turn, because it tends to be consolidated in periods when working-class organization is relatively weak, the reformist perspective is almost invariably associated with strategies for reform requiring minimal working-class mobilization — routinized (often symbolic) strike action, institutionalized collective bargaining, and above all the electoral road. Unable to carry out the class struggle in an all-out way, the workers seek *alternative* methods to defend their interests.

Nevertheless, reformism, like any other worldview, can command widespread acceptance only on the condition that it provide the basis for successful action. Thus, given even a minimum of working-class organization, reformism tends to be widely attractive in periods of prosperity precisely because in such periods the threat of even limited working-class resistance — symbolized by the resolution to strike or a victory at the polls — actually can yield concessions from capital. Since filling orders and expanding production are their top priorities in the boom, capitalists will tend to find it in their interests to maintain and increase production, even when this means concessions to workers, if the alternative is to endure a strike or other forms of social dislocation. In fact, as the economy expands, capitalist competition almost always drives up the price of labor, whatever labor does, and this gives an appearance of effectiveness to workers' organizations, and of the reformist perspective, even if these are actually quite weak. On the other hand, in periods of economic contraction and falling profits, the capitalists' first priority is to increase competitiveness in stagnant markets. Since increasing competitiveness depends on cost-cutting, employers will often choose to weather a long strike or social unrest if they can thereby achieve significant reductions in labor costs. Moreover, the very fact that capitalist profits are shrinking gives capital a tremendous weapon in periods of economic downturn. Since profits are the only category of income which can be assumed regularly to go back into expanding production and increasing employment, even workers find it hard to deny that the capitalists' share, above all others, must be protected as the pie shrinks, and tkat (by the ironclad logic of aritkmetic), the working class must be prepared to make sacrifices. *All else being equal,* declines in profitability and the general outlook for business actually tend, *in themselves,* to increase the power of capital vis à vis labor. Under conditions of economic crisis, then, unless an explosion of working-class struggle can radically transform their level of organization, power, and consciousness, workers will find reformist ideas decreasingly relevant or attractive. With strategies requiring class action against capital apparently impossible to implement, working people will increasingly find it reasonable to resort to individualistic and class-collaborationist strategies, and will adopt the pro-capitalist, right wing theories which make sense of these strategies.

Reformism as the Ideology of a Distinct, Non-Working Class Social Layer

Under conditions of low or diminishing struggle and minoritarian working-class activity, any working-class organization and leadership — trade union, political party, or whatever — will be obliged to make certain compromises with capital and to relinquish, for the time being, certain programatic ends and strategic options. To do otherwise would be to ignore the actual balance of forces and invite suicidal defeat. The recognition of this reality — which in certain periods is the dominant one — constitutes the critical point of departure for those who argue for building a new social democracy by entering into reformist organizations and by merging with reformist forces. The new social democrats view the conservative outlook and strategies of the official reformist organizations and their leaderships as *merely reflecting* the temporary balance of class forces and the momentarily reigning political consciousness. They logically conclude, therefore, that they should enter into and seek to build these organizations, since, on their assumptions, as working-class activity once again increases, and new strategies and ideas become more appropriate, these organizations and their leaderships will, more or less naturally, adjust their perspectives in a radical direction.

Nevertheless the view that the political limitations of today's reformist organizations and their leaderships simply mirror the political limitations of the rank and file of these organizations is partial and profoundly misleading. For it fails to take sufficiently into account those critical modern social forces which constitute the *permanent* social basis for reformist institutions and ideas, give to reformism its *consistent* character, and provide its chief sources of creativity — i.e. the trade union officials, the parliamentary politicians, and the petty bourgeois leaderships of the organizations of the oppressed. Any political strategy that seeks to revitalize social democracy from within must look to these elements. Now, the official representatives of the reformist organizations obviously do depend for their very existence upon the establishment of these organizations, and these are almost always initially created out of militant mass struggles. Moreover, as the class struggle dies down, the reformist leaderships tend to adopt political and strategic alternatives which appear quite similar to those adopted by the majority of the working class in such circumstances. Nevertheless, the reformist standpoint does not have the same causes or the same significance for the reformist officialdom as it does for rank and file workers. The majority of workers adhere *temporarily* to reformist perspectives because, under conditions of waning struggle and minority organization, they believe these perspectives are the best ones they can realistically act upon. In contrast, the official representatives of the reformist organizations tend to adhere to a reformist political worldview on a *permanent* bais. Constituting *a distinct social layer* with distinctive interests quite different from those of the mass of the working class, these elements adhere to reformism as an expression of their drive precisely to free themselves from dependence upon their working-class base and to secure their long term acceptance by capital. This fundamental difference becomes crystal clear when the level of working-class activity and organization begins to grow. As the class struggle heats up, the transformation of workers' self-activity creates the potential for the transformation of workers' consciousness in a radical direction. But for the reformist officials, the same is *not* true. As the class struggle intensifies, these elements do not dissolve or change their political approach. On the contrary, they seek to contain the struggle and channel it into the classic forms of reformist activity — forms which they hope will be acceptable to capital.

The Labor Officialdom, Parliamentary Politicians, and the Petty Bourgeois Black Leadership

Simply put, the labor officialdom, the parliamentary politicos, and the petty bourgeois leaders of the Black organizations adhere permanently to a reformist perspective because it offers them the theory, strategy, and tactics through which they can best pursue their own reproduction as they are. Labor bureaucrats, parliamentary politicos, and Black officials no longer work beside, or share the conditions of, those they represent. This is fundamental, as the requirements for *their* survival cease to be the same as those of the rank and file workers or the people in the community. They are not *directly* affected by the pressure from employers upon wages and working conditions or from the government upon social expenditures for the community. Nor is their ability to defend their own conditions of life, as it is for the rank and file they represent, *immediately* dependent upon their capacity to build a counterforce by organizing their fellow workers for struggle. Instead, the material base of the trade union bureaucrats, the party politicos, and the Black officials becomes the organizations for which they work, and, in turn, the increasingly self-conscious groups of officials who operate the union, the party, or the Black organization. The organization — and the bureaucratic group which founds itself upon it — not only provides the officials with their means of support, thereby freeing them from the drudgery of manual labor and the shop floor. It constitutes for them a whole way of life — their day to day function, formative social relationships with peers and superiors on the organizational ladder, a potential career, and, on many occasions, a social meaning, a *raison d'être*. To maintain themselves as they are, the whole layer of officials must, first and above all, maintain their organizations. It is thus easy to understand how an irresistible tendency emerges on the part of the trade union officials, the party politicos, and the Black leaderships to treat their organizations as ends in themselves, rather than as the means to defend their memberships — to come to conflate the interests of the organizations upon which they depend with the interests of those they ostensibly represent.

As representatives of the organized sectors of the working-class, the trade union officials have historically constituted the critical — and archetypical — social layer attached to reformism. The trade union officials naturally understand that the fundamental threat not only to the workers whom they represent, but also to the organizations upon which they depend, is the capitalist class — a class 'permanently' self-organized and 'permanently' dominant. The indispensable condition for the survival of the unions and thus of the officials' own continuing existence as officials is acceptance by capital —specifically, the capitalists' recognition of the unions and the capitalists' acceptance of the rules of parliamentary democracy. Ultimately, the capitalists' acceptance of the unions and of parliamentary democracy can only be assured by the organized power of the workers. Nevertheless, the trade union leaders are excruciatingly sensitive to the fluctuating strength and the potential weakness of the organized workers: they understand that even at the height of the class struggle, indeed especially at that point, there is an enormous risk of defeat, and thus of the destruction of their organizations. To the extent that they are able to do so, they increasingly seek to protect their organizations — and, in their minds, their memberships — by renouncing all those broader forms of struggle which provide the ground for broadly ranging attacks on capital and, in turn, the basis for socialist ideology — not only militant direct action, but organization which goes beyond the immediate workplace or industry to link organized with unorganized, employed with unemployed, workplace with community, etc. But even while undermining workers' militancy and self-organization, the officials must still appear to defend their constituencies, within the limits imposed by the requirements of defending capitalist profitability. This, in the end, is a difficult trick to pull off. But historically, the official labor movement has relied on two basic strategies as consciously-conceived *substitutes* for direct action: (1) constituting, with the help of the state, permanent institutions to regulate worker-employer conflict; (2) the electoral/parliamentary road.

Collective Bargaining

Establishing regular institutions for the (temporary) coexistence between capital and the labor officaldom — the traditional forms of collective bargaining — has, classically, depended on striking a 'deal' between labor officials and capital. The officials must be prepared to pledge to reduce labor disturbances and enforce labor discipline. In turn, the capitalists must be prepared to make regular concessions to the workers for which the officials can take credit, since this is the requirement for their being able to maintain the allegiance of the majority of workers and to isolate militants. This deal is not without cost to the capitalists and benefit to the workers, and the capitalists will therefore accept it only to the extent they are forced to do so, and to the degree it is worth their while to pay extra for labor peace in exchange for smooth production. Capitalist expansion and high profitability are, almost always, the necessary conditions for the deal.

In the context of this bargain, the union officials are free to develop their 'organization within the organization' and their own special role. They negotiate a contract; there is an agreement not to strike throughout its duration; instead, the officials settle disputes through the grievance procedure and ultimately compulsory arbitration. The officials 'service' the rank and file, enforcing the contract in grievance procedure. But as the other side of the deal, they must also compel the membership to adhere to the contract and limit any sort of shopfloor resistance. To this end, they must move to undercut all independent organization of the rank and file and to curb rank and file control over the trade union itself, curtailing union democracy.

Like reformist practices generally, collective bargaining in the context of the deal has a dual significance. On the one hand, it *does* reflect the momentary interests of the working class in a period of declining and minoritarian organization: under the circumstances, most workers see no choice but to accept it as the best they can get. On the other hand, the labor officials find in the ramifying institutions of collective bargaining, not only an essential *raison d'être,* but also an important basis for their material existence and a critical foundation for their *modus vivendi* with capital. In the hands of the officials, the functioning of collective bargaining ceases merely to reflect the momentary (unfavorable) balance of class forces between capital and labor; it serves to dissolve workers' self-organization and workers' power, and in this way has the effect of tipping that balance further in the direction of capital. Thus is produced, once again, the classic paradox of reformism: although the union officialdom may rise to great heights during the boom on the basis of its ability to secure labor peace and the apparent well-being of workers, it does so at the expense of the workers' self-organization and thus of its own power and position over the long term. As the expansion gives way to contraction, the officials are less and less able to make collective bargaining work for their constituencies or themselves: the employers break the deal and unleash their offensive; the workers see fewer reasons to support either the officials or their reformist strategies; the officials watch their organizations erode and their whole worldview lose its credibility.

The electoral/parliamentary road constitutes the definitive strategy of all those distinctive social elements characteristically tied to reformism, because it appears to provide the means to overcome the central dilemma they face: how to retain their mass working-class bases without having to organize their constituencies for direct action against capital. In election campaigns, isolated individuals can be mobilized to cast their ballots, privately and individually, in favor of pro-working class candidates around a reform program. In this way, it appears possible to amass power and win reforms without the risk of mass struggles like strikes or street confrontations.

Nevertheless, to adhere to a primarily parliamentary strategy is to fall victim to the classical social democratic illusion: that a balance of class forces favorable to the working class can be constructed inside the state by electoral/parliamentary means, apart from the massive strengthening of the workers against the capitalists in the shops and in the streets. The electoral approach is illusory because, contrary to appearances, power in capitalist society is not normally exercised through control over the state and through force. So long as capitalist property relations hold, the capitalist class, through its control over the means of production, retains control over the investment function, and thereby holds the key to the development of the productivity of labor, to economic growth, and to economic prosperity — and, on that basis, to employment, social stability, and state revenue. Since capitalist investment depends on the capitalists' ability to make a profit, short of revolution, all elements of society find it sooner or later in their own interest to ensure capitalist profitability. 'What's good for GM is good for the country' captures an important aspect of reality under capitalism.

In this context, it is clear why those who hold positions in the state, even those elected on programs representing the interests of workers, are under enormous pressure to 'be responsible,' to support policies that will safeguard profits. To do otherwise would risk the malfunctioning of the economy and all that entails. The politicians are aware that, short of challenging capitalist property itself — taking control of production away from the capitalists — it is impossible to carry out, over an extended period, an anti-capitalist program without inviting the withdrawal of investment funds and ultimately economic chaos.

Even so, it needs to be emphasized that, like collective bargaining, the electoral/parliamentary road has a dual significance. On the one hand, under conditions of limited working-class mobilization, the majority of workers *are* likely to favor the electoral road: electoralism appears to constitute a substitute for direct action, a way for workers to fight for their interests without having to face the enormous dangers of confronting the capitalists. Moreover, like collective bargaining, the electoral road can, under certain conditions, appear to function very well for the working class. In periods of prosperity, especially in the wake of fairly substantial working-class mobilizations, it is often in the interests of capital to accept reforms, rather than risk social disruption.

On the other hand, because the gulf which separates the social democratic parties' bureaucracies from the working class as a whole is even greater than that which separates labor officialdom from its membership, the social democratic party politicos are positioned to respond to the needs of capital even more sensitively and immediately than are labor bureaucrats. Union leaders must, in many cases, respond to the organized interests of (usually localized) groups of rank and filers who have been brought together in production and who have had the experience of collective struggle and collective self-organization in their union and on the shopfloor. In contrast, the party ostensibly represents the 'class as a whole,' but since workers are, *in practice*, able actually to organize themselves as a class only rarely, the official party and its machine are generally under little pressure from, or control by, their atomized electoral base. Nor (in the absence of mass working class direct action) can the periodically radicalized and aroused party rank and file generally exert more than the most partial and temporary pressure on the parliamentary delegation and apparatchiks who rule the party. This is, in part, because the professional politicos generally command an institutionalized apparatus explicitly designed to ensure their control over the organization and insulate them from the pressure of the party membership. But it is also because the politicos can, in most situations, claim with some justice to represent the party's real base — viz., the broader electorate, which is generally far more conservative than the rank and file party members and which will decide the one question of moment to the whole party: whether or not it will win the election. Free to accept the rules of the game, the reformist professional politicians may demand the workers' rightful piece of the growing pie in periods of prosperity, but as prosperity gives way to crisis, they will have little choice other than to translate 'fair share' into 'austerity' for their worker constituents. However, as the reformist politicians increasingly assume the role of restorers of capitalist profitability, the working class finds fewer reasons to prefer them to the outright representatives of capital, or even to distinguish between the reformists' perspectives and those of capital itself. Consistent reformism leads once again, to its own dissolution.

Rationalizing Capitalism Through Corporatism

Unable to confront capitalism, and acutely aware of their consequent dependence upon the health of the system, the official forces of reformism have been among those most concerned to understand the operation of capitalism and to devise plans to make it function better. Perhaps more than any other groups, the labor bureaucracy, reformist politicians, and the official representatives of the established organizations of the oppressed have been the leading proponents of conscious, society-wide attempts to regulate those economic dislocations which they see as caused by capitalism's anarchy and its unequal distribution of income. One need attribute no special cynicism to reformist officials in pursuing the policies they do. On the contrary, they view their interests as coinciding with those of (capitalist) society as a whole, and their ideology as expressing the general interest. Indeed, given the particularist interests of the individual capitalists and their necessary competition with one another, the capitalist class as a whole may actually be less capable than the reformist leaders of devising and promoting policies in the interests of overall capital accumulation. As is well known, the trade union officials, reformist politicians, and official Black leaderships have been the most consistent proponents of government intervention to regulate the economy. They were the prime apostles of Keynesian efforts to smooth out the cycle by means of regulating demand. They are today the leading exponents of industrial policy to make their own national capitalisms more competitive in the international economy. Through these approaches, the reformist leaderships strive to ensure and restore capitalist profitability and economic growth, for that, in their view, is the indispensable condition for the improvement of the condition of the working class, as well as of their own survival. Given their belief in the permanence of the capitalist property system, they have no other choice.

Neverthless, in order actually to have their policies put into practice, the official reformist leaderships know that they must secure the cooperation of the employers, for they have no intention whatsoever of imposing upon them (since this would require working-class mobilization). For this reason, as the economy enters into crisis, the official reformist leaderships seek, with increasing singlemindedness, to eschew all forms of resistance and to force corporatist or collaborative arrangements with the employers at the level of the shop floor, the firm, and the economy as a whole through which they can have implemented their rationalizing plans. But as the economic crisis appears more inexorable and as their own self-disarmament increases their weakness, their plans for the reform of capital appear ever more quixotic and their ability to influence the employers declines. As they forward ever more desperately their plans for collaboration, they encounter an increasingly ferocious capitalist offensive. Unless a revitalized workers movement deters them or the economy's miraculous recovery reprieves them, the reformist leadership will pursue to its conclusion their lemming-like drive to self-destruction.

IV   Two Cycles of Reform and Decline

The whole history of the relationship among the official leaderships of reformist organizations, the Democratic Party, and the movements for reform over the past half century in the United States illustrates the dynamic outlined thus far. Since the late 1920s, we have witnessed two great cycles of reform and decline, the first running from the 1930s to the early 1950s, the second running from the late 1950s to the present. During each of these cycles, workers and oppressed people won major reforms by means of explosive mass direct action against employers and the state — in the workplaces, in communities, in the street. Through these struggles, the working class and oppressed groups *imposed* reforms on hitherto do-nothing Democratic Party administrations *from the outside*. In each cycle, the Democratic Party profited from the reforms, the mass movements, and the liberalization and radicalization of consciousness which went with them, significantly expanding its electoral base. Nevertheless, the movements were obliged to develop almost entirely outside and largely against the Democratic Party and the established reformist organizations on the basis of new leaderships, because the established, official leaderships opposed them. As the movements developed, small sections of the traditional leaderships did 'go over.' But as they did, they functioned generally to domesticate these movements, specifically by turning them away from mass direct action and to dependence upon electoralism and the Democratic Party. In each cycle, as the movements declined — partly as a result of the officials' actions, partly for independent reasons — the leaderships succeeded in recuperating their bases for the Democratic Party, and working people and oppressed groups were left to depend upon it. But as popular militancy died down, the Democratic Party, despite its electoral majorities, was less and less successful in winning reforms. In the end, the Democratic Party's abject failure to deliver the goods opened the way to a new period of revival for the Republican Party.

The Movements of the 30s

Franklin Roosevelt acceded to the Presidency in 1933 as a pragmatist and moderate, with no clear reform program. Shortly after his inauguration, a wave of increasingly powerful workers' struggles shook the country, beginning in the auto industry in Detroit, spreading to the southern textile mills, the eastern coal mines, and the midwestern steel mills. But Roosevelt stood by and did nothing, as the companies and the local repressive forces crushed one strike after another. Meanwhile, the mediation boards set up under Roosevelt's National Recovery Act attempted, in almost every case, simply to get the workers back on the job for the employers without dealing with the issues at stake. But the strike wave continued to grow, and in 1934 workers won astounding victories in three great general strikes in Toledo, Minneapolis, and San Francisco — all of which were marked by the most massive and violent confrontations between workers and authorities. During 1935-1936, a mass rank and file movement of auto workers created the United Auto Workers and went out to defeat General Motors in the historic sit-down strikes of

December-January 1936-1937.[4]

The Democratic Party benefited from this broad labor upsurge and the transformation of political consciousness which it underwrote. This was evidenced in the party's unexpectedly massive and decisive midterm electoral victory in November 1934. Meanwhile, more radical forces were also gaining ground, with the Communist Party experiencing a massive period of growth and expanding influence, and the Socialists asserting themselves successfully in certain local electoral arenas. As a result of the sharp increase in the level of struggle and the consequent radicalization of the political mood, Roosevelt suddenly changed political course. In 1935, he pushed through the hitherto neglected Wagner Act and Social Security Act, the two main reform achievements of the New Deal.[5]

The great mass workers' movements of the 30s developed entirely outside and against the old AFL officaldom. Throughout the later 1920s, these officials watched passively as employers waged an all-out assault on the unions, exemplified in the union-busting American Plan. Even as their dues base declined, then shrank to insignificance after 1929, the bureaucrats were incapable of launching even a token counteroffensive. When the new workers' movement exploded onto the scene in 1933, the AFL tried to capture and domesticate it by seeking, in strike after strike, to get the workers to go back to work and to rely on the decisions of the courts and the federal mediation boards. With the help of AFL officials, the employers crushed the United Textile Workers strike of 1934.[6] Meanwhile, in the fall of 1933, John L. Lewis played a powerful role in limiting the militant struggles of coal miners which had spread to the captive mines (owned by the steel companies); shortly thereafter in early 1934, Lewis helped derail a nascent triple alliance of the miners, the steel workers, and the railroad workers. The auto workers succeeded in creating the UAW only by breaking from the AFL and building a powerful and independent rank and file movement, with an explicit program of refusing to depend on the officials, the courts, and the mediation boards, and of relying instead on militant direct action.[7]

Ultimately, as the movement threatened to get out of hand, a small section of the old AFL leadership, led by John L. Lewis, did see the handwriting on the wall and made a break from the AFL to help found the CIO. At the same time, however, they strove mightily to contain the movement's burgeoning militancy and turn its energies toward the Democratic Party. Lewis made himself a hero by standing firmly beside the GM sit-downers in January 1937. But immediately thereafter, he cut short the Chrysler sit-down which was threatening to win even greater gains than had the GM strike. During the spring and summer of 1937, Lewis and his cohorts bent all their energies to break the wave of sit-downs and wildcats that continued to shake the auto industry. Meanwhile, Lewis ensured that the critical campaign to organize the steel industry would end in disastrous defeat when he turned explicitly to top down, conservative methods of organizing and carried out the strike under the banner 'Trust in Roosevelt.' The defeat of the Little Steel strike in the summer of 1937, following the infamous Memorial Day Massacre and the betrayal of the workers by one after another Democratic Party mayor and governor, coupled with the officials' successful repression of the struggle in auto, marked a turning point. Especially with the onset of the new depression, beginning in mid-1937, the dynamism of the labor upsurge was rapidly dissipated and a long process of erosion initiated.[8]

As Lewis and Co. were stifling the movements of direct action, they were, simultaneously, attempting to reroute the CIO into electoral dependence on the Democratic Party. When the UAW voted not to endorse Roosevelt at its first convention in April 1936, Lewis personally intervened to get the decision reversed. Henceforward, the CIO leaders stuck ever more closely to a strategy of electoral intervention aimed at increasing their leverage on the Democratic Party. To this end, the unions established in 1943 the so-called Political Action Committees (PACs) as part of their general tactic of building local level machines to turn out the vote for 'pro-labor' candidates in order ultimately to strengthen their position inside the Party. But if the labor movement could not win a place as coequals with the Dixiecrats and big city bosses inside the Party during the period of mass labor upsurge and of the reforms which accompanied it, it was unrealistic to expect that they could do better as the movement waned and labor's real strength correspondingly declined. During the 1940s, despite the Democrats' overwhelming electoral/parliamentary hegemony for most of the period, the forces of reform became progressively weaker. As early as 1943, Congress passed the Smith-Connally Act, which curtailed some of labor's chief weapons of struggle (providing for 'cooling off' periods before strikes, injunctions 'in the public interest,' etc.)[9]

By the end of the war, labor was unable to prevent the passage of the viciously anti-labor Taft-Hartley Act, which in a single stroke wiped out much of what had been won in the 30s. By the early 1950s, the official forces of reform had presided over the total decay of the workers' movement of the 1930s, the consequent dissolution of the main forces for both reform and Democratic Party hegemony, the resulting dissipation of liberal and radical sentiment, and the inevitable return to power of the Republican Party.

The Movements of the 60s

The rise of a mass militant Black movement, originating in the buses and cafeterias of the Deep South, ushered in a new period of reform. The Black movement, which rose and fell in the period from the later 1950s to the early 70s, followed very closely the trajectory traced by the mass labor movement of the 30s and 40s. Thus, the historic civil rights movement, ignited by the Montgomery Bus boycott of 1955-1956, and, even more, the explosive movement of Black Power, which arose in the urban ghettos of northern cities in the summer of 1964, based themselves from the start on a powerful commitment to direct action and confrontation with the white power structure. In the civil rights struggles of the late 50s and 60s, tens of thousands directly stood up to the authorities in illegal sit-downs, provocative freedom marches, and unauthorized fights for the right to vote. Whole communities, especially in the South, organized themselves to resist. In the urban risings of the North between 1964 and 1967, hundreds of thousands of working-class and poor Blacks actively participated in the struggle. By the time of Martin Luther King's assassination in early 1968, the Black movement had shaken white society to its foundations, had inspired militant student and anti-imperialist movements in its wake, and had begun to ignite dynamic organizing drives in the labor movement itself. King was assassinated in the middle of an organizing campaign of primarily Black city workers in Memphis, Tennessee. A short time later, the League of Revolutionary Black Workers was founded in the inner-city auto factories of Detroit.

John F. Kennedy came to office, as had Franklin Roosevelt, as a middle-of-the-road and pragmatic Democrat. Interestingly, his narrow electoral victory over Richard Nixon was assured by the massive vote of newly-aroused Blacks which allowed him to carry certain key states. Nevertheless, during his three years in the Presidency Kennedy failed to achieve any significant social legislation, and his tenure in office was overshadowed by America's growing, if largely unheralded, involvement in Vietnam. It was clearly the deepening radicalization of the Black struggle, marked by the civil rights movement's growing opposition to the Vietnam War, and above all the urban rebellions in Detroit, Watts, Harlem, Newark and elsewhere which concentrated Lyndon Johnson's mind on his 'Great Society' and enabled him to inaugurate a new era of reform. In 1964, Johnson won a landslide electoral victory on a rising tide of liberal and radical sentiment rooted in the Black and newly emergent anti-Vietnam movements. Shortly thereafter, a suddenly reform-minded Congress passed the Civil Rights Acts, the Poverty Programs, and other important pieces of reform legislation. Once again, an independent mass movement had forced the Democrats to become reformers.

Like the workers' movement of the 30s, the Black movement grew up almost entirely on the basis of new leadership and new organizations. SNCC and CORE, not the NAACP or the Urban League, provided most of the dynamism that built the freedom struggles. The new Black militants had to create their movement largely over the resistance of the old, official leaderships. The NAACP refused to participate in the 1963 March on Washington unless it would be entirely legal and peaceful; it insisted that the Black movement support Johnson and his war in Vietnam; and it vehemently attacked Black Power. In the process, it precipitated a profound split between the new movement and the old guard. The chasm became unbreachable when the urban rebellions ignited the mass struggle for Black Power which ultimately issued in the formation of the Black Panther Party and the League of Revolutionary Black Workers.[10]

Treading the well worn path followed by trade union official-dom in the 30s, official Black leaders did what they could to steer the explosive Black movement toward the Democratic Party. In 1964, for the first time ever, the NAACP officially endorsed the Democratic candidate and organized a voter registration drive designed to channel the newly-unleashed energies of the Black struggle toward the campaign of Lyndon Johnson for President. Nevertheless, the new civil rights organizations continued to reject electoralism and remained almost obsessively devoted to militant direct action. When the civil rights movement sought to use the ballot box, it was, as a rule, to assert the right to vote, not to win an election. This is best seen in what was perhaps the civil rights movement's most dramatic electoral intervention: the struggle of the Freedom Democratic Party in Mississippi in 1964. There, against the violent resistance of the white power structure, organizers from SNCC, CORE, and other groups initially tried to compel the authorities to allow Blacks to register to vote in the Democratic Party. When they were prevented from doing this by a wave of repression, they turned to organizing an autonomous campaign to sign up Black voters for their own, unofficial Mississippi Freedom Democratic Party (MFDP) in order to challenge the official Democratic Party delegation which was, of course, firmly segregationist and reactionary. Lyndon Johnson and the Democratic Party refused to seat the MFDP at the national convention, despite the official Mississippi delegation's rejection of most of Johnson's program and their generally favoring the right wing Republican Barry Goldwater for President. Nevertheless, at the time of the convention and after, the official Black leadership called upon the MFDP to compromise. More generally, they demanded that the Black movement turn 'from protest to politics,' in Bayard Rustin's eloquent phrase, from the politics of the street to the politics of the ballot box. Nevertheless, the civil rights movement continued to reject electoralism. As Meier and Rudwick, the historians of CORE, sum up the position of both CORE and SNCC at this critical juncture: 'Social change could come only through an independent movement that would "remain a threat to the power structure." '[11]

As it had from the labor struggles of the 30s, the Democratic Party benefited greatly from the Black movement, as well as from the student movement, the anti-war movement, and the small but significant rank and file movement — all of which emerged in the middle 60s on the rising tide of Black militancy. The Party also benefited from the general trend toward political liberalization and radicalization which accompanied these movements. Indeed, despite Richard Nixon's victory over Humphrey in 1968, the Democratic Party appeared to some at this time on the verge of achieving a permanent electoral majority. This was largely because demographic developments were drastically sapping the Republicans' rural strongholds and feeding the Democrats' apparently permanently reformist working-class and Black electoral base. Cushioned from capital by the unprecedented prosperity and pressed for reform by the rising mass movements, the Democrats appeared capable of delivering the goods more or less indefinitely.

By the middle 1970s, the mass movements of the 60s had experienced precipitous decline and, with them, the impetus for reform. Significantly for the argument of this essay, the continuing strength of the movements and of the liberal and radical ideologies to which they gave rise propelled a dramatic continuation of the general wave of reform even through the first Nixon administration. The years between 1968 and 1972 witnessed the establishment of the Occupational Safety and Health Administration (OSHA), the creation of the Environmental Protection Agency (EPA), and dramatic increases in funding for Social Security and food stamps. But during the late 60s, the Black movement reached its zenith, and, unable to find powerful allies in a still largely dormant working class movement, found itself isolated, politically without perspective, and brutally repressed by local and national police. When Nixon began to withdraw the troops from Vietnam, the once powerful peace movement declined rapidly. For a brief period, militant rank and file movements exploded across industry and precipitated bitter struggles with employers; but they were unable in the end to produce a lasting impact on the political landscape.

Thus, by the mid-70s, the Democrats got the chance to prove once again that, in the absence of mass struggles, reformist electoral majorities bring little power to the forces of reform. As recently as 1976, the Democratic Party controlled both the White House and powerful legislative majorities. Many of its officials were committed on paper to widely ranging programs of social reform. Nevertheless, during the later 1970s, the Democrats were unable to pass a single significant piece of social legislation. Congress first gutted then passed the Humphrey-Hawkins bill for 'full employment,' as if to rub the noses of its sponsors in the dirt. The bill for common situs picketing was soundly defeated. National health insurance, the rallying cry of the Democratic left, never got a hearing. Perhaps most humiliating, the so-called Labor Law Reform bill, shorn of all serious anti-employer passages, was soundly defeated. Meanwhile, President Jimmy Carter put an end to the long period of rising expenditures for the urban poor, and was, after one term, succeeded by Ronald Reagan. Once again, the Democratic Party and the established reformist leaderships had succeeded in riding out the wave of mass struggle, depriving themselves of their own base and opening the way to the Republicans and the right.

V   Left Reformists in the Economic Crisis

The conservative tendencies of the trade union officials, the petty bourgeois Black leadership, and the Democratic Party politicos are often recognized. It is, nevertheless, widely assumed, especially by the new social democrats, that, given the proper backing from an active and politicized rank and file, at least the left wing among the reformist officials, under pressure from the capitalists, will take the lead in reviving mass movements. According to the widely accepted view, the trade union, Black politico, and Democratic Party 'lefts' cannot help but understand that capitalism is experiencing a long term economic crisis and that there is a wide-ranging employer offensive under way to restore profits. These leaders are acutely aware, moreover, that the employer offensive poses a mortal threat to the basic institutions from which they themselves draw their lifeblood — viz., the trade unions, the established Black organizations, and the liberal wing of the Democratic Party. On the rampage, employers have been discrediting the leadership with the rank and file, if not smashing the unions outright, thereby undermining the officials' cherished dues base. Meanwhile, through their PACs, the capitalists have been isolating the unions and the Black leaderships even inside the Democratic Party. Thus, according to this line of thinking the trade union, Black politico, and Democratic Party 'lefts' *have no choice* but to resist, if only out of self-interest, to protect their own positions. They will, sooner or later, have to initiate action, put masses into motion, or at least create the conditions which will bring this about.

This analysis is sadly mistaken conceptually, and has been massively refuted empirically in the recent period. The fact is that the reformist leaderships have a wide range of options in responding to the employer offensive. They can, in the first place, often carry on quite prosperously for extended periods, even while their memberships suffer heavy losses. Moreover, even when the employers attack them directly, the reformist leaderships are most unlikely to respond in kind. In periods of deepening crisis like the present, to fight back effectively against the employers requires organizing the most massive and militant mobilization of unions and other mass organizations in order directly to confront the employers. But as the reformist officials are aware, to carry through such a mobilization and confrontation, they would have to risk the total destruction of their organizations and their secure positions. As a rule, therefore, the trade union, Black official, and Democratic Party 'lefts' will choose to sustain even serious losses, if the alternative is to stand up and confront employers and risk total annihilation. It seems to them the better part of valor to preserve their own organizations and positions at least partially intact until a new period of economic expansion allows them to take up their old positions as brokers between capital and the working class. Of course, to the degree the crisis lengthens and the employer offensive intensifies, the reformist officials' strategy proves progressively less effective; so, over the long run, the officials tend to find the ground for their very existence cut out from under them. Nevertheless, *at any given moment,* it appears to the officials too risky to make a stand, so they are unlikely ever to take the initiative to reverse the trend. Even as the entire labor movement disintegrated under the employers' attacks during the 1920s, and with it their own organizations and positions, the old AFL officials never offered any serious resistance. Nor are things markedly different with the officials of the current epoch, despite the distant origins of their organizations in the CIO mass upsurge. When UAW President Doug Fraser made his dramatic exit from the Labor Management Advisory Board to form the Progressive Alliance in 1978, he warned that the bosses had broken their side of the deal and could expect swift retaliation from at least the left wing of reformist officialdom. But it is doubtful if Fraser's defiant posture struck much fear into the hearts of the employers. In fact, the 'one-sided class war' of which Fraser spoke had been going on for at least a decade with hardly a murmur of protest from the ranks of labor's officialdom, least of all from its ostensible 'left' or social democratic wing.

The Rank and File Revolt

The imposition of Nixon's 'New Economic Policy' in the wake of the recession of 1970-1971 was the definitive sign that the economy had entered a phase of protracted crisis and that the employer offensive was well under way. The NEP could not have been more clearly designed to redistribute income away from the working class toward the capitalists. Wages were frozen under the control of the wage-price board (assisted by hundreds of thousands of capitalists). Prices were allowed to rise (as no effective mechanism was provided to enforce the mythical freeze on prices).

Meanwhile, employers stepped up their attack in almost every industry. The response was a significant wave of worker rebellion. Nevertheless, in almost every case in order to struggle against the employers, workers had to act in defiance of — and in direct opposition to — their own officials. In March 1970, over a quarter million Post Office employees defied the law and the National Guard — as well as their own leaders — to shut down the mails in over 200 cities and win big gains. Some two months later, tens of thousands of teamsters covered by the National Master Freight Agreement conducted the first (effectively) nationwide truckers strike in history. It was no accident that this unprecedented action was strictly unofficial — and directed not only at employers but also the Teamsters bureaucracy. Over the next two years, there were numerous battles of this sort — for example, the wildcat strike in telephone in New York in 1971. But by far the most spectacular and far-reaching of these rank and file struggles was waged by the coal miners. Over more than a decade, between 1965 and 1978, the rank and file miners unleashed one after another wave of unofficial mass strikes against the mine bosses on the one hand and against a succession of sell-out leaderships on the other. For the present context, what is most significant about the rank and file movements among miners is that, by the end of the period, the UMW rank and file was no longer training its weapons on the gangster-type regime of corrupt Tony Boyle, but was having to assault a newly-ascendant group of self-styled reform officials, led by Arnold Miller, who had risen to power in large part on the basis of their close working relationship with key elements within the liberal wing of the Democratic Party, notably ADA lawyer Joseph Rauh. Entirely devoted, like the rest of reformist officialdom, to electoralist and legalistic methods, this new 'Miners for Democracy' leadership would prove no more willing than its predecessors to mobilize the ranks to stand up to the vicious assaults of the mining companies upon safety conditions in the mines. Like its predecessors, the Miller-MFD leadership had to be buried beneath a new wave of entirely rank and file-led resistance, which actually succeeded in holding back the corporations in the miners strike of 1977-1978.[12] The question still remains, however: were things different in the real bastions of the labor 'left,' above all the UAW and public workers unions, long associated not only with militancy and social unionism, but with social democracy.

The UAW

During the early 70s, in close conjunction with Nixon's NEP, GM introduced its famous GMAD speed-up system into its auto assembly operations. This made headlines around the world and helped make the question of work the center of national discussion. It also provoked a new wave of working-class revolt in auto. Most notable, perhaps, was the six month fight at Lordstown, Ohio, where GM tried out its 100 car per hour assembly line. But an equally long and bitter 26 week strike took place in Norwood, Ohio. Toward the end of 1972, rank and file pressure succeeded in forcing representatives from St. Louis Local 25 to demand a national strike of all GMAD plants. At a meeting of the UAW's GMAD council in Detroit, local presidents went so far as to ratify this plan.

The response of UAW President Leonard Woodcock and of the UAW staff could not have been more destructive. Instead of organizing the national GMAD strikes demanded by the members, they instituted the so-called 'Apache strategy.' This called for local strikes, announced in advance, to run in successive weeks at different GMAD plants for two or three days at a time. Given the advance warning and the shortness of the strikes, GM was easily able to adjust its operations to make sure that these were not disrupted. On the other hand, it was hard to conceive of a tactic better designed to disorganize and demoralize worker militancy. It broke their embryonic drive for unity; forced them to face the employers one at a time; and was almost calculated to prevent victory. It showed the workers precisely where their leaders stood, and succeeded in its purpose of breaking the movement.

If the auto workers had somehow failed to get the message that their liberal/socialist leadership was sympathetic to the corporation's problems, things were made perfectly clear over the next few years, as socialist Doug Fraser himself took center stage. In the summer of 1973, Black workers dramatically seized control of a Detroit Chrysler plant to protest deteriorating conditions, terrible overheating, and racist foremen. To everyone's surprise, they won an initial victory. But when they (ill-advisedly) attempted the same sit-in tactic a second time, union officials were ready. Fraser led more than 1000 UAW staff in smashing physically the picket line outside the occupied plant and dispersing the movement.

The process of social unionist sellout has, of course, reached its climax with the recent series of concessionary contracts. These began in 1978-1979, with the famous contract to save Chrysler, negotiated by Doug Fraser as part of the bailout engineered by the Carter administration. That agreement was followed in GM and Ford by a series of give-back deals, supposedly temporary, to tide the companies over the serious recession of 1979-1982. But with the return to prosperity and record profits in auto, union officials have failed to reverse their approach. On the contrary, in the contract negotiated in September 1984, the UAW gave GM the green light to pursue its far-reaching plans both to shift much of its production to Japan and Korea and to modernize drastically its remaining American operations, even though these policies will decimate the auto labor force. Once again, the utter dependence of the labor officialdom, left and right, on 'their' corporations' profitability could not have been more definitively expressed.[13]

The Public Workers Unions

The pattern in the public sector unions has paralleled that in auto. There, an explicitly 'social democratic' leadership has assumed command to an extent probably unequalled anywhere else in the labor movement. Jerry Wurf, president of AFSCME, and Victor Gotbaum, leader of New York's giant District 37, were both members of DSOC, and District 37 is loaded with DSAers at the local president and staff level. Nonetheless, these leftists constitute the hard core of the conservative wing of public sector unionism. Ironically, it was the 'apolitical' locals that were most responsible for the pressure from the ranks within AFSCME during the 70s. The militant strikes waged by public employee locals in response to the city and state governments' versions of the employer offensive during the middle and late 70s had to take place independently of the 'more advanced' and more 'radical' leadership.

This has been particularly true in New York, which entered the 70s as the nation's stronghold of public employee unionism. When the crisis struck in 1975, the rank and file responded vigorously, only to be crushed by their 'left' leaders. In that year, sanitation workers walked out on a nearly unanimous wildcat. The leadership, however, refused to budge, and allowed the strike to be smashed. In the teachers union, the membership voted an official strike, but were forced back to work after one week by their officials (this time headed by conservative 'socialist' Albert Shanker).

In the wake of these and other defeats, social democratic officials were free to help turn the city over to the direction of the banks and corporations via the Municipal Assistance Corporation (MAC). They have cooperated in the gutting of municipal services to the working-class poor with barely a rhetorical whimper. Tens of thousands of jobs have been surrendered, the remaining ones Taylorized. Class size of 40 or more in the New York City schools is common. Firehouses have been closed, while the number of fires grows. A large proportion of public hospital beds has been eliminated. Meanwhile, for their co-operation in saving the city from financial ruin, unionized workers have been compelled to accept a succession of increasingly concessionary contracts while watching their unions be reduced to a shell.

Winpinsinger, PATCO, and Solidarity Day

Although the images of the miners, auto, and public service union leaderships have been tarnished by their conduct throughout the employer offensive, International Association of Machinists (IAM) president William Winpisinger remains a hero of the new social democratic left. A member of DSA, Winpisinger will, at a moment's notice, call for just about any progressive reform measure and (between elections) will even demand that labor break from the Democratic Party. He remains a favorite speaker at DSA conferences, and at the roundtable discussions of the DSA intelligentsia.

But 'Wimpy' has never tried to conceal his contempt for rank and file organization, past, present, and future: 'The leadership of a union is almost always an accurate reflection of the view of the membership,' he said in an interview with *The Guardian* newspaper not long ago. What about the Teamsters, he was asked, surely a different case? 'Perhaps not,' he replied. 'It's up to the membership to change the situation.' Then, concretely, does Winpisinger support the rank and file movement in that union? No, the Teamsters for a Democratic Union (TDU) represents, in his words, 'outside forces.' 'They asked me to back them,' he said. 'But I asked myself, hell, what's to stop a bunch like that from coming in here and doing the same thing?' In addition, Winpisinger denounced moderate steelworkers union reformer Ed Sadlowski, and said he supported that union's notoriously reactionary leadership. He saw no merit, he said, in Sadlowski's charge that the USW staff had been undemocratically mobilized to stop Sadlowski, asking 'What's wrong with that? Doesn't the staff have democratic rights too?' Winpisinger added that Sadlowski had 'burned his bridges' by running for USW president on a 'screw management platform.' 'I view that as a kind of irresponsible populism,' said Winpisinger.[14]

Far more significant than his words, however, have been Winpisinger's deeds. Over the recent period, Winpisinger has shown that he and the rest of the labor officaldom, both right and left, are one when it comes to cutting short any movement toward a mass militant fightback against the corporations. In the summer of 1981, Reagan fired the opening shot in his newly stepped-up war against the labor movement when he simply abolished the Professional Air Controllers Organization (PATCO) for daring to go out on strike. Coincidentally, at about the same time, the AFL-CIO was planning its so-called Solidarity Day demonstrations, aimed at kicking off the traditional electoral/ legislative effort against Reagan. To everyone's surprise, some three quarters of a million workers showed their potential power by attending the March on Washington, while tens of thousands of others demonstrated at the largest local labor day demonstrations in decades. PATCO had large and militant contingents at all these demonstrations.

Here was a clear opportunity for the labor leadership to bring the spontaneously aroused labor movement behind PATCO and to launch a counter-offensive against the employers and Reagan. Not surprisingly, however, the AFL-CIO officials, across the board, failed to do anything. In particular, Winpisinger refused to call on his membership to honor PATCO's picket lines. The powerful IAM airline mechanics could certainly have shut down the airports and, had Winpisinger been willing to act, called upon the rest of the labor movement to rally behind them in support of PATCO and against Reagan. What was Winpisinger's excuse for scabbing on the pilots? Exhibiting the shopkeeper mentality for which the labor officialdom has become famous, Winpisinger explained that supporting PATCO would have been illegal and would have been risky for the union, threatening its apparatus, especially because the top AFL-CIO leadership had decided not to help (as if it ever had or ever would). In the upshot, the entire labor movement was, yet another time, shunted back onto the electoral road, initiating the ill-fated campaign which reached its predictable and disastrous *dénouement* in the recent Mondale fiasco.

A Two Pronged Strategy?

To the extent that the advocates of a new social democracy base themselves, as they must, on already-existing social democratic and reformist forces, particularly any wing of the trade union officialdom, they pose for themselves a classic dilemma. Historically, the trade union officialdom has furnished the 'political' proponents of a social democratic politics with a ready-made working-class base. But since the turn of the twentieth century, these same officials, in the U.S. and around the world, have asserted their sole right to speak for and to control this base within the party, while setting themselves systematically against those militant rank and file upsurges which have, periodically, offered social democracy in particular and the left in general its best opportunities for transforming working-class consciousness in a radical direction.[15] DSA leader Michael Harrington recognized the dilemma in an interview a number of years ago. 'If you say to me, is it possible that someone who is now a member of DSOC in the union movement will be so fixed and anchored in the bureaucracy that they will be appalled by that rank and file movement and try to put it down? I guess, sure, it's happened before and I suppose it will happen in the future. What will we do then? I hope we will go with the rank and file . . . but I'm sure that some of us might fail the test. There's no way you can anticipate.'

Less willing than Harrington to depend solely upon good intentions — and perhaps more concerned than he about a trade union bureaucratic interest within social democratic parties — some of the current advocates of a new social democracy have proposed a more nuanced, two pronged approach to the problem: ally with the 'progressive' officials inside the party, they suggest, but, at the same time, organize the ranks, independently and from below, in the workplace and the industrial context. This tactic might be worthy of consideration, if there already existed a strong independent rank and file movement which was in a position to act on its own and to influence political organizations. But today no such movement exists. The question, therefore, is whether at the present moment, when the key problem is precisely to bring such a movement into existence, it will be possible simultaneously to work with the trade union 'lefts' in building social democracy and to attack these same 'lefts' while building the rank and file movement. Can anyone seriously contend that the Frasers, Wurfs, Winpisingers and their ilk will, at this juncture, ally with people on a political project when they know that these same people are simultaneously opposing them in 'their own unions'? To ask this question is to answer it. This explains why even the embryonic social democratic movement in the U.S. has failed to challenge in the slightest way the hegemony of its trade union officials in their own special sphere, despite these officials' already long record of bureaucratic discouragement of independent rank and file initiative and militancy. The new social democrats have already, in other words, ratified the 'two pole' structure of separated jurisdiction which has marked social democratic parties from the beginning, and helped mightily to perpetuate their self-destructive dynamic.

VI The Electoral Struggle as Movement Building? The Jesse Jackson Campaign

In the wake of the precipitous decline of the movements throughout the late 70s and early 80s, the official reformist leaderships — the trade union bureaucracy, the established Black leadership, the liberal wing of the Democratic Party — have focused ever more narrowly on the electoral road. In this situation, those who would revive social democracy have had little choice but to make a virtue of necessity. They have themselves focused more and more on electoral campaigns and have justified this tactic either by claiming to use these campaigns to organize mass struggles, or simply by construing the campaigns themselves as mass movements. In the absence of already existing mass movements, such perspectives are delusionary. It is, of course, on occasion quite possible to translate the power accumulated through mass struggle into electoral victories and reform legislation; but the reverse is rarely if ever conceivable. Those who contemplate such a strategy can do so only because they mistake the meaning of the electoral struggle to both the Democratic Party leadership and its rank and file, and because they fail to take into account what is required to wage electoral campaigns successfully.

Winning Elections and Organizing Mass Movements

In part, as I've emphasized already, using the electoral struggle for mass organizing is problematic because the official reformist forces who provide much of the impetus behind Democratic Party campaigns conceive the electoral road explicitly as a substitute for mass organizing. To use Democratic Party electoral campaigns for movement building would have to be done, so to speak, over their dead bodies. Nor are the bureaucratic leaderships the only force inside the Democratic Party that opposes the use of electoral struggle for mass organizing or left politicking. In the continuing absence of major mass struggles, the Democratic Party rank and file and prospective recruits are no more likely than is the leadership to support such efforts. The most obvious, yet most important, fact about the reform-minded people who choose to work inside the Democratic Party or who are attracted to the campaigns of 'progressive' Democratic Party candidates is that they believe the electoral process provides an effective vehicle for winning reforms. If they felt, as do a number of those leftists behind the new social democratic movement, that the electoral road, in itself, cannot generate the power required to win reforms, they would not expend the tremendous amount of energy required to do electoral work. On the other hand, because they are serious about the electoral road, they want to win, and because they want to win, they will have no truck with leftist plans to use electoral campaigns for mass organizing or left propaganda. This is especially because they believe, quite correctly, that such plans would be counter-productive for their own aim of winning the election.

There is a strict logic to winning elections which is quite different from the logic of winning strikes or organizing success-ful mass militant actions of any sort. In strikes and analogous forms of protest which have the object of winning concrete gains from the owners or the government, it is not only the numbers of people involved which is critical, but *what they do*. Especially as the economic crisis deepens, in order to win, people have to construct a new and enormous power, for they have to *extract* the desired concessions, since these will be granted by the em-ployers or the state only under great pressure. If they are to win, then, they *have to* develop the most powerful solidarity; they *must* take risks; they *have to* make sacrifices; they *must* be prepared to take illegal actions and use force; and, in the end, they *need* to develop the ideas that explain and justify these actions to themselves and others. All this is necessary to win, because what is involved is a direct test of power with the employers and/or the state. Without such direct tests of strength little can be won, especially in periods of economic contraction like the present. For this reason, leftists have much to offer in strikes and analogous struggles — above all an understanding of what is required, both organizationally and theoretically, to build a successful mass movement, and a willingness to act upon this knowledge.

Winning an election is entirely different: it demands two basic things: 1) appealing somehow to 50% plus one of the voters; 2) getting potential supporters to the polls. Nothing else matters. Money and bodies, and little else, are required. It follows that the way to win is to adapt one's program to the existing conscious-ness of the electorate. The right has to move left; the left has to move right. The battle is for the votes in the middle.[16] This is not to deny that mass struggles and the transformations of political consciousness with which they are associated would in theory be of help to a liberal or left candidate. It is simply to point out that, in the short period of an electoral campaign, it is almost never in practice feasible even to try to call such a movement into existence. It can rarely be done, and it would be absurd to predicate a campaign on succeeding in doing it. To win an election, one must essentially accept consciousness as it is and try to adapt.

Naturally, there are limits beyond which candidates cannot go without turning off their core supporters; but these supporters are often quite flexible. In the first place, where else can they go? They are not going to support the opposition (to the right), for this would be self-defeating. At the same time, and equally important in this context, the supporters of the reform candidate almost always freely accept the necessity of moderating the candidate's image and program, for they, too, understand that this is required to win. Winning, moreover, is everything, for unless the candidate takes office, absolutely nothing can be gained. There is, for the overwhelming majority of leaders and followers in the campaign of progressive Democrats, no other payoff.

Because of this logic, the reform-minded rank and file Democrats can have little or no sympathy for radicals who want to use the campaign 'not only' to win, but to build organization and change consciousness. First, they understand that if the candidate were associated with radical ideas (as he/she would be if his/her followers were spouting left ideas in the campaign), it would be much more difficult to get the moderate vote. They understand, too, that the same is true, only more so, for any sort of mass organizing of militant direct action, for this is guaranteed to frighten moderate potential voters. It was on the basis of this sort of reasoning that some of the new social democratic forces 'understood' Mondale's move to the right in the recent presidential campaign. Given the righward political shift within the electorate, they ask, what else could he have done? Of course, it is precisely because the electoralist perspective must accept the state of mass movements and mass political consciousness as *given* that it is, in the end, like other reformist strategies, futile and self-defeating.

From Black Movement to Black Middle Class [17]

The supporters of Jesse Jackson's recent campaign for the Democratic Party's presidential nomination contended, not surprisingly, that his campaign was something different. Some argued that it was the *de facto* extension and logical culmination of the Black movement of the 60s. Others asserted that whatever Jackson himself intended, his electoral campaign had the objective effect of building a 'Rainbow Coalition,' which represented not merely the revival of the civil rights movement but the unification of the popular movements of the working class, women, gays, and Latinos, as well as Blacks. Still others, like Manning Marable, espoused both these positions and went on to assert that the Jackson movement actually represented an already crystallized 'Black social democracy' and the vanguard of the left.

Nevertheless on the eve of Jackson's campaign and after it, the Black movement was and is at its lowest ebb by far in several decades, with very few struggles of any scope occurring in the Black community — neither strikes, nor rent struggles, nor fights for services, nor other campaigns of that sort. It is the demise of the Black movement which, more than any other factor, has determined the character of Black politics in the recent period. During the 60s, the growing Black movement relied on militant mass direct action, not the ballot box, to extract significant reforms 'from the outside.' In the process, radical Black organizations like SNCC, CORE, and the Black Panther Party succeeded in loosening, partially and temporarily, the political stranglehold over the Black community long exercised by organizations more or less explicitly representing the Black middle class — the NAACP, the Urban League, and the like. These traditional organizations argued, even in the 60s, for toning down direct action and putting primary emphasis on legislative/electoral and lobbying tactics. But at least through the 60s, they saw their political influence waning within the Black community.

However, with the political repression of the late 60s and the economic crisis which followed, militant Black organizations found their options radically reduced and entered into a period of profound decline. Even at its height, the Black movement had not, for obvious reasons, been able to amass a power or consolidate a position at all comparable to that of the workers movement of the 30s; nor could it, correspondingly, maintain as much of its influence as it began to run out of steam. This was especially the case, since the decay of the Black movement occurred at a time of deepening economic contraction and accelerating employers offensive, while the decay of the labor movement took place during — and was obscured by — the spectacular postwar

boom. The fact that economic crisis and decline affected disproportionately precisely those heavy industries (auto, steel, etc.)
where Black workers had made their greatest inroads into the
workforce — and where Blacks had played prominent roles in
the short-lived militancy of the early 70s — naturally made
things even worse, increasing Black workers' economic insecurity and reducing the already rather limited potential for
linking Black aspirations to the struggles of the organized labor
movement. As it was, the skyrocketing Black unemployment —
running at rates double the national average and at 50% among
Black youth — was a further critical demoralizing factor, making
it that much more difficult for the Black community to launch a
fight back.

As the Black movement disintegrated, the Black middle class
was able, bit by bit, to reconsolidate its domination over Black
politics. Black professionals, small businessmen, government
servants, and politicos turned out to have been the Black movement's main material beneficiaries, as well as its major political
inheritors — even though they had not been its primary instig-
ators. They staffed the new poverty programs. They gained most
from the expansion of supervisory positions in state and local
government. They and their children assumed the lion's share of
the places opened up by affirmative action programs in the
universities and the professions. They, too, were hurt by the
diminished strength of the militant Black movement, as well as
by the deepening economic crisis of the 70s. But the Black middle
class was also able to adjust and make the most of the new
situation, while the income gap between them and the Black
working class and poor grew sharply throughout the 70s. Above
all, the Black middle class was able to reimpose its old political
line.

The Black middle class's increasing domination of Black
politics was manifested in the fact that, as the Black community
turned away from militant mass action tactics, they adopted
whole hog the Black middle class's preferred strategy: getting
Black progressives elected to office. The turn to electoralism was
dramatically symbolized by the retreat of the Black Panthers,
riddled by police repression and politically isolated, from their
former militant tactics to a purely electoral focus. When in 1972-
1973, Bobby Seale and Elaine Brown, symbols of Black Power,
ran for mayor and city council in Oakland, they were setting the
trend for what remained of the entire Black movement. Nor was

the political perspective of the Black middle class exhausted by electoralism pure and simple; it also involved establishing ties between the established Black organizations and large corporations in order to obtain corporate assistance for the economic development of the Black community. It was expected that local Black businessmen and professionals could play a profitable, if subordinate, role in this development. Black organizations sometimes took their own lead in establishing such alliances — as with the NAACP's agreement with Exxon or with the agreements made by Jesse Jackson's PUSH with Coca-Cola and other companies. But naturally, these alliances could best be consolidated when Blacks held leading urban offices; electoralism and the alliance with big capital generally went hand in hand.

The Black electoral effort has totally dominated Black politics in the 70s and early 80s.[18] Black mayors now govern four of the six largest cities in the nation — Chicago, Los Angeles, Philadelphia, and Detroit — and a total of twenty cities with populations over 100,000. In 1973, there were only 48 Black mayors across the country; today there are 229. The new Black mayors have nearly universally pursued the same strategy: a growing alliance with the corporations. Black mayors see to it that the local governments grant tax cuts, raise (regressive) sales taxes, and grant subsidies to corporations (including tax breaks, cheap loans, etc.) in order to create the conditions for corporations to invest. Black mayors like Maynard Jackson, Coleman Young, and Kenneth Gibson have, for at least a decade, been making corporate investment the keystone of their urban development strategies. Recently-elected Andrew Young also did not waste much time in emphasizing the need to seek private capital for his city's economy, and quickly pushed through a 1% sales tax increase as a token of his intentions. More left-talking politicos, like Richard Hatcher of Gary, have pursued essentially the same policies with a different rhetoric throughout the 70s. The hope, of course, is that if businesses are encouraged, they will invest, and the benefits will 'trickle down' to the Black community. Unfortunately, there is no lack of statistical data demonstrating that no Black mayor has succeeded in slowing down even slightly the downward curve of economic development for Black workers and the poor throughout the 70s and early 80s. Still, the Black middle class does benefit from this approach. The professionals get supervisory and managerial jobs, and small businessmen get subcontracts from the giant corporations.

The more candid and sober of the Black Democratic politicians do not make great claims for their strategy. They point out that they are highly constrained in what they can accomplish by the cutoff of federal funds and the erosion of the urban tax base due to capital flight and the economic crisis. Surely they have a point. For without the sort of mass struggles which can compel concessions from the government and corporations at both the national and local levels, the cities will be hostage to the corporations and their requirements for profits. Meanwhile, the Black mayors can adopt the words, though not the actions, of the 60s Black movements. Above all, they depict their entirely legalist voter registration drives and the push to elect Black Democrats like themselves as the extension of the old civil rights movements — neglecting to mention the mass mobilizations, illegality, and confrontational tactics which gave those movements their power (as well as the fact that those were *struggles for rights*, not electoral contests). As Joseph Madison, director for voter registration for the NAACP put it at the time of the 1981 meeting of the 'Black Leadership Family,' attended by over 1000 professionals, politicians, and government officials: 'The militancy of the old days is passé. We've got to develop technical militants out of those middle-class affluent Blacks who have received training, acquired good education, worked themselves into the mainstream of economic life.'[19]

Jesse Jackson's campaign for the Democratic presidential nomination represented the culmination of the electoralist strategy which the Black middle class has been implementing for more than a decade. Many of Jackson's leading supporters and advisors, such as Richard Hatcher of Gary and Harold Washington of Chicago, are reform-minded, left-talking Black mayors. Indeed, Washington's dramatic campaign for mayor of Chicago in 1983 was the immediate predecessor, and in many ways the model, for Jackson's own effort.

Washington's Campaign

As they would with Jackson's effort, many leftists insisted on calling Washington's campaign a mass social movement. The rallies were huge, the enthusiasm boundless, the rhetoric inspiring. But the fact remains that Washington's election campaign was simply that. It did not come out of, nor was it accompanied by, significant oppositional struggles of any sort in the Black community. There were no demonstrations (or demands) by Chicago Housing Authority tenants for improvement in their conditions; there were no strikes by workers demanding higher wages, better conditions or benefits, or that plants not be shut down. Material conditions in the Chicago Black community have deteriorated rapidly in recent years, but the level of Black militancy and political organization has declined with equal speed. In no sense did Washington ride to power on the crest of an already existing movement of Blacks organizing themselves against employers or the government. Nor did the Washington campaign — which, like other electoral campaigns, remained solely concerned with electing the candidate — seek to bring such a movement into existence. On the contrary, as one observer put it: 'Everything stayed well within the bounds of traditional politics — though a remarkably boisterous and rowdy brand of traditional politics. Everyone's hopes were in Harold Washington — no one had any hopes or expectations in themselves.'[20]

What has happened since the election? Despite dealing a powerful blow to the old machine and bringing many Blacks and Latinos into important official positions, the Washington administration has functioned much like other liberal regimes in the crisis. Immediately upon assuming office, Washington explicity called for 'austerity' and pushed through a reduction in the city's workforce. He did support a bill for collective bargaining for city workers, but only after seeking to pass legislation which would have taken away the unions' right to strike. Shortly thereafter, Washington forced the Amalgamated Transit Union to accept a plan to defer the payment of 26 million dollars into their pension fund, threatening that if they refused, 1500 layoffs would follow. Perhaps most important, Washington failed to give any support to the majority-Black teachers union in its bitter, unsuccessful, three week strike in October 1984. In fact, Washington's labor attorney, Richard Laner, helped the school board engineer the final settlement and defeat the union. Washington failed even to protest when U.S. Steel closed its southside Southworks plant (which only a few years ago employed some 5000-7000 workers), despite massive concessions from the United Steel Workers Union. Meanwhile, like Black mayors all over the country, Washington went about creating an economic development task force whose membership reads like a who's who of Chicago business — with top representatives from all the leading banks, manufacturing firms, and construction companies. Washington has admittedly been badly hurt by the obstructive tactics of what remains of the old white machine. On the other hand, he has not lifted a finger to aid himself, the Black community, or working people in general by helping them to organize themselves to fight to improve their conditions. A traditional liberal politician, Washington led no mass social movement in his campaign; has, in office, been bound by no social movement; and has done nothing to bring one into existence.

Jackson's Campaign

That Jesse Jackson was, intentionally and explicitly, carrying out the electoral strategy of the Black middle class and Black politicians to enhance their influence within the Democratic Party in particular and American society in general was made clear again and again throughout the campaign by his supporters and opponents alike. Jackson's overriding goal was to get millions of unregistered Blacks signed up for the Democratic Party. With this newly-created electoral base, Jackson hoped to use the primaries to amass the power to leverage the Democratic Party: Jackson and the Black politicians would deliver a much increased Black vote to the Democrats, if the latter would, in return, grant the Black politicos a greater role within the party and, more generally, make certain programmatic concessions. This is precisely the same strategy organized labor has followed for the past forty years, with progressively diminishing returns.

As should have been obvious to those who hoped the Jackson campaign would constitute an ongoing mass movement for social reform, Jackson's strategy did not require building mass struggles or even constructing much of an electoral organization. The be-all and end-all was to get Blacks registered and voting in the primaries for Jackson. No one should have been surprised, therefore, to find that Jackson's organization, to the extent it existed, was entirely top down. It was headed by elite figures, long influential in business and Black politics, who saw their goal as accomplishing certain clear-cut electoral tasks. There was no need to get feedback and input, let along to encourage the mass self-activity required for actual social struggles. Jackson did, of course, hold massive demonstrations and marches, and made hundreds of speeches in local community churches. He is a magnetic personality, and generated an enormous amount of enthusiasm. But despite the rhetorical verve, he did practically nothing to strengthen the existing grassroots organizations in the community, but, on the contrary, subordinated the already constituted organizations and their resources to the electoral effort.

Nor could those former leftists who flooded into the local Rainbow Coalitions, as they had into the Washington campaign, significantly reverse the direction. It is doubtful, in most cases, that they even tried. It was not that the official politicos exerted a stranglehold on the campaign organization and tactics — although this was a problem in some places, like Los Angeles.[21] It was, rather, that most of those from the Black community who came to build the campaign naturally did so with a single purpose in mind — to get out the vote and win the primaries. It is hardly surprising that, only a few months following the elections, most local Rainbow Coalitions have been reduced to hollow shells, manned by leftists and liberals. No more the launching boards for new social struggles than they were before the campaign, most are looking to survive by finding new electoral efforts in which to immerse themselves.

Jackson's Impact

Precisely because he did not build a movement with the capacity to exercise power outside the Democratic Party and outside the polling booth, Jackson failed badly even in his own terms. When the Democratic Party, in an arrogant display of racist *realpolitik*, refused to grant a single one of Jackson's key programmatic planks, he was nonetheless forced, ignominiously, to call for unity at the national convention and to back Mondale. Some leftists saw this as a sellout, but Jackson had, in effect, no choice, since he had no basis for breaking from the Party and going off on his own. First of all, Jackson himself never had any intention of splitting and had not prepared his followers to do so. But, equally important, Jackson's campaign had emerged in the wake of the decline of mass struggles in the Black community and had itself done nothing to bring about the emergence of a movement in any way independent of Jackson's electoral effort, or indeed, of Jackson the personality. This was why Jackson's more radical and impatient supporters were obliged to sit quietly by as Jackson capitulated at the convention. In possession of no mass base themselves, they had no means to pressure the candidate. In the absence of already existing mass movements, a critical source of Jackson's attractiveness, not only to his backers among the politicians and the bourgeoisie, but to the Black community as whole, was his apparent ability to offer a realistic strategy for reform. Consciously or unconsciously, the majority of Jackson's supporters saw in his plan to use the primaries to leverage the Democratic Party a credible substitute for the self-organization which seemed, at that moment, off the agenda.

Had Jackson sought at any point to build an electoral movement which claimed independence from the Democratic Party — and which had as its object a long term process of rebuilding the left — he would surely have lost the support of the Black middle class and, arguably, also the Black masses. As most Americans are aware, splinter parties have no hope of winning practical gains, given the winner-take-all electoral system, unless they are extremely large — larger, that is, than any which have appeared on the political horizon for more than half a century. The premise for a practical third party campaign would have to be the radical and massive transformation of the national political consciousness. This would depend, in turn, on enormous historical changes, not the least of which would be the rise of mass struggles of a magnitude not seen since the labor upsurge of the 30s. In the absence of such a transformation, any third party efforts will, of necessity, be confined to propaganda objectives — which is not to say they would be without value.

Because the whole premiss of the Jackson campaign was its claim to being practical, Jackson and his allies could not refuse to mobilize against Reagan after the convention, despite the Democrats' continuing failure to grant them the slightest concession. For, as the Democratic Party regulars realized, the Black leadership and the Black masses wanted to defeat Reagan more than did any other group in American society. To refuse this effort in order to punish the Democratic Party would have been to cut off their nose to spite their face. This, of course, has been the characteristic quandary of the official labor leadership which has for decades supinely backed Democratic Party candidates no matter how anti-labor. It follows strictly from the logic of the electoralist strategy.

A Black Social Democracy within the Democratic Party?

Despite the long term decay of the Black movements, Manning Marable, a prominent writer and national officer of DSA, has, in several recent essays, argued that the Black officials and the thrust they represent actually constitute an 'American version of social democracy' within the Democratic Party and society at large. What Marable means by this assertion is that Black politicians, virtually across the board, advocate social programs and give voice to ideas which are today far to the left of those in the white political mainstream.[22] This is undoubtedly true, as far as it goes. There is no question that the political sentiments of the Black community as a whole are far to the left of those common in the rest of American society. Indeed, one reason Jesse Jackson could adopt his radical-sounding program was that his electoral strategy required focusing, almost exclusively, on the Black community and did not necessitate a broad appeal to the far more conservative white electorate.

But to imply, as Marable does, that the Black electoral movement led by the Black middle class constitutes a powerful force for reform is highly misleading. Even had the Democratic Party adopted significant sections of Jackson's radical program at the convention, it would not have made a stitch of difference: the party has adopted countless, quite radical, platforms in the past, but unless mass movements acted effectively to 'keep the Party honest,' these platforms have remained only on paper. Indeed, throughout the 70s, Democratic Party majorities with on-paper commitments to reform retained control of Congress to no descernable effect. To bring this point home, one has only to refer to the obvious fact that what Manning Marable sees as Black social democracy — the Black politicos with their left programs and mass electoral 'movements' — has been in power in numerous places for at least a decade, but has done little either to challenge the powers that be or help the Black masses. Witness all the cities with Black mayors, including left-talking ones like Richard Hatcher and Harold Washington. Of course, social democratic parties also have been in power in quite a few nations around the world during the late 70s and early 80s, but have delivered only cuts in services and rising unemployment to their working classes. By conflating electoralism and program mongering with movement building, Marable perpetuates the myth that winning office is winning power, and that there is a shortcut to the long, hard, and daunting task of rebuilding the movements.

VIII   From Fair Share to Austerity: The Failure of Corporatism and the Opening to the Right

Throughout the 70s and early 80s, the official forces of reformism have become progressively more reluctant to combat capital. They are aware that the slowdown of the economy is, in the last analysis, a crisis of profitability and that this has consequences for their own strategic perspectives. Between 1965 and 1973, the rate of return on investment dropped from 16% to 9%, and it has declined even further since.[23] The crisis of profitability is, in the first instance, an expression of the long term crisis of the international economy — a crisis which has engulfed all of the capitalist nations. But it is also the case that the international crisis has been accompanied by a long term relative decline in the growth of the productive forces and the accumulation of capital in the American sector, and this has had vast implications for working-class politics. It is sufficient to note that over the long period between 1950 and 1976, the rate of growth in productivity in U.S. industry averaged 2.8% while the comparative figures were 5.4% for Germany, 5.0% for France, and 8.3% for Japan. Similarly, over this same period, the U.S. devoted on average 17.8% of GDP to investment in new plant and equipment, while the comparative figures were 24.3% for Germany, 23.2% for France, and 33% for Japan.[24] Over the recent period, the numbers have, if anything, become even more unfavorable for the U.S.

As the official forces of reformism are aware, these figures represent a huge decline in the competitiveness of the U.S. sector and, specifically, its declining attractiveness as a place for new investment. The declining relative efficiency of the U.S. productive system has meant that relative costs of production, especially in manufacturing, have continued to increase. The result, as most are now aware, is accelerating disinvestment, a massive flight of capital especially in the form of loans, and a preference for finance over manufacturing. This trend has reached a climax over the past several years, with large sections of what was the industrial core of the U.S. economy entering into serious crisis — steel, auto, textiles, consumer electronics, machine tools, etc.

These trends, in the context of the international crisis, have forced the official reformist forces drastically to reappraise the Keynesian approach to political economy which was their received religion throughout the postwar boom. By the end of the Carter administration, deficit spending was perceived not only as inflationary but as less capable of increasing employment. Equally salient, government programs which appeared to redistribute income away from capital came to appear increasingly counter-productive. Even the 'left' leaderships of trade unions, Black organizations, and the liberal wing of the Democratic Party have come to believe that forcing capital to give higher wages, better conditions, or more government services is likely to make things worse, harming competitiveness and generating reluctance to invest. Wedded to an ideology of 'fair share' within capitalism, the forces or reformism, both right and left, have been accepting austerity as the economy declines, just as they demanded a bigger piece of the pie in the period of growth.

The long term political consequences of this change in perspective are ominous. Unwilling to launch an attack on capital, the official forces of reform have moved rapidly toward devising strategies to help 'their own' capitalists protect their profits in order to safeguard their own and their memberships' position. They have sought to enter into tripartite partnerships with business and government to launch vast cooperative efforts to protect and revamp the American economy from to top to bottom. Pursuant to this strategy, the labor leadership has, with increasing unanimity, embraced protectionism for U.S. manufacturing. Beyond this, in tandem with certain minority representatives of capital — notably the investment banker Felix Rohatyn — they have been the arch-apostles of what has come to be known as 'industrial policy,' a hodgepodge of programs to encourage planning of and investment in new industry. At the level of the corporation, they have placed top labor leaders on boards of directors of corporations, while beginning more and more to accept corporate proposals for profit sharing. Finally, on the shopfloor, they have become backers of so-called Quality of

Worklife (QWL) programs, aimed at increasing worker participation to improve productivity.

Meanwhile, the decreasing numbers of liberal politicians who
have continued, as the crisis deepens, to demand improved
social programs from the government have failed, systematically, to show how the capitalists can be made to bear their
naturally high costs. In so doing, they have opened the way to
discrediting in advance any new offensive for reforms. Over the
past twenty years, no section of the reform establishment has
lifted a finger to oppose the dramatic long term decline in the
level of corporate taxation.[25] On the other hand, since the early
70s, the working class has had to accept a massive decline in their
disposable income: workers now get approximately 20% less
spending money per hour (wages minus taxes) than they did in
1972-1973, and approximately the same amount they received in
1961.[26] The great majority of workers have come to assume that
they themselves will have to pay for any increases in social
services won in Congress. As a consequence, many working
people have given up attempting to defend themselves through
the struggle for reforms and sought to ameliorate their condition
by trying to reduce taxes. Propositions 13 in California and 21/2
in Massachusetts were typical in this respect.

The reformist officials' increasingly desperate turn to corporatist solutions throughout the 70s and early 80s is understandable in view of their absolute refusal to confront capital, but
has nonetheless proven entirely self-destructive. By emphasizing both the impossibility of successfully resisting employers
and the self-defeating character of any effective resistance, the
official forces of reform have merely confirmed the workers' own
conclusions, derived from a decade-long experience of both
defeat at the hands of the employers and of the declining competitiveness of U.S. manufacturing. By recommending, on that
basis, policies which bring workers objectively into alignment
with capital and in *de facto* conflict with other groups of workers,
they have demonstrated the increasing irrelevance of strategies
based on collective organization by the working class, and, in
turn, the decreasing utility of their own organizations.
Ironically, to the extent that the trade union officials have
transformed their own organizations from weapons of class
struggle into instruments of collaboration in production, they
have been to that degree less able to assert their own place within
those corporatist arrangements through which they had hoped,

alongside the employers, to manage the crisis. Under no pressure to accept the trade unions as partners, the employers have seen no reason not to turn around and destroy them — and that is what they have done, with growing success, since Reagan ascended to the Presidency.

Finally, as class-based strategies for self-defense have become less practicable and as class collaborationist alternatives have appeared more inevitable, workers naturally have embraced the ideological conceptions which can make some sense of what they're actually doing.[27] To the extent that workers have supported protection, they have allied with their own capitalists against workers around the world. To the extent, moreover, that they have participated — at the level of the state, the corporations, or the shopfloor — in cooperative arrangements to improve productivity, they are actually helping their own employers defeat workers in other places. To the extent that workers have turned to tax cuts, they are unavoidably joining the attack on the living standards of those who are dependent upon welfare and other social services, above all Blacks and women. To the extent that workers are defending their own positions — in a 'colorblind' and 'sexblind' manner — through defending the seniority list against affirmative action, they are attacking Blacks and women in still another way. Many working people who attempt to defend their positions with these methods do not intend to profit their employers or to gain at the expense of other workers. But this is in fact what they are doing. Their actions are, in effect, chauvinist, racist, and sexist. Inevitably, therefore, they are opened up to the reactionary worldviews which will rationalize their conduct.

Ultimately, as workers cease to find any practical basis for the collective defense of their own lives, they cannot help but perceive the world as a dog-eat-dog competitive struggle, and, as a result, come to consider more attractive those pro-family and fundamentalist religious ideologies which make this perception their point of departure. Whatever oppression the patriarchal family brings, it can, with some conviction, still offer some of the only non-commodity, non-commercially competitive relationships which still remain intact — i.e., between husband and wife and between parents and children. It can, therefore, with some legitimacy, offer the reality of a (non-capitalist) 'haven in a heartless (competitive) world.' It need hardly be added that to the degree such a view of the world — as inevitably composed of families in cutthroat competion — carries conviction, that promise of community held out by the fundamentalist christian sects will prove ever more appealing.

From Mitterand to Le Pento . . .

The progression from reformism to corporate capitalist restructuring to the rise of the right is, unfortunately, no mere prediction. Throughout the later 70s and early 80s, it has been, and is being, played out in a variety of forms in the capitalist west, above all in some of those regions which have experienced the most thoroughgoing social democracy during the first stage of the global economic crisis. In June 1981, the Socialist Party of François Mitterand came to power in France in a smashing electoral landslide that gave it a massive parliamentary majority and uncontested control of the executive for seven years. The Socialists were committed at the start to a somewhat radical version of the traditional social democratic program: Keynesian reflation, mild increases for social welfare, and ambitious plans for economic modernization through state intervention and nationalization. Within months of their accession to power, the Socialists' attempt to implement their program had led to runaway inflation, massive capital flight, precipitously rising imports, the collapse of the balance of payments, and stagnating investment and growth. As a result, in less than a year, the Socialists had junked their reform program, devalued the franc twice, and embarked upon a vicious program of austerity, marked by severe fiscal restraint and huge cuts in government services. France's workers are today experiencing the highest levels of unemployment since the Great Depression, made worse by the decay of government welfare programs. Meanwhile, to counteract the disastrous effects of its own policies on its worker constituencies, the government has sought shamelessly to shift as much as possible of the burden of the crisis onto immigrant guest workers, while attempting to distract the population with Cold War polemics and imperialist adventures.

With their own political parties and trade unions implicated in what has been, in effect, an allout experiment in capitalist modernization, French workers have been compelled, not surprisingly, to rethink their political perspectives. With their traditional parties and trade unions making a mockery of class-based, collective strategies of self-defense, it is hardly unexpected that they are turning in increasing numbers to those political forces who will give coherent ideological rationalizations for the class collaborationist and individualistic strategies they have been forced to live by. Is it really surprising that Le Pen, with his barely concealed fascism, has emerged from the rubble of Mitterand's experiment in capitalist transformation under Socialism? Do today's American exponents of a revitalized social democracy from within social democracy believe they can achieve better results than did the French Socialists through the agency of Mitterand's feeble American counterparts and their even feebler reformist perspectives?

Notes

*I want to thank the editorial board of *Against the Current* for helpful suggestions and criticisms of earlier drafts of this paper. I wish to dedicate this essay to the memory of Steve Zeluck (1922-1985).

1. Stan Weir, Doug Fraser's Middle Class Coalition', *Radical America* (January-February 1979)

2. See 'The Paradox of Reform: Black Politics and the Democratic Party', *Southern Exposure*, 12 (February 1984), pp. 23-24; 'The Left in the 80s', *Changes* (March-April 1984).

3. *The Mass Strike* (1906).

4. On the mass strike upsurge of the 30s and the response of the employers and the government, see Art Preis, *Labor's Giant Step* (1972) and Irving Bernstein, *The Turbulent Years* (1969).

5. On Roosevelt's new activism, in response to the mass movements and radicalization of 1934, see W.E.Leuchtenberg, *Franklin D. Roosevelt and the New Deal* (1963).

6. On the trade union officials' passivity under the employers' offensive of the later 1920s and beyond, see Irving Bernstein, *The Lean Years* (1961), as well as *The Turbulent Years*.

7. S. Lynd, 'The Possibility of Radicalism in the Early 1930s: The Case of Steel', *Radical America* (November 1972); Roger Keeran, 'Communists and the Auto Workers. The Struggle for a Union, 1919-1949' (University of Wisconsin Ph.D. dissertation, 1974), chapter IV.

8. Keeran, 'Communists and the Auto Workers', pp. 292ff.; Preis, *Labor's Giant Step*; R.R. Brooks, *As Steel Goes . . .* (1940).

9. Keeran, 'Communists and the Auto Workers', p. 215; Bert Cochrane, *Labor and Communism* (1977), p. 107ff.; Mike Davis, 'The Barren Marriage of American

Labor and the Democratic Party', *New Left Review*, no. 124 (November-December 1980).

10. A. Meier and E. Rudwick, *Core. A Study in the Civil Rights Movement 1942-1968* (1975), parts II and IV; Clayborne Carson, *In Struggle. SNCC and the Black Awakening* (1981), esp. pp. 83-95 and 218-220.

11. Meier and Rudwick, *Core,* pp. 282, 272-281; Carson, *In Struggle,* pp. 111-129.

12. For a superb account of the miners' struggles of the 60s and 70s, see Paul Nyden, 'Miners for Democracy: Struggle in the Coal Fields' (Columbia University Ph.D. disseration, 1974).

13. For an interesting account of the latest, very important agreement in auto, see Eric Mann, 'Send in the Robots: How UAW sold out its membership in 1984 . . . ', *L.A. Weekly* (4-10 January 1985).

14. Ben Bedell, 'Winpisinger's Wimpy Socialism', *The Guardian* (20 February 1980).

15. For a classic account of these dynamics, see Carl E. Schorske, *Germ. an Social Democracy 1905–1917* (1955).

16. The pressure of this electoral logic is of course the greatest where there is a winner-take-all electoral system, as in the United States (in contrast to proportional representation).

17. For this and subsequent sections on the Jackson campaign, see especially Anthony Thigpenn, 'Jesse Jackson and the Black Movement', *Against the Current* 3, (Fall 1984)

18. For a fine analysis of the recent practice of Black electoralism, which forms the basis for this paragraph, see Monte Pilawski, 'The Limits of Power', *Southern Exposure,* 12, (February 1984).

19. Quoted in Thigpenn, 'Jesse Jackson', p. 16.

20. Dan Labotz, 'Harold Washington: The Hopes and the Realities', *Against the Current,* 3, (Fall 1984), p. 40. My discussion of Washington's campaign and its upshot depends very heavily on Labotz's excellent article, and I have appropriated a number of phrases from it.

21. Thigpenn, 'Jesse Jackson', p. 16.

22. Marable, 'Paradox of Reform', pp. 24-25.

23. D.N. Allman, 'The Decline in Business Profitability', *Federal Reserve Bank of Kansas City Economic Review* (January 1983).

24. Riccardo Parboni, *The Dollar and its Rivals* (1981), p. 93. Ira C. Magaziner and Robert B. Reich, *Minding America's Business* (1982), p. 45.

25. See Joseph A. Pechman, *Who Paid the Taxes, 1966-1985?* (1985), esp. chapter 5.

26. Samuel Bowles et al, *Beyond the Wasteland* (1983), p. 25. Wages per hour are about 10% lower today (before taxes) than they were in 1972-3.

27. For the following analysis, see Johanna Brenner and Robert Brenner, 'Reagan, the Right and the Working Class', *Against the Current,* 1, (Winter 1981) and 'The Right Wing and the Working Class', *Against the Current,* 1, (Summer 1981).

3.   Stumbling in the Dark:
American Labor's Failed Response

Kim Moody

The 1984 elections were a test for America's embattled labor movement. Many of the institutions upon which stable labor relations had rested in the U.S. lay in shambles. Union membership was shrinking in all but a few industries. The collective bargaining process was riddled with setbacks and organizing efforts were down for the count. Whether they believed it or not, the leadership of the AFL-CIO pinned all the blame on the Reagan administration and its policies. All hopes for a solution to labor's decline were pinned on the return of the Democrats to power in Washington. The road to that objective lay in choosing a mainstream, centrist liberal who could rally and reconstitute the decomposing base of the Democratic Party. That candidate was Walter Mondale — a proven economic liberal, political centrist, and Cold Warrior. Union leaders who might have backed a more liberal Democrat, perhaps even Jesse Jackson, fell into line in the hope that unity and a moderate candidate could defeat the right and restore the 'good old days' before Reagan. The maneuver failed. For the long-run, however, what may be more important is that the whole idea upon which this strategy rested — that labor's problems lay simply in the White House — embodied a misunderstanding of the situation, including of why the right was so powerful an electoral force in the first place.

The foundations of American industrial unionism and its political practice were built on a compromise with the capitalist state in the midst of World War II. As a mechanism for enforcing the new labor laws passed during the New Deal years, the National Labor Relations Board was largely a failure in the late 1930s. Mass strikes, sit-ins, and later the irresistible draw of war orders were the forces that brought America's industrial giants to heal before the CIO upheaval. But the top leaders of the CIO, men like John L.Lewis, Philip Murray and Sidney Hillman, never had it in mind to protect their new organizations with a permanent mobilization of the membership. They sought the sort of orderly system of bargaining that Hillman and the garment unions had reached with the clothing makers in the 1920s. When World War II arrived, these men turned to the Roosevelt administration and the state to find this stability. Historian Nelson Lichtenstein has summarized the process that focused largely on the War Labor Board:

> For the next four years, these boards were instrumental in setting for the first time industry-wide wage patterns, fixing a system of 'industrial jurisprudence' on the shop floor, and influencing the internal structure of the new industrial unions. They were a powerful force in nationalizing a conception of routine and bureaucratic industrial relations that the Wagner Act and the NLRB had thus far filled to implement fully.[1]

With this system in place, the commencement of the postwar boom rendered the NLRB and related state institutions sufficient to guarantee stability for both industry and labor.

Closely related to this new structure was the peculiarly American political alliance and organizational arrangement between the CIO and later most of the labor movement and the Democratic Party. This alliance was responsible for making necessary adjustments or fending off conservative attacks on the institutional basis of economic peace. It was unique to the United States because it did not include an independent political party of the working class. The formation of CIO-PAC in 1943 sealed the rejection of a class approach to the electoral arena in favor of a subordinate role within the Democratic Party as one of many allied, but also competing social groups. As Lichtenstein puts it: 'In launching the new Political Action Committee, the CIO leadership specifically rejected any 'ultraliberal political party in the name of the working man.' Instead, they sought to discipline the unruly left wing by channeling its energy into a firmly controlled political action group that could function safely within the two-party system.'[2] The acceptance of this limited political role implied a rejection of the European model in which organized labor sees the political party as the vehicle for mobilizing non-union as well as union workers on the basis of a class appeal. In the postwar American arrangement, labor functions not as a party of broad mobilization, but as a pleader for the interests of unions within the party. The political program is not something designed to inspire, even demagogically, or increase class consciousness, but something to be lobbied for in the higher circles of the party or the legislature in coalition with or opposition to other social and economic interest groups. While labor does often fight for the political goals of working-class people, in general its methods tend to reflect its bureaucratic style of bargaining with infrequent mobilizations: for example, Solidarity Day I in 1981, limited to its own members. With rare exceptions, the leaders of the AFL-CIO prefer to pursue their political objectives through negotiations and powerbrokering among allied and/or contending groups. The tactical change in the 1984 elections, when the AFL-CIO Executive Board endorsed Walter Mondale in the primaries, did not represent a departure from this practice so much as a public acknowledgement of it.

Both the industrial and political arrangements that emerged from World War II depended on more or less continuous economic growth and capital accumulation at competitive rates of return for the employers who dealt with unions. As the storm clouds of chronic economic crisis took shape in the second half of the 1960s, economic growth slowed down and falling rates of return led capital to seek new avenues of accumulation; the basis upon which the existing compromise rested thus began to change. The crisis of capital became labor's crisis as well. Outer symptoms of this crisis can be seen in the decline of union membership, first as a proportion of the workforce, then in absolute numbers. While unions represented 34.7 percent of the civilian workforce in 1954, the year the AFL and the CIO merged, they could claim only 20.9 percent in 1980. This gradual decline became a plunge when the proportion of union members fell to 17.9 percent in 1982. That two-year nose dive represented a net loss of 2.6 million members.[3] But serious as this decline in the level of unionization is, it is only one of a number of trends undermining the strength of organized labor and the working class as a whole. Most of these trends result from changing strategies of accumulation adopted by American-based capital in response to the crisis of its system. These trends have largely undermined the institutional basis of labor's industrial and political practice.

The last decade and a half have seen an accelerated restructuring and reorganization of U.S. industry. The restructuring that has produced 'deindustrialization' in the U.S. and much of Europe is part of a global transformation that has reduced the weight of traditional basic 'smokestack' industries in many of the more advanced capitalist economies as the locus of these industries shifts to a select number of Third World nations where labor is relatively cheap and thought to be under stable political control. Increasingly, the formerly industrial nations of the West have become service-based economies. In the U.S. during the decade of the 1970s, 13.4 million out of a total of 19.6 million new jobs were in the private service-producing sector.[4] The implications for highly unionized basic industry can be seen in Tables I and II. Alongside this development has been an almost continuous reorganization of corporate capital. Facing slumping profit rates in many traditional lines of production — the average rate of profit for non-financial corporations slumped from 16 percent in 1965 to 9 percent in 1970[5] — and an intensification of competition at home and abroad, many corporations sought to strengthen their position through mergers and acquisitions. Large corporations became diversified giants. In 1960, 28 corporations were worth $1 billion or more and controlled 27.6 percent of manufacturing assets. After the merger movement of the late 1960s, 102 billion-dollar corporations controlled 48.8 percent of assets by 1970. A second wave of mergers, again mostly conglomerate in nature, in the late 1970s produced 212 corporations worth $1 billion or more controlling 60 percent of manufacturing assets.[6] Even allowing for the effects of inflation, capital was precipitously concentrated during this period. This produced a shift in the balance of forces between capital and labor in the U.S.

For organized labor, the most obvious consequence of these changes was that unions with a shrinking membership and dues base faced employers who possessed far greater resources than the unions. But since the mergers were mostly along conglomerate lines, it also meant that the old match between union, corporation and industry established in the 30s and 40s was eliminated in many cases. New diversified corporations such as United Technologies dealt with a number of fragmented unions and with non-unions workers as well. No single union had the leverage over a company that the CIO unions had previously achieved over firms like General Motors, Ford, General Electric or U.S. Steel. To make matters worse, as the 70s wore on, the merger movements turned into rapid-fire reshufflings as production units changed hands regularly. A number of bargaining units became, in effect, moving targets. Most recently, even the more conventional setups, like those in auto and steel, have altered, as companies like GM and U.S. Steel have begun to diversify. To these changes in power relations must be added the fact that most of the corporate giants had become international in scope and could draw on resources from abroad. Perhaps the most typical impact of these trends was exemplified by those unions dealing with small manufacturing firms that became targets of corporate acquisition. Struggles by workers in various unions against corporations like Gulf & Western, which tried to close its once independent Morse Tool plant, or Greyhound, which sold its Armour meat packing plants out from under the United Food and Commercial Workers, exemplify the problem.[7]

By the mid-1980s, the direction of corporate mergers and acquisitions took a turn away from diversification toward the strengthening of corporate positions in one line of production. *Fortune* magazine noted this change in its 1983 survey of the 'Deals of the Year.' Daniel Weiner wrote: 'The movement away from conglomeration was evident in 1983's grand-scale deals. Corporate acquirers tended to go for the industries they knew best — their own. Among the mergers and acquisitions in *Fortune*'s directory, same-industry deals predominated.'[8] In the early 80s this type of merger movement was particularly strong in oil refining and steel. The effects of these same-industry mergers on both employment and union membership for these industries can be seen in Tables I and II. According to the Oil, Chemical and Atomic Workers, 25 unionized plants employing about 5,000 workers were closed in the early 80s.[9] An example in the steel industry is the merger of LTV and Republic which, they announced in 1984, would be accompanied by the combination of compatible operations and the elimination of duplicate ones.[10] Not even the recovery of 1983 buoyed employment and union membership levels in many industries. The AFL-CIO reported that in the 1981-83 period, 55 affiliated unions reported losses in per capita dues, while only 13 registered an increase.[11]

This changing balance of forces gave business the club it needed to obtain sizable contract concessions from unionized workers. The willingness of the United Auto Workers' leadership to grant concessions three times as a result of the Chrysler bailout that began in 1979 was the signal that even the most powerful unions would give concessions if the company's problems or the general economic conditions were bad enough. Once they gained momentum, however, concessions spread to healthy industries and firms as well. Average first-year wage increases in major contracts covering 1,000 or more workers fell from 10.2 percent in 1981, to 3.2 percent in 1982, and 3.4 percent in 1983, a recovery year. In manufacturing, where concessionary bargaining tended to be concentrated, the effect was even more dramatic. First-year wage increases in manufacturing fell from 7.2 percent in 1981, to 2.8 percent in 1982, and 0.4 percent in 1983.[12]

Concessionary bargaining has also altered working conditions and shop floor relations in manufacturing during the first half of the 1980s as management was granted greater 'flexibility' in the workplace. Ironically, concessions, often made in the name of job security, provided funds for the introduction of new technology in many industries — another source of job elimination. In some industries the effects on productivity have been substantial. In auto, productivity rose 14.2 percent in 1983, in steel an unprecedented 27.7 percent, while several other 'smokestack' industries showed gains of over 10 percent.[13] Productivity almost always increases during the first phase of a recovery, but these levels were unusual.

Many of the concessions that management demanded in the first half of the 80s, and continues to demand now, are meant to reintroduce or intensify competition among workers. By establishing uniform wage rates, working conditions and production standards, unions have attempted to eliminate or suppress competition, at least between members of the same union. Management, by introducing two-tier wage systems, undoing pattern-setting contracts, and even establishing job bidding between units within the same firm, attempts to undermine the foundation of union solidarity. Under the pressure of international competition, capital is also trying to shift the burden of this competition onto the shoulders of labor. Speaking about the impending 1985 negotiations, William Angell, chief negotiator for General Electric, told the *Wall Street Journal:* 'The name of the game in 1985 negotiations is to negotiate contracts that will allow the company to be competitive.'[14] Mr Angell is not alone in this approach, and it appears to have yielded results. Charles Lieberman, an economist for Shearson/American Express, said: 'Unlike the major industrial economies of Europe, the U.S. labor market is becoming progressively more competitive. This development reflects the gradual erosion of the power of labor unions as well as the impact of deregulation.'[15] The implications of this new situation were drawn out, in very polite language, by the Conference Board in its predictions for bargaining trends in 1984. They stated:

> Labor-market competition will affect bargaining . . . even during the recovery. Companies will be attempting to cut labor costs by hiring more part-time employees and more temporary employees. They will press for two-tier pay systems in which new hires (or rehires) come on the payroll at far lower rates. And, finally, an abundant supply of labor makes it more possible than ever before to operate during a strike. This possibility constrains union demands. Moreover, the additional risk that the company may emerge without a union-represented work force is also a constraint on union leaders in the mid-80s.'[16]

Ironically, while many companies did turn to the confrontational approach implied in the Conference Board's predictions, another major weapon in management's campaign to introduce competition among the workers was cooperation. This came to light in the General Motors management memo entitled, 'Actions to Influence The Outcome of Bargaining.' This memo was obtained and published by Local 160 of the UAW; it enumerated various demands that would increase competition among GM workers. Its approach to influencing the union was through 'joint problem-solving,' i.e., giving the union leadership the feeling of participation in solving the problems that confront the company. An aspect of that approach which reaches down to the shop floor is GM's Quality of Work Life program; for higher ranking union officials a variety of joint committees were to be established. The goals of this cooperative approach, however, are identical to those sought by outright union busters like Phelps-Dodge: worker competition and ineffective unions.[17]

In spite of all the language of cooperation that clutters much of the literature on labor relations these days, the trend has been toward greater employer hostility to unions. This fact was detailed in a 1984 paper issued by the House Labor-Management Relations Subcommittee. In this paper, Professor Richard Freeman wrote: 'managerial opposition to unionism has increased by leaps and bounds. In the 1950s many managements did relatively little to discourage their workers from unionizing — after all, did not the law specify that the decision was the workers' to make? In ensuing decades, however, management has come to contest hotly nearly every significant NLRB election.'[18] The results of this resistance show up clearly in the percentage of representation elections unions have won. During the 1960s, labor won, on average, 58-59 percent of NLRB conducted elections. By the end of the 70s, this declined to 45 percent, while in the early 80s it fluctuated between 43 percent and 47.7 percent. By 1984, however, the number of elections held had dropped to half the level of 1970, as labor became discouraged with the results.[19] Growing employer resistance also shows up in the figures for Unfair Labor Practices, most of which cover unionized workers. The number of Unfair Labor Practices filed against employers rose from 7,723 in 1960, to 13,601 in 1970, and 31,281 in 1980.[20] These figures indicate management's growing proclivity to play hardball on the shop floor.

The decline of the NLRB as an instrument of mediation between capital and labor means that, along with a number of other institutional arrangements such as pattern bargaining, the institutional foundation of the post-World War II system of labor relations has collapsed. The state could act as the guarantor of labor peace only so long as both sides agreed to play by the rules. As capital increasingly ceased to do so, the state lost — and under Reagan, freely abandoned — its ability to appear as the protector of the organizational stability of the labor movement as a whole. While this institutional collapse pre-dates the Reagan administration, it has accelerated under Reagan. The leadership of the AFL-CIO has interpreted this institutional transformation as simply an act of political will by the Republicans. Unable to conceive of any way of reversing the setbacks they have suffered in industry without the aid of the state, the leadership of the AFL-CIO has put its most concentrated effort into rebuilding the political unity and influence that have dwindled since the late 1960s. The model on which the new tactics and increased investment in politics have been based remain essentially that created in the 1940s.

In the view of most labor leaders, the defeat of Ronald Reagan was a priority that justified new levels of political spending, directing staff efforts away from organizing and contract enforcement into the electoral arena for most of 1984, and a level of political conformity among the leadership not seen since the 1950s. The decision of the AFL-CIO Executive Board in October

1983 to endorse Walter Mondale in the primaries was meant not only to increase labor's influence in the Democratic Party, but to avoid a repeat of the 1972 and 1980 debacles. The AFL-CIO leaders have always felt that the strength of the Democratic Party lies in its political center and organizational hierarchy. The ability of Lane Kirkland to convince the entire AFL-CIO leadership — plus the United Mine Workers, the National Education Association, and the National Organization of Women — to endorse Mondale was a coup for the political center of the labor leadership. Fear of a second Reagan administration was, of course, the force behind the unified endorsement of a candidate who had no clue about how to handle economic crisis, who stood firmly in the hawk wing of the party, and who had been associated with the numerous disasters of the Carter administration. If the primary goal of this tactical innovation had been achieved and Reagan defeated, there would have been much for Kirkland and the AFL-CIO Executive Board to chortle about. It didn't happen. Instead, the dismal political realities behind Reagan's victory and the continued decomposition of the Democrats as a national party were buried in a sea of self-congratulation.

On 8 November 1984, the AFL-CIO's Committee on Political Work, the leadership group charged with implementing the 1983-84 maneuver, met to assess the results. Bill Keller of the *New York Times* described the mood of the meeting as 'one of determined self-congratulation.'[21] Victor Gottbaum, writing before the elections in a paid advertisement to be placed in the *Times* afterward, claimed that, regardless of the outcome, labor had taken 'a quantum leap forward in American politics in 1984.'[22] The perception that the labor leadership had emerged victorious from electoral defeat was justified by the narrowest possible reading of the election results.

In the first issue of the *AFL-CIO News* to appear after the elections, Lane Kirkland voiced the official pride in labor's role in the elections. This pride was justified by the fact that union households voted for Mondale-Ferraro by a 17-18 percent greater margin than the electorate as a whole. As interpreted by Kirkland, labor had clearly done its job. Pride in his own organization led him to point out that AFL-CIO members voted 60-40 for Mondale-Ferraro, in comparison to a 57-41 split for union members generally.[23] Subsequent analysis of the union vote shows that AFL-CIO households voted 67 percent for Democratic House candidates, and 70 percent for Democratic Senatorial candidates.[24] In other words, as long as the figures for union members and families still looked respectable, the leaders of the AFL-CIO reasoned they had done their job. The fact that the percentage of union household members who voted for Reagan actually increased from 43 percent in 1980, to 45 percent in 1984, was ignored, as was the fact that 53 percent of blue collar workers voted for Reagan in 1984, as compared to 47 percent in 1980. The fact that Mondale-Ferraro did better than Carter-Mondale is partly explained by the shift of those unionists (6 percent) who voted for John Anderson in 1980, to Mondale in 1984. The unspoken secret behind both the shift in blue collar votes toward Reagan and the improved turnout for Mondale-Ferraro is racial polarization. On the one hand, more whites voted for Reagan in 1984 than in 1980 — 68 percent of white men in '84, compared to 59 percent in '80, 64 percent of white women in '84, compared to 52 percent in 1980.[25] On the other hand, the numerical increase in Black voters due to the registration drives associated with the Jackson campaign undoubtedly helped improve union household figures.

The fact of the matter is, labor's efforts, which were intense in their own terms, did nothing to reverse the political trends that were undermining labor's political influence. For example, in spite of vigorous efforts by labor — and probably more so by Black and women's organizations — voter turnout remained at historically low levels. In 1984, 52.9 percent of those eligible voted in the Presidential election compared to 52.6 percent in 1980, and 62.8 percent in 1960.[26] In fact, of the 12 million people registered since 1980, only 4 million — one third — bothered to vote. Labor saw voter registration essentially as a technical question, not one of political content and inspiration. Jesse Jackson, during the primaries, and the political right throughout the elections, had shown that voters could be mobilized around a political vision — if not quite a program. But Jackson's effort could not save the day for the Democrats. On the contrary, it appears that the Republicans may have beaten the registration drives of all those in the Democratic camp. Of the 4 million new registrants who did vote in 1984, 61 percent voted for Reagan and only 32 percent for Mondale-Ferraro.[27] Seeing its job as a technical one of halting the shrinkage of the union vote through registration and turning out the vote by means of phone banks and electronic mailings, labor eschewed any programmatic vision different from the vague and crumbling liberalism of the

Democratic Party's mainstream. To this failure, and no doubt related to it, may be added the fact that the whole strategy for 1984 was bureaucratic from start to finish. Except for a couple of unions that polled their membership, no pretense of membership involvement was made beyond enlisting them in phone banks or last minute voter turnout efforts. The AFL-CIO Executive Board attempted to stem the political momentum of the right with bureaucratic technique and failed.

The drift to the right in American politics, like the decline of organized labor and its sustaining institutions, has many roots in the global nature of the current economic crisis and its accompanying industrial restructuring. At the level of ideology, American liberalism is stuck with a Keynesian and Neo-Classical framework that analyzed and proposed policy in terms of a basically autonomous national economy. But the global nature of today's markets, particularly capital and financial markets, has confounded the macro-economic policy options inherited from the New Deal and Kennedy-Johnson eras. For many mainstream liberals, including most of the AFL-CIO's official theorists, the major updating of this body of theory consists in amendments, not real changes. The major amendment is protectionism, sometimes coupled with the sort of industrial policy advocated by financier Felix Rohatyn, and aimed at preserving as much of basic industry as possible. For other liberals, and particularly for the more aggressive neo-liberals, the amendments are more sweeping — a supply-side version of industrial policy directed at improving America's competitive position by accelerating the restructuring process away from 'smokestack' production to high tech, communications, and services.[28] Mainstream liberalism attempts to maintain an untenable position, while neo-liberalism represents an adaptation to the political initiative the right has held for several years. Both represent a marked drift to the right within the Democratic Party.

The broader rightward drift in American politics is not primarily a result of ideological shifts within existing electoral constituencies, but of a complex interaction between the relative size of certain active constituencies and organizational/political changes within various class groups. Within the working class, for example, traditionally well-organized blue collar workers were shrinking as a group, while unorganized white collar and service workers were growing as a proportion of the class, as we noted earlier. One consequence was a decline in the percentage of working-class voter participation. As Walter Dean Burnham has noted: 'Sociologically, this decline in the post-1960 participation levels has been particularly concentrated among working class Americans who already vote least. Thus by 1976 blue collar and service workers constituted only 48.5 percent of the active electorate, but fully three-quarters of the 'party of non-voters.'[29] This is not only a reflection of the decline of unionism, but also of the collapse of the New Deal coalition. While this coalition is often depicted these days as a coalition of labor, Blacks, women and liberals, the fact is that the Democrats' ability to mobilize a national majority rested on the organizational pillars of the old northern urban machines and the 'Solid South,' i.e., the white South. By 1960, both of these institutions were well into their decline. For half a century, the skeleton in the closet of labor's national influence in politics was its dependence on the ability of an alliance between southern racism and northern machine politics — itself ethnically based and normally racist toward Blacks — to produce a national legislative majority and a favorable White House. While few progressives would mourn the passing of that setup, none has yet conjured up an alternative model for mobilizing a Democratic majority.

If the working-class vote has been on the decline for two and one-half decades, the participation of both old and new upper-income groups has been on the rise. One of the products of Imperial America's position at the center of much of multi-national capital has been the growth of a well-heeled middle class. In 1978, for example, 15 percent of the American work force earned over $41,000 per year. By 1982, the proportion was 18 percent.[30] The growing number of self-employed, well-to-do mini-entrepreneurs whose new life-style is in part subsidized by the very growth of (non-voting) low-income service workers is also part of this trend toward economic polarization.[31] That these voting groups are not highly committed to the welfare state or organized labor is not surprising. For these largely professional people, the admonition to 'vote your pocket-book' is an invitation to vote for Ronald Reagan or, if they are Democrats, a Gary Hart. Given their view of their own economic self-interest, it is no surprise that 35 percent of those who voted for Gary Hart in the Democratic primaries voted for Reagan in the general election.[32] Furthermore, the turnout rate is much higher for upper-income groups than for working-class people. The percentage difference in the turnout rates of white collar professionals and blue collar operators, for example, grew from 24.2 percentage points in 1968, to 33.0 points in 1980. In the primaries, which are important in determining the political direction of the party, the results of this differential translate into even more disproportionate representation for middle-class voters.[33] Of course, middle-class voters may be liberals on a variety of questions, but the evidence points toward the rise of newer middle strata who are quite hostile to labor and willing to 'vote their pocket-books' even when it conflicts with some liberal values on social or foreign policy questions.

Shifts in electoral constituencies do not necessarily bring immediate or clear policy changes such as those that took place toward the end of the 1970s. But as was the case in investment, finance, technology and corporate organization, big business saw in politics an opportunity to open new avenues for capital accumulation. Long-standing policy goals of business like tax relief, deregulation, and the thwarting or reversal of pro-labor legislation appeared increasingly viable as liberal policies crumbled under Carter. During the 70s, business changed its mode of intervention in politics and the legislative process. As Thomas Byrne Edsall has put it: 'During the 1970s, business refined its ability to act as a class, submerging competitive instincts in favor of joint, cooperative action in the legislative arena.'[34] So far as labor issues are concerned, the landmark event was the formation of the Business Roundtable in 1972. Other business organizations like the U.S. Chamber of Commerce also modernized their political functioning during the 70s, but it was the Roundtable that spoke for the Fortune 500. To present the appearance of a unified, aggressive class, the Roundtable also set out to mobilize its smaller colleagues around specific campaigns.

The effects of the Roundtable-led campaigns on labor's political agenda during the 1970s are well known. Most of the AFL-CIO's important initiatives were either chewed to pieces, as was the Humphrey-Hawkins Bill, or defeated outright in spite of Democratic control of Congress and the White House, as was the Common Situs Bill in 1977, and the Labor Law Reform Bill in 1978. For a brief period, some labor leaders began to ask hard questions. Pointing to the failure of the Democrats to pass any of their major platform promises of 1976, UAW President Doug Fraser asked: 'Why, with Democrats in control of more than two-thirds in the Congress and in the executive branch, has so little progress been made toward adoption of the Democratic platform the party worked so hard to develop?'[35] In a similar vein, the AFL-CIO leadership noted in its *Memo from COPE*: 'If any more evidence were needed that the 2-1 Democratic majority in the U.S. House is a pure illusion, it was provided by a recent series of votes on minimum wage.'[36] The explanation went far beyond the usual presence of conservative southern Democrats; it lay in the rightward motion of more and more Democrats, including liberals and neo-liberals in the 'class of 74,' who composed the two-thirds majority. Symbolic of the shift on economic and labor policy was the Joint Economic Committee of Congress' Report for 1979. This was the first time in history the Democrats and Republicans issued a bipartisan report. As JEC Chairman, Democrat Lloyd Bensten, wrote in his introduction to the Report: 'This year's report illustrates an emerging consensus in the Committee and in the country that the federal government needs to puts its financial house in order and that the major challenges today and for the foreseeable future are on the supply side of the economy.'[37] Few Democrats, and by no means all Republicans, would want to be stuck with the 'supply side' label anymore, but the underlying concept has carried the day.

The pressure tactics of organized business were one cause for this shift, as was the collapse of liberal theory as a policy guide. Big business money was another. Along with the growth of a unified business lobby, the 1970s saw the development of the corporate Political Action Committee (PAC). The importance of business PAC money has often been correlated with the rise of media politics. The enormous expense and strategic importance of TV time in particular has raised the cost of running for national office and created a greater dependence on those who are able to dispense funds. To be considered a viable candidate for a Congressional primary, one must demonstrate the ability to raise big money. Obviously, office seekers are influenced by those who finance their campaigns. In addition to this general effect, which works on both parties, there is a specific way in which PAC money has effected Democrats. Ironically, the Congressional reforms of the mid-70s, which produced a proliferation of committees and sub-committees, and therefore of influential committee chairs, encouraged business to target incumbent Democratic committee heads and important members. The number of important Democrats who receive business PAC money grew in the 70s, as did the amounts they received. By 1978, the *Wall Street Journal* observed:

> Business PACs aren't experiencing any difficulty in finding out-stretched hands, and they seem to be getting their money's worth from a growing contingent of Democrats. Many observers, looking at the pro-business tone of the current Congress, have concluded that PAC dollars have something to do with it. Says one Democratic member of the House Ways and Means Committee: 'These PACs are influencing a lot of Democrats. You're seeing people from main-stream Democratic districts, elected with labor support, who are now voting with business.'[38]

In the 1981/82 election cycle, after the Democrats lost control of the Senate, contributions to Democratic Senatorial incumbents fell considerably behind contributions to Republicans, $2.6 million to $4.2 million, respectively. But for House Democrats, business contributions remained high and much closer to Republican levels, $6.2 million to $8.5 million.[39] In the 1984 elections, while most of big business was rooting for Reagan's re-election, business PACs increased their contributions to Democrats, nearly equalling what they gave to Republican Congressional candidates. Business PACs gave Republicans $23.6 million and Democrats $20.7 million — three times what they gave the latter in 1981-82. In 1984, labor PACs gave Democratic Congressional candidates $14.7 million.[40] Much of this money went to the same people the business PACs were financing. Business was simply outbidding labor.

The combination of the idological/theoretical collapse of traditional liberal economic policy with the growth of the affluent as a proportion of the electorate (particularly as a proportion of the Democrats' active base), and the well-directed flow of corporate campaign money have been crucial to the shift to the right within the Democratic Party, particularly with regard to labor policy. Far from being a reversal of this trend, the Mondale-Ferraro campaign of 1984 presented itself as an endorsement of liberal retreat. Labor united in accepting this context. Far from being the mobilizer of the working class and oppressed, the AFL-CIO appeared on the field once more as the powerbrokering 'special interest' *par excellence*. Gone were the sweeping social programs that had formerly characterized labor's platform, if not always its practice. It was not simply that the Democratic Party and its candidates had dropped such ideas as full employment or national health insurance in favor of budget-balancing and Cold War rhetoric. The labor leadership, almost to a man (and, more rarely, a woman), had ceased to demand those things from the party it regarded as its own.

The twin shocks of right-wing business political ascendancy and accelerated industrial restructuring that hit labor in the late 70s and early 80s led most of the labor leadership to abandon any real effort to implement its broader social program. The anti-corporate rhetoric that characterized Doug Fraser's 'one-sided class-war' speech in 1978, when labor walked off the Carter administration's Labor-Management Group, or the Progressive Alliance's call to 'implement new programs for achieving social, political and economic justice in America'[41] gave way to talk of a new era of labor-management cooperation, even as business intensified its economic and political attack on unionism. The sole culprit for all injustice became Ronald Reagan, while, except in specific cases where the immediate interests of a union were involved (for example, at J.P.Stevens, Litton, or Coors), big business was simply let off the hook. While the AFL-CIO still supported initiatives by other groups, like the campaign for the ERA, it ceased to exert pressure for any specific legislative goals that could inspire or mobilize working-class people. The AFL-CIO/COPE assessment of the 98th Congress was emblematic of this direction. Of the 13 votes named key in the House, where presumably the Democrats could still get their way in 1983-84, only one, the Jobs Bill, represented a positive program in the general social interest. Seven of the 13 dealt with narrow issues of trade protection or limitations on foreign workers and immigration. The others involved defensive votes again Republican initiatives.[42]

The future direction of the Democratic Party is almost certainly toward further compromise with the right. When the votes were in, the party pundits, who care about electoral majorities and not visionary programs, drew the lesson that the Democrats would have to regain the white male vote, north and south, if it was to regain its status as the majority party. The Black vote did not save the day. Among white voters, still the vast majority, the gender gap all but vanished in the Presidential race. Labor delivered only 60 percent of those among its dwindling membership who chose to vote, but was not able to stem the flow of blue collar votes to Reagan. The loyal groups — Blacks, dedicated union-ists, liberal women — had nowhere else to go and would vote Democratic in any case. It was the white blue collar workers in the North, all kinds of whites in the South, and the affluent Democrats who won the attention of the party. Mainstream liberals of the old stamp were dead, defeated, or had resigned from politics. The future of the party was passing to people like Richard Gephardt, Chairman of the House Democratic Caucus for the 99th Congress, and Tony Coehlo, Chairman of the Demo-cratic Congressional Campaign Committee. Both are neo-liberals keenly aware of their middle-class base and anxious to garner corporate money for their party. Coelho, in fact, is credited with bringing in much of the business PAC money that Democratic House candidates got.[43] All signs point toward a bleak future for labor as long as it clings to its half-century old position of dependence inside the Democratic Party.

Democratic Party politics have been based on the cobbling together of majority coalitions on the basis of existing conscious-ness. It is painfully appropriate that in this era of electronic politics, the political pollster should take his place among the framers of party strategy. It should be evident, however, that a political strategy based on existing consciousness, rather than on the more difficult job of changing or raising consciousness, will not take labor or any other social movement beyond the right-ward moving morass of American politics today. Indeed, it is this approach to politics that has created the 'party of the non-voters.' Viewing this phenomonon from the other side of the coin, Walter Dean Burnham notes: 'It follows that a political system with *no* organized working-class left will be marked by heavy abstentions among the lower classes.'[44] As Burnham's analysis generally suggests, the way out of this situation lies through the development of a class-based politics. As he argues, the Democrats are incapable of such an approach by virtue of the social harmony themes of American welfare state liberalism.[45] Additionally, the Democratic Party is a capitalist party not only in the ideological sense, but because it counts among its members, politicians, leaders, and financial supporters a sig-nificant section of America's capitalist class.[46] A political realign-ment along class lines requires a new political organization and an approach to programs that challenge corporate prerogatives and power. Simply registering new voters, even millions of them, changes nothing so long as no clear alternative exists, as the 1984 elections demonstrated. Without a dramatic break toward an independent, class-based political organization and program, the balance of power within the U.S. will continue to shift in favor of capital. Indeed, by mid-decade, capital had achieved a latitude for unrestricted action in the U.S. not enjoyed since the 1920s. The greatest barriers to accumulation facing American capital were its economic competitors and the rebellion building in the Third World.

'Capital acts, labor reacts,' goes the old saying. But taken as either a movement or an institution, American labor has yet to react on a scale commensurate with the problems it faces. The framework of a forty-year old social contract has come apart in both the industrial and political arenas. As is always the case with a strategy based on class collaboration, both sides of the compact must agree to collaborate. When the deal ceased to be profitable in the late 1960s, business began withdrawing its cooperation. By the early 80s, it was on the rampage. While thrashing about for new techniques, organizational improvements, or tactical innovations, the American labor bureaucracy continues to cling to the old framework, even as its undoing pulls them down with it. With rare exceptions, these top union officials view any sort of innovation solely in the context of the bureaucratic hierarchy that characterizes most unions. In discussing some changes in union practice proposed by Harvard University economist James Medoff, for example, Murray Findley, President of the Amalgamated Clothing and Textile Workers Union, said that any fundamental changes in labor's practice would require 'a strong consensus.'[47] But bureaucratic consensus is what stifles change. Ironically, bureaucratic resistance to real change may produce the forces that make change possible by provoking the sort of rank and file rebellion that began to appear in the late 60s and early 70s.

The American labor movement is not a monolith, nor, in spite of extensive bureaucratic restraints, is it the exclusive property of its leadership. While nothing that amounts to a rank and file rebellion is on the immediate horizon, an increasingly self-conscious, overlapping series of networks of militants, union reformers, and political leftists touches most of the major unions in the U.S. While organizational expressions are rare — the only existing national rank and file organization in the U.S. is the Teamsters for a Democratic Union — genuine debate and discussion about new directions exist among these networks. The activities of unionists involved in these debates vary. They can be seen in temporary caucuses at various international union conventions, in the new cross-union strike support committees that have sprung up in the wake of the PATCO and Greyhound strikes, in monthly meetings of organizers from different unions in the New York City area, in the unemployed committees, in the unique labor radicalism that has appeared in the steel-producing Mon Valley, in the national and regional conferences held by *Labor Notes,* and in the daily work of countless caucuses and groups in local unions that push for a new standard of militancy, democracy, and — at times — political consciousness. While these forces — essentially leadership groupings in search of an active base — are small, they have captured a place in the American labor movement.

While no political consensus among these dissident forces currently exists — indeed, many would reject the title dissi- dent — there is an implied agenda that points away from the framework in which the top leaders still tend to discuss things. Increasingly, the cooperative or 'joint problem-solving' approach embodied in QWL is being rejected as a false promise. Membership involvement and democracy are seen as essential elements in renewing labor. The organization of the unorgan- ized is viewed as a priority that requires rank and file parti- cipation, a stress on social issues that can attract minority and women workers who compose the strategic core of non-union industries and occupations, and a willingness to operate outside the law when necessary. In terms of both organizing the un- organized and what might be called reorganizing the organized, there is a general commitment to the idea that labor's ability to survive and grow depends on its willingness to become less an institution and more a crusade for social change that can inspire millions of unorganized working-class people. At least implied, if not always consciously accepted, is the notion of independent political action — the idea that labor has to act as a class move- ment and not a special interest, and that this would require an independent political organization and program: something like a labor party with a program well to the left of anything the Democrats could adopt. Taken together, these directions point toward the concept of class struggle unionism, although the term is not used outside of left circles. These simple, minimal ideas are strong stuff in today's labor movement. They run counter to bureaucratic practice, to politics as usual, to non-adversarial

106

unionism, and to any attempt to cling to the decaying framework of post-World War II labor relations. Whether the debate becomes a conflict, the conflict an upheaval, remains to be seen. The one thing certain is that the rules of the game have changed in industry and politics, and that unions are no longer to be allowed the luxury of business as usual.

Notes

1. Nelson Lichtenstein, *Labor's War at Home: The CIO In World War II* (New York, 1982), p. 51.

2. Lichtenstein, p. 173.

3. Thomas Byrne Edsall, *The New Politics of Inequality* (New York, 1984), p. 142; *Directory of Labor Organizations*, 1984-85 Edition (Washington, DC), p. 2.

4. Mike Urquhart, 'The Employment Shift to Services,' *Monthly Labor Review* (April 1984), pp. 15-21.

5. William D. Nordhaus, 'The Falling Share of Profits,' *Brookings Papers on Economic Activity* 1 (1974), p. 180.

6. *Federal Trade Commission Quarterly Financial Report for Manufacturing, Mining and Trade*, 1977-79; *Statistical Abstract of the United States* (Washington, DC 1978', p. 578.

7. See 'Labor-Community Unity: The Morse Strike Against Disinvestment and Concessions,' *Labor Research Review* (Fall 1982), pp. 5-17; and *Labor Notes* (20 December 1983).

8. Daniel Weiner, 'Deals of The Year,' *Fortune* (23 January 1984).

9. Interviews with OCAW officials and members, 1984.

10. *Business Week* (6 April 1984).

11. *Directory of Labor Organizations*, p. 3.

12. BLS, *Survey of Current Wages* (October 1984), p. 45.

13. BNA, *Labor Relations Reporter* (13 August 1984).

14. *Wall Street Journal* (11 December 1984).

15. *WSJ* (18 June 1984).

16. Audrey Freedman *et al.*, 'Labor Outlook, 1984,' *The Conference Board Research Bulletin* 150 (1983), p. 11.

17. *Tech Engineer*, UAW Local 160 (January-February 1984).

18. 'Report By The House Labor-Management Subcommittee on Failure of Labor Law,' *Daily Labor Report* (4 October 1984), p. D2.

19. Edsall, *New Politics of Inequality*, pp. 151-4; 'Report By House,' pp. D2-D6; *Wall Street Journal* (2 October 1984).

20. 'Report By House,' p. D3.

21. Bill Keller, 'Labor Leaders Assess Their Drive For Mondale,' *New York Times* (9 November 1984).

22. *New York Times* (11 November 1984).

23. *AFL-CIO News* (10 November 1984).

24. *AFL-CIO News* (1 December 1984).

25. New York Times/CBS Poll, *New York Times* (8 November 1984).

26. 'Elections Turnout Shows Slight Rise,' *New York Times* (8 November 1984).

27. *AFL-CIO News* (19 January 1985).

28. Kim Moody, 'Industrial Policy: Can It Capture The Workers Votes and The Bosses Hearts?' *Changes* (January-February 1984), pp. 14-19.

29. Walter Dean Burnham, *The Current Crisis in American Politics* (New York, 1983), p. 262.

30. Harold Meyerson, 'Labor's Risky Plunge Into Politics,' *Dissent* (Summer, 1984).

31. See Mike Davis, 'The Political Economy of Late Imperialist America,' *New Left Review* 143 (January-February 1984).

32. *New York Times* (8 November 1984).

33. Edsall, *New Politics of Inequality*, pp. 179-87, 245-6.

34. Edsall, p. 128.

35. *UAW Ammo* 19, 6, (1978).

36. *AFL-CIO Memo from COPE* (26 September 1977).

37. *Joint Economic Report*, 1979, Report No. 96-44 (22 March 1979), p. 3.

38. *Wall Street Journal* (11 September 1978).

39. Edsall, p. 133.

40. *New York Times* (6 November 1984).

41. 'Statement Adopted By The Progressive Alliance,' (15 January 1979).

42. *AFL-CIO News* (20 October 1984).

43. *New York Times* (6 November 1984; 8 November 1984; 2 December 1984; 9 December 1984; 11 December 1984).

44. Burnham, *Current Crisis*, p. 262.

45. Burnham, *passim*.

46. G.William Domhoff, *Fat Cats and Democrats* (New York, 1972), *passim*; Laurence H. Shoup, *The Carter Presidency and Beyond* (Palo Alto, CA, 1980), pp. 21-62.

47. *Business Week* (17 December 1984), p. 35.

Table I

Production Workers By Industry (in 000s)

Industry & SIC	12/78	12/82	8/84	Net Loss/gain
Auto (371)	832.7	491.7	654.8	-177.9
Steel (331)	449.7	242.6	260.6	-189.1
Meat Packing (2011)	136.4	119.1	120.8	-15.6
Petroleum Refining (291)	103.2	93.7	84.0	-19.2
Chemicals (28)	629.7	580.8	597.3	-32.4
Aircraft (372)	307.8	296.1	276.2	-31.6
Machinery (35)	1607.2	1183.4	1358.1	-249.1

Sources: *Supplement To Employment and Earnings*, BLS, July 1984; *Employment and Earnings*, BLS, October 1984.

Table II

Paid Union Membership, 1967, 1979, 1980

Union	1967	1979	1983	1979–83 Loss/Gain
UAW	1,325,000	1,499,000*	1,010,000	-489,000
USWA	952,000	964,000	707,000	-257,000
URW	166,000	158,000	108,000	-50,000
IAM	740,000	664,000	596,000	-68,000
IUE	304,000	243,000	192,000	-51,000
IBEW	658,000	825,000	820,000	-5,000
OCAW	142,000	146,000	124,000	-22,000
UFCW	892,000**	1,076,000	993,000	-83,000
AFSCME	297,000	889,000	959,000	+70,000
SEIU	328,000	528,000	589,000	+61,000
CWA	315,000	485,000	573,000	+88,000

*1978, **Combined paid membership of Packinghouse Workers, Retail Clerks, and Meatcutters who merged during the 1970s to become the UFCW.

Source: Directory of U.S. Labor Organizations, 1984-85 Edition, BNA, 1984, pp. 3, 51-53.

4. Democratic Dilemmas

David Plotke

'The choices this year are not just between two different personalities, or between two political parties. They are between two different visions of the future, two fundamentally different ways of governing — their government of pessimism, fear, and limits, or ours of hope, confidence, and growth.'

Ronald Reagan, acceptance speech at the 1984 Republican National Convention, 23 August 1984

I   Why Reagan Won

When a presidential election is won by almost 20 points, across all regions and most social groups, reasons are not far to seek. The result seems to have been inevitable, even though there were moments in the campaign when it did not. Following the California primary, Mondale moved to within 9 points of Reagan in several polls — not a great distance. And in mid-July, the nomination of Geraldine Ferraro momentarily seemed exhilarating; the normal calculations were thrown out, and new possibilities were created.

It is still worth trying to sort out the reasons for what happened, because they imply judgments of how those who opposed Reagan in 1984 should proceed. It is easy to say: Reagan won because he is charming and popular; his campaign was well-organized and well-financed; he benefited from a lucky economic upturn; and he had the good fortune to be running against a weak candidate.

There's some truth in each of these reasons. The danger is that taken together they may, in 1985 and 1986, divert attention from problems with the organization, policies, and views of those who opposed Reagan. Or they may encourage the sort of pseudo-reflection which made the Democratic response to Reagan's 1988 State of the Union address so depressing (most viewers chose *Dynasty* instead).

In the aftermath of the major defeat suffered by Democrats of all stripes (and those to their left), many groups fear that a public analysis of the weaknesses of their efforts would only weaken them. Such fears are reasonable, since there are many Democrats who would be happy to dispense with discussions of the gender gap, or distance the party from labor unions, or reduce the role of the groups most active in the Jackson campaign. Yet defensiveness doesn't encourage clarity about the causes of Reagan's victory, and implicitly tends to treat that victory as an approval of an unusual individual.

Reagan's personal charms are considerable, but his personal performance during the campaign was hardly devastating. He was widely criticized for avoiding the press in favor of 'morning in America' events. In the two presidential debates, he managed one mediocre and one very poor performance. On a deeper level, focusing on Reagan's personality as though it were mainly a private matter, is misleading. Reagan has been a major public political figure for several decades; his personal traits and political themes have become intertwined. If he is now so personally popular, it is wishful to claim that this popularity is innocent of strong political associations.

Winning on Issues

Well into the presidential campaign, polls began to reveal a surprising result, apparently full of contradictions. Some people claimed to feel less confident in Reagan's personal abilities than in the direction of his policies; others claimed to disagree with many of his specific policies, yet to agree with his overall direction. Were these results the residue of a chaotic political moment, without much significance, or even the sign of a secret sympathy for liberal to left positions?

Such confusing findings can be explained by distinguishing between specific policies and broad political direction. On the former, Reagan had mixed success, and continues to encounter problems, especially where issues of 'fairness' are involved. On the latter, however, the Reagan administration was successful in framing the terms of political debate and sustaining substantial popular identification with its overall direction.

Reagan and the Republicans won debates on two of the three main clusters of issues in the campaign. Winning such debates, given their sprawling, multisided quality — and the presidential-congressional division of power which makes a 'mandate' easy to contest — does not give programmatic license. It does offer the power to set a general political direction through the Presidency. Reagan knows how to do this.

On the economy and taxes, the Reagan administration has generally been successful. Most people now believe that the economy will perform better with less government intervention than more; with lower taxes rather than higher taxes; and with lower social policy expenditures for jobs, welfare, and housing. Most people, across most social groups, believe that economic growth is essential both for their personal futures and for the future of the nation as a whole. Here the left's willingness to credit the 1984 economic upturn for Reagan's victory is too simple. Obviously this prosperity was crucial, and without it Reagan would have faced a much tougher race. There is a strong connection between how people vote and how they perceive their economic condition to have changed in the recent past — and what they expect it to be in the near future. Yet there was an even stronger connection, in this case, between voting and perceptions of whether the economy as a whole was likely to improve, irrespective of individual prospects. The two patterns are related, but more is going on than short term calculations of economic self-interest. People — again, across social groups with the exception of the lowest 10% or so in income — have come to perceive Reagan and the Republicans as more likely to produce sustained economic growth.

Democratic attachments linger; in registration terms it remains the majority party, though by a relatively small and declining margin. And the Democratic Party is still perceived as more interested in the less privileged, in the condition of 'ordinary' Americans. Yet if these same Americans view the choice as one between growth with insufficient attention to social equality, and short term efforts at greater social equality with little attention to growth, they now tend to choose the former. All the arguments of conservatives have not been persuasive: witness the opposition to some proposed budget cuts.

Yet inattention to growth is seen as irresponsible, and many — once again, across classes — feel that without growth inequality cannot be reduced.

On foreign policy, Reagan was also successful. Most people believe that peace is more likely to be achieved by sustaining a high level of defense spending (though not granting Secretary of Defense Weinberger every request) and by adopting a tough stance toward the Soviet Union than by cutting defense spending and pursuing detente. The campaign's dynamic demonstrated that there is a strong popular sentiment in favor of arms control. Imagine the costs to Reagan had he not attempted to respond to that sentiment! At the same time, the Democrats — much less those to their left — were and are perceived as too weak to get a solid arms control agreement from an adversary who can't be trusted. Another tension: there is widespread support for Reagan's general stance toward radical regimes in the Third World, and he continues to benefit from comparison with Carter. Yet there is no enthusiasm for direct military intervention in Central America, a line which Reagan has recognized as one that the Republicans would cross with grave domestic political consequences. If the population is not eager to fall into line behind every Republican foreign policy initiative, the Reaganite identification of security and tranquility with military strength has been persuasive. By the end of the campaign, the Democrats had even lost their position in the surveys as the party better able to avoid war.

In a third cluster of issues, Reagan was less successful. The 'social' agenda of the new right now shapes the Republican Party platform. It has substantial public support; its adherents were an important part of the coalition which reelected Reagan. Public debate has been moved significantly to the right on many of these issues, from abortion to crime. Yet there is certainly no popular consensus on behalf of Reagan's approaches, and disagreement extends to the Reagan electoral coalition itself, notably among many young first-time Republican voters.

By any standard, winning on two of three major sets of issues is a good performace. It's crucial to discuss why people now believe many of the things which Reagan and the Republicans would like them to believe; and in doing so, we should be careful not to assume that the agreement is a durable new fact of American political life. But it's also plainly realistic to recognize that people now do believe these things. Today, there is no automatic liberal (much less left) consensus on policies which got obscured by Reagan's personal appeal.

A New Electorate

Reagan's victory was also a loss for all sections of the Democratic Party and those to its left. Some reasons for the Democratic loss have to do with misunderstandings or lack of attention to major socioeconomic and demographic changes in the U.S. in recent decades. Democratic strategies, with the partial exception of Gary Hart's campaign, paid little more than lip service to these changes beyond those which have directly involved women. The Democratic campaign — and not just its Mondale centerpiece — seemed to combine the rhetoric of the 1930s with some of the movements of the 1960s.

Someone listening to a Mondale speech might have thought that most people in the U.S. are very poor or on the verge of becoming so; personally threatened by the decline of traditional industries; living in the northeast and industrial midwest; and eager to pay taxes to expand government social programs. None of these things is true, though there are millions of poor, some of whom have become poor as a result of Reagan's policies. And millions of people, from unemployed auto and steel workers to women and children in poverty, have been hurt by chaotic economic dislocation.

Yet the electorate has changed dramatically over the last several decades. First, there has been a major economic shift away from the industries of the first half of the century, toward new industries from computers to services. With this sectoral shift has come an occupational shift, so that industrial labor has declined relative to technical, service, and sales work, even within the 'traditional' industries. The socioeconomic configuration which provided the basis of Democratic power from the 1930s through the 1960s has been eroded; the groups which were both numerically and strategically crucial for the New Deal coalition, especially industrial labor, no longer play the same role.

Second, there has been a major population shift. The East and Midwest have declined relative to the South and West, while central cities have declined within larger metropolitan areas. These changes have much the same effect as the economic changes, because Democratic power was concentrated in the urban, industrial North and Midwest.

It is not exactly news to note these developments. But to go from recognizing them to taking them into account politically is no easy matter, especially when doing so involves costs and risks. This is particularly true when many of the calls to recognize these new realities have until recently come from the right and center of the party, often with the implicit message that Democrats ought to curtail their support for unions, government social programs, and welfare policies. The Democrats have been unsuccessful at winning the allegiance of new social groups or growing regions in ways which would replace the decline in political support caused by the weakening of traditionally Democratic groups. The result means political trouble for Democrats under any circumstances, but it spells disaster when Democrats act as though there is still a natural Democratic presidential majority, and the party's main task is to activate and mobilize it. That is demonstrably no longer true. For large new groups —from technical and professional workers in Silicon Valley, to office workers in Boston, to industrial workers in the Sunbelt —possess no automatic Democratic identification, even if Democrats think that they should.

In 1984, Democrats and independent voter registration groups affiliated with them expected new voters to fill in the gaps in the old electoral majority: 'The prospect that new voters and old ones who are reenergized can provide a constituency for progressive politics in the 1980s is lending a fervor to voter registration drives unmatched since the crusading days of the civil rights movement'. (Hulbert James and Maxine Phillips, 'The New Voter Registration Society,' *Social Policy* [Winter 1984], p. 2.) Without the registration efforts, things would have been even worse for the Democrats in 1984. Yet new Republican registrations approached those of the Democrats. The ability of Democratic and left independent organizations to mobilize new voters was no greater than that of the Republican Party. Reagan was supported by 60% of first-time voters, a figure almost identical to his overall support (59%).

The disappointing outcome of voter registration efforts underlines the new reality: a Democratic presidential majority now has to be rebuilt, not just activated. This requires persuading people who have stopped being Democrats and people who have never been Democrats that they should vote Democratic in presidential elections.

What did Reagan Win?

Reagan didn't win a mandate to do anything he pleases, although he did win broad approval for his foreign and economic policies. In his second term he seems determined to press forward with his overall program. His vagueness during the campaign may haunt him, because it will be hard to claim that his massive vote means approval for x rather than y. Yet he can reasonably claim, for example, to have been elected in order to try to reduce the growth of social spending. He can claim support for relying more on spending cuts and efforts to sustain growth than on tax increases to reduce the deficit. And he can claim approval for maintaining a high level of defense spending, though public reaction to further dramatic increases has been mixed.

Perhaps the most valuable commodity Reagan earned is an opportunity. In 1980, many read Reagan's victory as principally a vote against Carter, not a vote for Reagan. Whether or not that judgment was true, his current position is stronger. Reagan now has the chance to turn his two victories into a lasting Republican regime. Republican presidents and Senates could become routine for decades, with the Democratic Party restricted to the House and to some state and local governments. Whether Reagan and the Republicans can take advantage of that opportunity is not a foregone conclusion. A shift to the right has demonstrably occurred, but it has not yet been consolidated, either organizationally or ideologically.

II Democratic Options After 1984

For everyone who opposed Reagan's reelection, preventing the consolidation of a Republican regime should be the main point of reference for the next several years. Taking that goal seriously means engaging in a politics concerned with reshaping the direction of the Democratic Party. To focus on blocking a Republican realignment is both realistic and desirable. It is

desirable because a durable Republican regime would undermine many of the most important democratic achievements of
recent decades, from civil rights to union recognition. A Republican realignment would block further progress across a wide
range of issues, from the environment to many international
issues to education to the condition of the nation's economic
infrastructure. It is also realistic to try to block a Republican
regime, since, while popular ideological shifts to the right are
more substantial than the left likes to acknowledge, the situation
yet remains fluid. New socioeconomic groups are not 'naturally'
Republican any more than they are 'naturally' Democratic. They
can develop political identities entirely different from those
offered by Reagan and the Republicans, but only if those identities make sense of their experiences and values, and seem to be
linked to a positive vision of the future, not just economically but
socially and culturally as well.

In 1984, however, the Democrats — from left to right — failed
badly. For the most part, they tried to win an election by relying
on their traditional 'natural' sources of support, adding some of
the movements and interest groups which arose in the 1960s and
1970s. This strategy seemed to offer the best chance of beating
Reagan in late 1983 and early 1984, when Mondale seemed likely
to be the Democratic nominee. It was attractive to many whose
enthusiasm for Mondale himself was limited. When groups like
the National Organization for Women (NOW) and Friends of the
Earth signed on early, organizational self-interest was only part
of the reason. They sought, as well, to intervene in the most
effective manner. In the crucial case of the AFL-CIO, broad agreement with Mondale's positions was also important. But these
conceptions of the campaign assumed that the old Democratic
coalition was much stronger than it is. Imagining that coalition
to provide a solid electoral base amounted to ignoring demographic and social changes, and hoping that the campaign would
be won by appeals to 'natural' or traditional loyalties. This
strategy too quickly assumed that the official organizations of
various social groups could deliver 'their' voters. This proved
chimerical to the degree that would have been necessary to
defeat Reagan. The AFL-CIO could help produce a reasonable
margin among union households (45% for Reagan, 53% for
Mondale,) but not nearly so large a margin as required. And
increasingly the AFL-CIO's political influence seems to end at its
own organizational boundaries: nonunionized workers were

not persuaded to vote for Mondale (53% of blue-collar workers voted for Reagan.) NOW and other women's organizations could make a significant difference among women voters, especially the working and unmarried, but there is no homogeneous 'women's vote' to be delivered for the Democrats (57% of women voted for Reagan). A grand coalition of coalitions did not materialize in actual voting. The most Democratic social groups were blacks (90%), Jews (66%), and the unemployed (68%). (These and preceding figures taken from the *New York Times*-CBS Poll, *NYT,* 8 November 1984.)

Given the ineffective Democratic strategy, what political direction does the election's outcome suggest? Would moving toward Reagan help block a new regime? During the 1984 campaign, part of the Democratic Party advocated this course, and its candidates — John Glenn, Reuben Askew, Ernest Hollings — failed to win a significant primary vote. Yet a straightforward Democratic conservatism has powerful adherents, and after the election debacle they will surely find a wider audience. This tendency criticizes Mondale as the captive of liberal special interests, such as the women's movement and the unions; claims the party as a whole has moved too far away from the center to win a national election; and castigates the Democratic leadership for its foreign and military policies:

> With peace and prosperity in the land, Reagan might have been unbeatable in 1984, but his landslide was something the Democrats brought on themselves . . . The message for the Democrats was simple: what they were selling, the voters were not buying.
> The Democrats were offering peace and fairness. But what the McGovernized Democrats mean by peace is military weakness and a retreat from global responsibility.' (Joshua Muravchik, 'Why the Democrats Lost,' *Commentary* [January 1985], p. 25.)

The failures of this tendency's candidates in the Democratic primaries attest to the improbability of a prospective center-right Democratic presidential majority. The neoconservative Democrats who advocate this course miss the ways in which the traditional Democratic voters they have in mind have been relocated—ideologically and often literally—by the last two decades' socioeconomic changes. Moving right, the better to oppose Reaganism, also runs a major risk: that the popular left, from unions to the gay movement to environmentalists, will be demobilized by uninspired campaigns in which 'their' issues are ignored, while the Democrats fail to gain enough center votes to compensate.

Conservative strategies will continue to hold certain attractions. This is partly because many prominent Democrats agree with them in principle. Among this stratum, a number of influential office-holders in the South and the West, having survived two Reagan landslides, now gain considerable credibility as advocates of a different Democratic course. There are, however, major differences between southern and western critiques of the Mondale campaign. The latter — exemplified by Governor Bruce Babbitt of Arizona, or by Gary Hart himself — are often significantly to the left of the former in crucial ways: on the means to limit growth in social spending; on environmental issues; on foreign policy; and especially on the so-called 'social issues,' with Christian fundamentalism and other conservative tendencies playing a more modest role in most western states than in the South. For the moment, a rough working alliance exists between southern and western Democratic leaders, despite obvious areas of disagreement. Even for those not entirely approving a conservative strategy, this direction offers at least a politically attractive change of course.

One alternative to this view, usually implicit in organizational behavior rather than articulated as a coherent strategy, is to retreat into the trenches, defend existing positions, and prepare for a national campaign without Reagan's haunting, powerful presence. It would be unfair to call this strategy do-nothingism, since it requires enormous efforts to wage the defensive battles now on the agenda, such as those over abortion rights. Yet the labor movement, and parts of the women's movement, have already given an account of the 1984 defeat which amounts to calling for a replay of Mondale's campaign. The hope is that in 1988 success will be achieved against a less attractive Republican, perhaps with a more telegenic or at least more eloquent Democrat, perhaps with the assistance of more troubled economic times. Mario Cuomo is the obvious candidate, with his insistence that 'we must be the family of America, recognizing that at the heart of the matter we are bound one to another . . . ' (Keynote Address, Democratic National Convention; quoted in NYT, 17 July 1984). If Mondale's defeat had been narrow, this strategy might have dominated. Given the result, however, this view must remain an undercurrent, even though it represents the implicit choice of powerful Democratic forces. It is, however, likely to fail as an electoral strategy for all the reasons that the Mondale campaign failed.

Another possible strategy has been suggested by elements on the left of the Democratic Party, as well as by left groups outside the party. This strategy proposes that the party move substantially to the left. In a modest version, this shift would follow the successful Senatorial campaigns of Paul Simon in Illinois and Thomas Harkin in Iowa. The claim is that despite neoconservative critiques, Mondale suffered by moving too far toward Reagan, and that greater success could be achieved by a candidate who tried recapture a more militant and populist spirit for the same coalition Mondale appealed to unsuccessfully. Such a campaign would defend social spending more aggressively and attack Reaganite foreign policy with less reserve. In a more radical version of this strategy, Democrats are advised to move sharply to the left to take up the positions expressed in Jesse Jackson's 1984 campaign.

The evidence for the strategic merit of the first type of left shift is mixed. Simon and Harkin won against weak opponents—but they did defeat incumbents in a difficult year. In other races, a more aggressive populism would have gained some votes, but the question is how many, weighed against the considerable potential losses.

The prospects for the second type of shift are bleak if the aim is to win a presidential election in the near future, rather than to build a left faction in and around the Democratic Party. Jesse Jackson and George McGovern together represented at most 30% of the Democratic primary vote, and failed to win any primaries in the larger states. Further, Democratic primary voters make up a smaller group, as well as one more to the left, than the 41% of those voting who preferred Mondale to Reagan. Neither Jackson nor McGovern could have transformed the political scene dramatically in a short period, and both would have run much further behind Reagan than Mondale did.

In 1984, the lines between the left inside and outside the Democratic Party were more blurred than has been true for many years, and this for two reasons. The Jackson and McGovern candidacies were quite radical, especially by American standards; a section of the Democratic Party has moved well to the left, and expresses many positions with which those to its left have relatively little disagreement. From the other direction, among those who once disdained participation in the Democratic Party, the threat and the reality of Reaganism persuaded most to support the Democratic efforts. The movement into the Democratic Party from the organized left, and much more important, from the social and political movements of the last decade, has influenced most sections of the party. This influence has helped shift much of the organized party to the left of its traditional positions, especially on international issues.

Another effect of relations between the organized party and popular social and political movements has been the dispersion of the Democratic left among three of the main tendencies in the party, represented in 1984 by Mondale, Gary Hart, and Jackson. Leftists inside and around the Democratic Party were by no means unanimous in supporting Jesse Jackson, especially after Jackson's failure to deal adequately with charges of anti-Semitism. Feminists divided their support among Hart, Mondale, and Jackson; labor activists mainly supported Mondale, but there was some support for Jackson, and in the West, sympathy for Hart (especially in the service sector unions). Chicano activists were also divided among the campaigns, despite the overtures made by Jackson's campaign that they participate in a 'Rainbow Coalition'; this reluctance was due in part to a widespread perception that Jackson's campaign was basically a Black ethnic politics, with limited possibilities for becoming much broader.

Boundaries have broken down on the left of the party. There is more debate, and it sometimes unfolds in language which even the socialist left finds familiar. Yet there is no unitary 'left' with a clear, coherent position on the main issues confronting the Democratic Party. Various left currents (inside and outside the party) face most of the same problems as those to their right, with no apparent solutions.

One problem facing all the 'lefts' is that some of their core positions are politically so unpopular that they were among Reagan's favorite targets, even when Mondale did not really share them. The Democratic left's positions on defense, for example, are still framed by opposition to the Vietnam War, or to overt American intervention in Latin America on the side of the dictators. For many, including people highly critical of Reagan, these positions appear exclusively negative, or passive and indifferent to the course of events outside this country.

The policies of the left are also a source of problems in social and economic policy. This is not due so much to wild popular enthusiasm for Reaganite budget-cutting, as to the perception that Democrats are far more concerned with distributing wealth than with generating it. Many regard Democratic policies as aimed at preserving positions of relative privilege for industries (and unions) which are competitively inefficient—in effect, as efforts to force taxpayers to subsidize powerful special interest groups.

Interest Groups

The negative public reaction to calls for protectionism from within the Democratic Party — calls from its left as well as on its center — is connected to a central problem which will confront Democratic efforts for the rest of the decade. Antiwar activists, feminists, environmentalists, and unionists share this image with those who guided the Mondale campaign. In recent years it has become known as the problem of 'special interests,' a term which the left has understandably resisted when it is applied to labor, the women's movement, and environmentalism. Gary Hart raised this issue effectively, and was rewarded with almost as many primary votes as Mondale, over 35% of those cast. Reagan amplified this theme in his criticism of Mondale, and used it to pad his victory. He charged that rather than having any firm principles or overall political direction, Mondale sought simply to please a range of powerful constituency organizations in order to obtain political resources for his campaign. Thus Mondale's connections were treated, not as evidence of success-ful coalition-building, but as signs of political and even moral weakness. Reagan and Bush added that Mondale's inability to withstand interest group pressure was another sign of his 'wimpiness,' and exploited the growing racial polarization of the electorate, especially in the South.

On the left as well as the center, anti-Reagan efforts were often oblivious to the popular perception of these issues. Most efforts, assuming that 'natural' Democrats still constitute a majority, also conceived the Democratic vote as a collection of blocs to be delivered by their nominal leaderships, from NOW to the AFL-CIO. And while Hart's charges were bitterly resented by many on the left who defended Mondale's ties with the AFL-CIO, NOW, etc., Mondale's campaign was vulnerable because it really was a collection of pressure groups, tenuously allied. A weak Democratic apparatus tried to coordinate their efforts or at least keep them from attacking each other in public, but without success.

Blaming all this on Mondale would unfairly continue the tendency among Democrats and the left to excuse their own weaknesses by vilifying a recent unsuccessful Democratic presidential candidate (McGovern, Carter, or Mondale, depending on who's doing the accusing). In the wake of the decline of the Democratic political order, which had lasted from the 1930s through the 1960s, little holds together the remaining sections of the old coalition or the new groups around it. And neither old nor new groups' main organizations can easily deliver 'their' constituencies for Democratic presidential candidates. Nor is this situation just a problem for centrist Democrats. The left — inside and outside the Democratic Party — is no more able to present itself coherently than was the Mondale campaign.

Two levels of political discourse now predominate within the Democratic Party and to its left. One centers on very general statements of principle about democracy, equality, and social justice. The other makes specific programmatic commitments arising from the immediate demands of a multitude of groups, from comparable worth to toxic wastes programs. The general principles remain essential. And most of the immediate demands are worth defending. But there is painfully little to connect them. There is little sign of a political vision which mediates between the two levels, concretizing general principles and clarifying the rationale of specific policies. This weakness means at the extreme a lack of politics; in its place, moral exhortation or programmatic detail.

In this setting, Republicans claimed — and continue to claim — that Mondale and the Democrats lack any real political or moral core, and that governance based on interest-group coalitions is bound to be ineffectual and erratic. The political effectiveness of this critique raises a difficult problem for the left. From the 1960s to the present, the major accomplishments of the popular left have been achieved by a succession of mass movements which have fought to be recognized as an autonomous source of legitimate political and social claims. From the civil rights to the gay and lesbian movements, new social and political forces have developed through a logic of identifying and articulating particular grievances and developing distinctive collective identities. The modest power of the popular left in the U.S. still lies mainly in this richness and diversity among its voices, which have articulated a repeated, creative expression of novel demands. New forces have often refused to subordinate their programs to claims about a general political interest, which have often seemed to threaten the loss or political marginalization of painfully won new identities and forms of organization.

This approach worked well in establishing the right of new forces to exist. Further, it was strategically fruitful when a Democratic political order affirmed the legitimacy of such efforts, and, however grudgingly, made concessions for both moral and instrumental reasons. The decay of the Democratic order and the triumph of Reaganism have created a new situation to which the popular left has been painfully slow to respond.

Calls for coalition ('progressive,' 'Rainbow,' or whatever) usually avoid a key question: what is the glue for any such effort? What political conceptions can now provide a bridge between general statements of principle and specific programmatic points? This question has been relevant for years, but it is unavoidably urgent given the success of Reagan's campaign — against which a more left-leaning version of Mondale's collection of interest groups would have suffered even more devastating defeat.

Various groups and individuals — from the AFL-CIO to NOW to Jesse Jackson — may now continue rushing to exonerate themselves, blaming others for Reagan's landslide victory out of fear that they will be blamed and abandoned. This tactic will prove no more fruitful than clichéd Reagan-bashing accompanied by hopeful waiting for the next recession.

If such responses are all the popular left can manage, the special interest problem will be defined and handled by relatively conservative forces in the Democratic Party. For these groups, the lesson of 1984 is that 'special interest' politics should be abandoned in favor of a centrist appeal to a 'national interest' based on the needs of partly imaginary 'middle-class' constituencies. Thus labor, Blacks, and women as groups should play a more modest role — and such a change should be made structural by deemphasizing caucuses within the organized party. This argument has exerted considerable influence on national debate within the Democratic Party since the election. If its prescriptions were adopted, the result would probably be further Democratic defeats. Yet such an approach may prevail, particularly if the popular left has no alternative which goes beyond congratulating itself on its diversity and occasional capacity to make fragile alliances. The problem faces all parts of the Democratic Party, though it is formulated differently by different fractions. *The New Republic's* view, for example, is less conservative than others which may gain increasing power: 'Somehow, the Democratic Party must find a way to represent a national interest that transcends the mere sum of these perfectly legitimate but still comparatively narrow group interests. And it must divorce the goal of representing the aspirations of minorities, working people, women, and other groups from the tendency to obey every demand of interest group spokesmen.' ('Now What?' *New Republic,* 26 November 1984.) Reagan's re-election shows that a collection of Democratic and left-independent interest groups will not now defeat a much more coherent conservative political force. Calling for 'unity' among those opposed to Reagan will accomplish little without a sustained, open debate aimed at defining a political approach which could provide a credible alternative to Reaganism. Such an alternative requires a shared political and moral vision beyond a laundry list of complaints and demands. The left's political vision is now as fragmented as that of the center of the Democratic Party. There is only vagueness at the crucial level between general principles — equality, decency, justice, democracy — and particular demands.

III An Alternative Course

Those who oppose the direction of the Reagan administration and want to block its consolidation need to formulate a position which takes account of, instead of simply denouncing, the socio-economic and demographic changes of the last few decades. To do so requires reshaping elements from several points on the Democratic spectrum. This isn't a matter of changing basic principles: commitments to social justice, to racial and sexual equality, to protecting the environment, to peace, to democratic procedures, remain fundamental. But we do need a new political vision; its absence made the 1984 Democratic platform a bloated, shapeless document.

The national Democratic Party contains many tendencies which were broadly represented by the presidential candidacies of Glenn, Hart, Jackson, and Mondale. Most of these tendencies present ideas relevant to a new direction, and all try to represent electorally important groups. While not excluding any of these alternatives completely, the only way to shape a new direction is to begin with a more limited focus, to which other elements can be added. The best such focus at present aims to rearticulate democratic principles politically by linking themes suggested by Hart's campaign with themes from Jackson's campaign. Starting from Glenn's campaign would mean a dramatic and electorally fruitless turn to the right; starting from Mondale's campaign would mean duplicating its incoherence.

Hart's campaign recognized and made an effort to come to grips with new socioeconomic and political realities on a national scale. His actual program did not lack substance, so much as it lacked a broader democratic political vision within which his many specific proposals could be argued. In a sense, his campaign filled an empty space, signifying by its success the size of the absences in Democratic thinking and activity. Combining Hart's themes with Jackson's means linking a commitment to economic growth with a defense (and reshaping) of social programs as both economically efficient and morally correct. It would mean combining a commitment to expanding political participation and broadening the range of individual choice, with respect for individual loyalties to conventional social institutions. Even more difficult, it would mean combining restraint in the use of American military power with a rejection of naive beliefs about the nature of Soviet foreign and military policy.

The Problem of Growth

These syntheses are hard to achieve, for they involve issues over which there are deep divisions. Yet there may be more of a chance to create new perspectives than recent history suggests. One crucial example concerns the problem of growth, an area where Reagan enjoyed a virtual monopoly in 1984. For Democrats, and those to their left, one obvious difficulty in dealing with this area is that conflicts between environmentalists and trade unionists have often been severe, while both groups make strong claims to shape the direction of the Democratic coalition. The unions are for economic growth, while many environmentalists still cringe at its very mention. Beyond the unions, growth remains politically popular for most of the population — which, on the whole, prefers growth to protectionist policies that could retard economic prosperity in the name of limiting some of its negative effects.

A democratic political effort now has to define a rational and politically viable growth model. Opposing a Reaganite growth model, which relies on the market with minimal intervention to protect the environment and thereby promises destructive results, is insufficient. Nor was the Mondale growth strategy significantly more appealing. Mondale initially gave strong support to environmentalists' demands, but these themes later dropped out of his campaign. In part this was because he was allied with forces in the Midwest and East — not only labor — for whom environmental issues are not a priority. Mondale's growth model was protectionist with regard to existing industrial constituencies. From an environmental perspective, it had the serious problem of tending to favor some of the industrial activities hardest on the environment. And from a broader perspective, it had the problem of seeming unlikely to produce growth at all, but would, instead preserve positions for supportive constituencies. The protectionist edge of Mondale's campaign — duplicated in many more radical programmatic proposals floating around the left of the Democratic Party — was so politically unpopular that many viewed the Reaganite course as a better alternative.

In order for a left politics to have any prospect of winning majority support in the contemporary U.S., it has to combine a serious commitment to equity with a persuasive argument about growth. Without an economic and social growth model, the left in all its variants will be at the mercy of forces which claim to have workable strategies. There is now a basis for a growth strategy which could overcome some of the divisions that have plagued the Democratic Party. This strategy would develop Hart's emphasis on high-tech change, but broaden it beyond claims about the employment possibilities in high-tech industries per se. In direct terms, the latter will be more modest than their advocates sometimes claim. What is important is the restructuring and expansion of existing industrial and service activities, using not only the technical advances made available by the high-tech industries but the expanded organizational capacities for flexibility, communication, and development which can accompany those advances.

Hitherto, much of the left has mainly offered a critique of

high-tech growth, trying to dismantle simplistic claims about a bright new future. The critique of high-tech boosterism has effectively raised questions, but has not ever shown convincingly that the new forms of emerging stratification are dramatically worse than those of industrial capitalism. Thus the left has tended to become identified as a protection agency for the mass production industries and some of their unionized workers. This stance suffers all the liabilities of the Mondale campaign, and also appears passive, never posing the problem of how to influence as much as possible the course of post-industrial (capitalist) growth. The similarities between Mondale and Jackson on this point stand out in Jackson's explicit statements about jobs:

> There is nothing more basic to the dignity of an adult than having a job. Military spending creates fewer jobs than any other kind of spending. A cut in the defense budget will allow us to put people to work. The Democratic Party must have a plan to rebuild America. We must put people to work rebuilding our nation's infrastructure —our roads, our bridges, our cities. We need 250,000 bridges rebuilt. That's how you put steelworkers back to work. They don't need training; they need contracts. (Jesse Jackson, speech delivered before the 13th Annual Convention of Operation Push, Inc., 7 June 1984, quoted from *Black Scholar* [September/October 1984], p. 5).

Such statements discredit what remains of the Democratic commitment to reducing unemployment in their naivete about social and industrial change.

To return to the environmental example, intensive post-industrial growth contains serious environmental risks (as in toxic waste disposal), but it is not necessarily environmentally destructive (certainly not on the scale of the traditional industries which are being restructured or have gone permanently into decline). Active government policies very different from those of the Reagan administration are required to contain the dangers which will arise. And in many cases, the main environmental dangers stem from human error and technical failures; these problems can only be reduced by a broadly expansive strategy of upgrading labor skills and capacities. Those problems of Three Mile Island or Union Carbide which are in principle soluble — and some aren't — cannot be handled by traditional industrial deskilling and rationalization.

Hart's presentation of a postindustrial growth strategy was

framed in a way which offered much less than it could have to the labor movement and to some of the constituencies represented in the Jackson campaign. Hart may simply have intended to be provocative for purposes of short term electoral gain but future Democratic politics cannot afford the luxury of fragmenting its elements. An effective postindustrial strategy requires, for example, an expanding public provision for education and social services to cope with growing needs for training and retraining. The human capital side of such a strategy can offer genuine opportunities to those threatened with increasing marginalization by a Reaganite growth strategy, especially parts of the inner city minority populations. Such opportunities are more promising than those offered by the Reaganite strategy, with its reduction of social services and labor rights, or the Mondale strategy aimed at expanding traditional industries. What a post-industrial growth strategy cannot offer is guaranteed protection for narrow sections of the population; efforts to do so are perceived as a virtual anti-growth strategy aimed at preserving 'privileges.'

After Sharing the Blame . . .

Unions, along with other forces who opposed Reagan, were badly defeated in 1984. The Black political leadership also suffered a severe defeat, when an extraordinarily unified Black vote went to a candidate who suffered one of the worst losses in modern history. Both groups want to defend their basic positions, against Reaganite efforts to attack their legitimacy, and against intra-Democratic efforts to blame them for the outcome. Defensive impulses are understandable for the union leadership, Black political leaders, feminists, and others. If unchecked, they may exact a high cost: every group denies responsibility for the outcome, defending the legitimacy of their perspective, and blaming others. Political discussion disappears, and those who unsuccessfully opposed Reagan continue to do what they were doing for lack of any alternative.

Developing a new Democratic course requires a political climate within which reflective, self-critical discussion can occur. This has not yet emerged. The labor movement, for example, has issued an interesting document proposing reforms aimed at improving its ability to recruit new members. At the political level, however, the unions have claimed that they were successful because union members were significantly more likely than nonmembers to vote for Mondale. This defense is at most half true. Union efforts did help persuade union members to vote Democratic, though the figures are less impressive when one subtracts Black union members who would have voted against Reagan in any case. Yet the labor vote is in serious decline, not only in terms of the relative weight of union members, but in terms of large sections of the working and middle classes who once made their political decisions partly under the influence of the labor movement. In 1984, this positive effect had all but disappeared; in many cases, it was even reversed when people voted against Mondale partly because of his labor ties.

The point is not to berate the unions, who made a massive effort to defeat a president whose policies have hurt them and their memberships badly. Yet the defensiveness born of defeat can only lead to further defeats. Precisely because almost everyone's reason for Reagan's victory contains a kernel of truth, there is plenty enough blame to go around. Without a real shift in the political mood among Democratic groups, the angry exchanges of the first months after the election could be a sad preview of further decline.

Stopping the onset of a durable Republican regime remains central; to prevent this outcome, environmentalists, feminists, antiwar activists, and others will have to make many compromises. Compromises are difficult, and often distasteful for representatives of social movements whose experience have led them to view political compromises as abandoning their movements' basic goals. In this context, one possibility which may tempt sections of the Democratic Party's left is to focus on consolidating its mainly secondary positions of power within and around the party. In pushing hard for its programs, and in the process entering into sharp conflicts with the center and right of the party, the Democratic left could probably make organizational gains, especially given the weakness of the formal Democratic organization in most parts of the country.

There are serious dangers that lie along this course. It risks confusing organizational advances with the much broader processes of political change necessary to rebuild a popular Democratic — and democratic — majority. Given the character of the Democratic left, such a course would be apt to maintain the form of interest-group conflict which now dominates the party. Placing the main emphasis on building a (Democratic) left force would probably mean, in a world where it is hard to do everything at the same time, downplaying efforts to force a broad alternative to Reaganism. If this happened, and a durable Reaganite realignment occurred partly as a result, the Democratic left would in the short run enjoy at least modest growth. It might become a political force with considerable power inside and around the Democratic Party, and electoral strength equal to perhaps 10-15% of the general vote.

Yet this growth would be small consolation for the marginality which the left in all its forms would face during a Republican regime that could last into the first decades of the next century. The fluidity of the political moment, when an old order has been finally destroyed, but not replaced, combined with the scope of ongoing socioeconomic changes, offers a more attractive option. There exists a serious chance of fusing democratic, egalitarian, and modernizing themes in a political project aimed at shaping the forms and direction of postindustrial growth; this project could unify large sections of existing Democratic constituencies, and provide a framework for creating new ones. This is not a project for a postindustrial utopia, but for selecting one of the more decent of postindustrial alternatives now available, and for creating a dynamic in which more ambitious goals can become politically realistic.

5.   No Alternative

Reagan's Reelection and the Democratic Party

Stephanie Coontz

With 52.9% of adult Americans voting, Ronald Reagan handily defeated Walter Mondale in the 1984 election, garnering 59% of the vote to Mondale's 41%. How should we interpret this seeming mandate for a man who has gutted social welfare and environmental programs, surrounded himself with individuals facing charges of corruption, presided over gigantic give-away programs to the rich, worked so little that he has been called the most ill-informed president in American history, and left the public believing, by a margin of 2 to 1, that 'the risk of war remains as great as ever as a result of Reagan's policies' (*Business Week*, [6 August 1984])?

Before trumpeting the dangers of a new mass-based right wing, we should recognize the limits of Reagan's victory. Only 30 percent of the adult population voted for Reagan. Since the 47 percent not voting is predominantly working class or poor, there is good reason to suppose that a majority of Reagan's support came from upper-income Americans. Moreover, even those who voted for Reagan did not necessarily support him on the issues. National polls have consistently shown that a majority of Americans oppose intervention in Central America, oppose school prayer, favor the ERA (though this has been dropping from its high point in the late 1970s), favor at least some access to abortion, support a nuclear freeze, and oppose deep cuts in spending for health and education. In Thurston County, Washington, a referendum against U.S. military involvement in Nicaragua and El Salvador outpolled Mondale by 6,000 votes and came within 150 votes of matching the vote for Reagan, who carried the county. A similar Boston measure received more than 62 percent of the vote. Regional Republicans were not carried along on Reagan's coat-tails. Indeed, Republicans faced a net loss of two Senate seats and failed to offset their House losses from 1982. In the first months after his inauguration, Reagan's attempt to paint the Nicaraguan government as an evil band of terrorists left 70 percent of the American people opposed to attempts to topple the Sandinista regime (*The Olympian* [3 March 1985]). It is difficult, then, to see Reagan's election as any decisive mandate for the right.

Neverthless, the win was impressive. Approximately 67 percent of whites who voted cast their ballots for Reagan, and that included significant numbers from the working class. Despite the impressive formal support of organized labor, NOW, environmental groups, and the freeze network, Mondale lost in every area except the District of Columbia. The 90 percent support he received from blacks who went to the polls could hardly compensate for his total failure to mobilize the rest of the population.

But it is the Democrats' failure, not Reagan's success, that really stands out in any examination of the election. Reagan won the 1980 election with the support of only 50.7 percent of those voting — i.e., 25% of the adult population — and he won it against a thoroughly discredited president whose austerity measures and failure to cut unemployment had antagonized many who had voted Democratic in the last election. Yet within two months of his inauguration the Democrats had pronounced his programs unbeatable, and the media had followed their lead in completely ignoring the vulnerable areas of his administration, from the tax giveaways to the rich to the proliferation of malnutrition among the poor, from the lies about Soviet arms build-ups to the corruption surrounding his closest confidantes and appointees. By 1984 they had helped create a president whom people overwhelmingly perceived as 'above it all,' while the Democratic nominee refused to take up any of the issues on which Reagan lacked support. It was the Democrats, gratefully followed by a press eager to get back to convivial relations with the Washington power structure, that made Reagan 'above it all.'

Those who argued that the primary task in 1984 was to 'dump Reagan' or to build an alternative within the Democratic party ignored the dialectic that gave rise to the Reagan victory. Two factors are at work here. The first is the number of people who are alienated from the electoral process. Almost half the adult population doesn't vote. These are people whom some liberals and leftists hoped could be mobilized to revitalize New Deal issues and dump Reagan. But this ignores the second factor: the extent to which the electoral system in general, and the Democratic party in particular, cannot raise the kind of issues that could cut across this alienation or address the similar feelings that have led those who *do* vote increasingly to vote on image rather than issues (*Discover*, November 1984). What has clearly emerged, and what an orientation toward the Democratic Party does not grapple with, is that electoral victories cannot be explained by the idea that a well-organized and self-conscious section votes its interests while a disorganized and apathetic section sits on its hands. Nonvoters show the same interest in the news as do voters, while voters often report that they vote out of a sense of civic duty rather than any concern for the substantive issues (see Angus Campbell et al., *The American Voters* [New York, 1960], pp. 103-106; and *New York Times* [5 September 1976; 31 August 1984]). Both nonvoters and the majority of voters who vote for a presidential candidate's perceived personality rather than his program are reflecting their appreciation that 'candidates say one thing and do another' or that 'it doesn't make any difference who is elected because things never seem to work right,' a view expressed by two-thirds of the voters interviewed in a detailed 1976 study (*New York Times*, [5 September 1976]).

Americans have good reason to hold these views. Time and time again they have seen politicians reverse their platforms. It was Johnson the peace candidate who escalated the war in Vietnam, just as it was Nixon and Reagan the fiscal conservatives who upped the federal deficit to unprecedented levels. Americans also have some reason to believe that 'things never seem to work right.' Pollution measures are often paid for by the loss of workers' jobs, while efforts to conserve energy in the 1970s 'energy crisis' led to skyrocketing ultility rates. Consider briefly the history of some favorite liberal programs.

The income tax, of course, was a great liberal triumph. But its history has been one in which, through both Democratic and Republican administrations of the last thirty years, the corporations and the rich have shifted a larger and larger share to working, middle-income Americans. By 1983, corporate income taxes produced just 6.2% of federal government revenues, compared with 32.1% in 1952 (*The Olympian*, [1 December 1984]). Corporate tax preferences and write-offs divert from $77 to $91 billion a year from the budget, and Michael Parenti claims that 'if the top one hundred corporations were taxed at the same rate as the average middle-income family there would be enough revenue for all federal expenditures on behalf of the poor, education, housing, environmental protection, medical care and much more' (*Democracy for the Few* [New York, 1980], p. 96). Families making more than $100,000 per year receive tax breaks of more than $11 billion annually, and it was liberal President Carter whose 1978 tax plan broadened the capital gains loophole. A 1980 treasury study found that more than two-thirds of all capital income is exempt from individual income tax, despite the nominally high tax brackets of the people who receive this income (*Dollars and Sense* 68 [1981], p. 9). In 1982, the latest year for which figures are available, 299 couples and individuals with incomes of more than $200,000 per year used deductions and tax credits to avoid paying a single penny of federal income tax (AP wire service report [9 January 1985]). The biggest single tax paid by working people is social security, which is quite openly regressive. There is a single tax rate up to the ceiling of $29,700, and no tax on anything above the ceiling.

No Democratic president or Congress has made any serious effort to correct this inequity. At the same time, much publicity is given to the nominally high rates, up to 77%, for example, on estates in excess of $10 million, while there seems to be a conspiracy of silence on the actual inheritance tax collections amount — only 0.2% of net wealth (Lester Thurow, 'Tax Wealth, not Income,' *New York Times Magazine* [11 April 1976]). Add to this the fact that most families are house-poor, and one recognizes the reasons for the general refusal to support Mondale's tax proposals and the hope that Reagan's jiggery-pokery can really freeze taxes. The typical American family saw its paper wealth increase by more than one-third between 1970 and 1983: the catch is that 63% of such a family's net worth came from equity in the family home, hardly a liquid asset but instead a tax burden. (Federal Reserve Board study, reported in *The Olympian* [4 December 1984]). Small wonder that taxpayers are willing to give the rich sizeable tax breaks if they can, in turn, be given a measure of relief themselves.

What, after all, have high taxes actually achieved in terms of social equality? The wealthiest 10% of families in 1983 controlled almost 60% of net worth, while the poorest 20% had a zero or negative net worth (*The Olympian* [4 December 1984]). Welfare, meanwhile, has been more of a bonanza for the rich than the poor. The richest fifth of the population receives more than twice as much in housing subsidies as the poorest fifth. A careful study of the welfare system in Oakland, California, revealed that 'the public policy process generally has tended to *increase* the incomes of the rich and the nonincomes of the poor . . . In urban renewal, a $2 million subsidy was deliberately given to local business, while the poor were driven out of the demolition area . . . Federal job programs . . . resulted in guaranteed profits to corporate employers who took trainees, but have not increased job supply' (Edward Hayes, *Power Structure and Urban Policy: Who Rules in Oakland?* [New York, 1972,]p. 198).

Arguments over school lunch programs fade beside the $25 billion per year that the U.S. Treasury distributes to business in direct and benefit-in-kind subsidies, or the $26 billion in research and development grants to big corporations, which then keep the patents that were developed at taxpayer expense (Parenti, pp. 76, 79). It was the liberal President Kennedy who turned over the satellite communications system to AT&T even though the taxpayers had funded the initial $20 billion, and even though AT&T decided not to use the sytem to cheapen U.S. long distance calls. And it was liberals, too, who first rolled up the deficits whose interest payments absorb more than twice the amount of federal money than is earmarked for the poor. Just as it was liberals who, under the guise of foreign welfare, channeled tax monies into aid programs that subsidized American companies while improving the delivery of food to the international poor not a whit (see, for example, Francis Moore Lappe and Joseph Collins, *Food First: Beyond the Myth of Scarcity* [New York, 1977], and Harry Magdoff, *The Age of Imperialism* [New York, 1969]). How many liberals are willing to admit that the riots and revolutions in underveloped countries receiving foreign 'aid' are in part caused by structural flaws in the 'aid' system? And in the absence of such an admission, is it pure selfishness for people to conclude that 'we might as well save our money'?

I am not suggesting that the people who refuse to vote, or the ones who vote against traditional Democratic Party candidates, command all this data. They have, however, noticed what liberals and leftists calling for a return to New Deal policies have simply refused to face: big spending programs have accomplished little in relation to the higher interest rates, higher taxes, and tremendous corruption they have spawned. On their own, or with the help of right-wingers, people can draw some wrong conclusions about this — that the problem lies with the welfare chiselers, or subversives, or affirmative action programs. But how can they not draw such conclusions as long as the Democrats keep defending the programs that have had such consequences? Only a radical critique of the welfare state can provide a convincing alternative to the right wing account.

Such a radical critique would have to start by pointing to the structural constraints of the American economic system on electoral reform. The entire process is set up to effect the merger of political and economic power, and this merger takes place, for the most part, outside the framework of the electoral process altogether. G.William Domhoff has shown how the general issues of American foreign and domestic policy are resolved through a seldom-studied sequence which begins in corporate board rooms and exclusive private clubs (where 'issues' are identified as 'problems' to be solved), moves to charitable foundations and special corporate discussion groups (where solutions to the problems are discussed), and winds up in the government (where the corporate solutions are adopted by executive order or congressional legislation). (Domhoff, *Fat Cats and Democrats* [Englewood Cliffs, 1972], p. 146). The Trilateral Commission and the Council on Foreign Relations are nonelected assemblies that play a crucial role in formulating and coordinating U.S. international policies. Their composition and influence have remained unchanged through successive Democratic and Republican administrations. Individuals such as James Schlesinger are equally at home advising Nixon, Reagan, Carter, and Mondale, while at least one Secretary of State under every President since Truman has been associated with the Rockefeller Foundation or the law firms of Rockefeller oil companies.

The Pentagon Papers reveal that not a single person involved in the discussions about escalating the war in Vietnam was an elected official. The Federal Reserve Board, which determines the interest rate and the money supply, is composed primarily of bankers whose records and books are off limits to Congressional committees or the White House. Just as a fail-safe device, in the unlikely event of the election of a populist, the Federal Reserve Board members are appointed to staggered fourteen year terms, and a president may make only two appointments during a four year term of office.

Business control over the social interest begins with the first drafting of legislation. Consider, for example, the role of the

American Bar Association. The ABA writes public laws and provides much of the personnel for their administration. Most people regard it as reasonable that laws should be drafted by the 'experts.' But it's instructive to make a list of recent chairmen of the law-drafting committees of the ABA and the clients whom they have represented: the chairman of the Committee on Environmental Controls was a lawyer for Humble Oil and General Motors; the Drug Law Committee was headed by an employee of the Pharmaceutical Manufacturers' Association; the Aviation Law Committee by an Eastern Airlines executive; the Committee on Railroads by the vice-president and general counsel of Gulf Mobile and Ohio Railroad Company; the Section on Anti-Trust Laws by an IBM and Shell Oil executive; the Section on Public Utility Law by an AT&T employee; the beverage law committee by a lawyer for Coca-Cola. As for the ABA's committee on banking law, its newsletter has been written by registered lobbyists for the banking industry since 1959! (*Washington Monthly* [Summer 1974]; Joseph Goulden, *The Superlawyers* [New York, 1971], pp. 383-84).

Another example of business control over public policy is found in the activities of the regulatory commissions that are supposed to regulate various industries in both their own interests and those of the consumer. In a system of production for private profit, these are hardly compatible mandates. Consumers are unorganized and unable to concentrate their energies on any particular industry. The industry involved has more time, money, and expertise to present its side of the case to the commission's members. These are all the more likely to identify with industry's point of view since almost half the members of such regulatory commissions have previously held, or can be expected to move on to, high level jobs in the industry they are supposed to be supervising.

Under these circumstances, and considering the role of business in underwriting party conventions, campaigns, and campaign debts (see Domhoff, *Fat Cats and Democrats*, pp. 28-29), it is difficult to see how the capitalists and their allies in the party machine could lose control over the election process. It may be true that the nomination of George McGovern in 1972 represented something of a breakdown in machine politics, though it is more likely that, as Walter Karp claims, McGovern's nomination was meant to keep party dissidents in line, after the earlier challenge to machine control mounted by the McCarthy candidacy. Either way, the machine demonstrated its ultimate control by openly conniving at McGovern's defeat, despite his abject attempts to prove that he would be a good organization man (*Indispensable Enemies: The Politics of Misrule in America* [New York, 1974], pp. 67-73). Even if a candidate did get past the party machines and the capitalists, his or her lack of an independent base would simply allow them to reassert control through the decision-making process described above.

Most leftists, of course, recognize these aspects of capitalist rule, but some argue that working within the Democratic Party can expose the facts to others, radicalize them and lead them to challenge capitalist control over the political system. The problem with this analysis is that the majority of Americans *know* that 'special interests' control politics. They lack a systematic analysis of *how* this occurs and a program for changing it. This tends to make them cynical (and therefore complacent) about human 'corruptibility,' as well as vulnerable to right-wing demagoguery about labor unions, who get equated with (and then substituted for) big corporations as the villains of the piece. As someone once remarked, running better individuals for office as a solution to political corruption is rather like trying to stop prostitution by putting virgins into brothels.

The structure of the American two-party system does not even have the merit of allowing individuals who work within it to expose capitalist control of the government or to organize people against that control. First, unlike a labor party, the Democratic party is not based on any organizations with the potential to bring workers together to elect delegates or call representatives to account. This makes it possible to obscure the capitalist decision-making process and blame its results on bureaucracy or big government. Parenti gives a telling description of how the system works in the absence of accountability to constituencies, using as an example the way that the committee system has been replaced by the subcommittee system:

> The fragmentation of power within the subcommittees simplifies the lobbyist's task of controlling legislation. *It offers the special-interest group its own special-interest subcommittee.* To atomize power in this way is *not* to democratize it. The separate structures of power tend to monopolize decisions in specific areas for the benefit of specific groups. Into the interstices of these substructures fall the interests of large segments of the unorganized public.
> With its fragmented pockets of special power . . . congressional

factions achieve working majorities through various trade-offs and mutual accommodations, a 'logrolling' process that is not the same as compromise . . . The net effect is not a *check* on competing claims but a *compounding* of claims against the interests of an unorganized public.
(*Democracy for the Few*, pp. 225 and 236; emphasis in original)

A peculiar accompaniment to this phenomenon is that the leadership of the parties may decide that winning an election in any particular area or year is less important than maintaining their control over the 'old boy' network this pork-barrelling entails. Candidates considered untrustworthy or threatening to an established bipartisan back-scratching operation may be sabotaged by the party leadership. Leaders are also free to maneuver with their so-called political opponents in elaborate charades where each can blame the other for blocking the program he would have otherwise carried out. John Kennedy was notorious for this kind of spectacle, for example, in his all but open support of Republican conservative Everett Dirksen, whom he then used as an excuse to water down social programs and build up missiles (see Karp, pp. 104-07).

A second characteristic of the American two-party system that militates against its effective use of radicals is the absence of proportional representation. A party that garners 49% of the vote is left with nothing. This raises a different pressure among the ranks, inimical to radical organizing: since a loss leaves neither an organizational structure nor any kind of political foothold for future organizing, the rank and file themselves, no matter how sympathetic they are to radical issues, will engage in censorship of ideas that might threaten electoral victory. The reason they are in the Democratic party at all is to be 'practical'; they are unlikely to accept any proposal to take risks, and may indeed be more hostile to radical ideas raised inside their ranks than to ideas raised from the outside. Democratic party activists during the Vietnam war gave a more receptive hearing to outsiders who asked them to participate in the antiwar movement than to insiders who asked them to run on an antiwar platform and thus jeopardize their support in pro-war sectors. As a local activist and socialist in Thurston County, I find myself being asked more often to present my views to Democratic party luncheons and gatherings than do the socialists within their ranks, who are hurriedly shushed for fear they will taint the whole organization.

Paradoxically, the Democratic Party leadership's very pre-

cariousness as an independent power bloc makes it less susceptible to reform from below. The place of Democratic party bosses
in the power structure is only occasionally assured by their
independent ownership of resources. More often, it comes from
making themselves indispensable in the political and economic
maneuvering that inevitably accompanies an unplanned
economy. The Democratic bosses must constantly juggle special
interests and renew their usefulness to the capitalists. To do this,
they often *initiate* the corrupt interactions and special favors that
are sometimes thought to be simply imposed upon them. If the
parties were simply hostages to big business, the left might
make some gains by entering them to show well-intentioned
leaders how they are manipulated by the capitalists. But the
leaders often maintain their positions of power by actively
seeking ways to put capitalists in their debt. They must create
corruption where it doesn't already exist, in order to maintain
and reconfirm their usefulness to the various corporations on
whom they depend.

The go-betweens in this process are the lawyer-lobbyists who
make up what David Osborne calls 'the Permanent Party,'
arranging matches between firms looking for special privileges
and politicans looking for special financing (*Mother Jones*
[August-September 1984]). The fact that some marriages fall
through, or that there are on-going tensions between the
partners, in no way challenges the system.

The next issue raised by those who advocate working within
the Democratic Party, of course, is whether there is a split in the
ruling class that reflects itself, at least periodically, in the two-
party system. If so, there should be some way for us to take
advantage of this split. The historical record, however, does not
suggest that the Democratic Party represents a strategically
distinct wing of the ruling class. Franklin Delano Roosevelt, of
course, is always held up to illustrate the progressive possibilities of the Democratic party, but a closer look at his achievements calls this into question. Roosevelt was swept into office in
a period when radical solutions seemed the only salvation to
millions of Americans, including business leaders. He moved
very cautiously at first, and it was the Republicans who first
attacked him for not instituting social security. One historian of
the period concludes that Roosevelt did the absolute minimum
necessary to preserve the system, fighting against more radical
proposals that had strong popular back (Barton Bernstein, 'The

New Deal: The Conservative Achievements of Liberal Reform,' in Bernstein, ed., *Towards a New Past: Dissenting Essays in American History* [New York, 1969]). It is also worth remembering that the greatly exaggerated conflict between FDR and business primarily involved *small-town,* not national, businesses who were squeezed by 'reforms' that traded moderate unionization for protection of corporate profit rates.

Roosevelt, of course, also led America into war, as did the Democrats Truman, Kennedy, and Johnson. There has been no difference in the number or importance of anti-trust cases filed by Democratic and Republican administrations, and the trend toward concentration has proceeded without setback, so that today the top 200 corporations own more than two-thirds of all corporate assets, a share equal to that controlled by the top 1,000 corporations in 1948.

Most important, the two parties are far too respectful of each other's needs to give much credence to the idea that they represent warring or even separate wings of the capitalist class. The Democrats have consciously maintained their Dixiecrat wing as a hedge against having to present a full program of social reform, while the Republicans have never tried to drive out their moderate wing: 'The Southerners have to stay Democratic so that politics don't polarize around issues,' a Republican political scientist explained to Domhoff (*Fat Cats and Democrats*, p. 96). Liberal Democrats agree. They routinely give Southern Democrats key committee chairmanships, even though the Democratic leadership is under no obligation to do so. Meanwhile, both parties have always united to defeat any third party upsurge, something neither would do if it seriously wanted to weaken the other.

While it is certainly true that Reagan has presided over a more ruthless dismantling of social service programs than any previous president, this should be related to changes in the world position of capitalism, rather than to changes in the power relations within the capitalist class. 'The American Century' heralded by Luce in 1941 is definitely over. After postponing overproduction problems, such as those that triggered the Great Depression, by a combination of international expansion and heavy investment in non-consumer items, the U.S. economy faces the collapse of the international economy and a profit squeeze at home. The U.S. trade deficit has ballooned from $36.5 billion in 1982 to $125 billion in 1984, while the 'compensating' influx of foreign investment in government securities has led to a distortion of economic development, making fights over acquisitions of more interest to many firms than creation of new productive capacity. The debt crisis has created a highly explosive political and economic situation. All these things add up to a need for retrenchment at home and increased intervention abroad, despite the continuation of the 'Vietnam syndrome' that is the legacy of the antiwar movement of the 1960s and early '70s.

Reagan did not begin the retrenchment policy. It was started by the corporations in their union negotiations, acquiesced to by the trade union leaderships who proved themselves wholly incapable of dealing with the breakdown of labor-management harmony, and politically spearheaded by the Carter administration. It was Carter's 'human rights' administration that backed the butcher of Iran to the point of provoking the embassy takeover and then helped to orchestrate hysteria about 'America held hostage.' The Carter administration initiated a government offensive against social services, proposing cutbacks in public service jobs, subsidized housing, lunch programs, and disability benefits. Carter raised the military budget by $10 billion and signed Presidential Directive 59, which authorized the formulation of a first-strike policy with nuclear weapons.

When Reagan was elected by a narrow margin in 1980, the Democratic party fell all over itself helping him get through his escalation of this austerity program, appointing Democratic supporters of the same policies to important committees and sending the leaders responsible for mobilizing opposition to his program on tour to Australia and New Zealand. The Democrats also promoted a plan known as 'budget reconciliation,' which allowed the budget cuts to be lumped together in omnibus legislation and then cut into separate portions (containing a little bit of each issue) to be discussed by each committee (*Harper's* [July 1984], pp. 53-4). The effect was to make it almost impossible to highlight the effects of any particular cut, as well as to create an impression of inevitability about the whole process, an impression aided by Democratic pronoucements about Reagan's invincibility. The Democrats then proceeded to sit on their hands instead of offering any alternative to Reagan's grossly unfair tax proposal, while they shielded him from the impact of his initially unpopular MX proposals by letting the final decision come as a recommendation from a bipartisan committee of 'defense experts.'

Writing in *The Nation* (6 October 1984), Thomas Ferguson and Joel Rogers suggest that there was indeed a tactical difference among businessmen that expressed itself in the 1980s. While there was strong bipartisan support for domestic cutbacks and increased military spending, some businessmen were concerned about the amount of increase in the military spending, the problem of interest rates, and the need to conciliate labor. Within a short time, however, the failure of labor to mobilize any significant opposition to the take-back movement convinced business that they didn't need to deal with labor, while the differences over the deficit and over protectionism tended to recede as the recovery spread and it appeared there was not a serious threat from the peace movement. The consequence was a Democratic campaign that was a lack-lustre imitation of Reagan's, offering just enough concessions to the trade union leadership to anger non-unionists and too few to mobilize the union ranks.

As this example shows, the relations among Democrats, Republicans, and social movements are often misinterpreted by those who claim that the Democratic party represents an alternative to the Republican. The gains that Democratic administrations have granted generally came only after mass pressure from outside that party. In the absence of such mass pressure, the Democrats have never taken the lead in pushing for reform. They have not attempted to mobilize mass support for reforms and in fact they have consciously attempted to substitute themselves for the mass movement. As McGovern's campaign manager put it in 1972, 'Our strategy all along was to coopt the left.' Conversely, Republicans have not initiated moves toward conservatism so much as they have reaped the advantage of the Democrats' failure to combat offensives by the bourgeoisie.

Instead of proposing major reforms or mobilizing a mass movement of its supposed constituencies, the Democratic party has relied on discrete concessions to distinct groups, avoiding conflict with capitalists by financing these through taxes or deficit spending. Once real wages began to decline, however, as they did through the 1970s, and workers came to see taxes as the one part of their paycheck that might be susceptible of control, state spending could now be seen as taking from one group to pay another — which, of course, it is. Since the Democrats have been no more willing than the Republicans to finance their spending by taxing the rich, they have been unable to counter the growing reluctance of all working Americans to pay taxes and high interest rates in order to finance social services. While organized labor, as long as its power position was protected, continued to support such programs, other sectors of the working class, unprotected and not unionized, grew to resent these policies. In this sense even Jesse Jackson's eloquent pleas for 'the rejected' failed to make a decisive impact. In the absence of a movement that could provide a coherent analysis of the economic system, in the context of a party whose ability to hobble any independent action has been amply demonstrated, Jackson's proposals often sounded like pleas for charity rather than appeals to the collective interests and self-organization of the entire working class. It remains to be seen if the Rainbow Coalition can break with these limits and stimulate any independent organizational and political alliances.

Meanwhile, the narrow attitude of the trade union leadership has only exacerbated the growing fragmentation within the former allies of the Democratic party. Reports of labor's demise are greatly exaggerated, but it remains true that only 20% of the work force is organized, while take-back campaigns and two-tiered wage contracts have greatly weakened labor's support among working youth. While the *social* weight of the organized labor movement would still be decisive in open struggle, its *political* weight within the electoral process is dropping. Yet the AFL-CIO leadership has abstained from serious organizing efforts, continued to support the Cold War, supported trade protectionism and subsidies to benefit the few against the interests of other consumer-workers, and lent its support to short-sighted exclusionary measures designed to protect craft jobs. No wonder the growing number of minority and female workers, especially those in the ill-paid and nonunionized service fields, feel little inclination to fall in behind the labor bosses' political initiatives. The creation of a new electorate out of the current nonvoters will not be achieved by traditional Democratic interest group politics. The trait non-voters share is their lack of affiliation with any organized group — be it union, church, social club or fraternal organization (*New York Times* [5 September 1976]). The Democratic party offers no political platform, social vision, or organizational vehicle to lift these people out of their powerlessness.

The candidacy of Geraldine Ferraro was a last-ditch effort to mobilize the female constituency, but it also failed. Certainly there is a gender gap in American politics. The Democratic-oriented feminists, however, have little hope of touching it. The fastest growing poverty group in America today is women with children. One in five children (and one in two black children) now live in poverty-stricken families. The single mothers who comprise a large proportion of this group had little to relate to in the candidacy of Ferraro, with her wealthy, high-rolling husband and her right-wing opposition to busing. Women who work because their husbands' wages no longer suffice are not to be won over by liberal promises of equal access to male jobs. These women are not joining men in traditional work, but are being drawn into new areas of work characterized by low pay and underemployment for all who work there. Only a fundamental challenge to the dual labor market, with concrete actions on its behalf, could have won these women and their husbands over, and the Democratic party did not organize such action.

In my opinion, many of the people who voted for Reagan did so for one of two reasons. Some have correctly concluded that issues are not being discussed in campaigns any more, and that even if they were, our voting system provides no way of calling to account those politicians who break their campaign promises. We live in a world that seems to many ordinary citizens out of control, where actions often have the opposite effect from that intended, and where political platforms are discarded the day after the elections. It is not entirely irrational to search for a candidate who projects a moral quality. Carter's religion and Reagan's projected sincerity were important factors in their election. As one man told me when I was canvassing for an anti-war referendum: 'I don't agree with everything Reagan's done, but I think he believes what he says. He's not just a mouthpiece for someone else.' The Democrats must accept considerable responsibility for allowing Reagan to appear this way.

Others have taken the Democrats at their word and found them inconsistent in carrying it out. If the American system of private enterprise is superior, if profits are the key to progress, if our world standing is important, then we don't need to pussy-foot around about it. Capitalism needs some harsh measures to survive, though they be unpalatable. Trade union officials who ask workers to take wage cuts to keep 'their' companies 'competitive' shouldn't be shocked when Republicans cash in on their promise to keep *America* competitive in the world. Another memorable quotation from my canvassing, this time from an unemployed housewife: 'Well, Reagan's policies will hurt me a little, and I really feel sorry for people who don't have anything at all to fall back on, but he's going to get the economy back on track, and that's better for everyone in the long run. Just like Roosevelt did.'

The Democrats, even their most liberal wing, have come up with no alternative to these ideas. Mondale couldn't let go fast enough of the issues he had support on, issuing instead empty calls for a return to liberal programs he admitted would require a tax increase. The Democrats have yet to propose a program for making the rich pay for their proposed projects, and Mondale retreated from even the most shallow suggestions for guaranteeing full employment. At the same time, while occasionally muttering about Reagan's bellicosity, Mondale and Ferraro were at least as fervent as Reagan in asserting America's need for a strong military and a forceful presence in defense of 'our' interests abroad.

It is as if a fierce battle were going on and the foot soldiers are asked to choose between two generals. One of them declares: 'Look, we have to win this war, but I want you to pick up the packs of your fallen comrades and share your rations with them.' The other replies: 'That's false sentimentality that will harm more people than it helps. If we really want to win the war, we have to push through to higher ground, regroup, drive back the enemy forces, and then go get our wounded.' So long as the need for the war is taken for granted, it is not unreasonable for those of the unwounded who have the energy to vote to choose the second position. The first ceases to be ineffective sentimentality only if you couple it with an immediate call for a cease-fire. Without the vision of peace, without the vision that there's no need to fight this war, the first general's proposals only strengthen the hands of the second. The battle here, of course, is the battle for corporate profitability, and both Democrats and Republicans accept the need for the war. Even if it's true that the Democrats are more concerned with the wounded than the Republicans, their proposals are shallow and become unworkable any time a setback such as the deterioration of America's international economic position occurs.

But what are our alternatives? A labor party or a mass socialist party is not on the agenda in the near future. Moreover, the left remains remarkably isolated in America. But the pull of the Democratic party on the left is part of the problem, not part of the solution. The marginalization of the American left has been created and sustained by a number of historical and structural features in American society. It will not be ended by attaching ourselves to organizations or movements whose ideological and organizational underpinnings assume the *perpetuation* of that marginalization and require us to cover up our politics. It can only be attacked by seeking arenas in which we can prove the relevance of our politics to everyday struggles. We need to find arenas in which we can show that a left perspective answers questions of concern to the people with whom we work, and that gives them effective strategies and tactics for organizing.

The two-party electoral arena is, right now, the place where the left has the *least* to offer to independent activists. All of our strengths become weaknesses in this arena. Our structural analysis of the American economy sheds little light on the questions facing Democratic Party activists: which lawyer-lobbyists are most likely to set up fund-raising events for the particular candidate? what is the best way to prevent right-wing PACs from flooding an opponent with last-minute contributions and mud-slinging ammunition? Indeed, our structural analysis is an *embarassment* in Democratic party campaigns, as it opens the candidates to attacks from the right. The strategy that flows from our radical analysis also has little to offer. At best, experienced leftists can offer excellent tactical advice about how to win concessions from the party bosses in the early stages of a nomination fight. After that, we either help decide when to stop demanding concessions and start being 'team players', or we offer good but unwelcome advice about how to go down fighting. Either way, our work is explicitly divorced from our long-range goals and strategies. To independents committed to winning an election, our long-run perspective is at best idealistic and unrealistic; at worst, it is seen as divisive and a liability.

We should concentrate our energies in places where our socialist vision and the strategies to enact it can answer the questions of most concern to activists, win some concrete gains, and build people's confidence in their own abilities to make and implement decisions. Right now, these places are in concrete social struggles over particular issues, or sets of issues, from antiwar work — a key priority in this period — to strike and labor solidarity work (internationally as well as nationally), campaigns for the rights of oppressed national minorities, and struggles for child care and abortion. In these struggles, the questions that preoccupy activists are ones that we can answer best: how and why did the U.S. get involved in Central America, and what's at stake there? doesn't labor really need to moderate its demands to ensure continued investment and jobs? why, after all the gains in civil rights legislation, does one in every two black children grow up in poverty, while the unemployment rate for blacks remains at more than twice the level of whites during Democratic and Republican administrations alike? Our answers here are more realistic than those proposed by liberals or the right-wing, and they are also more persuasive to activists, whose experiences confirm our explanations. Our answers also have tactical consequences that work: don't support the elections in El Salvador or get sucked into supporting a 'moderate' such as Duarte; never turn over labor negotiations to supposedly neutral arbitrating bodies; build picket lines, demonstrations, community support organizations for your demands and don't rely on any politician, judge, or statute to defend your rights for you. There is thus no inherent contradiction, as there is in working within the Democratic party, between our interests as socialists and our interests as day-to-day activists, and no reason not to build our own socialist forums, campaigns, and organizations.

In addition to the opportunities offered us right now, issue-oriented struggles allow us to advance our long-range goal of convincing people to begin to exercise power on their own behalf. In all truly revolutionary upsurges, social change has come when people have broken away from the existing institutions that were structured to serve the needs and favor the strengths of the ruling groups, when people have begun to make and implement decisions in their own organizations. From the New Model Army of the English Civil War, which usurped Parliament's old prerogatives of debating war, finances, and national policy, to the Committees of Public Safety and Committees of Correspondence in the French and American revolutions, from the Soviets in revolutionary Russia to the French worker-farmer committees in May 1968, these institutions of 'dual power' have been the route to serious and effective social struggle. There is, of course, nothing on this scale right now, but as Sam Adams once remarked: 'We cannot make events. Our business is wisely to improve them.'

There are plenty of events, modest though they may be, that we can improve with wise intervention. The copper miners of Arizona, on strike since 1 July 1983, against the vicious repression of Phelps-Dodge (aided by a Democratic governor), could use an international solidarity campaign linking their struggle to that of the British miners. Surely we could have some role in driving home the lessons to be learned from the Canadian GM workers, who rejected an offer based on the U.S. auto settlements and who won a better contract than U.S. workers. We could have publicized and aided strikes like that of the 6,000 nurses in Minnesota who walked out last summer because less than 30% were working full-time, and this action could have been coupled with the general question of the dual labor market for women in America. And we might have done a lot more with the Las Vegas food and commercial workers strike last spring, where workers defied court injunctions and used mass pickets to win a partial victory against a two-tiered wage contract.

Consider what might have been done if the energy poured into dumping Reagan had been used to organize more antiwar referenda like those in Boston and Thurston County. For one thing, the antiwar movement would have come out of the elections with concrete gains rather than widespread demoralization. For another, we would have been able to oppose a specific mandate to Reagan's claim that he has the confidence of the American people. For a third, this would have had *more* effect on politicians, both Democratic *and* Republican, in pressuring them to end support for intervention, than a Mondale victory. It is significant that two months after the victory of the anti-intervention measure in Thurston County, Republican Senator Slade Gorton, in 'a surprise change of position,' announced that he would end his support for the Contras in Nicaragua, acknowledging that the referendum 'had some weight' in his decision (*The Olympian* [9 January 1985]).

As this example shows, an argument against work in the Democratic party is not an argument against influencing politicians. The question is how to influence them best: do we agree to play by their rules, so that even an impressive mobilization like the Jackson campaign ends up with no alternative but to support a Mondale campaign that involved the dismissal of every demand on which Jackson had garnered support? or do we build our power base outside their ranks so that, whatever the fate of any particular candidate, we have a viable organization beholden to no one? No revolution in history, nor any major reform, has been won without some kind of split in the ruling class. But those splits have only emerged when movements outside ruling class institutions have become so powerful that the elites begin to divide over how far to modify their institutions or grant concessions. Let us not confuse the tactical differences between the Democratic and Republican parties with a split in the ruling class. Those differences are part of their normal decision-making apparatus, and they aren't going to start splitting over how to relate to us as long as we're directing the bulk of our energies figuring out how to maneuver inside their apparatus.

To those who argue that most people are inside the Democratic party, we should reply in two ways. First, every mass movement starts with just a few who have the courage to break with the routinized institutions to which the majority give lip service. Even when radicals don't win their full program, they do more to win specific reforms than those who are constrained by working within the system. It was the small group of the Congressional Union who revitalized the woman suffrage campaign, and it was the Women's Party, condemned as divisive by the larger NAWSA, whose demonstrations finally embarrassed Wilson into cabling two key senators to let the suffrage bill come out of committee. It was Blacks who refused to cancel the March on Washington during the patriotic fervor of W W II who paved the way for the civil rights movements of the 1950s and '60s. And it was the Immediate Withdrawal wing of the antiwar movement, originally a minority, who galvanized the antiwar movement into a social force that, as the Pentagon Papers reveal, greatly reduced the response options of the U.S. government to the Vietnamese revolution. Negative examples also abound, as in the way that NOW has frittered away the political capital of its majority support for the ERA in backroom deals with politicians who broke their promises again and again. NOW's only major victory in the past years was the extension of the ERA, which was gained by going outside the political process — and promptly wasted in more maneuvering within the Democratic party.

Second, not every place where numbers of individuals come together is a mass movement. Many are simply mass spectacles. The people watching them, paying admission at the door, even voting for them, are not learning anything about self-empowerment. They will relate to us, even if we get on stage, as merely one more piece of entertainment. Our job must be to help people break out of the spectator mentality and teach them to act directly in their own behalf. We should take the small steps that we can make toward that goal in this period and resist the temptation to take big leaps where there is nothing for us to land on. The Democratic party is not the place for the left in the 1980s. If any lesson emerged from Campaign 84, surely it was that.

SECTION TWO

Politics and Culture in Central America

1. Poetry and Revolution in Central America

John Beverley

It might be useful to begin by invoking Fredric Jameson's remark that 'the whole so-called "crisis of Marxism" is not a crisis in Marxian "science" but rather in Marxist "ideology," which has everywhere abandoned any attempt to project politically and socially gripping visions of a radically different future.'[1] 'Everywhere' is too pessimistic. What I want to examine here is the way in which poetry has been a *materially decisive* ideological practice of Central American revolutionary movements. I'm going to consider in particular the cases of Ernesto Cardenal in Nicaragua — Cardenal is the Sandinista Minister of Culture today — and of the late Roque Dalton, a major figure in the development of the revolutionary New Left in El Salvador in the 1960s and 70s. I choose Cardenal and Dalton because they are perhaps the most important Central American revolutionary poets, but with the understanding that this choice involves an important distortion of perspective: the political valence of poetry in Central America is not simply the effect of individual writers like Dalton or Cardenal, however influential they might be; it depends also on the operation of poetry as a generalized discursive-ideological space engaging directly or indirectly very broad sectors of the population, including those elements which constitute, potentially or in fact, the revolutionary vanguard. This is what has made poetry a key sector of struggle in Central America — a situation which must seem at first sight anomalous given the relatively marginal status of poetry in metropolitan imperialist culture.

Aesthetics and Ideological Practice

A few general points about art and ideology and their relation to revolutionary mobilization are in order, with apologies to those for whom some or all of this will be old hat. The first concerns the problematic status of the traditional distinction between aesthetics and ideology. I think it's clear that the major tendencies within Marxist aesthetic theory — at least within 'Western' Marxism (e.g. Marx and Engels themselves, Lukács, Brecht, the Frankfurt School, Della Volpe, Althusser and Macherey in their early work) — whatever their differences on other matters, all maintain some form of this distinction, with a characteristic ethical-epistemological privileging of the aesthetic *over* the ideological. What is involved here, it seems to me, is the survival within Marxism of an idealist *ideology of the aesthetic,* rooted in Kant's distinction between aesthetic and teleological judgment and taking the form in everyday culture of common-sense notions of the 'humanizing' properties of works of art and literature, their 'timelessness,' etc. (as for example, in the Euro-centric, petty bourgeois Hellenism of Marx's remark about the 'eternal charm' of Greek epic poetry). I don't want to question the political usefulness of such a view in certain contexts. Most of you will be aware of Herbert Marcuse's paean to the counter-culture (and of its source in the 19th-century critique of bour-geois philistinism), which was a powerful component of New Left politics in the 60s. But it also may impose limitations on cultural practice: for example, a general contempt for the forms of mass or popular culture as degraded or fetishized; or the sense — Marcuse again — that art can only be a radical negation of the imperialist status quo when it is not being used directly for utilitarian political ends. The problem with poets like Dalton and Cardenal, however, is to understand how they stake the success or failure of their poetry as art on its effectiveness as a means for building and maintaining a revolutionary movement; how, in other words, they produce a kind of 'party literature,' to invoke a much-abused concept of Lenin's (with the qualification that both the 'party' and the 'literature' involved are quite different than those usually associated with Leninism).

The article by Althusser on ideology and 'ideological state apparatuses'[2] allows a different way of conceptualizing the relation between art and ideology. If ideology, in Althusser's central thesis, is what constitutes the subject in relation to the

Real (of, e.g., a particular set of relations of production), then the domain of ideology is not a world-view or set of 'ideas' or 'principles' which has the masses in thrall, but rather the ensemble of social signifying practices: the cultural. If it is true that bourgeois ideology is a kind of 'false consciousness,' in the sense that it 'misrepresents' the location of the subject in society (denying exploitation), socialism is no less an ideology in that it must also construct an 'imaginary' representation of/for the subject (new forms of heroism, sensibility, ethics, new senses of history and destiny, etc.). From the point of view of science (*connaissance*), all ideologies involve a structure of misrecognition (*méconnaissance*) analogous to Lacan's idea of the mirror-stage in the formation of the psyche; on the other hand, collective or individual subjects are conscious of themselves as such (i.e., as 'subjects of history') only through an ongoing process of ideological interpellation. Class struggle takes place not between ideology and science, as if bourgeois ideology were ideology as such — what Althusserians call *Ideology in general* — and the working class its opposite in science, but rather between working class and bourgeois ideologies.[3]

In Althusser's own early essays — 'A Letter on Art to André Daspre,' for example — art was said to occupy an intermediate position between science and ideology, since it involved ideology (as its 'raw material,' so to speak), but in such a way as to provoke an 'interior-distancing' from ideology, somewhat as in Brecht's notion of an 'alienation effect' which obliges the spectator to scrutinize and question the assumptions on which the spectacle is proceeding. In the ideology essay this Modernist concern with estrangement has been displaced by what is in effect a Postmodernist concern with fascination and fixation. The issue is no longer *whether* ideology is happening in the space of the aesthetic, or whether there is a 'good' or 'great' art which transcends ideology (and a 'bad' art which doesn't), but rather *what* or *whose* ideology is happening, because the art work is precisely one of the places *where ideology happens*. The aesthetic effect — what the Russian Formalists called *ostranenie* or the 'deautomization' of perception — is an ideological effect. Even in the constitution of what is and is not 'artistic,' we are never *outside of* ideology, though we may be outside of the dominant ideology.[4]

We can combine this sense of the way art functions *as ideology* with the problem of how revolutionary subjectivity is formed.

We have known, at least since *What Is to Be Done?*, that socialism is not in any ontologically essential way inherent in capitalism (although the notion that socialism is 'inevitable,' that it is a consequence of the very unfolding of capitalism, is an important ideological effect in various forms of Marxist *historicism*). Revolutionary consciousness does not directly emanate from exploitative relations of production. Like bourgeois forms of hegemony, it has to be invented, articulated and disseminated in already existing or new practices and institutions, in the case we have before us, the institution of poetry in countries like Nicaragua and El Salvador.[5] As Lenin suggested, actual socialist revolutions or revolutionary movements in this century, particularly in the Third World, have involved in one way or another the fusion of working class (in the broadest sense) forces with a radicalized intelligentsia, drawn partly from the educated working class, but also from the petty bourgeoisie and *déclassé* upper class elements which have become imbued with socialist theory, culture, organizational ideas, etc. Whatever their originality, the Central American revolutions have been no exception to this rule. But if it is the case that this fusion is somehow decisive in creating revolutionary movements, then the question of what practices produce a radicalized intelligentsia doesn't 'fall from the sky.' Note, however, that this may be a somewhat different issue from what practices produce a revolutionary consciousness in the exploited classes themselves, in part because one of these practices is that of the already constituted radicalized intelligentsia (the ideological practices which produced 'Lenin', for example, are not necessarily the same as those which might make a Petrograd factory worker join the Bolsheviks —but most Marxist discussion of cultural politics proceeds on the assumption that they are or should be the same).

Literature is, at least in the form we confront it, a determinate product of a prior bourgeois ideological class struggle against feudal culture. Its generalization as a cultural form depends on: 1) its ideological utility as a surrogate for religion and oral poetry; 2) print technology and the emergence of the book as a commodity with the requisite networks of production and distribution; 3) new forms of mass democracy and education. All of these can be unevenly developed between one nation-state and another, between regions of the same state, between classes, etc. Though it is part of the ideology of the literary that literature is a *universal* form of expression, *who* literature forms is not 'mankind' (much less 'humankind') or the 'nation' or the 'people,' but rather the 'reading public,' that is, in all class societies, the 'educated classes.' In Third World countries like Nicaragua and El Salvador, the 'educated classes' are, it scarcely need be said, a small fraction of the population.

Both Cardenal and Dalton produce in their poetry a revolutionary articulation of what Gramsci called the *national-popular*.[6] But they are only heuristically genuinely national or popular poets, given, among other things, that illiteracy, partial literacy, even the very institutionalization of a national literature, are problems the Central American revolutions can solve at the mass level only after taking power. The direct audience for the work of Cardenal, Dalton and their fellow poets is, even more than in a country like the United States, a very small one. This is not to minimize it, however. The 'educated' spans a series of contradictory socio-cultural locations which can be mobilized for or against a revolutionary anti-imperialist movement. Students, teachers, professionals and technicians, seminarians and clergy, social workers, functionaries and bureaucrats of all sorts, even young army officers — for such members of the middle strata in Third World countries, as well as for important sectors of an actual or would-be national bourgeoisie, there is not always an identity of interests with the oligarchic-imperialist power bloc. In particular, this non-identity may assume the form of the feeling that the dominant bloc retards precisely the development of the *cultural*, or art, literature, music, education. For the 'educated,' poetry can be a passionate concern and a stimulus for political and personal consciousness-raising, a way of producing the 'subject-form' of a radicalized intelligentsia, of giving form and direction to the awareness of exploitation, injustice, and underdevelopment, of linking pleasure to politics.

Why poetry in particular, though? To insist on the centrality of cultural and artistic practices in revolutionary struggle, even in the sectoral way I am doing here, is not to say that any and all of them are equally relevant in a given context of struggle. What counts as an important cultural signifier (and for whom) is mediated by national and regional traditions and their complex interactions with international cultural forms, contingencies of race, class, gender and generation, 'fashion,' etc. The centrality of poetry as a cultural form in Central America has to do with the contradictory effects of combined and uneven development, which has left intact elements of earlier cultural formations and

160

practices that have become extinct or anachronistic in the Postmodernist mass culture of the imperialist metropolis. These
include: the rural tradition of songs and story-telling (e.g., the
corrido or narrative ballad) with roots at once in survivals of
pre-Colombian cultural forms and Catholic-*mestizo* Spanish folk
poetry; the special status of *belles lettres,* in particular the
Baroque style in poetry (*culteranismo*), as a sign of metropolitan
and caste authority in the Colonial period (where literacy itself
was a mark of distinction between the colonizer and colonized);
the role of the *criollo* writer in the epoch of the Wars of Independence as a sort of Liberal-Romantic Moses, 'informing'
through his rhetoric the processes of national liberation and
identity formation; the cultivation of aestheticism and of poetry
as a private and elite language by the organic intellectuals of the
landowning oligarchy displaced by imperialism and its attendant ideologies like positivism around the turn of the century in
Central and South America. In societies where illiteracy is widespread, song and rhetoric have the virtue of being susceptible to
oral recitation and transmission. The spoken word conjures
together the presence of the communal, the erotic and the sacred.
At the same time, even among those who may be functionally
illiterate or who have only limited access to literature, the writer
and writing are endowed with an aura of authority and
charisma. The *letrado* or 'man of letters' as revolutionary leader
has a long and important tradition in Latin America, which goes
from Tupac Amaru, to Padre Hidalgo and Fidel Castro. The
letrado and his or her text (*obra*) is the place where the 'unlettered'
voice of the people can become or find itself mirrored in a
discourse of power equivalent to and thus capable of displacing
the official culture of the exploiting classes.

Ruben Dario and Sandinismo

The founder of modern Latin American poetry, Ruben Dario,
was a Nicaraguan, a fact that has made the figure of Dario and the
practice of poetry as such signifiers in Nicaragua of the national.
The style Dario created was called *modernismo,* and involved an
adaptation into Latin American poetry of French Parnassian and
Symbolist models. The cultural sign of *modernismo* was the figure
of Ariel in Shakespeare's *The Tempest,* celebrated by Dario's
contemporary Rodo, as the incarnation of the refinement of the

Latin American creole elite as against the menacing and vulgar Prospero represented by the United States. But whatever the political and artistic limitations of Dario as the poet laureate of the *fin de siècle* oligarchy, fascinated and repelled by the U.S. at the same time, revolutionary Sandinismo has invented a cult of personality around him similar to the cult of Jose Marti in the Cuban revolution. Sergio Ramirez, recently elected Vice President for the Frente Sandinista (and not incidentally one of Nicaragua's most important novelists and literary critics), explains:

> the revolution has rescued Dario, not from oblivion but from false idolization, because Dario has always been authentically present in the popular imagination as the source of a pride more intuited than understood, as the figure of the 'great poet,' the genius of unknown acts who could triumph over any rival, over death itself: the poet of poets, the fabulous creator of impossible rhymes and images. Because poetry as such, and inspiration, are values which the Nicaraguan people esteem without limit.[7]

Sandinismo itself could best be defined ideologically as a revolutionary populism with a Marxist core. Carlos Fonseca Amador and the founders of the Frente Sandinista (of whom only Tomas Borge survives) developed politically in and around the orbit of the Nicaraguan Communist Party — the Partido Socialista Nicaraguense (PSN) — in the mid 1950s. Their break with the PSN came not so much out of the opposition of a petty bourgeois nationalism to Leninism (as in the prior cases of APRA in Peru or Accion Democratica in Venezuela, for example). It stemmed, rather, from their belief that the PSN was incapable of making a revolution in Nicaragua, that it was too closely tied to the ameliorist strategy of the bourgeois opposition to the Somoza dynasty. What was needed, they felt, was not only a new vanguard party but also a new form of revolutionary ideology specific to Nicaragua's cultural and political experience.[8] Fidel Castro's 26th of July Movement in Cuba (1956-59) was a suggestive model for a revolutionary movement of a new type; but there was also a native source that could be revived: the ideological and organizational forms developed by Augusto Cesar Sandino in his successful struggle in the 1920s against occupation of Nicaragua by the U.S. Marines. Representing itself as a direct continuation of Sandino's popular army, the Frente Sandinista came into being as a military-political organization in 1961.

It has been common for Frente cadre to insist that they were not 'socialistas' but 'sandinistas,' that 'socialismo' was a foreign ideology and that 'sandinismo' was 'their way.' There is no doubt a certain tactical caution in this: it is useful not to be branded too quickly by imperialism; moreover, decades of in-doctrination and Marxism's own well-known birth pains have created strong anti-communist prejudices even among some of the more exploited sections of the population. But there was also a recognition that in any case orthodox Marxism-Leninism was going to be at best one strand of anti-imperialist consciousness in Nicaragua, not *the* necessary and sufficient ideological sig-nifier for all the social forces in the country potentially mobiliz-able against imperialism and for the hegemony of the working class (as we'll see, this problem comes out a bit differently in El Salvador).

This slippage between a specifically class-based ideology — socialism and more particularly Marxism-Leninism — and the notion of a broad, 'national' anti-imperialist constituency, was already implicit in the central signifier of revolutionary San-dinismo, Sandino himself. Sandino typified, on the one hand, the provincial Jacobin nationalism that developed among sectors of the Latin American petty bourgeoisie in the 19th and early 20th century (Sandino was the bastard *mestizo* son of a provincial landowner). On the other hand, there is the image of Sandino as *artesano*, the mechanic and former oilfield worker of the Huasteca Petroleum Company, aware from the start that the war against U.S. occupation would be betrayed by the Liberal bour-geoisie, that it depended finally on the peasants and workers, that it would have to be not only an anti-imperialist war but (and this becomes a central theme in later Sandinista ideology) a '*revolutionary* anti-imperialist war,' implying a transformation of class relations inside Nicaragua. Ideologically, Sandino drew on both modern and traditional strains of revolutionary collec-tivism: socialist and anarchist ideas (partly derived from the IWW and the Flores Magon brothers in Mexico); the Latin American Jacobism mentioned above; the Mexican Revolution; millen-arian religious elements in earlier Central American revolutions; revindications of indian ethnic pride; etc. What he specifically rejected in a famous debate with the father-figure of the Salva-doran revolutionary movement, Farabundo Marti, was the official Marxism-Leninism of the so-called 'Third Period' of the Comintern (the period of Stalin's rise to power in the Soviet

Union, of forced collectivization and of the doctrine of 'social facism' as applied to the non-Communist left). This has led to attempts to make Sandino an anti-Marxist (for example, by supporters of the Sandinista renegade and current *contra* leader, Eden Pastora). But it would be more correct to see Sandino as a forerunner of Popular Front Marxism of the sort represented by Mao or Ho Chi Minh.

In the years following the withdrawal of U.S. marines in 1933, the specific form of imperialist penetration and domination of Nicaragua was the Somoza dictatorship, which was not only a personalist, dynastic regime, but also a party dictatorship to the extent that the Nicaraguan Liberal Party had been transformed by the Somozas into their political machine (Sandino had been a Liberal too). Somocismo invoked ideologically the great themes of 19th century Liberalism to justify its own monopoly of power and its alliance with imperialism. This meant that Catholicism, even in the patrician and reactionary forms left over from the colonial and early independence phases of Nicaragua's political economy, came to constitute at both popular and elite levels an ideological space where an anti-bourgeois, anti-imperialist ethics could be preserved and broadened. This peculiarity of Nicaragua's uneven cultural modernization dovetailed in the 1960s with the emergence of Liberation theology and the *comunidades de base* movement (*comunidades de base* are in effect Christian soviets) in Nicaragua and Latin American in general. This is the nexus that has produced the poetry of Ernesto Cardenal.

Cardenal's Sandinista Poetics

They've told me I talk only about politics now.
It's not about politics but about Revolution
which for me is the same thing as the kingdom of God.

Ernesto Cardenal
'Epistle to Coronel Urtecho'

For those who are not familiar with him, the best way to introduce Cardenal is to note that he is a Catholic priest, a religious mystic, a Beatnik and a communist. He comes from the Conservative landowning dynasties which the Somoza regime displaced. His roots as a poet are in the *vanguardista* movement of the 1920s and 30s, which flourished in the provincial city of Granada, the cultural and economic center of the great Conservative families (the northern city of Leon was, in contrast, the Liberal capital). His mentors include Jose Coronel Urtecho, the founder of the *vanguardistas* and an admirer of Ezra Pound and T.S. Eliot, as much for their poetry as for their ultrareactionary politics.[9] Through Coronel Urtecho, Cardenal came into contact with U.S. poetry; he lived for many years in this country, studying for a time with Thomas Merton and developing a connection with some of the Beat Generation poets (Cardenal's U.S. publisher is New Directions). During the 1960s and 70s, he served variously as fellow traveler and roving ambassador of the Sandinista Liberation Front, moving from what he calls 'contemplative pacifism' to direct participation in the armed struggle after the destruction of the Christian utopian community he created on the island of Solentiname by the Somoza *guardia.* Cardenal's work ranges from the formative text of cultural Sandinismo, *Zero Hour (La Hora Cero),* which appeared in 1960, coincident with the founding moment of the FSLN itself, to his current projects as Minister of Culture of the revolutionary government, including the *poesia de taller* (poetry workshop) movement.

In ideological terms, the basic achievement of Cardenal's poetry has been to interpolate a Marxist vision of class and national struggle through the belief structures and corresponding discursive practices (prayers, sermons, psalms, homilies, etc.) of Catholicism. To understand the importance of this idea in political terms requires a brief parenthesis on Liberation Theology. Without the new kind of religious experience and activism represented by Liberation Theology and related tendencies in the Latin American church, neither the victory of the Nicaraguan nor the present strength of the Salvadoran revolutions is conceivable. How explain the metamorphosis of at least a significant part of Latin American Catholicism into a politically progressive and revolutionary force? Part of the answer must lie in the ambivalent relation between Catholicism and capitalism, noted by Max Weber among others. The Counter Reformation was an ideological counter-revolution against those doctrines which in mature form would become a century or two later the Liberalism of the great bourgeois revolutions. Liberalism, at least in its initial stages, carried in consequence a strongly anticlerical bias in Catholic countries, and the Church, on the whole, remained tied to the patriarchal culture and politics of the Conservative landowners. In the early 19th century, Liberal historicism became the dominant ideological expression of an emerging Latin American creole bourgeoisie, located in the mercantile centers of the colonial economy. Liberalism was tied to Latin American revolutionary nationalism in the sense that it projected, along with liberation from colonial domination, a vision of a new American cosmos and of corresponding political, administrative and cultural structures. Within this cosmos, the human and natural elements of the new republics were to find their proper place and use in terms of their coincidence with the evolving project of the creole bourgeoisie, a project which, in the fashion of French Jacobinism, envisioned itself as a movement of universal human emancipation. The characteristic narrative *epos* of dependent Liberalism was thus the account of the conquest of the interior (the frontier or 'backlands,' seen as a historical space bound to anachronism) which elevates the values and ambitions of the urban elite to the level of a national enterprise. By contrast, the force of evil in Liberal narrative is the reactionary egotism of local groupings (priests, provincial caudillos, bandit heroes, etc.), which fragments the potential unity of the body politic and leaves it in a state of cultural and economic childhood.

In practice, Liberal optimism about the providential wisdom of the 'unseen hand' of the world market produced contradictory results in Latin America — as elsewhere. Most notable among them, the living standards of the masses declined both relatively and absolutely during the 'century of progress' from Latin American independence to the First World War (the time span of Garcia Marquez's *100 Years of Solitude*), particularly as the organization of agriculture and trade becomes more capitalist in character. The 'highest stage' of the Liberal agro-export model may thus be seen, for example, in the present situation of Central America where a peasantry that previous to Independence had at least a modicum of ownership or effective control of land and resources (through the surviving Indian *ejidos* or the plots available on the big estates to the *colonos* or serfs) has been reduced to a landless, immiserated rural proletariat. *Laissez faire* meant not industrialization, as in the case of the United States or Japan, but rather Central America's specialization as a producer and exporter of foodstuffs and raw materials (coffee, sugar, cotton, beef, and leather) at structurally disadvantageous terms of trade, a constant pressure against the traditional forms of land tenure and livelihood of the rural masses, and a gradual erosion of national autonomy.

In such a situation, where Liberalism has rooted late and unevenly, the possibilities of a crossover between Catholic traditionalism — historically a breeding ground of reactionary ideologies and movements — and popular, 'folk' insurrections have been rich and varied. The Spanish Communist leader La Pasionaria recounts in her autobiography that her uncle, who had been a Carlist guerrilla as a young man, ended his life as a Socialist trade union leader in the coal mines of the Basque country. Michael Taussig notes similarly of the Afro-American peasantry of the Cauca valley of Colombia: 'Their hatred of racial and class privileges was nourished by a radical reinterpretation of Catholicism in which the peasant's fight for land was sanctified . . . The relation of God to the underworld remained forever fraught with the violence of the master-slave bond. When the blacks broke that bond, they recruited God to their side and let their masters go to the devil.'[10]

Cardenal inherits from Liberal nationalism the responsibility to produce in his poetry an image of Nicaraguan national destiny, but precisely in a context where the founding assumptions of Liberal historicism have collapsed, where the expected apotheosis of democracy and 'modernization' reveals instead the death squads of what Noam Chomsky and Edward Herman call the 'Pentagon-CIA Archipelago.' In Cardenal's poetry, the image of the imperialist present is of time-without-hope; the pseudo-eternity of the Somoza regime, the sense of a past which has been cancelled, the 'unsatisfactory' epic of a dominated and dependent Banana Republic. This is the corollary of the apocalyptic ending in the Latin American *boom* novel where, as in *100 Years of Solitude*, the text collapses into a sort of Black Hole. But there is at the same time a counter-motion in Cardenal, which derives from his representation of history through the narrative frame of primitive Christianity. Despair is lit up from within by the promise of an imminent redemption from evil, a time when 'the last shall be first,' when we will attain a new community and a new body:

> They are enlarging the concentration camps
> they are inventing new tortures
> new systems of 'investigation'
> At night they sleep not making plans

plotting how to crush us further
                                how further to exploit us
but the Lord laughs at them
for he sees that they shall soon fall from power
The arms they manufacture shall be turned against them
Their political systems shall be erased from the earth
and their political parties shall exist no longer
The plans of their technicians shall serve for nothing
The great powers
                                are as the flowers of the field
The imperialisms
                                are as smoke

                                                'Psalm 36'[11]

Zero Hour was an attempt to portray Sandino's war against the
United States and his assasination by Somoza as the central
passion — in the evangelical sense — of modern Nicaraguan
history. The poem is in four parts: a short introduction describing the mood of Central America during the 'night' of the dic-
tatorships in the 1920s; 2) a textual collage on the economics of
the Banana Republics (histories of United Fruit, etc.); 3) a long
central section reconstructing Sandino's struggle, culminating in
the description of his assassination; 4) a final episode describing
an anti-Somoza conspiracy in the 1950s (the so-called Con-
spiración de Abril of 1954) in which Cardenal himself took part
and in which his close friend Adolfo Baez Bone was captured
and in which his close friend Adolfo Baez Bone was captured and
tortured to death by the Somocista police. The 'zero hour' is the
moment of death, but also the time before dawn, the moment
which separates disaster and redemption, the point where
history turns on its axis:

Tropical nights in Central America
with moonlit lagoons and volcanoes
and lights from presidential palaces,
barracks and sad bugle calls for curfew.
'Often while smoking a cigarette
I've decided that a man should die,'
says Ubico smoking a cigarette . . .
In his pink-wedding-cake palace
Ubico has a head cold. Outside, the
people were dispersed with phosphorous bombs

. . . .
Watchman! Tell me of the night?
Watchman! Tell me of the night?

Like the Christian passion, Sandino's story is an annunciation, the figuration of heroism and community that will reappear in a new epic of national liberation. His 'barefoot army' prophesies the Sandinista guerrilla army, still at the moment of the poem's appearance in 1960, to be created:

> and though they had a military hierarchy they were all equal
> with no distinction of rank when they shared their food
> and their clothes; they all had the same rations
> And the leaders had not adjutants:
> it was more like a community than an army
> and it was not military discipline that unified them but love,
> though there was never such unity in an army.

This concern with recovering and giving poetic form to a tradition of struggle reflects the experience of a national history which has been falsified, driven underground, marginalized, forgotten. Cardenal's poems are a sort of palimpsest in which fragments of a past that has been 'written over' by imperialism resurface. Imperialism in the realm of culture depends on the destruction of collective memory, the imposition of forms of amnesia, the corruption of language and values under the pressure of commercialization and modernization. 'There are also crimes of the CIA in the realm of semantics,' writes Cardenal in his 'Epistle to Coronel Urtecho.' In the official history of Somocista Nicaragua, Sandino figures as a renegade and an outlaw. (How many of *you* know that Sandino forced the Marines to evacuate from Nicaragua? That the U.S. has *already* suffered a military defeat in Central America?) The loss of the past is the loss of revolutionary possibility; the revolution is therefore the return of the repressed. The classless society is *inside* history, prefigured in the communitarian societies of pre-Colombian America or of primitive Christianity:

> At mass, we discussed the Gospels
> with the peasants
> in the form of a dialogue
> and they began to understand the essence
>   of the divine message:
> the heralding of the Kingdom of God.
> Which is the establishment on earth of a just society
> without exploiters and exploited
> like the society of the early Christians

'The Meaning of Solentiname'

The point here is different from Roger Garaudy's proposal for a Christian-Marxist 'dialogue' based on converging ethical humanisms. Cardenal is more of a mystic than a humanist. Like Liberation Theology theory, he is concerned with fusing Christian eschatology with a Marxist sense of contradiction and dialectical transformation in history and nature. What he is creating, in other words, is an *ideology*, a new sort of revolutionary historicism that shuttles between the cosmic and the immediate, the individual and the community, the raw data of history and its transfiguration, death and renewal, nature and culture:

> I said that iguanas spawn . . . It's the process. They
> (or the frogs) in the carboniferous silence
> >   emitted the first sound
> >   the first love song over the earth
> >   the first love song under the moon
> >   it's the process
> The process emanates from the stars
> >   New relations of production: that
> too is the process. Oppression. After oppression, liberation.
> The Revolution began in the stars, millions
> >   of light years away. The egg of life
> >   is one. From
> the first gaseous egg, to the egg of the iguana, to the New Man.
> Sandino boasted of having been born from 'the belly of the
> oppressed'
> >   (from the belly of a Niquinohomo Indian woman)
> From the belly of the oppressed will be born the Revolution.
> . . . .
> In death Che smiled as if he had just left Hell.
>
> > > > > > > > > > > > > > > 'National Song'

Roque Dalton (1933-1974)

Dalton is different from Cardenal in a way that reflects a specifically Salvadoran national-popular ideology rooted in the symbolization of the revolutionary past by the Communist leader Agustin Farabundo Marti, rather than by the populist Sandino. Dalton writes as a Marxist-Leninist within the ideological and organizational horizons of Marxist-Leninist sectarianism (though not without, as we'll see, a sort of revisionism). His tone, partly derived from Brecht and Nazim Hikmet, partly from the cynical 'anti-poems' of the Chilean Nicanor Parra, is both self-absorbed and self-mocking, secular, antiprophetic, aphoristic, didactic. The Poetic was his favorite genre:

> Well you see here there was this poet
> from here, this country
> who wasn't no beauty but wasn't real bad either
> like Satan (who he dreamed he was)
> just sort of ugly and chicken-chested and a real nice guy
> who found it rough finding time to write
> between studying bookkeeping
> and working in the Courts.
>
> 'The History of a Poetic'[12]

That's fairly typical Dalton, offering the persona of the battered, loveable mug, half Cantinflas, half *film noir* tough, aesthete turned terrorist, 'national' — Salvadoran — in his very imperfection and idealism, in his oscillation between machismo and sentimentalism ('a real nice guy'). Behind the pose and the self-mocking humor, though, there lies a deadly seriousness and a life put on the line in the face of one of the most violently repressive regimes in Latin America. The traumatic political unconscious of Dalton and his generation was the failure of the 1932 uprising led by Farabundo Marti, and the subsequent massacre of some 30,000 peasants, workers and indians by the dictatorship of General Maximiliano Hernandez Martinez, an event expunged, like Sandino's struggle, from the official history of the subsequent 'civico-military' regimes, as they came to be called in El Salvador. 'We were all born half dead in 1932,' Dalton wrote in one of his most famous poems, 'All'; 'we survive only half alive.' There is a harsh lesson to be learned from this:

> There have been good people in this country
> ready to die for the revolution.
>
> But the revolution everywhere needs people
> who are ready to not only die
> but also kill for it.
>
> 'Old Communists and Guerrillas'

Dalton belongs to a generation of Latin American poets —Otto Rene Castillo, Ibero Gutierrez, Javier Heraud, Victor Jara, Cardenal's protege Leonel Rugama, Ricardo Morales, Francisco Urondo, and Jacques Viau are some of the others — who began to write a new kind of revolutionary lyric in the 60s: colloquial, self-conscious, youthful, sometimes brittle with anger or irony, sometimes suffused with fraternal tenderness, in Roberto

Fernandez Retamar's phrase, a 'conversational poetry.' Mario Benedetti — who anthologized their production in one of the great books of contemporary Latin American literature, *Poesia trunca* (Truncated Poems) — spoke of them as poets who no longer wrote *for* but rather *from* the people ('el poeta ya no escribe *para* sino *desde* el pueblo').[13] They are the voices of Latin America's New Left in the period between the Cuban Revolution and the Sandinista victory of 19 July 1979. As Benedetti's title indicates, the event that seals the poet's work and stamps its influence on posterity is a premature martyrdom in the guerrilla *foco* or in the urban 'popular organization.' The death of the poet 'rewrites' the poems, giving them a new urgency, relevance, and power of expression, so that poet and poems together come to constitute not only a new way of doing poetry, a counter-hegemonic canon, but also a revolutionary hagiography.

The tragedy of Dalton's death, however, is that it came not at the hands of the class enemy — those death squads and counter-insurgency 'special forces' the Alliance for Progress made ubiquitous in Latin America in the 60s — but rather from his own comrades. Dalton joined the Salvadoran Communist Party in the late 50s, sharing the usual misfortunes — jail, torture, death threats, exile — with that 'patience and irony' which is supposed to be the mark of a good cadre. Between 1969 and 1972, however, the Salvadoran CP split under the impact of new generational and ideological tendencies which argued the necessity of armed struggle on the Cuban model rather than the party's cautious reformism. In 1972, the CP and the Salvadoran Socialist and Christian-Democratic parties formed an electoral coalition, UNO, around the presidential candidacy of Jose Napoleon Duarte, the popular mayor of the capital city. UNO was crushed in a massive and blatant electoral fraud, followed by a wave of repression against the political opposition and the trade unions. The bubble of an electoral challenge to the power of the Salvadoran oligarchy burst. This is the context for the emergence of armed struggle in El Salvador in the 1970s.

Returning from exile in Cuba and Czechoslovakia, Dalton got involved with what has become perhaps the largest of the guerrilla groups today: the Ejercito Revolucionario del Pueblo (ERP—Revolutionary Army of the People), founded by young Fidelista Marxists and Liberation Theology activists. After some initial success with hit-and-run actions, ERP got badly bogged down by 1974. Dalton and a faction of the organization close to him argued the need to supplement *foco*-style guerrilla activity with the development of legal mass organizations: unions, neighborhood associations, student groups, etc. In the sectarian hothouse of Salvadoran politics and in a very down period for the Latin American left in general (Allende and the Unidad Popular went down to defeat in September 1973), the debate turned bitter. Dalton's opponents accused him of trying to split the ERP. He persisted in his critique of their strategy, only to find himself charged by the ERP leadership with treason. Along with several of his allies, he was summarily tried and executed, and the rumor spread that he was working for the CIA. His murder provoked a split in ERP, out of which emerged a new guerrilla organization dedicated to his line, Resistencia Nacional (National Resistance).

Dalton was a hard-luck case from the start. At least, that's part of the persona he liked to project: the tender idealist just beginning to rise on wings of song when he crashes into the brutal philistinism of everyday life in the backyard of the American Empire:

> You've scorned my love
> laughing at its small bashful gift
> not wanting to understand the labyrinths
> of my tenderness
>
> Now it's my turn
> the turn of the offended after years of silence

'You've Beaten Me'

A passion for beauty and justice denied (Dalton was trained as a lawyer) turns into hatred, hatred into political militancy, militancy into revolutionary violence:

> Now it's too late
> Now tenderness isn't enough
>
> I've had a taste of gunpowder.

'Terrible Thing'

Dalton's persona — oscillating between 'nice guy' and commissar — merges here with the terms of the great debate on the Salvadoran and Latin American left over the strategic wisdom or necessity of armed struggle. Dalton's position is clear: the 'peaceful road to socialism' is the lyrical illusion, the temptation based on the very feelings of love, humanity and democracy which the revolution stands for. Softness — Dalton feels a great softness and tenderness inside himself — is a danger to oneself and to the movement:

> Commander Ernesto Che Guevara
> called by the pacifists
> 'the great adventurist of armed struggle'
> went and applied his revolutionary concepts
> in Bolivia. Testing these concepts out
> he and a handful of heroes lost their lives.
>
> The great pacifists of the prudent way
> also tested their own concepts in Chile:
> now more than 30 thousand are dead.
>
> Imagine what the dead would say
> on behalf of those concepts
> if they could relate to us their experience.
>
> > 'Ways of Dying'

Dalton will insist on a poetry of 'ugly words,' *palabras feas*: 'worm-eaten scream,' 'asphixiating skin,' 'face of bread out of ovens,' 'hell of quicklime,' 'eyes and ears pierced with needles,' etc. There is an urgency to wound — to wound himself — and then to reject consolation, to keep the wound from healing too quickly, to use the pain to generate insight and militancy:

> Matter is hard
> matter is indestructible
> therefore matter is unsympathetic
> matter is cruel.
>
> > 'Head Against the Wall'

To the poet as the patriarchal-populist seer of the national liberation struggle in the fashion of Neruda or Cardenal, Dalton, in his manifesto 'Poetry and Militancy in Latin America,' counterposes 'the poet as a scrutiniser of his own time . . . because, like it or not, by insisting too much on what will come we lose at some level our immediate perspective, and we run the risk of not being understood by all the people who find themselves immersed in everyday life.' Strategically, the problem is to raise 'to the category of poetic material the contradictions, disasters, defects, customs, and struggles of our present society,' a task, Dalton admits, 'involving a great deal of destructive activity.' Only after the work of destruction is finished 'is it possible to begin constructing, without major obstacles, the prospectus of the future.' Moreover, this position is 'valid in the preparatory stage, the insurrectional stage and the triumphal stage of any Latin American revolution.'[14]

'Destructive activity' — that is the essential stance of Dalton's poetic and the place where it dovetails as a means of the class struggle in language with his defense of and involvement in armed struggle in El Salvador. The unremitting mocking/self-mocking which composes the verbal texture of his style is meant as a tactic of personal liberation and disenchantment (*desengaño*) addressed to his contemporaries who are the potential constituency of the revolutionary organizations. Its function is to chastise the poet's own petty bourgeois Imaginary and guard against its return, to deconstruct the mendacious 'humanism' of the official culture, to tell 'the other side of the story.' But Dalton's humor is not just directed against the ruling class; it is also concerned with redefining ideologically the sense of Marxism-Leninism and revolutionary militancy in order to bring them closer to the sensibility and spirit of the new generation emerging in El Salvador, and in the rest of the Americas, on the heels of the Cuban Revolution. (Demographically, Latin America has become a continent where the majority of the population are now under 20, making youth culture a critical area.) Dalton's audience, like Dylan's in the United States or the *nueva trova*'s in Cuba, is generationally specific: that is why his poems often carry generational markers (e.g., 'Old Communists and Guerrillas' cited above). His poetic persona is in effect a new model of subjectivity for a 60s radicalism: the 'nice guy,' the non-heroic hero. Humor provides the distance-effect necessary to revive a Marxism which has become official and officious. That is the sense of Dalton's best-known poem, 'On Headaches':

> It's beautiful being a communist
> though it brings on many headaches.
>
> And communist headaches
> are supposed to be historical, meaning
> aspirin won't cure them
> only the realization of Heaven on earth
> So it goes.

Under capitalism our head aches
and they cut it off.
In the struggle for revolution
the head is a time-bomb.

In the stage of socialist construction
we plan the headache
which doesn't make it go away, quite the contrary.
Communism will be, among other things,
an aspirin the size of the sun.

The appeal here lies in how the poem allows one to be playfully
serious about Marxist ideas — here the idea of stages — which
get 'cancelled and preserved' in such an operation. The ideological effect is to create a kind of aporia: on the one hand
orthodox Marxism-Leninism — what Brecht liked to call the
Classics — is maintained as the 'untranscendable horizon' of
praxis; on the other, the deconstructive ironizing gives expression to the more skeptical, antidogmatic spirit of 60s leftism.
There is a gentle but evident allusion to the problems of actual
Socialist societies; but Dalton as someone who has lived in the
Socialist world as an exile, is not unmindful that these same
societies have been the principal material and ideological
support for Third World liberation movements. Like 'Headaches,' all of Dalton's poems seem to involve an almost continuous dialogue between New and Old Lefts, entwined and
alternating with the different aspects of his own persona to
create a new mode of revolutionary sensibility and activism.
This is not an inconsiderable achievement when one considers,
for example, that the disasters of the U.S. and European left at the
end of the 60s were predicated on the inability of Marxist-
Leninists and SDS-style youth movements to come together.
Dalton, like Cardenal, always conceived of his poetry as a
theoretical-practical contribution to building a successful revolutionary movement in his country; the present strength of the
Democratic Revolutionary Front is in part an effect of his work.

There are some problems, too. Dalton's persona depends in
part on activating — albeit sometimes self-critically — the
image of the charming but sentimentally unreliable revolutionary Don Juan. The dominant sexual mood is hip machismo:
the aesthete-idealist 'scratches his little violin/like a pedarast/
until he smashes his face/against the barracks wall.' The homo-
phobia is directed against that tenderness the poet is afraid will

reappear, will take away his anger, 'unman' him, make him a dupe and victim again. There is something immature and unresolved here (something, it should be added, not peculiar to Dalton but characteristic of the Latin American male left). There is also something peculiarly and intimately Salvadoran (again from a male point of view) about this interplay of toughness and sentimentality. For all his posing as a lady-killer, Dalton is really a poet of male-male relationships, for whom the imperfect fraternity of the guerrilla *foco* and the imagined equality of communism are both, in the end, utopias of male-bonding. Women enter his poems usually in the 'conflictive' zone of domesticity. In writing about and for other men, Dalton sometimes allows his vulnerability to show through and harmonize delicately with the revolutionary punk, as in his beautiful 'Love Poem,' where he declares his solidarity with

> those who rotted in prisons in Guatemala
> Mexico, Honduras, Nicaragua
> for stealing, smuggling, swindling
> for starving
>
> . . . .
> those who pack the bars and whorehouses
> in every port and capital
> ('The Blue Grotto,' 'The G-String,' 'Happyland')
> the sowers of corn deep in foreign forests
> the crime barons of the scandal sheets
>
> . . . .
> the spongers, beggars, pot-heads
> the stupid sons of bitches
> those who were barely able to get back
> and those who had a little more luck
> the forever undocumented
> those who would do anything, sell anything, eat anything
> the first ones to pull a knife
> the wretched the most wretched of the earth
> my compatriots
> my brothers.

Although one of the strengths of Dalton's poetry as an ideological practice is its oscillation between alternatives — nice guy and terrorist, macho and lover, bohemian and commissar, old and new leftist, Marxism and the colloquial voice — there's also a sense in which it stays locked within this specular dialectic and doesn't ever really become 'popular' in the ways he suggested it should in the 'Poetry and Militancy' theses quoted above. Dalton's audience was and will be people much like himself. Given our previous remarks about the formation of a revolutionary intelligentsia, this is an important, perhaps decisive, constituency for a Marxist poetry in Central America, and poetry is a language which addresses it with special directness. But this audience is not 'the people,' especially in Latin America. Dalton is finally the poet, as well as the victim, of cadre micro-politics.

Conclusions and Projections

The ideal of Central American political and cultural unity is a key feature not only of the ideology but also of the strategy of the Central American revolution. What is curious in the case of Dalton and Cardenal is that neither really translates well into the other's national context, at least as the strong force for ideological conversion they have been in their own. That is how nationally specific their poetic work is. The Frente Sandinista and the Salvadoran Democratic Revolutionary Front have been molded by quite different traditions of struggle and political-cultural backgrounds. Dalton's poetry is inflected by the particularities of El Salvador, it is written in what Ileana Rodriguez has called a 'creole-mestizo voice.'[15] The populist, intertextual Modernism of Cardenal's 'documentary poems,' in turn, responds to the concrete evolution of poetry in Nicaragua, from Dario through the Granada *vanguardistas* and the testimonial lyric of the period of resistance to the Somoza dynasty. That is why it would make no sense to pose the alternative, Dalton or Cardenal, (as in say, Kafka or Mann, Brecht or Lukács), because the political significance of their poetry depends on its *specificity*, not its universality. Within what might be called the fraternal polarity of their two poetic modes may be located most of the other major aesthetic-ideological discourses at stake in the Central American revolutionary movement today.

Most, but not all. Missing in both Cardenal and Dalton — as we've already noted apropos of Dalton's machismo — is any significant sensitivity to the situation of women and to their role in struggle. As might be expected, Cardenal is adept at evoking 'suffering womanhood,' but one also senses the paternalism of the priest. Dalton is more 'liberated,' but also more problematic, because of the misogynistic strain in his poetry. At least he tries. In a long poem called 'For a Better Love,' he proposes ambitiously to develop Kate Millet's feminist slogan, 'Sex is also a political category.' But this principally involves evoking the struggle of women 'in the rearguard of household work/in the strategy and tactics of the kitchen' — hardly the sort of interpellation calculated to turn on the schoolteacher or the nurse or the compañera shop steward in a textile mill. (Providentially, the Central American revolution has also brought forward a strong and politically significant movement in women's poetry with figures like Claribel Alegria, Gioconda Belli, Rosario Murillo and Michele Najlis.)

The problem of sexism in much of Latin American revolutionary culture will not be solved easily. It would be a kind of idealism, I think, simply to abandon machismo as an ideological signifier to imperialism and its local allies like D'Aubuisson and the death squads, because it is a concept closely bound up with *both* male and female ideas of personal integrity and commitment in Latin America. Indeed, Dalton's particular brand of machismo might be appealing to young males and thus prove a positive factor in his poetry's political usefulness (to the extent that we agree that convincing young men to join the struggle against imperialist domination is a good thing). On the other hand, machismo, even in such a left-populist mode, involves an inevitable devaluation of the feminine, and thus produces an inhibition of the drive to women's self-actualization. A revolutionary movement that cannot involve women fighting *for themselves* as well as for the 'class,' 'national,' etc. will fail. If in a given situation there is a need to suspend judgment and tolerate tension, difference and unevenness which reflects the uneven development of education and consciousness in the revolutionary bloc, then it is only on the understanding that at some other moment the working out of these 'contradictions among the people' *will* become the politically and historically decisive task.

A way of returning to the problem posed by Jameson in the quotation cited at the outset: when I presented this paper as a lecture, someone asked afterwards what it implied for cultural struggle in the United States. What was the 'key sector' here? Poetry has been important politically, of course, in the Black, Chicano and Puerto Rican movements (and in parts of the Women's Movement) for reasons similar to those in Central America. But I didn't answer poetry, I answered rock music. The moral of this story for North American activists searching for effective ways to intervene in their own historical conjuncture may be: learn from Bruce Springsteen.

Notes

Portions of this paper have appeared previously in the Chicano journal *Metamorfosis* (Fall, 1984), and in *the minnesota review* (Spring, 1984).

1. Fredric Jameson, 'Morality Versus Ethical Substance,' *Social Text* 8 (Winter 1983/84), p. 152

2. 'Ideology and Ideological State Apparatuses (Notes Towards an Investigation)' Louis Althusser, *Lenin and Philosophy and Other Essays*, trans. Ben Brewster (New York, 1972).

3. Ernesto Laclau makes the point that while Marxism is the 'science' of revolution in the modern world — i.e., the expression of its general conditions of being and possibility (class struggle, imperialism, crisis theory, etc.) — it is not necessarily nor even usually *the* ideology of revolutionary movements. Mass politics, whether of the right or the left, has for Laclau a *populist* form in the sense that the 'people' is the *subject* of political struggle. Both Facism and Maoism are forms of 'populist rupture' with a dominant power bloc, but with very different consequences in terms of class hegemony. See Laclau, 'Towards a Theory of Populism,' in his *Politics and Ideology in Marxist Theory* (London, 1977).

4. An Althusserian restatement of the ideology/aesthetics issue is Pierre Macherey and Etienne Balibar's article 'Literature as an Ideological Form: Some Marxist Propositions,' translated by James Kavanagh in *Praxis* 5 (1981).

5. Michel Pêcheux clarifies: 'ideologies are not made up of "ideas" but of practices . . . it is impossible to attribute *to each class its own ideology*, as if each existed "before the class struggle" in its own camp, with its own conditions of existence and its specific institutions, such that the ideological class struggle would be the meeting point of two distinct and pre-existing worlds, each with its own practices and "world outlook." ' *Language, Semantics and Ideology*, trans, H. Nagpal (New York, 1982), p. 98.

6. In Gramsci's view, a social class or intra-class *bloc* achieves hegemony when it can appear as the necessary embodiment of popular will and the national interest and tradition. The terrain of the national-popular is that of culture, of the reproduction of 'common sense' seen as a layered and contradictory totality.

7. Sergio Ramirez, *Balcanes y volcanes* (Managua, 1983), p. 198; my translation.

8. For Sandinista ideology, see Fonseca Amador's 1969 manifesto, 'Nicaragua: hora cero,' available in translation in *Sandinistas Speak* (New York, 1982); David Nolan, *FSLN: The Ideology of the Sandinistas and the Nigaraguan Revolution* (Miami, 1985).

9. Sergio Ramirez notes of the Granada *vanguardistas*: 'The movement was nationalist, anti-bourgeois, catholic and later on reactionary. If these positions seem dissimilar or contradictory, they have to be situated in the class context which gives rise to the movement; the young *vanguardistas* were attempting to break open the oligarchic culture they themselves belonged to by insisting, against the vulgarity and opportunism of the times, on restoring ideologically a concept of tradition which carries in it the notion of the conservation of the

national culture as a patriachal legacy . . . This will lead them, paradoxically, to favor Sandino's struggle' (*Balcanes,* p. 61).

10.   Michael Taussig, *The Devil and Commodity Fetishism in South America* (Chapel Hill, 1980) p. 67; an essential book for understanding religion and the religious imagination as modes of ideological class struggle in Latin America. For a useful introduction to Liberation Theology, see the Summer 1984 special issue of *Monthly Review* 'Religion and the Left', and the essay by Paul Buhle and Thomas Fiehrer printed below.

11.   For this and other translated versions of Cardenal's texts, I am using *Zero Hour and other Documentary Poems* (New York, 1980); Roberto Marquez, ed., *Latin American Revolutionary Poetry* (New York, 1984): and B. Aldaraca, et al. eds., *Nicaragua in Revolution: The Poets Speak* (Minneapolis, 1980).

12.   This and other translations of Dalton poems are my own or are taken from Roque Dalton, *Poems,* trans. Richard Schaff (Willimantic, Connecticut, 1984).

13.   Mario Benedetti, introduction to *Poesia trunca* (Havana, 1976).

14.   Dalton's essay appeared originally in the Cuban literary journal *Casa de las Americas* in the mid 60s. I cite the translation by James and Arlene Scully in their R. Dalton, *Poetry and Militancy in Latin America* (Willimantic, Connecticut, 1981).

15.   See her fine essay on Dalton, 'El texto literario como expression mestizo-creole: in memoriam,' *Casa de las Americas* 126 (1981).

2.   Lessons in Liberation:

The Fiction of V. S. Naipaul, Joan Didion and Robert Stone

John McClure

'It is very interesting,' remarks a character in Don Delillo's recent novel, *The Names*, 'how Americans learn geography and world history as their interests are damaged in one country after another.'[1] Delillo's novel is about the damage being done to American interests in the Middle East and Africa; but these days Americans are also learning something about a region closer to home, the Caribbean Basin, where American interests have been challenged in places like Jamaica, Grenada, El Salvador and Nicaragua. Those Americans who read contemporary fiction have had three main lines of imaginary access to the region, three literary guides to the sights and sounds and significance of its recent history. Though one guide, V.S. Naipaul, is Trinidadian by birth and has lived for most of his life in England, he is at least as familiar to American readers as the other two, Joan Didion and Robert Stone. And all three novelists have much in common besides their status as major figures on the American literary landscape. They all write in English, and all acknowledge Joseph Conrad, with his dark portraits of an earlier imperial epoch, as their master. They are all aware, too, of one another: Didion has reviewed Naipaul's work in *The New York Review of Books*, to which he frequently contributes; Stone cites Naipaul in a recent interview and has reviewed Didion's *Salvador*.

They have also found similar ways of writing about the third world. Naipaul and Didion have written politically focused travel reports, Naipaul about India and the Islamic world, Didion about El Salvador. And in their novels all three focus on privileged Western travellers who get entangled in revolutions they don't really understand. These situations are framed in similarly circumscribed ways. None of their novels have the range of Conrad's magnificent *Nostromo*, with its particularized portraits both of the parties directly engaged in battle and of the captains of finance and industry who direct some of these forces from afar. And none provide a particularized view of indigenous revolutionary communities like that offered, for instance, by Manlio Argueta's *One Day of Life*. All tend to confirm, then, Fredric Jameson's thesis that the social frame of the present world system is so vast, its circuitry so complex, that 'lived totalization' of it in narrative is no longer possible.[2]

A final point of comparison between Naipaul, Didion, and Stone will provide the point of departure for this essay. All three of them, I will show, focus their evaluation of the revolutionary movements they describe in a similar way, by testing the discourses that characterize these movements. 'Occasionally,' Althusser has written, 'the whole class struggle may be summed up in the struggle for one word or another.'[3] Naipaul, Didion, and Stone all write as if this were the case in Latin America today and as if the word to be struggled for, or against, were 'liberation.'

Their focus on this term is certainly justifiable. Liberation is a key word in a whole range of contemporary discourses of revolution, discourses identified with Latin Americans such as Fanon, Guevara, Freire, and Gutierrez. And it rings through the speeches, songs, and slogans of the Latin American movements themselves. There are, of course, several different theories of liberation in circulation, each with a somewhat different definition of liberation, analysis of the obstacles to be overcome, and approach to overcoming them. But the different theories have much in common. All characterize the third world as a realm of oppression dominated by and dependent on Western capitalist economies. All define the task of liberation as one of overcoming the economic, political, social, and psychological manifestations of this dependency. All insist that this process will require but by no means be completed by radical political change. And all draw on two massive discourses, the Judeo-Christian and the Marxist. ' "The last shall be first and the first last." Decolonisation is the putting into practice of this statement'[4] — so wrote Frantz Fanon in *The Wretched of the Earth*.

In this context, to defend the notion of liberation, to use the word without dismissive quotation marks, is to indicate that the dream of radical and beneficial social change must be taken seriously, to affirm the vision that has sent hundreds of thousands of people into the streets and the mountains over the last twenty-five years. Conversely, then, to dismiss the notion, to insist on putting quotation marks around the term or on voicing it with contempt, is to dismiss these people, their efforts, and the very hope of radical social change. Two of the novelists under discussion, Naipaul and Didion, try to imprison liberation within the quotation marks of contempt and incredulity. This is to be expected, I suppose, not only because they bear personal grudges against the forces that use the word, but also because many book-buying Americans are finding it hard to believe in, or convenient to dismiss, the very notion of profound social progress. What is surprising, then, is that Robert Stone, arguably the most artistically accomplished novelist of the three, should be ready to give sympathetic voice to the voices of liberation, that he should allow these voices, as Naipaul and Didion do not, to interrogate their interrogators. In the discussion that follows, I will be looking first at Naipaul's and Didion's attempts to discredit the project of liberation and then at Stone's attempts to do justice to its vision and appeal.

I

Naipaul's *Guerrillas*,[5] published in 1975, depicts a popular uprising on an island which resembles Jamaica and Trinidad. The main characters are two white Western visitors, two members of the country's bourgeoisie, and Jimmy Ahmed, a local exponent of 'black power' and 'revolution based on the land.' The first part of the novel establishes the characters and their relations to one another. Peter Roche and his girlfriend Jane are newcomers to the island. Peter, a liberal white South African who has been part of the anti-apartheid movement, is working as a public relations man for Sablich's, an old slave trading firm now assiduously courting island radicals like Jimmy Ahmed. Jane, Roche's girlfriend, is a London political groupie; disappointed with Roche, and fascinated with Ahmed, she becomes his lover. In the meantime, Jane and Roche's more privileged friends, the businessman Harry de Tunja and the politician Meredith Herbert, are looking for the kind of security their country can hardly offer. Harry is quietly transferring his funds, and his citizenship, to Canada. Meredith is looking for a post in the higher reaches of the government.

The second part of the novel is concerned with the social

explosion that has been building in the background all through the first. The island, with its American-owned extraction industry showering little more than a cloud of bauxite dust on the population, is a social tinderbox. When one of Jimmy's colleagues, or rivals, is ambushed and killed by the police, Jimmy uses the incident to set the tinderbox afire. Almost immediately, however, he loses control of the insurrection. And after a couple of days of violence the United States sends in helicopters and special forces: peace is restored.

Naipaul's portrayal of American power is persistently critical. On the plane that brings Jane to the island, two American bauxite officials are reading pornographic magazines with titles — *Easy Lay* and *Sucked Dry* (p. 156) — that betray their relation to the island. The terms of this relation are summed up in a different manner by Harry de Tunja: 'One factory, one rich white businessman, one rich black politician' (p. 156). And when U.S. forces intervene to stop the insurrection, Harry draws a lesson: 'The Americans are not going to let anybody here stop them lifting bauxite,' he remarks, 'You see, Jane? They don't just read pornography' (p. 223). But the Americans are not, in any dramatic or thematic sense, the villains of *Guerrillas*. The characters who are most consistently criticized and who suffer punishment in the last part of the novel are all identified, in fact, with opposition to American domination. Roche is publicly humiliated, Jane sexually humiliated and murdered; Jimmy Ahmed is left to face the wrath of the government he has failed to overthrow.

One way to explain this curious deflection of attention, anger, and retribution from the powerful forces of oppression to their all but powerless opponents is to recall that *Guerrillas* is based on an actual incident which Naipaul followed closely and discussed in an essay, 'Michael X and the Black Power Killings in Trinidad.' But both in the essay and in the novel, Naipaul makes the weakness of the radicals who took part in this incident the basis for a generalized condemnation of radicalism, uses the single sordid affair, as Edward Said has put it, to exorcise 'all the 1960s devils — national liberation movements, revolutionary goals, Third Worldism.'[6] Thus if at times he seems to be condemning specific misapplications of liberation discourse, ultimately it becomes clear that the discourse itself is under attack.

One of his lines of attack is to suggest that the new discourse of liberation is little more than a mask behind which visitors and local people alike are playing out a familiar drama. At times the disguised drama is depicted as that of tourist and tout. Westerners working with third world revolutionaries are simply tourists in disguise, 'people who keep up with "revolution" as with the theatre . . . who visit centers of revolution, but with return air tickets, the people for whom Malik's kind of Black Power was an exotic but safe brothel.'7 And revolutionaries like Malik (Michael X) are simply a new sort of hustler, picking up the right words, assuming the fashionable poses, and being rewarded with a season's patronage.

But the more persistent and wounding insinuation is that beneath all the rhetoric of liberation, the old relations of domination persist, and persist not only on the economic and social levels, in the form of new structures of exploitation and domination, but also on the psychological. It is no accident, surely, that *Guerrillas* opens on a world ringing with defiant black power slogans and closes with a single word from an older discourse, 'Massa.' For between the first lines and the last, Naipaul builds a case for seeing the discourse of liberation as nothing but a vehicle of self-deception, a way of denying realities and even desires that are more accurately expressed in the language of slavery. Naipaul's chief charge is that not even the people making the revolution believe that radical change is possible. 'Those guys down there don't know what they're doing,' declares Harry de Tunja, gazing out over the burning city, 'All this talk of independence, but they don't really believe that times have changed. They still feel they're just taking a chance, and that when the show is over somebody is going to go down there and start dishing out licks. And they half want it to be over, you know. They would go crazy if somebody tell them that this time nobody might be going down to dish out licks and pick up the pieces.' (pp. 216-217) The people are torn, in other words, between the dream of liberation — 'all this talk of independence' — and the older attitudes, social relations, and discourse of slavery, the world in which 'dishing out licks' is a familiar phrase and a feature of daily life.

Much of what Naipual says about the people's ambivalence to the idea of liberation has of course been said before by proponents of liberation. Frantz Fanon and Paulo Freire have both charted the psychology of colonized peoples in ways that anticipate Naipaul's dramatizations: both acknowledge the power of older constructions of reality and the battle that must be waged against these constructions during the struggle for political liberation. But because they view people and the societies they construct as unfinished structures, open to self-transformation, they do not reduce a dynamic process of struggle, as Naipaul does, to an eternal opposition, a matter of flattering dreams and dismal realities.

Naipaul argues not only that the people have no faith in the discourse of liberation, but also that this discourse contains within itself a dream of dependency. This dream, he suggests, lies hidden in the millenarian elements of liberation discourse, elements which he highlights in a number of ways in *Guerrillas*. '*In my father's house are many mansions, I remember that from my schooldays, they'd "bust your tail" with licks if you didn't go to church. But the house is full up now . . . there are no more mansions,*' writes Jimmy Ahmed to a friend. Then he continues, reflectively, '*I suppose like everybody else I fooled myself that there was a mansion waiting for me, but I didn't really fool myself*' (p. 94). Once again in this passage Naipaul juxtaposes a discourse of liberation with a discourse of domination, and once again he has a proponent of liberation testify to the deceptiveness of its promises, the weakness of its hold. But the passage also calls attention to the patriarchal elements of Christian liberation discourse, a discourse subsequently linked, in *Guerrillas*, to the more secular versions of liberation espoused by Jimmy in his public declarations. Naipaul draws the same damning connection between contemporary discourses of liberation, older millenarian discourses, and unacknowledged dependency in his essay on Michael X. In Trinidad, he writes, Black Power 'added something very old to rational protest: a mystical sense of race, a millenarian expectation of imminent redemption.'[8] This addition represents, he continues, 'a deep corruption: a wish to be granted a dispensation from the pains of development, an almost religious conviction that oppression can be turned into an asset, race into money. While the dream of redemption lasts, Negroes will continue to exist only that someone might be their leader.'[9] As Naipaul presents it, then, utopian and millenarian visions are not useful inducements to people mobilizing for struggle and sacrifice, not a way of imagining a social order in which the inevitable pains of labor could become productive. They are simply and inevitably ways in which people deceive themselves and testify to their moral unreadiness for freedom.

What is more, they make 'rational protest' and progress impossible. 'This place could be a paradise, man,' exclaims Harry de Tunja, slipping himself for a moment into the millenarian mode, 'if people really planned. We could have real industries. We don't have to let the Americans just take away our bauxite' (p. 156). Meredith Herbert agrees, but insists that the people 'want other things' and that their millenarian 'madness' makes even Harry's rational dream unrealistic.

Things, in other words, simply aren't going to change. The people are wise only in their self-suspicion, foolish in their hopes. Naipaul's pessimism, focused in *Guerrillas* on the countries of the Caribbean, expands in more recent works to encompass virtually the entire third world. Only India is exempted from the general vision of a world of 'half-made societies' that seem 'doomed to remain half-made.'[10]

Naipaul writes about contemporary movements of liberation with a vengefulness resulting from personal experience. Born in Trinidad in 1932, Naipaul grew up in a colonial world. His immediate environment was Indian, his birthplace a mainly Indian settlement where Hindu and Moslem festivals were celebrated regularly. His ancestors had been brought from India to Trinidad, both colonies in the British Empire, to cut sugar cane. His mother's family had risen, by the time Naipaul was born, to become wealthy landowners and local leaders; Naipaul's father, from a less successful family, was a journalist with an insecure post on an English-language newspaper. Naipaul was educated in colonial schools which whetted his appetite for England; when he won a government scholarship for higher study, he used it to read English at Oxford.[11]

In a remarkable passage of recollection, Naipaul recalls that the post-war politics of decolonization threw him into a 'political panic': 'To be a colonial was to know a kind of security; it was to inhabit a fixed world . . . But in the new world I felt the ground move below me. The new politics, the curious reliance of men on institutions they were yet working to undermine, the simplicity of beliefs and the hideous simplicity of actions, the corruption of causes . . . these were the things that began to preoccupy me.'[12] A great deal is revealed here in a very few words. Naipaul tells us that he knew himself as a 'colonial,' rather than as a Trinidadian or an Indian or an Englishman, and this makes sense, for only the imperial term encompasses the culturally diverse elements of his constitution. But for this very reason, the political attack on the British Empire became, for Naipaul, a personal attack on his identity and home. The attack was strong enough to induce a 'political panic' because it fell on a man haunted, as Naipaul tells us elsewhere, with a pathological 'fear of extinction.'[13] And it left Naipaul furious at its sponsors, the people who had demanded independence.

By the time Trinidad became independent, Naipaul had been in England for years. By the time England began refusing entry to East Africans of Indian extraction who held British passports, making it clear that the old imperial channels of movement were closed, Naipaul was established. But an old dread of being trapped in provincial Trinidad, among 'family and clan' and 'negroes,'[14] seems never to have left him. It emerges in *Guerrillas* entwined with the dream of vengeance against those who shook his world and go on shaking newer worlds. The imperatives of both dreams are satisfied in the disposition of Jane. She has no need to endure island life: her passport reads, as Naipaul reminds us more than once, '*Holder Has Right of Abode in the United Kingdom.*' But Jane doesn't appreciate her privileges; indeed, she flaunts and from Naipaul's perspective forfeits them by playing with the enemies of security. In killing her, then, Jimmy acts as Naipaul's surrogate. But as a figure of revolution, a force for chaos, Jimmy too is a target of vengeance. His punishment brings the two dreams together: an islander, he is left alone — abandoned — among enemies by a European patron who is returning to England; a revolutionary, he is made to suffer the consequences of his mad talk of liberation.

II

In a 1980 review of Naipaul's essay collection, *The Return of Eva Peron*, Joan Didion declares her sympathy with the harshest aspects of Naipaul's vision. She praises him as a man daring enough to refrain from offering even 'token applause in the interests of social progress'[15] and respectfully recapitulates his case against the discourse of social possibility. Naipaul, she writes,

> renders societies in which the dynamic of change opens new frontiers only for opportunists, 'half-made societies . . . doomed to remain half-made.' . . . He persists in translating underdeveloped into underequipped, undereducated, undone by imported magic and bor-

rowed images, metaphors, fantasies and applauded lies, fairy tales. He posits what has been the controlling historical trope of our time — the familiar image of the new world emerging from the rot of the old, the free state from the chrysalis of colonial decay — as a fairy tale, a rhetorical commodity, and his contempt for those who trade in it is almost total.[16]

Didion's talk of translation and tropes makes it clear that she sees Naipaul as fighting a discursive war, attempting to substitute one set of terms, with their connotations of permanent disability, for another, more hopeful, set. What emerges when this substitution is made, she suggests, is a rendered world 'dense with physical and social phenomena, brutally alive.' Naipaul displays this world, she proclaims, 'without regret or hope,' offering its 'intense radiance' as a kind of substitute for more traditional satisfactions: 'The actual world has for Naipaul a radiance that diminishes all ideas of it. The pink haze of the bauxite dust on the first page of *Guerrillas* tells us . . . who runs the island and for whose profit the island is run and at what cost to the life of the island this profit has historically been obtained, but all of this implicit information pales in the presence of the physical fact, the dust itself.'[17] In describing Naipaul Didion also describes herself: her vision, her objectives, and the rhetorical devices she uses to achieve them. In her political journalism and fiction she acknowledges that oppression exists, insists that it is permanent, and suggests that given this fact, the only authentic experience of transcendence lies in the apprehension of the actual in all its brutal radiance.

Didion began her career writing about local 'fairy tales', the California dreams of her childhood in *Run River* (1963), the California dreams of the sixties in *Slouching Towards Bethlehem* (1968). More recently, though, she has turned her attention to Central America, in *A Book of Common Prayer* (1977) and *Salvador* (1983), and to the American-dominated Pacific Basin, in *Democracy* (1984). But she is still exposing fairy tales. In each work an American woman receives abroad an education in 'the hardness of the world'[18] which reveals the foolishness of her American optimism and sense of exemption.

Didion characterizes Charlotte Douglas, the protagonist of *A Book of Common Prayer*, as a 'not atypical *norteamericana*.' 'As a child of the western United States,' the novel's narrator observes, 'she had been provided . . . with faith in the upward spiral of history . . . She understood that something was always going on in the world but believed that it would turn out all right' (pp. 56-57). In Boca Grande, the fictional Central American state to which Charlotte comes in the wake of innumerable personal disasters, she learns, perhaps, that this is not so. At least we learn it as we watch crates of desperately needed American vaccine being used as targets by depraved oligarchs, an 'empty revolution' (p. 254) playing itself out in blood, and Charlotte staying on to be arrested, tortured, and killed.

In *Democracy* a similar point is made in a similar manner. The heroine, who bears a striking resemblance to Charlotte Douglas, also comes to terms with reality in the third world. 'What difference did it make,' she muses in her Hong Kong outpost, while waiting for the CIA agent who is her lover to bring her daughter out of Vietnam, 'what difference did it make in the long run what she thought, or Harry thought, or Jessie or Adlai did? The world that night was full of people flying from place to place and fading in or out and there was no reason why [they] should be exempted from the general movement . . . Just because they were Americans.'[19] What is being dramatized here is the by now familiar argument that Vietnam shattered a national illusion of invulnerability, cancelled our collective subscription to the fairy tale of an 'American exemption'[20] from historical failure. Ever the ironist, Didion seems to have named her novel *Democracy* in part because it denies this American dream of privileged exemption.

Salvador too takes aim at national illusions, demonstrating clearly and effectively that the Reagan administration's rhetoric bears only an 'hallucinatory'[21] relation to actual events in El Salvador: ' "The new Salvadoran democracy," Enders was saying five months after the election, not long after Justice of the Peace Gonzalo Alonzo Garcia, the twentieth prominent Christian Democrat to be kidnapped or killed since the election, had been dragged from his house in San Cayetano Itepeque by fifteen armed men, "is doing what it is supposed to do — bringing a broad spectrum of forces and factions into a functioning democratic system." '[22] This is effective political polemic, and there is much of it in *Salvador*. But here, as in the novels, Didion's disdain for a discourse of progress which has often been used to sponsor oppression is extended to all affirmations of social possibility, including those which are inspiring the oppressed to rebel.

A Book of Common Prayer, for instance, portrays a social reality in which all political parties and discourses are contemptible. At home in California Charlotte's daughter Marin is swallowed by the newly fashionable discourse of liberation much as her mother was by an older 'faith in the upward spiral of history.' The new discourse breaks violently into the verbal field of the novel, as it does in *Guerrillas*, but this time in the form of a taped communiqué, read by Marin, in which her group explains why it has set off a bomb, hijacked an airplane, and blown it up. '*All class enemies must suffer exemplary punishment*' (p. 76), Marin delcares; '*We shall reply to repression with liberation. We shall reply to the terrorism of the dictatorship with the terrorism of the revolution*' (p. 78). In Didion as in Naipaul, the discourse of liberation is represented only by such shrill and fatuous pronouncements as these.

The third world radicals portrayed in the novel are as offensive in their behavior, motives, and pronouncements as Marin. Decadent oligarchs or intellectuals, they stir up trouble to stave off boredom or satisfy vanity, and the revolutions they make have nothing to do with the ideas they espouse. Indeed, they can hardly be called revolutions at all, as the narrator, a member of the nation's most power family, makes clear. For her, they represent only an all-too-familiar family drama: 'The *guerrilleros* would stage their "expropriations" and leave their communiques about the "People's Revolution" and everyone would know who was financing the *guerilleros* but for a while no one would know for whose benefit the *guerrilleros* were being financed. In the end the *guerrilleros* would all be shot and the true players would be revealed.

Mirabile dictu, People we knew.' (p. 214). Didion suggests, as Naipaul does, that there are no authentically progressive forces in the Caribbean Basin, and that none will emerge: 'Boca Grande is. Boca Grande was. Boca Grande shall be' (p. 244), chants the narrator, as if the nation (The Great Mouth or Maw, in English) were a dark devouring deity.

In *Salvador* Didion mounts virtually the same sweeping attack on all notions of social possibility. The whole book can be read as an extended ironic play on its own title, also the name, of course, of the country it discusses. 'Salvador', the name given to a divine agent of redemption, expresses a hope which Didion deplores. She plays mockingly on the term throughout the book, referring to Reagan, for instance, as '*el salvador del Salvador.*'[23] 'Solucion,' another important term in the lexicon of hope, is similarly savaged. The people Didion most admires don't talk, she remarks, about solutions, and those who do are dismissed with contempt. These people, Didion declares inaccurately, are 'mainly somewhere else, in Mexico [the left] or Panama or Washington.'[24] This distance keeps them from seeing or enables them to deny what is apparent to Didion: El Salvador, like the fictional Boca Grande, isn't going to change. In a conjugation that echoes the 'Boca Grande is' chant from *A Book of Common Prayer*, Didion informs the reader that 'if it is taken for granted in Salvador that the government kills, it is also taken for granted that the other side kills; that everyone has killed, everyone kills now, and, if the history of the place suggests any pattern, everyone will continue to kill.'[25] Messages of despair are everywhere, even in the Metropolitan Cathedral, where a less confidently disillusioned visitor might pause to reflect on the hopeful words and luminous example of the late Archbishop Romero. The message of the cathedral, though, for Joan Didion, is that 'at this time and in this place the light of the world could be construed as out, off, extinguished.'[26]

It is not political hope then, or even a quest for signs of hope, that produces Didion's preoccupation with third world settings and situations. On the contrary, she turns to those scenes and settings in order to find images for a discourse of political despair. Or rather for two discourses, one fashioned around the familiar tale of apocalyptic disintegration, the other around the notion of enduring barbarism.

Didion as much as acknowledges this in *Democracy*. The narrator of that novel, a character named Didion, recalls that 'in 1975 time was no longer just quickening but collapsing, falling in on itself, the way a disintegrating star contracts into a black hole.' The 'falling capitals' of Southeast Asia provided then, she continues, 'a graphic instance of the black hole effect,' a way of representing a particular experience of history. Or they did, at least, for her: 'I said "falling," ' she recalls, 'Many of the students to whom I spoke said "being liberated." ' Because she felt she already understood their historical significance, the narrator of *Democracy* studied reports of these falling capitals in a certain way: 'I would skim the stories on policy and fix instead on details: the cost of a visa to leave Cambodia in the weeks before Phnom Penh closed . . . the colors of the landing lights for the helicopters on the roof of the American embassy.'[27] It is from just such a perspective and in much the same manner that the Didion of *Salvador* examines the country she visits. The ideas and interests of the various warring parties are dismissed as insignificant, the physical features of the war itself brought forward to confirm an already established vision of a world without hope.

If there is something melodramatic about Didion's vision of the world going down in flames, there is also something sentimental and familiarly 'American' about it. Having 'seen through' the American myths of guaranteed progress and special exemption, Didion does not accept the responsibility of mature political analysis, and so attempt a particularized vision of the complex social world she might have discovered. Instead, she simply affirms the counter-myths of apolcalypse and punishment. The world turned upside down is still the same old un-nuanced world of myth, now gone all dark and demonic. And Didion's tone is still the same old, offensively confident, arrogantly dismissive tone.

What is more, there remains a certain nostalgia for what has been lost, a certain inclination to cast America and Americans as benign innocents suddenly confronting 'the hardness of the world.' In *Salvador*, for instance, Didion takes it for granted that American policy makers have simply been duped by El Salvador's crafty reactionaries, 'drawn, both by a misapprehension of the local rhetoric and by the manipulation of our own rhetorical weaknesses, into a game we did not understand, a play of power in a political tropic alien to us.'[28] And in both *Salvador* and *Democracy* she balances her more cynical assessments of American action — assessments which cast Americans as 'players' in an international game with no ethical dimension — with images of American officials doing their best to help. Thus Ambassador Deane Hinton is seen struggling manfully 'to keep Salvadorans from killing one another,'[29] but his equally manful efforts to provide the government with the means to kill its opponents go unrecorded. And the hero of *Democracy*, a CIA agent who speaks the morally sanitized argot of the Company, spends much of his time on stage rescuing various 'refugees,' including the wealthy protagonist and her daughter. Didion's escape from the flattering American illusions she deplores is far from complete.

Didion's apocalyptic propensities and aversion to the discourse of social possibility reflect important early experiences. When she writes, in the review of Naipaul cited above, of 'societies in which the dynamic of change opens new frontiers only for opportunists,' she is referring to the third world. But the phrase aptly describes the post-war Californian society depicted in her first novel. *Run River* portrays the decline of a family of wealthy ranchers in the Sacramento Valley, a decline ascribed both to internal failings and to the emergence after World War II of a new ruling class linked to industry, real estate, and democratic rhetoric. When the patriarch of the family loses his seat in the legislature, it is to an 'Okie' who talks of 'the new California . . . the California of jobs and benefits and milk and honey and 160 acres for everybody equably distributed, the California that was promised us yessir I mean in Scripture.'[30] And when the patriarch's daughter, having married into another old ranching family, takes a lover, he is an unscrupulous speculator from out of state who has been drawn to California by the promise of 'the biggest boom this country had ever seen.'[31] The violence this man works on the two old families is made to represent the larger violence his fellow 'developers' visit on the community and the land: post-war California is portrayed as a place where politicians spouting promises of liberation open the way only for rapacious opportunists.

The social experience of privilege, dislocation, and loss dramatized in *Run River* seems to have been Didion's own. She comes from one of the old families of the Sacramento Valley, a wealthy farming and ranching clan which was already mourning the loss of its 'finest hour' when Didion was born and was further upset by the post-war boom. The atmosphere of family life during her childhood was, Didion recalls, one of melancholy and 'Chekhovian loss.'[32] Perhaps these experiences help explain her interest in other embattled oligarchs further down the Pacific Rim. In any event, the contemporary calls for liberation she excoriates in her work must evoke for her, as they do for Naipaul, the cries of older, more intimate, antagonists.

In a revealing exchange published some years ago in the *Paris Review*, an interviewer asks Didion, 'What misapprehensions, illusions and so forth have you had to struggle against in your life?' 'All kinds,' Didion replies,

> For example, it may not be true that people who try to fly always burst into flames and fall. That may not be true at all. In fact people *do fly*, and land safely. But I don't really believe that. I still see Icarus.[33]

Icarus alone, without Daedalus who flew on and made good his escape from captivity — Icarus is all Didion can see. And seeing only Icarus, she hears only madness or malevolence in all invitations to fly. Hence the works we have examined, to which the best rebuttal, perhaps, is Didion's own: 'In fact people *do fly* and land safely.'

III

There is nothing 'dialogic' about Naipaul's and Didion's fiction, no strong elaboration and fair competition of antagonistic discourses. The languages of liberation are introduced only to be parodied, humiliated, disgraced. *Guerrillas,* Didion writes, is a kind of curse: it is Naipaul's way of 'wishing bad cess . . . to all those who continue to simplify the world and reduce other men — not only the Negro — to a cause.'[34] But as we have seen, the way of Didion and Naipaul works cruel reductions of its own, the reduction of a complex human cause to a set of slogans, mentally unbalanced and deluded human beings, and empty revolution. The result may indeed have the bitter eloquence of a heart-felt curse, but it does not lack a curse's savage one-sidedness.

No such spirit of reduction and revenge dominates *A Flag for Sunrise,* Robert Stone's powerful novel of revolution in yet another fictional Central American nation. On the contrary, Stone succeeds in 'giving voice' both to those who speak articulately for liberation and to their opponents. He draws out the discourse of liberation reduced to a few slogans by Naipaul and Didion, and draws in the discourse of despair, situating it within the world of the novel, where it can be interrogated.

A Flag for Sunrise charts the paths of three Americans as they are drawn into the revolution. Frank Holliwell, an alcoholic anthropology professor 'without beliefs, without hope — either for himself or for the world'[35] is the most persistently present of the three. His despair is at least partly a result of his experiences in Vietnam, where he did some work for the CIA. Now the agency would like some help again. Frank has been invited to deliver a lecture in Compostela, a Central American nation: would he be willing to stop over in the neighboring state of Tecan for a few days to check on some American Catholics who seem to be mixing politics with religion? Holliwell declines at first, but by the time his sojourn in Compostela is over he has found reasons to go on to Tecan. 'It would be strange,' he thinks, 'to see people who believed in things, and acted in the world according to what they believed. It would be different' (p. 101). And so, knowing better but telling himself, like Naipaul's Jane and Didion's Charlotte, that he is only a tourist, he heads south into trouble.

His contacts in Tecan are of two kinds. He is taken in, treated as 'one of us,' by the counter-revolutionary community, who assume that he is on assignment from Washington. But he is also taken in by Sister Justin Feeny, the protagonist of the second narrative line. Justin, a young American nursing nun working in the mission Holliwell has been asked to investigate, is the beautiful vessel of commitment and hope that he has been looking for. But for this very reason she is also the enemy he has been sent to ferret out, an active collaborator in revolution. Unwilling to abandon her to his teammates on the right or to commit himself to the struggle that ennobles her, Holliwell tries to play both sides and winds up betraying everyone. Tecan explodes, the revolution triumphs, and Holliwell survives, but his spirit is darker than ever. Adrift in an open boat with Pablo Tabor, a Coast Guard deserter and the third central figure in the novel, Holliwell reflects on his experience: 'He had undertaken a little assay at the good fight,' he concludes, 'and found that neither good nor fight was left to him. Instead of quitting when he was ahead, he had gone after life again and they had shown him life and made him eat it' (p. 426).

If Justin embodies possibilities that Naipaul and Didion deny, Frank Holliwell embodies their denial. His perspective resembles Naipaul's: he disapproves both of the status quo of oppression and of those who proclaim their determination to transcend it. Nobody in the novel, not even the CIA agents and U.S. military advisers, has any respect for Tecan's government. Captain Tom Zecca, a Vietnam veteran attached to the embassy in Tecan, admits that, 'there's a basic, quite justified piss-off all over the country . . . anyone with a brain or an honest buck to turn hates the government' (p. 167). And yet if a revolution breaks out, Zecca is ready to work with the Guardia: 'We put this government in for our own interests,' he explains, 'We trained the Guardia . . . The Guardia will have American weapons and support' (p. 168). Zecca justifies his own participation in this sordid business by proclaiming that he has acted honorably. 'I conducted that fucking war honorably,' he says of Vietnam, 'I took an oath . . . I fulfilled it and I fucking fulfilled it without compromising myself' (p. 169). But Holliwell isn't buying any such rationalizations:

> Excuse me . . . Do you expect to conduct your career in one American-sponsored shithole after another, partying with their ruling class, advising their conscripts in counterinsurgency and over-seeing their armaments, and not compromise your oath or your honor? Because that sounds very tricky to me. (p. 170)

Although Holliwell disapproves of the status quo in Tecan, he is not ready to support those who would change it. Marty Nolan, the CIA agent who arranges his trip to Tecan, asks him a key question:

> 'What side are you on then? Do you really think the other guys are going to resolve social contradictions and make everything O.K.? Worker in the morning, hunter in the afternoon, scholar in the evening—do you really believe that's on, Frank?'
> 'No,' Holliwell said. (p. 23)

What he does believe in is a world much like that described by Didion in her review of Naipaul's *The Return of Eva Peron*, a world of aimless physical processes and endlessly deluded humans. Within the frame of such a vision, the hopeful appear to be among the most deluded and dangerous creatures of all: 'How could they?' Holliwell wonders,

> How could they convince themselves that in this whirling pool of existence, providence was sending them a message? Seeing visions, hearing voices, their eyes awash in their own juice — living on their own and borrowed hallucinations, banners, songs, kiddie art posters, phantom worship. The lines of bayonets, the marching rhythms, incense or torches, chanting, flights of doves — it was hypnosis. And *they* were the vampires. The world paid in blood for their articulate delusions. (p. 244)

This is as eloquent and disturbing a denunciation of the dream of liberation as any offered by Naipaul or Didion. But in Stone's work, as opposed to theirs, such denunciations are themselves denounced, and with equal power. Holliwell, trying to persuade Justin to abandon the 'articulate delusion' of liberation, insists that 'God doesn't work through history . . . That's a delusion of the Western mind' and that 'the things people do don't add up to an edifying story. There aren't any morals to this confusion we're living in. I mean, you can make yourself believe any sort of fable about it, They're all bullshit' (pp. 387-88). Justin responds by suggesting that Holliwell himself is story-telling. 'We don't think much alike,' she remarks, 'I don't have your faith in despair' (p. 388). And she goes on to wonder out loud about Frank's motives: 'I think despair and giving up are like liquor to you. You get high on it. But it's not for me Frank, I don't have the temperament. I don't have the sophistication to bring it off' (p. 389).

Like Didion and Naipaul, Stone does a better job of drawing counter-revolutionary characters than revolutionary ones. His portraits of U.S. embassy personnel, CIA agents and contract men, and Tecanecan Guardia officers are superb. Like Didion and Naipaul too, Stone seems to feel most confident working with bitter cynics and the mentally disturbed: Holliwell resembles Roche and Pablo Tabor has a good deal in common with Naipaul's Jimmy Ahmed. But Stone, unlike Didion and Naipaul, also creates intelligent and principled radicals, people who believe in things and act in the world according to what they believe. Like her sisters in the darker novels of Naipaul and Didion, Justin is a privileged Westerner who comes south and learns about the hardness of the world. Like them, she projects an aura of inviolability that infuriates the dark men she encounters. And like them she suffers violation: one can see here the tracings of a sexual fantasy which gets written out endlessly in our culture. But unlike Didion's Charlotte or Naipaul's Jane, Justin comes south to work, puts in years of effort, and finally discovers a community, and a way of life, that she can respect. Stone portrays the revolutionaries who contact her, Christians and secular leftists alike, as strong, intelligent, and reflective people. And he allows them to triumph, the revolution to succeed. Through Justin, then, Stone testifies to the existence of personal qualities, social forces, and political possibilities that are denied in Didion's and Naipaul's fiction. And by so doing he lends a legitimacy to the discourse of liberation which they vehemently deny.

A Flag for Sunrise is almost certainly the first North American novel to try to communicate the spirit and speech and political impact of liberation theology. Stone, who was raised a Catholic and educated in Catholic schools, is still struggling with the faith. Of working class origins and with roots in the sixties, he is also struggling with the dreams of the left. He went to Vietnam as a journalist in 1971 prepared to see the Viet Cong and North Vietnamese as heroes, but became disillusioned when he discovered that they too were committing atrocities.[36] The rise of the Christian left in Latin America seems to have rekindled social hopes that the Vietnam experience all but destroyed. And it brought to realization an alliance which Stone was dreaming of as early as 1963, when in *A Hall of Mirrors* he described a wild attack on a phantasmagoric right wing rally by two utterly isolated fanatics, one an old red and the other a Christian. In that earlier novel, both characters are portrayed with a great deal of contempt, and their assault is ill-advised and ineffectual; Stone is clearly both entertaining a dream and mocking himself for doing so. He must have found it intriguing, then, when secular leftists and Christians began working together in Latin America.

In *A Flag for Sunrise* his hopes for the movement are expressed through a number of characters. When, at the beginning of the novel, Justin confesses to another nun that she plans to leave her order, the woman replies, 'Justin — something special is happening now. The church is really turning back to Jesus. It's gonna be great and it would be a shame to miss out on it' (p. 34). Justin pays a dreadful price for staying on, but her final words, drawn from a favorite Biblical text of liberation theology, testify to the power of the calling she has accepted. And even the rugged old communist who is orchestrating the Tecanecan revolution is excited by the movement. He remembers with regret fighting against utopian Christians in the Spanish Civil War, 'men who in their hearts believed much of what we believed, who should by rights have been shoulder to shoulder with us' (p. 208). And he predicts to a skeptical comrade that the Christians now joining the revolution may become 'the best revolutionaries, the first Communists' (p. 208).

If Stone writes out of a strong sympathy for Christian leftists, he remains skeptical of the very millenarian impulses that appeal to him. And if his work testifies to the appeal of a Christian and Marxist synthesis, it also illuminates the difficulties of integration, the radically unfinished and all-but-unimaginable nature of the project. The play of voices in his book is likely to remind some readers on the left of the play of voices in their own minds, the ongoing dialogue between doubt and hope, religious kerygma and rational analysis. To have captured this play with so much power and complexity is a tremendous achievement.

IV

Yet even in its account of Justin, Stone's story is unable to disengage completely from the more completely tainted vision of Didion and Naipaul. In tracing the treatment of liberation through *Guerrillas, A Book of Common Prayer,* and *A Flag for Sunrise,* I have noted but not explored the fact that all three tell a similar story: in each a privileged white woman is captured by dark men who torture and murder her. (In two, the woman is 'delivered' to her persecutors by her white lover.) This is, of course, a story which transports the protagonist, and her audience, toward bondage rather than toward liberation. And it is a familiar story, a neocolonial version of tales sponsored by older forms of oppression, in which the dark men were slaves or 'natives' and the whites slaveowners or settlers. A basic function of the story is to legitimize oppression by painting the oppressed as savage, evil, the enemy.

In Naipaul's and Didion's fiction the elaboration of arguments about liberation within a drama of bondage makes perfect sense, for both writers hold that liberation is illusion, bondage reality. But in Stone's work, where liberation is taken seriously, there is a tension which Stone only partly resolves by transforming the basic story. Justin is captured, tortured, murdered, but in the course of her suffering, at the very edge of death, she experiences liberation through faith. Stone finds a way, in other words, to loosen the grip of the dark dream he is recounting. But he loosens it only slightly, for Justin's liberation coincides with her bondage and is realized only at the moment of death. (And although the revolution, like Justin, is said to triumph, it does so off stage: Stone shows us only the piles of rebel corpses, the Guardia torture cell.) Furthermore, the basic distribution of roles within the drama remains the same: a white woman, the vessel of beauty and morality, is still turned over to dark men, the vessels of evil. Stone's good Tecanecans are all one-dimensional characters; Lieutenant Campos, Justin's tormenter, is a vivid presence, the very quintessence of evil.

It would seem, then, that once the novelist surrenders to this particular story, lends his energies to recounting it, it becomes difficult, if not impossible, for him to dramatize *social* liberation. And it also becomes impossible to present a balanced view of third world men. To tell this story, then, is to reinforce attitudes of fear and hatred and hopelessness all of which in turn underwrite the status-quo of oppression. Stone alone of the three novelists we've discussed clearly wants to oppose these attitudes and policies, but he will have to break the spell of bondage over his own imagination in order to do so.

Notes

1. Don Delillo, *The Names* (New York, 1982), p. 58.
2. Frederic Jameson, rev. of *The Names*, by Don Delillo, *The Minnesota Review*, N.S.22 (Spring 1984), p. 116
3. Quoted in Stuart Hall, 'The Battle for Socialist Ideas in the 1980s,' *The Socialist Register*, ed. Ralph Miliband and John Saville (London, 1982) p. 12.
4. *The Wretched of the Earth* (New York 1966), p. 30.
5. *Guerrillas* (New York, 1976). Subsequent references to this edition appear in the text.
6. Edward W.Said, 'Bitter Dispatches from the Third World,' *The Nation* (30 May 1980), p. 523.
7. V.S.Naipaul, 'Michael X and the Black Power Killings in Trinidad,' in *The Return of Eva Peron* (New York, 1981), p. 31.
8. Naipaul, *Eva*, p. 41.
9. Naipaul, *Eva*, p. 74.
10. V.S.Naipaul, 'Conrad's Darkness,' *Eva*, p. 233.
11. V.S. Naipaul, 'Prologue to an Autobiography,' in *Finding the Center* (New York, 1984).
12. Naipaul, *Eva*, p. 233.
13. Naipaul, *Center*, p. 72.
14. Naipaul, *Center*, p. 32.
15. Joan Didion, 'Without Regret or Hope,' *The New York Review of Books*, 12 June 1980, p. 21.
16. Didion, 'Regret,' p. 20.
17. Didion, 'Regret,' p. 21.
18. Joan Didion, *A Book of Common Prayer* (New York, 1978), p. 243. Subsequent references to this edition appear in the text.
19. Joan Didion, *Democracy* (New York, 1984), p. 208.
20. Didion, *Democracy*, p. 211.
21. Joan Didion, *Salvador* (New York, 1983), p. 39.
22. Didion, *Salvador*, pp. 90-91.
23. Didion, *Salvador*, p. 29.
24. Didion, *Salvador*, p. 35.
25. Didion, *Salvador*, p. 34.
26. Didion, *Salvador*, p. 79.
27. Didion, *Democracy*, pp. 72-73.
28. Didion, *Salvador*, p. 96.
29. Didion, *Salvador*, p. 97.
30. Joan Didion, *Run River* (New York, 1978), p. 42.
31. Didion, *River*, p. 147.
32. Joan Didion, 'Notes of a Native Daughter,' in *Slouching Towards Bethlehem* (New York, 1981), p. 174.
33. 'Joan Didion,' *Paris Review*, 74 (Fall-Winter 1978), p. 162.

202

34. Didion, 'Regret,' p. 20.

35. Robert Stone, *A Flag for Sunrise* (New York, 1981), p.24. Subsequent references to this edition appear in the text.

36. Charles Ruas, 'A Talk with Robert Stone,' *New York Times Book Review* (18 October 1981), pp. 34-36.

3. Liberation Theology in Latin America:

Dispensations Old and New

Paul Buhle and Thomas Fiehrer

In 1654, the missionary Antonio Mavila addressed the Captain-General of Guatemala in eloquent defense of his Salvadoran 'poor charges' and in thorough condemnation of the presiding *alcalde,* José del Portal:

> Sir, His Majesty does not assign his *alcaldes* to these provinces so that they might proceed destroyers and scavengers of the earth's goods and benefactors of the sweat and blood of the poor. Apparently, the *alcalde* of this province fails to understand the *cedula* last directed by His Majesty. For somehow the very priesthood, with its doctrines and moral authority, counts for nothing. The religious, with his example and admonishments, reaps no fruits. The sacred is shorn of its immunity; the noble of its due respect; and the proper is out of use. Rights are ignored, while the poor are trampled under. The law of both God and His Majesty is violated and contorted because this is the will of José del Portal. [1]

The multi-layered appeal to authority and the complaint against abuse of both traditions and morals is classic in the Latin American vernacular. Substituting the Papacy for the Spanish crown, the words could have been repeated almost literally by Salvadoran Archbishop Oscar Romero, before his 1981 assasination at the hands of today's expropriators. Not far ahead of Mavila's day, the conditions of the masses would dramatically worsen with the conversion of subsistence land to export staples (notably indigo), with halting reform, swift change in political perceptions, and sharp population growth. [2] Then, as in the twentieth-century conversion of cropland to coffee and cotton, semi-starvation and unrest mounted. Likewise, the middle class, small and fragile, could not find its way. And the sole protector of the masses remained — the Church.

Such are the continuities in a region so different from European and North American social organization and *mentalité* that five centuries of intimate contact have failed to reduce the distance. No wonder U.S. policy experts from liberal to conservative betray a fundamental ignorance of the undiminished difference; no wonder arch-reactionaries view the appearance of Liberation Theology as a mere smokescreen, while left-wing support movements find Revolutionary Christology ideologically impenetrable.[3] Nothing in the bourgeois democratic tradition explains the continuity of the Latin American corporate state through colonization, de-colonization, neo-colonialism and insurrectionary transition. Nothing familiar allows us to view eras of relative pluralism within that larger history and its tradition as mere fragmentation, in which the dissolution of old power formations paves the way for a newly emergent new corporate synthesis.[4] Europeans may gaze backward at their feudal traditions; but what do we make of a Radical Reformation where the rebels situate themselves strategically within the Church's demographic future and where the Papal Father joins them, however ambiguously, in condemning the earthly Empire? The apparent Vatican shifts, now Right, now Left, now Right again, take place against an almost unchanged religious ideology: some of the world's most sophisticated revolutionary movements rally themselves under the flag of First Century millennialism.

To paraphrase Argentinian José Míguez Bonino, leading light of Liberation Theology, our present task is all prolegomenon[5]: we will attempt here to describe and place the specific economic-social and religious processes underway in Latin America in their special relation to both the widely misunderstood Iberian influence and to the enduring force of the world market. Liberation Theology may then be identified as a loose and shifting synthesis of religious, aesthetic and political moments; then, too, we may suggest the paths which a comprehensive analysis would have to take towards a larger perspective.

The key determinants of the unique synthesis which constituted Iberian colonialism may be succintly summarized: Counter-Reformation, acculturation, and social-religious syncretism. The omnipresence of the clergy in the emergent Spanish nation-state, at once institutionally jealous and other-worldly, shaped the colonial adventure from the beginning. The character of Iberian society — Christian, Muslim, and (until the Inquisition) overtly Jewish, prepared even the most dogmatic Church zealots to accept forms of essential cultural diversity. The overwhelming preponderance of Indians, Africans and later mestizos over identifiable Europeans in the New World, and the tenacity with which the indigenous inhabitants clung to their cultural forms, necessitated the construction of a syncretic religious practice, with Christian symbols as stand-ins for little-altered beliefs.[6] In the long run, the unwillingness of the indigenous to accept a materialist world combined with the willingness of the Church to accept the legitimacy of the native idiom resulted in a shared suffering and, eventually, a common protest.[7] Thus, by one of modern history's strangest turnabouts, the Church of the Inquisition and the culture of revanchist reaction become the seedbeds for the revolt against the fruits of bourgeois pluralism.

In Iberian society the second half of the sixteenth century and the beginning of the seventeenth saw an increase in the social power of the Church, both cause and effect of the clerical enrollment and acquisition of expanding real estate holdings. Inducement to join religious orders may not be wholly explicable in modern terms. The Counter Reformation, with its stout infusion of Renaissance Humanism, offered an inestimable stimulus. Newly reformed orders, (the Observant Franciscans, the Augustinians and Carmelites) alongside new ones such as the Jesuits, drew a spiritual elite to monastic life. But all classes of Iberian society showed a decided propensity for religious life; and despite reform initiatives, the Church remained what it had long been, a center of idealism, corruption and privilege.

To the second sons of aristocrats, excluded from inheritance by primogenitur, a vocation was an honorable career with upward mobility. For the mass of extremely poor in this period, holy orders offered an escape from misery, a form of social insurance and a surprisingly egalitarian opportunity for advancement. A remarkable number of humble men attained the pinnacle of influence through ability, chance and favoritism. Peasants often sacrificed all to prepare one son, through university training, to qualify for competition as prebend or other benefice. The widespread contempt for both business (associated with Jews) and manual labor (associated with moriscos) left no other route in any case. For all these reasons, then, in all their admixtures and permutations some 200,000 clerics can be counted in 1625 Spain alone, out of a total eight million population, drawing down into their expanded ranks something like one-third of all land rents in the nation.[8]

Whether in Spain or the American empire, the Church showed two contrary tendencies which encompassed such a range of the total society's behavior and personnel that we still gasp at the consequences. At the top, high office in the secular clergy remained for the elite; as a consequence archiepiscopal palaces and other amenities became so sumptuous and corrupt as to lose their religious significance entirely. Meanwhile, at the bottom of the hierarchy many priests retained exemplary practices. Yet simultaneously, as religious life became tantamount to living without labor, considerable numbers of other priests without religious intent or interests cohabited with concubines ('the devil's mules'), especially in the Americas, and generally made the good life accessible to themselves: *Me comí como un señor cura*, 'I ate like a priest,' was for centuries a customary post-repast comment in Cuba.

Meanwhile, convents burgeoned with the unmarried daughters of the nobility, generally deposited without their consent. Early widows made other nuns, and a relative minority entered vocations out of commitment to religious ideals. The luxury and worldly activity within sophisticated convents could be far removed indeed from contemplation and penitence; more common still was the practice of *galantéo de monjas*, paying court to the nuns, a romantic escapade which made for frequent escapes and seductions.

So, it was not surprising that the parish priest and monk enjoyed center stage in the satirical literature of the seventeeth century and the reformist critiques of morality during the Enlightenment. Philip II's determination to expressly prohibit the coexistence of the sexes in religious establishments was abandoned when it was determined 'not to oppress clergy any more than other men.' Popular faith so buoyed up the social system that no amount of scandal could undo the Church, unworthy clergy being the proof of an almost fond human frailty. In this clerical society, common immorality could actually bind the clergy to the masses.

Yet these bulky ecclesiastical bodies also proved a heavy social burden, of course, oppressing the secular working class to maintain a sufficient surplus, degrading all labor by way of religious pretensions. Physical misery proliferated rapidly throughout Spain's old and new world during the sixteenth and seventeenth centuries on the level of individual behavior. At the same time, exemplary sacrifice and powerful public imagery, the Church's role in providing non-punitive hospices, orphanages, hospitals and asylums to all localities created just the opposite impression. Monasteries throughout the Imperium practiced the tradition of 'sopa boba,' or dummy's soup, a thin broth prepared by the brothers and accompanied with huge baskets of bread — generally the sole sustenance for thousands of destitutes thronging the narrow streets of the Old and New World. Daily the great gates of the monastery swung open to the sound of the Angelus, permitting the exit of monks in daily contact with beggars, ascetics, war veterans and numerous students.[9]

Fanatical attachment to the images of charity and feminine humility (*i.e.*, the virgin-goddess) suffused these and other rituals. In some places, notably Mexico, she replaced a pantheon of feminine deities suppressed by the missionaries and the Inquisition.[10] Events and occasions such as canonizations, the transfer of relics, and the celebrations in honor of martyred members of religious orders might last days and involve the influx of pilgrims into small towns and villages. Meanwhile, in spite of Church efforts to control the multiplication of mystical and occult manifestations, the number of stigmatics steadily increased, especially among humble women; while *alumbrismo* or illuminism, a cult flourishing in reaction to Protestant emphasis on 'good works,' devolved into a pure contemplation rivalling the old gnostic heresies, Jewish Hasidism, and Islamic dervishes. From illuminism came not only legendary seductions, but also demonism and sorcery. With a widespread phenomenon of possession, Exorcism likewise flourished. But the Inquisitional courts were rather less severe than their secular counterparts.[11] With Protestantism effectively exorcized, the Church lacked substantial victims, although a few hundred put to death over several centuries sufficed to terrorize the fearful masses.[12] In any case, the overall result of all these tendencies and practices, like the public religious ceremonies that temporarily reduced rich and poor to the same spiritual status, was to undercut the normative basis for commercial capitalism.

It may seem perverse to suggest that a hierarchical society with a totalitarian centralization of religious hegemony actually promoted a sort of democratic ethos verging on anarchy. But the parallel structure of ecclesiastical institutions alongside and within the social hierarchy at the very least constituted an ambiguously anti-bourgeois force. That force had a special purpose (or 'mission') on the fringes of the Empire where utopian expectations and cruel realities exceeded the range of possibility within Europe.[13]

The Franciscans, for example, The New World's first missionaries, had been schooled in the apostolic traditions of Joachim.[14] Themselves products of the Inquisitorial bloodbath which swept potential reforms back into religious orders, they saw in the propertyless open spaces and innocent communal virtue of the natives, the lost tribes of Israel, *i.e.*, the last chance to build the terrestrial paradise before the divine curtain lifted upon the world stage for good.[15] Here the mendicant orders would both teach and learn, re-establishing society in the primitive simplicity of the early Church.

New World frontiers beckoned with messianic visions for natives, too — especially as their other options dwindled. And for those aborigines who survived the pestilence of the post-Conquest, few choices remained. The Tupinambas of Brazil, disoriented and disrespectful of the Portugese, trekked in 1539 from the east coast of the continent to the Peruvian lowlands, where they encountered the greedy Spaniards. Besieged on all sides, they understandably acceded to Jesuit conversion, a path other tribes followed with a mixture of resignation and authentic chiliasm. Other natives fled from their first encounters with the invaders back to traditional communities, often utilizing the techniques and language of European agriculture and crafts. Still others remained, adopting European ways, alien speech, dress, manners and religious behavior, including the exploitation of fellow Indians and a host of previously unknown European vices.[16] Pressures such as labor exactions, tribute and forced contributions compelled them to consider ladinization as a survival mechanism. From the beginning of the Iberian colonization, moreover, as Frank Tannenbaum once quipped, 'The Spaniards conquered the Indian empires, but the native women conquered the conquerors.' Across the continent the first full-blown colonial generation sprang from the loins of white fathers and native mothers. From cuisine to clothing, the domestic skills of the outnumbering females left a decisive mark upon the entire culture of the descendants. The catastrophic population reduction of the early years — in Mexico alone, a reduction from perhaps twenty-five millions in 1520 to a lone million in 1640 — guaranteed a mixed order.[17] Even where, as in El Salvador, strict laws and segregation of Indian communes from other communities forbade miscegenation, human contact gradually bred amalgamation. New communities of ladinos appeared along the roadways alive with the cries of muleteers, teamsters and herdsmen connecting distant villages to the capital, diffusing the emergent 'creole' culture and their own relation with the thriving profit system.

At no other time, not even during the Crusades, had European millenarians such an expanse of territory and such pliable 'children of nature' to prepare a heaven on earth. The Englishman Thomas More had located Utopia somewhere in the Western Hemisphere. And although the Humanism of Erasmus and others enjoyed a vogue of no more than a half-century in the Hispanic world, it issued directly in the creation of myriad 'millenial kingdoms' throughout the American hemisphere under the tutelage of the mendicant orders. Later on, the Jesuits established the most business-like agricultural enterprises and the most elite of creole educational institutions. Long-robed holy men interpreted the meditations and prophetic visions of Spanish mystics, while proselytizing tirelessly from the banks of tropical torrents and desert wasteland oases. Communalist experiments flourished among the Guaraní in the Paraná and Paraguay valleys in the spirit of the Counter-Reformation.[18]

During the following centuries, the formulae for conversion and salvation became fixed and stylized. The religious frontier — violent, dominated by a merciless nature — held predators larger and more fearsome than any known in Europe, but by the same token every flower could be held a world of wonder. Here, Renaissance men and noble savages dwelt together (at least in myth) with monastic certitude. So the surviving sermons and guides to spiritual exercises, the literary and institutional records, tell a story starkly different from the contemporary Reformation in Europe and North America. The Puritan obsession with Satan, his wiles and images in the forest, is here transmuted into humility before forces great and inscrutable, indulgence with human failings and emphasis upon God's equal salvation of all willing human types predominate.[19]

Likewise, while the Reformation cast mediaries aside, most notably in England, the Catholic counter-tendency responded with a tidal wave of grandiose artistic output, the baroque and rococo extremities found so often in Latin American ecclesiastical structures. Thousands of craftsmen went scrambling atop their scaffolds in a burst of aesthetic energy unmatched anywhere.[20] Yet no features of Latin American religiosity so exhibit the oriental qualities of southern European Christianity as the cult of the virgin and the saying of the rosary or 'telling the beads.' Luther was correct in complaining that the intercession of saints had little authority in scripture, but he showed a naive disdain for the religious universality of devotional objects such as relics and their mediatory powers. From Brahmic India the necklace of beads spread through Buddhism and Islam to ninth-century Spain, probably adopted by crusaders from their antagonists. Through the Imperium, then, vast syncretic possibilities loomed: Aztecan clergymen taught Latin rhetoric and the logic of Aquinas at the University of Mexico; Garcilazo, son of an Incan princess, drafted the first epic history of the South American conquest and Alarcón, hunchbacked son of a Mexican Indian mother, penned the bitterest satires of Golden Age Hispanic literature. A new people — and a newly complex cultural synthesis — were aborning.[21]

The impact of this interpenetration of cultures may be gauged in a number of ways. One local indication is a rapid decline of eight native tongues in the Salvadoran area, of which the chief language was Pipil, a form of Nahuatl. Social advancement naturally grew easier for those versed in Spanish, and by the late eighteenth century Indian tongues faced obsolescence even in the native pueblos.[22] Native participation in traditional practices and lore nevertheless persisted. 'Idolatrous' rites based on the cyclical phases of the life process could never be fully suppressed. Observers were dismayed by the waywardness, profligacy, vices and evasiveness of the natives. Reform measures to ease exploitation and encourage moral improvement failed at both ends of the scale. In spite of exceptional measures, for example, widespread nudism remained an open symbol of the older ways. Likewise marriages continued to be generally casual unions, easily sundered by indifference or the simple effects of the labor rotation which kept men at some distance from their homes for protracted periods. Nor did the Church lack its own participants in these activities. In the early eighteenth century the Holy Office of the Inquisition, seated in Antigua, Guatemala, reviewed the high incidence of *malas prácticas* in San Salvador, not least of which were the ubiquitous 'propositioning of women in the confessional.'[23]

What the Church took to be an inability of native men to

control their female counterparts had more likely developed from a traditional matrifocality, now adjusted to the new system. For economic and cultural reasons, women continued and indeed expanded their practice of changing mates, choosing fathers for the children from among distinguished colonists, and generally making the best of a difficult life. And life for most was difficult: it is noteworthy that the first European accounts made no mention of poverty, while this condition became endemic and universal during the centuries succeeding the introduction of Western modes of land use and economic production.[24] Not unreasonably did the subjugated masses associate Europeans with coercion, degradation and extermination. Not unreasonably did they console themselves with now-legendary music, dance, alcohol — and the Church, which for all its faults, made room for their miseries.

The Spanish decadence following the end of Charles II's reign inevitably weakened the hold of the Church by severely decreasing the number of missionaries, intensifying the isolation of the colonies, and promoting a fractious localism. Evangelization continued, but only in limited regions. Bourbon expulsion of the Jesuits in 1767 obliged more than 2,000 priests of the order to leave Latin America, with their communal *reducciones* snatched up by avaricious colonists and their ambitious planned economies with the Indians utterly wrecked and abandoned. But loss of control had also a positive side. The advance of Catholicism via the colonists in new towns and villages inevitably intensified laicization and a further syncretism among Africans, Europeans, surviving Indians and above all creoles. Latin American Christendom experienced what Enrique Dussel calls 'the release of a pent-up paganism,' further merging rural Iberian and Islamic-influenced beliefs into a common faith. The creation of a highly educated intellectual class — as, for example, at the University of Córdoba, where the doctrines of Descartes were spread — offered no contradiction to these developments, because a coherent and homogeneous culture could not be found in colonial society anyway. The loss of the Church as central directing authority essentially exacerbated a naturally chaotic condition, and freed Latin American Christendom to develop autonomously — for better and for worse.[25]

Meanwhile, changes in the colonial economies prepared yet

more devastating defeats for the Church. Highly extractive monopolies in the advanced sector quickly grew to depend upon more traditional European and native peasant agricultural components to supply low-cost food requirements as well as feed the rural population.[26] In the evolving logic of underdevelopment, agriculture was typified by 'labor scarcity,' a description that concealed native disinclination to work for specie, and consequent labor coercion in more and less successful forms. The upland and temperate region estates were manned by peasant cultivators driven from their own communal holdings and usually incorporated into estates constructed on the feudal model by the conquerers. The lowland tropical production was organized into plantations using first native slaves and later Africans. The basis for mercantilist accumulation of capital over these colonial centuries was thus in essence two-fold: silver bullion and cheap labor. Each colonial sub-economy exchanged to a modest degree with one or more of the others in the Hispanic system and each possessed both an archaic or semi-feudal arrangement along with an altogether modern one — slavery.

The rise of a creole oligarchy, enraptured with liberal or physiocratic ideals as the key to futher economic development, characterized the final stage of Iberian decadence. The aggressive importation of such mental constructs rested directly upon growing economic ties with Britain, whose markets increasingly absorbed Argentine beef and wheat, Mexican silver and wool, textile dyestuffs of cochineal and indigo from Central America.[27] Political independence came to Hispanic America (less Cuba and Puerto Rico) by the 1820s, thanks to British naval assistance and economic aid, without which the insurgency would have collapsed.[28] Black emancipation, fostered and directed by urban creole elites, ended the old systems of legal subordination. Neo-colonialism grew in a rush, with buyers of British manufactured goods pressured to expand production of raw materials fixed at artifically low prices. Neo-colonial leaders suffered both the myth of world-market competition (i.e., successful development) and the temptation of statutory secularization.

The widespread influence of the Encyclopedists, Mill, Bentham and even the Masonic Lodges upon the educated population pointed up the collapsing *élan* of the Church. Positivism entered Latin America as a quasi-religious philosophy but became increasingly a bludgeon against institutional religion. Essentially conservative nationalist governments, financially desperate from their first days, turned swiftly to Church properties and anti-clerical rationalizations. Convents in some places fell to plunder in the 1820s, state expropriation of Church holdings became official Colombian policy as early as 1861, and agricultural properties disappeared across the continent. Church political power likewise disintegrated. Hierarchical support for royalism sealed the Church's fate as far as the emerging bourgeoisie was concerned; only where Church leaders proved conciliatory and political figures (such as Bolivar himself) showed extraordinary sensitivity to the complexity of conditions, could familiar links be easily maintained.[29]

A hardening from Rome also played a baleful role. Pope Pius VII, in 1813, proposed an encyclical supporting Nationalist revolutions, but committed himself only a few years later to the Holy Alliance, commanding (but hardly receiving) obedience to royalism. Revolt against Ferdinand VII therefore became revolt against the Vatican. Later, especially after Ferdinand himself broke with Rome, the Holy See took a more constructive attitude and most of the new governments established formal relations. Yet the clinging of the Church hierarchy to the most conservative factions coincided with the post-colonial disappearance of new missionaries in what Dussel calls 'an agonizing period not unlike the barbarian invasion of Europe.'[30]

The British economic protectorate, which came to own what little infrastructure could be established in these turbulent, impoverished nation-states, set the pace of continuous economic dislocation and peripheral repercussion.[31] The dream of imported parliamentary institutions, of liberal, rational societies, died slowly, hard, and utterly. Between 1830 and 1920, the tendency of capital to concentrate and centralize within the state apparatus resulted in concerted imperialist efforts — increasingly North American in origin — to capture high rates of profit through more direct forms of investment. By the end of the nineteenth century, the U.S. financial institutions and industrial plant had begun to supplant Britain's monopoly; and the First World War supplied the *coup de grâce*.

This imposition of rapid development (or underdevelopment) fostered a new and utterly unique disaffection and armed resistance, one conditioned both by material conditions and by syncretic intellectual patterns centuries in the making. Now, the Iberian connection cut the other way, for the invasion of the market economy could never be accepted outside limited circles as the greater good for the greatest number. Bourgeois aspirations notwithstanding, alien it came and alien it remained even in sway.

Church historians now recognize that disestablishment actually formed the conditions for a monumental comeback. The conspicuous role of the radical clergy in the local insurgencies, both national-bourgeois revolts and internal rebellions, has yet to be systematically examined. But such historical deities as Fathers Miguel Hidalgo and José Mariá Morelos of Mexico, José Matiás Delgado and Jose Simeón Canas of El Salvador, pioneers of independence and abolitionism, carried the germs of an intellectual ferment probably French in origin, but reworked and transformed in novel and complex ways. Hidalgo had been a prize student of José Pérez Calama, Bishop of Quito and a powerful force for regional autonomy.[32] Morelos himself wrote characteristically, 'The Gachupines [Europeans] have always sought to abase the Americans to the point of regarding us as brutes, incapable of initiative or even of the waters of Baptism, and therefore useless to Church and state. But I see the opposite . . . '[33] Morelos sought to defend Mexican religious orthodoxy from French rationalism cloaked in 'enlightened' Bourbon robes. He waged a holy war against the extraneous forces of secularism, 'idolatry' and double-entry accounting. To the Bishop of Puebla he exclaimed in 1811, 'we are more religious than the Europeans,' capable of fighting to the death for 'la religión y la patria . . . nuestra santa revolución.'[34]

Thus, when revolutionary hubris collapsed into mechanical cynicism in the second half of the nineteenth century, the Church increasingly became the haven of the lost, notwithstanding its formally reactionary politics. Influential secular intellectuals in various countries proclaimed the inherent inferiority of the stubborn Indian masses and preached their ultimate disappearance according to Darwinian principles. Even the Indians' familiar allies, the liberals, undermined their actual security by seeking legislation to dissolve traditional communal holdings so as to make them more thrifty, productive and self-reliant landowners—with a resulting devastation of native society and aggrandizement of the already extensive latifundia. The toleration of subcultures broke down increasingly as American competition and collateral diplomacy nudged out the dominant British capital. The republican dream of races and cultures democratically mingling had ended. Within and against the context of these brutal developments, patrons of a more paternalistic, harmonious attitude meanwhile had the encouragement of the Church hierarchy, which refused to acknowledge the ongoing transformation of colonial castes into sharply divided classes. The charitable impulse alone gave the Church a unique status. But it not only wished to save the poor; it desperately feared the tide of anarchism and Marxist socialism would carry from Europe to the New World. Unlike the feckless bourgeoisie, the Church could accept neither the logic nor the consequences of market behavior. Salvation, the eschatological mission, remained a numinous alternative to secularity of all kinds.

In the same era, a modest renaissance of Catholic thought and deed arose from the renewed emphasis the Vatican placed upon the Americas and from a resurgence of Hispanic intellectual idealism. On Christmas Day, 1898, the first Continental Council of the Church opened, six years after Pope Leo XIII had celebrated the Americas' four centuries of Christendom. The mood of this gathering recalls Ortega y Gasset's lament: 'The Creole soul is full of broken promises; it feels pain in members which it does not have and which it never has had.'[36] Latin American bishops proposed a renewed defense of the faith against the sundry enemies of paganism, socialism, Freemasonry and the uncontrolled press. At the same time, resurgent Church determination to evangelize rural districts arose from a keen awareness of the growing secularization among the urban middle classes. Reactionary in ideology, the national churches nevertheless moved to embrace their last human resource — the alienation of the Indian, the peasant, the humble and the beaten, from the logic of bourgeois civilization.

Intellectuals who designated themselves 'Arielists' after Rodó's literary manifesto *Ariel* (1901), came to symbolize the region's emerging opposition toward both Yankee imperialism and local positivism on grounds inconceivable outside the Third World. The basic flaw in U.S. culture, according to the Arielists, consisted in its materialist concern with development for its own sake. Only a thoroughly benighted materialism could endure the madness of democracy and the concept of one man, one vote. An obsessive concern for *things* led the polity to grant equal political privileges to those who produced things and those who produced ideas alike. Production and consumption, the lowest common denominators, thus ruled supreme. Local bourgeois leaderships, tampering with traditional organization through the introduction of acquisitive, competitive, individualistic capitalism, had opened a Pandora's Box.[37]

The Iberian (and for that matter, Islamic) hostility to manual labor can be readily detected here, alongside strands of German Romanticism, *fin de siècle* decadence, and other more insular Latin American influences. Just as a similar impulse to valorize artistic creation over creeping mechanization turned contemporary Yiddishists toward anarcho-socialism, and U.S. literary fugitives such as Lafcadio Hearn (or later, Ezra Pound) away from Western Civilization entirely, in Latin America the weird syntheses of positivism, anti-positivism, Bergson and Thomas Aquinas brought romantics close to the Christian socialist-corporatism of Leo XIII's famous *Rerum Novarum*.[38]

The Church, lacking any serious intellectual rivals, thus emerged from potential inner crisis triumphant over philosophical secularization. It would face future political struggles armed with a renewed sense of purpose. Even indigenous anti-clericalism could be coopted, rejecting the Church's anemic pursuit of mission but not the mission itself, joining the struggle within the confines of the existing religious institutions against the common enemy of Protestant-style evangelization and scientism. An early apprehension of undervelopment by the rising intellectual classes permitted no other serious choice for national (or regional) purpose and identity. Wretched economies which promised only decay from within and further economic invasion from without, reinforced the sense of futility in advance toward any alternative framework. Thus the arch figure of a Thomist revival, Jackson de Figueredo, was said to have fretted, 'Dissolvent socialism and iconoclastic bolshevism are nibbling away at the European organism like leprosy. But Europe is prepared to defend itself. What will happen to us, I wonder, when we have to defend our poor bones against these evil assaults?' The Church triumph could never be truly comfortable so long as the causes for socialism's threat remained.[39]

The turn-of-the-century Spanish novelist Miguel de Unamuno, struggling with the fate of the spiritually faithless but humanistic local parish curate in the famed work *San Manuel Bueno*, predicted the future perspective.[40] The protagonist gains vindication because his 'faith in faith' permits him to sacrifice his personal needs and desires to the collective requirements; his individual personality virtually dissolves into service of his flock. The sacrificial figure is of course *the* stock character in the Hispanic pantheon, not so far from Don Quixote of La Mancha. But the peculiar crisis facing the Latin American intellectual gave the concept of sacrifice to faith an unpredecented emotional significance. The intellectual must find somewhere the faith for this personal transformation, and he is unlikely to find it in Rome, or (it almost goes without saying) Moscow. Of all the restless intellectuals in the world, he will be most ripe for doctrines hostile to the logic of modernization, and open to doctrines descended from the monastic ideal of Man and God sharing solitude in the wilderness; in the more updated versions of these doctrines, he may even be urged to take upon himself the communal poverty of the urban slum.

A full working-out of this sacrificial perspective continued to be blocked for the first half of the twentieth century by the desperate fear of public unrest. Intellectual and cultural elites who might have led the hungry masses in the repatriation of national resources clung to the forces of order. Crying anti-Yankee slogans, they cheered as the guns turned repeatedly against the starveling victims.[41] Their generation retreated to something between romantic flight and irrelevant rationalizations, as meanwhile, the Church began successfully promoting a middle-class party of order with working class roots, the Christian Democracy. Workers Clubs and youth organizations were gradually nurtured out of the tumultous subsoil of the early years of the century. The ascendance of Pope Pius XI channeled their energies squarely against the fiercely anti-clerical Mexican Revolution, without the slightest recognition of previous Church abuses or of any leftist motives other than monstrous atheism. Pius's fanatical anti-communism made the Vatican a zealous backer of Franco, partner to Mussolini, and even non-opponent to Hitler's pre-war Reich. But his willingness to take sides in the Mexican events, despite its reactionary overtones, cracked the historic Leonine non-partisanship. Christian Democrats confidently defined themselves as the mainstream Latin American alternative to military dictators and rebel nationalists, helped to facilitate the creation of important new Catholic universities, and prepared the way for younger thinker-activists.[42]

The Great Depression had a strengthening effect upon such developments. Catholic Action, influenced first by Italian and later by French examples, carried the torch of Jacques Maritain's 'New Christendom.' The universities in particular became hotbeds of a peculiar idealism bent upon evangelization and laicization. The Church thus planted roots into the sinkholes of spreading poverty, and with new material resources of its own, moved towards completion of its centuries-old quest for a clerical society led at the grassroots by non-clerics. The increasing friendliness of the economic and political Right towards such presumably stabilizing Church activities guaranteed (only for the time being, but seemingly forever) an end to the official anti-clericalism of the bourgeois national era. It thus seemed that the Church needed only to thread its way through the maze of development to gain a victory of historic proportions.[43]

Yet material conditions deceived the corporatist dreamers, just as they had so often deceived the expectant bourgeoisie. Following the Second World War, the dream of modernization within a religious context raced towards and down the U.S. Alliance for Progress *cul-de-sac*. At first the post World War II years seemed to promise a moment of triumphant florescence for the Church; the founding of the General Conference of the Latin American Episcopacy (CELAM) in 1955 marked the full recovery of Latin American Christendom from the post-colonial problems, a recovery that shamed the post-Reformation European Church by contrast. Not since the fifteenth century had Catholics so ruled a continent. Seminaries found new life, theological journals blossomed, biblical institutes arose at the popular level, and even parish life enjoyed a limited revival. By its founding conference, CELAM could claim that Latin American outnumbered European Catholics for the first time in percentage of world Church population.[44]

However, the progress of poverty, and the very strength accumulated by the Church, cast increasing doubt upon the religious function of civil order and upon the purportedly holy mission of rightwing caudillos or U.S. puppet governments. Moreover, after 1950 transnational capital immensely accelerated the erosion of those peasant land holdings which had survived earlier depredations and attacks. Multinational agribusiness, among other enterprises, usurped the most productive and accessible lands across vast expanses of Latin America, driving millions of tenants and squatters literally to the margins of life. Although Latin American in-migration is not generally associated with the world-wide growth of beggared refugee populations, the rural-to-urban movement of these years into its desperately overburdened cities has had much the same result.

Such people flee land and food pressures on subsistence farming without, however, abandoning their rustic habits or acquiring new skills to participate economically and politically in urban life; their sheer numbers thus depress wages in the service sector and stimulate the state's police terror against the inevitable unrest that results.[46]

The post-war economic world recovery upon which Christian Democrats based their hopes had, then, very nearly the opposite effect for the forty to seventy percent of peasant land-dwellers living in a condition that ranged from subsistence to starvation. From 1950 to 1963, annual international public investment to Latin America increased six times, from $177 million to $1 billion, 22 million. Net direct investment declined in the same years from an annual average of $309 to $283 million. A rapid and intensive expansion of U.S. subsidiaries seemed too attractive a prospect to turn or slow down, thanks to their great economies of scale, their exclusive access to the latest technology, and, consequently, their ability to soak up scarce local capital. The World Bank and the Inter-American Development Bank assisted this process by serving as agencies of credit between Latin American governments and world capital markets. Since the early 1960s, the tendency toward multi-national corporate control of key sectors in particular economies emerged and grew. The bulk of these MNC investments have been financed by profit retention and domestic savings. This trend contrasts ominously with the state of rural society and economy, where agricultural production levels per capita have seldom regained their pre-1940s equivalents, even to the present. The transition from semi-feudal estates to large-scale commercial farms converges with the devolution of the peasantry toward dependent status to form a historically new pattern of land tenure and functional dualism. That is, the continued provision of cheap labor for external accumulation under a local regime that fails to intercept local markets or to compete for investment has resulted in a lopsided capital market in the form of 'disarticulated accumulation.'[47]

Scarcities of land and water, labor and fuel resources have never yet been obstacles to Latin American development. Indeed, the very notion of 'underdevelopment' seems at best ambiguous in light of the boom-and-bust 'over-development' among large sectors of mining and staple export economies over the centuries.[48] Thus such cities as Mexico City, Quito or Potosí, once exporters of grain, meat, wood, gold or silver bullion and specie, are today net importers of beans, corn, and most of what they once produced in surplus. Intensive production of the more dynamic cash crops has likewise brought with it the breakdown of traditional patron-client relations. Capitalist labor arrangements have largely replaced semi-feudal ones. Food crops are now supplied by importation or by peasant subsistence production. This blend of commercial cropping and small peasant production hardly meets the demands of the national or regional food market, which includes peasant food, wage food, industrial and wage crops, and exports.[49]

The transition from servile-dependent labor on archaic private estates to landless proletarian labor in agribusiness was gradual at first, but has accelerated greatly during the last two decades. Although working conditions and labor relations differ widely between center and peripheral political economies, the increasing velocity of post-industrial capitalist processes impinges forcibly upon both components. In the periphery partial, lopsided, ill-planned 'development' has cut back previously high mortality without however supplying the social incentives that induce adults in the center to reduce family size. The effect has been increased fertility and a surplus of labor where there had always been a 'scarcity of hands,' to use the colonial phrase. Moreover, the state now possesses the technical capacity to handle normal protest, and thus to take on a function which devolved in the past upon landlords and entrepreneurs themselves, and which therefore formerly required a modicum of paternalistic caution.[50]

In the center economies, the proletarianization process is far more advanced, and requires real wage levels be sufficient to cover complete subsistence costs of laborers and their families. Though employers pay for only those hours actually punched in, the relatively high wage insures maintenance and reproduction. In the periphery, by contrast, proletarianization has meant that wages could be paid far below the actual cost of labor power, because the peasant economy has been able to absorb these costs through surplus, cheap, super-exploited domestic/family labor. The peasant family, especially the mother and numerous children — all unpaid for their services — thus subsidize both the modern capitalist sector of the local economy and the accumulation of capital at the center of the system.[51]

The progressive degradation and consequent mass destitution in the peasant sector results from the impossibility of their ever entering into the commercial/capitalist sector. As foreign and domestic capital brings ever more peasant holders and landless workers under its aegis, peasants are forced into fierce competition for steadily falling wages and markets in which to sell their small products. They themselves must search intently for additional resources such as increased terrain or the labor power of their own families in order to increase productivity.

The volume of misery has increased dramatically, whether or not (as experts debate) actual peasant lifespan has been shortened or lengthened. The Economic Commission for Latin America, UNESCO, and various private agencies have charted the downward trend in peasant production over the past two decades. Their surveys show that by the mid-sixties, at least sixty percent of rural households regionwide earned less than \$300/year, or an annual per capita income of less than \$60 for some sixty to seventy million people. In 1978 ECLA estimated that fully sixty-two percent of rural households regionwide could not meet the most basic nutritional requirements. In countries like Honduras the situation is worse; in others like Brazil the spectacular development of the urban sector remains shadowed by massive rural malnutrition, illiteracy, and minimal life-expectancy. In any case, whatever its local inflections, nothing in Marx's lengthy analysis of rural immiseration caused by land enclosure and geographical displacement can equal the scale and depth of agony throughout the continent and isthmus.[52]

Indeed, today a formerly somewhat independent peasantry is rushing toward catastrophe. The ravages of pollution, overgrazing, soil mineral exhaustion, timber depletion and erosion degrade and destroy natural resources with increasing, astonishing speed; destruction of the material base chokes off the flow of accumulation derived from cheap labor and cheap food production in the family; technological and financial transformation of the cities begets endemic crisis which must finally rebound to the countryside as well. Peasant life has always been hard, but never has it been so thoroughly marginalized, isolated from any and all cultural, physical, psychological, institutional and other aid. Population growth, meanwhile, shows little sign of abating, since family planning is in reverse ratio to poverty. Women in rural areas require children for help in labor-intensive cultivation, in cities for supplemental income (although fertility here declines considerably). Children leave rural homes for the city at ever-earlier ages, prompting more pregnancies in the attempt to compensate for their departures. To these interlinked dynamics of poverty and population growth there seems no end in sight.[53]

Even by the mid-1950s, these trends had become sufficiently marked to alarm Church officials and prick the consciences of many lesser clerics. Religious faith first engaged, then merged with and extended a psychology of survival among the teeming millions in the countryside and the semi-urban barrios of the continent. The fabric of ecclesiastical authority has been stretched if not riven by intimate contacts between the poor and young priests in particular, including foreign missionaries. Yet the most decisive changes in ecclesiastical behavior have perhaps been pedagogical. Formal rites and practices themselves changed little between the sixteenth century and the 1960s; but in the past, the cleric preached and the faithful listened with heads bowed in resignation. Now, over the past quarter-century, priests have begun to learn directly from the mouths of the poor how misery and oppression act upon Christian faith. The religious constituency has become a political constituency as well.

As early as 1954, Church opposition to the arbitrary Peronist style in Argentina breached the historic tradition of Church support for anti-Communist dictators. Religious youth in particular embraced popular opposition, forcing urban bishops to take a stand or risk the embarrassment of running behind their charges. As leader after leader fell across the continent over the next half-dozen years, the military emerged a most dubious messiah. The stark failure of the Kennedy reform program increased the danger from the Right, and brought the Church hierarchy to search for new long-run alternatives. In this context, many younger intellectuals, influenced by French liberal Catholicism or German Christian Socialism, met the new Papal dispensation with open arms.[54]

The Second Vatican Council, 1962-65, ratified the changes left pending at the 1955 CELAM conference, thus legitimating and reinforcing a progressive tendency which belonged to Latin America more than to Rome. Yet in doing so the Council took its warrant from John XXIII, Pope in an era of unprecedented world prosperity, who emphasized the essential human rights of decent livelihood, education and political participation. John XXIII also articulated the first serious doubts in the Holy See about unconditional opposition to Communism. Seeking to cool the historic differences between Rome and Eastern Europe, no less between the Vatican and reform-minded Western Marxist parties, his *Pacem in terris* went so far as to separate the false 'origin and inspiration' of Marxist atheism from the Marxist movements' real social contribution. John asked rhetorically, 'who can deny that those movements, in so far as they conform to the dictates of right reason and are interpreters of the lawful aspirations of the human person, contain elements that are positive and deserving of approval?' In short, while emphasizing peaceful change, John codified Vatican policy to allow the possibility that revolutionary motives could be admirable, and that (as Aquinas had said) unjust laws could be so far from the laws of nature as to constitute forms of violence in themselves. It was but a short step from such propositions to the inference that violence against such violence might merit the Church's sympathy, if not its support.

The Council faithfully registered this philosophical revolution, with all its ambiguities and implications. A 'sign of the times' had revived the sacrament as earthly salvation; and Latin American Church leaders recognized the signal. When Pope Paul VI extended such teachings in his *Populorum progressio*, granting the justice of some leftwing armed struggles, he seemed to vindicate Christian revolutionaries once and for all. 'If a person is in extreme necessity, he has the right to take from the riches of others what he himself needs,' read the new Pastoral Constitution. Dom Helder Câmara, the Brazilian Bishop who first invoked Vatican II's ideals in the defense of human rights against the highest levels of national government, turned them towards this conclusion in 1966: 'A greater danger than Communism threatens the world. It is the capitalist system.'[55]

The second CELAM conference, at Medellín in 1968, took place against the backdrop of the French May events, massive anti-war uprisings on U.S. campuses, and a promised trip by Paul to Latin America. By this time, the stakes in the conference's proceedings had risen considerably. Numerous younger theological graduates doing field work had interacted with the Latin American student movement, reaffirmed their own instinctive radicalism, and not infrequently gone to jail for political causes. Likewise, on the other side of the ideological fence, the CIA and conservative Catholics had supplied lavish resources for Belgian Father Roger Vekemans to rally the Right around the familiar symbols of order. Towards both sides in the dispute the Pope delivered a by-now-familiar litany of Church responsibility toward the poor, and rejection of violence in the face of even the most severe oppression. Meanwhile, the budding radicals held open meetings with students, sometimes broken up by the police, to discuss the meaning of the sessions while the bishops fumbled toward compromise. Ultimately, the bishops did acknowledge the solidarity of the Church with those suffering the unfolding tragedy in Latin America, noting the costs of dependency for economics, politics and culture, describing injustice and exploitation as 'institutionalized violence.' And they urged a 'liberating education,' the nearest official endorsement heretofore of Liberation Theology.

By recognizing more clearly than ever the connection between their faith and their regional identity, the Church leaders had taken a great step forward in Medellín.[56] And in the years that followed, the continuing pattern of right-wing violence continued to pull the Church into an adversary position. In Argentina, Brazil, Peru, Paraguay and even Haiti, individual priests and sometimes bishops protested shameful conditions. *Coups détat* accompanied by mass imprisonment and torture shocked even Church moderates; the occasional murder of a priest by these brutal powers-that-be gave the faith a new class of martyrs. Camilo Torres, the most famous of these, exemplified the growing, spreading notion that 'love of neighbor' demanded open combat with the privileged elites. Though Torres' own guerilla campaign failed and his actions were deplored by calmer heads, he demonstrated the capacity of the radical Church for life-or-death commitments.[57] Divine imperatives similarly supplied ideological legitimacy for many more patient but no less radical strategies. The sacred symbols of the liturgy drew masses into a mobilized posture, relating their religious vision of universal human equality to movements for temporal, political power.

In the late 60s and 70s, the failure of the guerilla focos and electoral strategies alike almost uniformly across the continent thrust the Church Militant into the cockpit of history. Although a 'Christians for Socialism' movement allied with Allende evoked deep mistrust among the hierarchy, Pinochet's arrests of priests and expulsion of a prominent bishop challenged established Church-state traditions and aligned the Church in an almost Social Democratic role in fundamental opposition to the Right. The case is quite different, of course, in Central America where a scant tradition of civil society buffers the conflict between armed supporters of socialism and bourgeois barbarism. By the late 1950s, young Salvadoran Christian intellectuals had drifted from a conservative Italian-style Catholic Action to a more liberal French-Belgian variety. These prospective social leaders joined the U.S.-sponsored efforts at land reform, only to be met with oligarchic defiance and repression. Thus, when the Salvadoran Communist Party fragmented over support for the 'Soccer War' against Honduras, Christian activists ascended to the leadership of armed resistance. Meantime, Medellín brought lay people and radical priests (one prominent figure, David Rodríguez, became known as 'the "Che" of the Bible') into Salvadoran villages where conscientization and mobilization evoked the right-wing slogan 'Be a Patriot! Kill a Priest!' The 1980 assassination of Archbishop Romero, a moderate turned militant opponent of the military, both silenced the official Salvadoran Church and ensured the radical character of its Christian message.[58].

As throughout Latin American history, however the balance of the faith depends upon the laymen more than Church institutions or individuals. Nothing dramatizes this development more than the appearance of a Nicaraguan 'People's Church,' engaged in symbolic and real political conflict with the Church hierarchy. The Sandinista government which recalled Ernesto Cardenal from his Solintiname solitude immediately fell under suspicion from the Nicaraguan Bishops' Council both for Marxist ideas and for actual (if numerically quite limited) Cuban presence. The Nicaraguan bishops had sought consistently to separate 'class struggle' (necessary for even the middle classes under Somoza) from 'class hatred,' and the vision of a better social system from strategies of violent or sudden change. Early and often in the wake of Somoza's overthrow they pressed for priests' resignation from government offices, as a violation of religious practices but more realistically as disruption of hierarchical discipline. More recently they have echoed the restlessness and discomfort of the middle class with the revolutionary process, the fervent if futile hope for amicable solutions. The resistance of both the Sandinista Government and the 'People's Church' to Papal authority has, for them, the scent of heresy. Yet even today the ambiguous unsettled positions of all involved parties in particular remains, to this writing, the predominant and astonishing fact of modern Nicaraguan Church history.[59] Whatever the attitudes of more secular Sandinista officials, the country has become no less Catholic, and of course no less

Christian since the victory of July 1979; Christian conscientization walks together with literacy and better medical services,
more effective transportation and communication. For its part,
the Vatican itself has likewise avoided the risk of spreading
heresy by declining the sort of modern Inquisition which the
Opus Dei would no doubt relish. Indeed, one imagines that an
all-out military invasion of Nicaragua backed or blessed by
Rome could easily provoke the kind of Christian war-
communism reminiscent of the Muenzerites' final months, and a
martyrdom whose flames would smolder on for generations to
come.

Throughout most of the continent itself, meanwhile, a somewhat less immediate millenarian spirit can be found. Church
officials, echoing the Pope, assail imperialism and denounce
injustice but speak far less often or specifically of alternatives.
Yet for the millions of peasants who have flocked to the *com-
munidades de base*, the rural and urban settlements embracing
20-50 people, the chiliastic spirit thrives. Within these communities the Church focuses upon both the people's desperate
material plight and their spiritual condition. Passing from
prayer meetings to self-help, building schools and clinics, community members construct for themselves a group identity and
solidarity which in their turn breed a will towards larger and
more drastic change. The Church hierarchy frequently attempts
to exercise a manipulative top-down control over such communities, yet the shock of awakening from centuries of self-
abnegation, fatalism, ignorance and indifference to offical
politics, cannot be overestimated or, ultimately, controlled.[60]

In and through this context, too, the Vatican threads a winding
course. The condemnation of 'imperialistic selfishness' is more
qualitatively unique in the Holy See than the condemnation of
Marxist notions such as class struggle; the acceptance of Marxist
economics by the Jesuits (notwithstanding the Jesuit discipline
visited upon Sandinista Fernando Cardenal) is yet more unique.
Perhaps most unprecedented of all, however, is the political
minuet carried on between Leonardo Boff and John Paul II in the
fall of 1984. Boff, perhaps the foremost Brazilian exponent of
Liberation Theology, represents the Left of the greatest population base in the Catholic world, that is to say the future of the
faith; John Paul, perhaps the final European Pope, and almost
certainly the only Eastern European pontiff, represents the collective past. Called to question on his Christology, Boff held his

ground and returned from the Vatican openly confident of his vindication.[61] Papal acceptance of Boff's position (or silence toward it) as legitimate if open to question, stands in utter contrast to Papal persecution of (for example) U.S. nuns openly supporting women's reproductive rights. No 'disobedience' could be found in a figure of so much political substance within the Church. If since Fall 1984 John Paul has spoken repeatedly against the dangers of class conflict and Marxist atheism, his phrases against Liberation Theology as such have been noticeably muted. Liberation Theology has become part of the Church; now the only question concerns the line between its proper applications and its misuse.[62]

On an immediate, ideological level the uniqueness of Liberation Theology's 'materialism' and praxis must be put against the Vatican heritage of Constantinian idealism. Roman academic tradition derives from an authoritarian strain of the first four centuries A D, together with the Church's domestication of the philosophic tradition running from Aristotle through Aquinas. The classic theological system thus stands clearly revealed as a fixed set of ideal truths to be taken naturally or *a priori*. By contrast, a modern materialism can be found in Baroja's 'hombres de carne y hueso,' working through the locus of social relationships, processes and products toward a view of how spiritual and ideological insights reflect the mundane.[63] Did not Jesus, the contemporary disciples ask, analogize always from the familiar elements in the immediate peasant environment? Did He not stay the course of evil-doers and their intended scenarios so as to demonstrate the immediate application of other-worldly ideals? Ideals and principles He illustrated through loaves, fishes, the olive and grape vine, the lillies of the field and the wayward sons of the plutocrats? Against such rhetorical questions Cardinal Ratzinger, master of Church conservatism, can only charge that the poor 'lack the capacity for discernment' and can only harm the Church in a campaign against 'the hierarchical structure . . . which was willed by the Lord himself.'[64] Meanwhile, denying the assertion that the ideals of social justice necessarily give rise to class struggle, Liberation Theologians uphold the reality of their constituents' daily lives and the enduring truth of a Church tradition running back to the ninth century, which has it that an exegete must embrace both God and the totality of the human race.

On a more abstract level, Liberation Theology represents the recuperation of the category of totality from a tradition both spiritual and secular, passing from nature-religion through German philosophy, aesthetic romanticism, Marxist and anarchist thought to the revived religious radicalism of the present. It grasps at the interrelation of all phenomena, the correspondence of all human manifestations — the rhythm of movement, the imaginative pattern of thought — to the cosmic context. It seeks to resolve the age-old problem of evil in a manner reminiscent of Gnosticism, yet poses its solution in sophisticated, modern socioeconomic terms. It is a holy pheno-menology which offers the twentieth century, and the West, a last chiliastic opportunity before the threatening fire of divine retribution consumes the beneficiaries of sin.

Liberation Theology in this sense might best be approached via the mythological interpretations and poetic metaphors of some of its most formidable articulators. J. Severino Croatto, Argentine biblist, speculates that according to the spiritual beliefs of the Fertile Crescent, the gods themselves rebelled against their leaders, after which it was resolved that 'humans bear the labor of the gods' (or, more picturesquely, 'I have transferred your screams to humanity'). Later, according to this same construction, the human masses themselves rose up in protest, inspired by that earlier rebellion. Although they were crushed, the memory of their revolt was preserved and revived several times over in Judeo-Christianity, in its own rebellion against the Empire of Rome.[65] The parallel to early socialist millennialism—with its invocation of anti-imperial solidarity in revolt, its visionary moment of spiritual-political triumph, its persistence in the face of ongoing failure and/or betrayal — is abundantly clear.

And the deeper theological implication of this parallel should not be neglected. Frei Betto, Brazilian author and former political prisoner, says flatly that for Latin American spiritual rebels such as himself, 'god is revealed in the negation of god,' the deity who shows himself to the seeker not as patriarchical Jehovah but rather comrade in the struggle.[66] Similarity of such perspectives to the Radical Reformation mentality, and specifically its philo-sophical legatee Jakob Böhme, is not accidental. For Böhme, influenced by the traditions of Gnosticism and the upswelling of Jewish mysticism, the deity arises from the *turba*, the dark turbulence of the cosmos, to find self-consciousness through Man his creation. God, himself in process, thus becomes at any given point the unity of all contradictions, but not their transcendence or resolution. Inspiration to Blake, Novalis and indeed the entire Romantic movement, Böhme was also seen by Hegel as father of German philosophy, reformulator of the dialectic lost to wisdom since the Ancients. For Böhme, schooled in the Radical Reformation revolt *against* history, the truth lay in a return to the beginning where reality (including the sexual polarization of woman and man) had been undifferentiated, where the animals spoke with humans and all lived in a cooperative peace. Although recognizing history's irreversibility, Hegel recast Böhme's notion of the dialectric into a new light in which revolutionary dreamers could bathe.[67] Yet now ironically it is precisely the descendants of the Counter-Reformation, the only strand in the West surviving Capitalism's dispersion of the numinous, who have re-engaged the tradition of the dialectic and its links to a Golden Age somewhere in humanity's past and future.

Thus we hear Ernesto Cardenal, arguably the most important literary figure to hold revolutionary office in the twentieth century, on pre-Colombian history. Student of Thomas Merton, inspired by Ezra Pound's great purpose of returning poetry to its original history-telling function, Cardenal delineates the Mayan example prior to Toltec rule:

There are no names of generals on the stelae.

Their language had no word for 'master.'
Nor a word for 'city-wall.' They did not wall their cities.
Their cities were cities of temples, they lived in the fields,
among the palm groves and the milpas and the pawpaw trees.
Their temple-arch was modelled on their hut.
Highways were for processions.
Religion was the only bond between them,
But it was a religion freely accepted,
imposing no burden. No oppression.
Their priests had no temporal power
and the pyramids were built without forced labor.
At its height their civilization did not turn into an empire!

They had no metallurgy. Their tools were of stone —
they never left the Stone Age, technologically speaking.
But they computed precise dates going back

four hundred million years into the past.
They had no applied science. They were not practical.
Their progress lay in religion, mathematics, art,
astronomy. They had no means of weighing.
They adored time: the mysterious
effluxion of time.
Time was holy. Days were gods.
The past and the future intermingled in their songs.
They used the same katuns for past and future,
in the belief that time was re-enacted
like the motions of the heavenly bodies they observed,
Yet the time which they adored abruptly ceased.
Stelae remained unfinished,
blocks half-cut in quarries —
and there they lie.[68]

By comparison, the Incas ('the Inca god/was Stalin') are already part of a cruel history continued under the Conquest. And if so, the judgment and the salvation of the biblical promise is as much as specifically Latin American as European and white. A new katun will come to pass, but only after Babylon falls:

And [the angel] said unto me: 'the nations of the world are divided
into two blocs (Gog and Magog)
yet the two blocks are in truth but one
(which is against the Lamb)
and fire will fall from heaven to consume them
both.'[69]

We need not take this fire-and-brimstone literally. But we are enjoined to regard very seriously indeed the vision of the very real Sandinista revolution, a revolution which, Cardenal says, has been made for the rivers, the tropical birds, the fish and the air no less than for the Nicaraguan people. The *earth* 'wanted the revolution,' Cardenal writes; and the assertion reminds us that 'revolution' originally meant return to a beginning, *i.e.* to the conditions of the Garden.[70]

This ecological revolutionism has a more literal and urgent aspect in Brazil's great Mato Grosso, where Bishop Pedro Casaldáliga struggles to restrain capitalism and prevent the devastation of surviving Indian tribes. Cardenal writes to his friend:

The tribe is moving up the river.
The Companies come putting up fences.

Across the Mato Grosso sky move the landowners in their private
planes.
And they don't invite you to the big barbecue with the Minister of the
Interior.
The Companies sowing desolution.
They bring in the telegraph to transmit false news.
The transistor to the poor, for murmured lies.
Truth is forbidden for it makes you free.
Desolution and division and barbed wire.
You're a poet and you write metaphors.
But you've also written: 'Slavery is not a metaphor.'[71]

For Bishop Casaldáliga who shows himself in public defiance of
corporations and government, wearing the bloodied shirt of an
assistant killed in an attempt on his life, the struggle of the poet
and the struggle of the Church are one. But his Church is not the
Constantinian Church, whose resistance to Liberation Theology
and bureaucratic manuevers to evade the central issues he finds
tragic and comical:

The matter is so serious
that it must be carried to Rome
    to the Rome of the Popes,
    as the oldest known custom.
It must be carried to Rome,
    via diplomatic channels, by sacred assumption.
Or it must be carried on one's back,
like one of many crosses, with no great heroism
As one carries a child, a wounded man, a hoe.
Or like a banner of natural green,
apace with many others,
    natural banner of the Third World, walking palm tree!
    with the green hope —
very natural, very high —
that we shall all be,
a little,
each day
    Vatican I, Vatican II, Jerusalem I, Bethleham I,
    Bethleham II—
more free, more human, more brotherly, more renewed:
the faithful, the little ones above all;
even the bishops
    once again fishers of horizons
    once again tanners of the gospel,
    once again beheaded, unmitered, in the main

squares of the Empire, to give testimony.[72]

In this vision the Martyr Church makes amends for its own past perpetuation of evil by sacrificing the dignity of Rome (*i.e.*, the West) to the redemption of the rural people:

> I rain down tears and protests,
> and I hear a voice crying in the backwoods:
> 'Prepare the way of the Lord, say the people.
> Make way for his people, which is the people.
> We have spoken.
>
> I make way for my people, he says,
> brimming with anger, the God of the humble ransomed ones.
> I will dry up the Stock Market like a bed of cursed sand,
> and my people will pass onward, treading dry-shod
> on your programs of high economic development . . . !
> The foot of a free man is worth more than an Empire, pharaohs!
> I have spoken!
> Put on me a tumankura of human dignity,
> like a seal on my arms and my legs,
> mother Tapirape, mother village, land still free, still human.'[73]

Do such poets sound more like transhistoric mystics than intellectuals of the modern world? Actually, they constitute part of a rapidly growing class of mental workers. According to recent figures, the seminaries swollen almost to bursting by the influx of youthful idealists in Argentina, Brazil, Colombia, Mexico and Peru, offer a sophisticated variety of economics, anthropology, communication and psychology along with the usual theological-philosophical fare. Figures such as Cardenal and Casaldáliga, models for many such students, hold out the promise of combining learning and faith. Rather like the Leninist formula on the nationalism of the oppressed ('national in form, social in content'), their assimilation of knowledge emancipates them from Third World intellectual underdevelopment en route to their religious vocations. In their words, however, nationalism never ceases to be more than mere form; nor does the Christological context dissolve into Marxist sophistication. Rather, they strive consciously and unconsciously for something new.

Their essential precursor in this project, Peruvian José Carlos Mariátegui, might properly be called the Ernst Bloch of syncretism, or the Bolivar of Latin American Marxist interpretation.

A lower-middle class, crippled boy rising from the print room of a Lima newspaper to the columns of prestige magazines, Mariátegui swiftly became a noted stylist beloved by young intellectuals. Drawn to the anti-censorship press in 1916, he soon went over from aesthetic decadence to the labor movement and thence to a heterodox Marxism. During the second half of the 1920s, until his untimely death, Mariátegui directed a literary journal which approached a surrealist perspective. In the Peruvian revolutionary movement, he helped the varied forces make a smooth transition from anarchosyndicalism to the Third International; while at his passing, he himself could rightly be called a Trotskyist, though a most distinctive one.[74]

Mariátegui's most important intervention in Latin American radical and religious thought is his *Seven Interpretive Essays on Peruvian Reality*. In it, he asserts that 'Socialism regards mere anti-clerical activity as a liberal bourgeois pastime,' and describes the renovation of myths (here he approvingly cites Sorel) as the true task of modern revolutionary practice. The Conquest which broke up the pre-existing religions and their regional theocracies, he argues, also used up the last of the true European Crusaders. Exhausted into each other, the two remnants transmuted into something utterly unique. Land policy, education, regional culture proved in general, all the necessity to recuperate pre-Colombian socialisms and the Jesuit *reducciones*, to rescue the communal meaning of *indigenismo* for the civilization about to ascend. In a phrase that might have been borrowed from Aimé Cesaire, Mariátegui proclaims, 'The universal, ecumenical roads we have chosen to travel, and for which we are reproached, take us ever closer to ourselves,' to an unrealized but inevitable Hispanic self-identity.

Today's Liberation Theology is in the process of filling out Mariátegui's dream through the only vessel available, the Church.[75] And, like Mariátegui's thought, Liberation Theology for all its intellectual sophistication remains in the idealist or non-historical materialist tradition which has been an uncomfortable partner to Marxist movements since the mid-nineteenth century. In those days, anarchists, syndicalists and quasi-Marxist romantics took the initiative in defending the peasantry's capabilities, in exalting will over material conditions, and in praising the post-revolutionary model of autonomy and decentralization. Now Liberation Theology texts stand unconsciously close to Gustav Landauer's *Skepsis und Mystik*, a nineteenth-century work which reflected Nietzsche's motto, 'when skepticism mates with yearning, the progeny is mysticism.' Landauer's own atheism forbade his allowing a world-spirit which could be personified as today's radical theologians do the revolutionary-insurrectionary Jesus.[76] Yet in his word as in contemporary Liberation Theology, the impulse toward 'inner feeling' which communally unites the anomic individual to others through love remains the basis for a trans-class, even trans-historic, unity of the human condition. Thus, however helpful modern texts by Ernst Bloch, Karl Rahner, Jurgen Moltmann and Rudolph Bultmann may have been to the Liberation Theologians, their culturally and theologically unique position is, from Old and New World perspectives alike, both immensely surprising and hardly new.[77]

How, indeed, could it be otherwise? Not for centuries, except within Black Christianity, has Western theology been primarily focused upon human liberation and cultural revolution. If even today, with widespread European and American religious involvement in peace activities, the main function of church and synagogue is balm upon the restive secular mind, how great the distance remains to a spirituality centered on the experience of catastrophe and the redemptive project of utopian renewal. Reactionary charges that Liberation Theologians are converts to Marxism are similarly parried: possessed of their own religion, they have no need for a new one. The centering truth evades Moscow, Rome and Washington alike, Liberation Theology articulates the consciousness of a continent alien to them all.

The future of Liberation Theology doctrine — and even more, the future of its practice — in the face of an avalanche of accumulated and steadily accumulating human misery remains to be seen. But no force, not Opus Dei nor the U.S. State Department, can root out the unique traditions which shape the collective response to this misery. So as Rome and its loyal opposition continue ideological negotiations we may watch the drama's daily unfolding with some faith in the deep historical and social embeddedness of Liberation Theology's redemptive, revolutionary instinct and urge.

Notes

1. *Archivo General de Centro America* (Guatemala), doc. no. Al.31-355.

2. Bishop Cayetano Francos of Guatemala made a personal inspection of the diocese in the 1780s, charging that the alcaldes and local judges 'care only to become wealthy by means of Indian sweat,' that the natives 'have no tongues with which to complain, knowing only acrimony, cruelty, and abuse,' that they are 'whipped right to the quick and, sometimes left near death.' Hence the saying, 'It is all right to take from the Indian everything from his money to his hide.' *Archivo Eclesiastico de Guatemala*, Visitas de los arzobispos, 'Francos y Monroy, (1778-1792)'.

3. See Michael Novak, ed., *Liberation South, Liberation North* (Washington, 1981) which displays an inspiring and unprecedented conservative interest in Liberation Theology. The volume's major critique is by a Latin American advisor to the Reagan White House. See Novak's *Capitalism and Socialism: A Theological Inquiry* (Washington, 1979) for the general argument.

4. T.Fiehrer and M. Lodwick, 'Iberic-Latin Corporatism: Heuristic Uses of an Ideal Type,' *Human Mosaic* XI (1977).

5. 'Historical Praxis and Christian Identity,' in Rosino Gibellini, ed., *Frontiers of Theology in Latin America*, tr. John Drury (Maryknoll, 1979), p. 260.

6. Tzvetan Todorov, *La conquête de l'Amérique: la question de l'autre* (Paris, 1982), pp. 66-69.

7. Silvio Zavala, *Ideario de Vasco de Quiroga* (Mexico City, 1941), pp. 34-50.

8. Mexico City, for its part, had over 8,000 clerics out of a white population of no more than 60,000, during the late eighteenth century. Charles Gibson, *Spain in America* (New York, 1981), p. 64; Marcelin Defourneaux, *La Vie Quotidienne en Espagne au Síecle d'Or* (Paris, 1966), pp. 105-08.

9. Marcel Bataillon, *Aspects du Libertinisme au XVIe siècle: Actes du Colloque international de sommière: exposés* (Paris, 1974), p. 43; Bartolome Bennassar, *The Spanish Character: Attitudes and Mentalities from the Sixteenth to the Nineteenth Century*, tr. Benjamin Keen (Berkeley, 1979), Ch.I.

10. Marina Warner, *Alone of All Her Sex: The Myth and Cult of the Virgin Mary* (London, 1976), pp. 320-21.

11. Cecil Roth, *The Spanish Inquisition* (London, 1937), pp. 44-56.

12. Powell notes that barely more than 100 persons were executed in Spanish America during the 250 years of the Inquisition's formal existence. *Tree of Hate* (New York, 1971), p. 26; Henry Kamen, *The Spanish Inquisition* (New York, 1965), Ch.IV and VI, finds Inquisitorial Spain comparatively 'enlightened.'

13. Gibson, p. 80.

14. Marcel Bataillon, *Erasme y Espana, estudios sobre la historia espiritual del siglo XVI* (Mexico City, 1966), pp. 31-34.

15. Robert Ricard, *The Spiritual Conquest of Mexico: An Essay on the Apostolate and the Evangelizing Methods of the Mendicant Orders in New Spain, 1523-1572*, tr. Lesley Byrd (Berkeley, 1966).

16. William B.Taylor, *Drinking, Homicide and Rebellion in Colonial Mexican Villages* (Stanford, 1979), especially pp. 160-70.

17. Sherburne F. Cook and Woodrow W. Borah, *The Aboriginal Population of Central Mexico on the Eve of the Spanish Conquest* (Berkeley, 1963).

18. Silvio Zavala, *La 'Utopia' de Tomas Moro an la Nueva España, y otros estudios* (Mexico City, 1937); John L. Phelan, *The Millenial Kingdom of the Franciscans in the New World* (Berkeley, 1956).

19. For the contrasting picture in contemporary North America see Sacvan Berkovitch, *The American Jeremiad* (Madison, 1978).

20. See the classic work on religious parallels: Rudolf Otto, *The Idea of the*

Holy, tr. John W. Harvey (New York, 1958).

21. Bonzalo Aguirre Beltrán, *Regiones de refugio* (Mexico City, 1967).

22. Francisco de Solano, 'Población y áreas lingüísticas en el Salvador, 1772,' *Revista Espanola de Antropología de América* V (1970).

23. Ernesto Chinchilla Aguillar, *La inquisición en Guatamala* (Guatemala City, 1953), p. 66.

24. Victor H. Acuña Ortega, 'Capital commercial y comercio exterior en centroamerica durante el siglo XVIII,' *Mesoamérica* IV (Dec, 1982).

25. Enrique Dussel, *A History of the Church in Latin America: Colonialism to Liberation*, tr. Alan Neely (Grand Rapids, 1981), pp. 100-05.

26. Eric R. Wolf, *Europe and the People Without History* (Berkeley, 1982).

27. Stanley J. Stein and Barbara Stein, *The Colonial Heritage of Latin America: Essays on Economic Dependence in Perspective* (New York, 1970), pp. 124-55.

28. The fullest account in English, minus economic dimensions, is John Lynch, *The Spanish American Revolutions, 1808-1826* (New York, 1973).

29. Dussel, *A History*, Ch. VII-VIII.

30. Dussel, *A History*, p. 100.

31. Richard Graham, *Independence in Latin America* (New York, 1972), pp. 113-25.

32. Archivo General de Indias (Seville), *Audiencia de Quito*, Leg.589, J. Pérez Calama to M. Hidalgo y Castilla, Valladolid, México, 8 October 1784; Germán Cardozo Galué, *Michoacan en el siglo de las luces* (Mexico City, 1973), p. 89.

33. Ernesto Lemoine Villacaña, *Morelos, su vida revolucionaria a través de sus escritos* (Mexico City, 1965), pp. 439-41.

34. Lemoine Villacaña, pp. 184-85.

35. Graham, pp. 106-11.

36. Quoted in Dussel, p. 30.

37. Frederick B. Pike, *Spanish America, 1900-1970: Tradition and Social Innovation* (New York, 1973), pp. 20-25, 88-89.

38. Harold Eugene Davis, *Latin American Thought: A Historical Introduction* (New York, 1972), pp. 174-81

39. Dussel, p. 107.

40. Mario J. Valdes, *An Unamuno Source Book: A Catalogue* (Toronto, 1973).

41. Frederick C. Turner, *Catholicism and Political Development in Latin America* (Chapel Hill, 1971), pp. 15-18.

42. Christine Gudorf, *Catholic Social Teaching on Liberation Themes* (Washington, DC, 1980), p. 189; Dussel, pp. 106-09.

43. Dussel, pp. 107-12.

44. Dussel, pp. 113-16.

45. Andrew Pearse, *The Latin American Peasant* (London, 1975), pp. 37-41.

46. Ernest Feder, *The Rape of the Peasantry* (New York, 1971).

47. Alain de Janvry, *Agrarian Reform in Latin America* (Baltimore, 1982) pp. 13-17, 54-59, 67-70.

48. Pearse, pp. 40-59.

49. James B. McGinnis, *Bread and Justice* (New York, 1971), pp. 39-41.

50. See Peter Dorner and Rodolfo Quiros, 'Institutional Dualism in Central America's Agricultural Development,' *Journal of Latin American Studies* V (1973), pp. 217-32.

51. de Janvry, pp. 67-90. See also Stephen Gudeman, *The Demise of a Rural Economy: from Subsistence to Capitalism in a Latin American Village* (London, 1978).

52. See Mary Kay Vaughan and Ahmed Idris-Soven, eds., *The World as a*

Company Town: Multinational Corporations and Social Change (Hague, 1978), Introduction.

53.   Pearse, pp. 46-56; Andre Gunder Frank, *Critique and Anti-Critique: Essays on Dependence and Reformism* (New York, 1984), pp. 56-60.

54.   Dussel, pp. 140-47.

55.   Gudorf, pp. 121, 220-23, 230-31; see also Dom Helder Camrara, *The Church and Colonialism: The Betrayal of the Third World* (Denville, N.J., 1979).

56.   Dussel, pp. 145-47.

57.   See *El Padre Camilo Torres Restrepo, por Camilo Torres* (Cuernavaca, 1969).

58.   Phillip Berryman, *The Religious Roots of Rebellion: Christians in Central American Revolutions* (Maryknoll, 1984), Ch. 5; also Plácido Erdozaín, *Archbishop Romero, Martyr of Salvador*, tr. John McFadden and Ruth Warner (Maryknoll, 1981).

59.   Berryman, Ch. 8.

60.   Alvaro Barreiro, *Basic Ecclesial Communities: The Evangelization of the Poor*, tr. Barbara Campbell (Maryknoll, 1982).

61.   See Penny Lernoux, 'Debate's Less on Theology Than on Who Runs the Church,' *National Catholic Reporter* (14 September 1984).

62.   Penny Lernoux, 'Pope Deplores Social Inequities, Urges Obedience in Peru and Ecuador Visits,' *National Catholic Reporter* (2 February 1985).

63.   *Paradox rey* (Buenos Aires, 1932).

64.   *Instruction on Certain Aspects of the Theology of Liberation* (Vatican City, 1984).

65.   J. Severino Croatto, 'The Gods of Oppression,' in Pablo Richard, et al., *The Idols of Death and the God of Life: A Theology*, tr. Barbara E. Campbell and Bonnie Shepard (Maryknoll, 1983), pp. 30-32.

66.   Frei Betto, 'God Bursts Forth in the Experiment of Life,' in *Idols of Death*, p. 161.

67.   See, e.g., Walter Feilchenfeld, *Der Einfluss Jacob Boehmes auf Novalis* (Berlin, 1922); Peter Schaublin, *Zur Sprache Jakob Böhmes* (Winterthur, 1963), pp. 2-5.

68.   Ernesto Cardenal, 'Lost Cities,' *Apocalypse and Other Poems*, tr. Robert Pring-Mill (New York, 1977), pp. 62-63; also see Pring-Mill's sensitive introduction.

69.   'Apocalypse,' *Apocalypse and Other Poems* p. 91.

70.   'Ecology,' tr. Alejandro Murguía, in *Volcan: Poems from Central America*, ed. A. Marguía and Barbara Paschke (San Francisco, 1983), pp. 146-49.

71.   Ernesto Cardenal, 'Prefatory Poem: Letter to Bishop Casaldáliga,' in Teófilo Cabestrero, *Mystic of Liberation: A Portrait of Pedro Casaldáliga*, tr. Donald D. Walsh (Maryknoll, 1981), xii.

72.   *Mystic of Liberation*, pp. 50-51.

73.   *Mystic of Liberation*, pp. 108-09.

74.   Jorge Basadre, 'Introduction,' to José Carlos Mariátegui, *Seven Interpretive Essays on Peruvian Reality*, tr. Marjori Urquidi (Austin, 1971), ix-xxxiv.

75.   Jose Carlos Mariátegui, 'The Religious Factor,' *Seven Interpretive Essays*, pp. 127, 134-35, 145, 152.

76.   Charles Maurer, *A Call to Revolution* (Detroit, 1971), p. 65; for another fascinating parallel, see Henriette Roland Holst, *Herman Gorter* (Amsterdam, 1973).

77.   For the 'scriptural' use of European theologians and secular intellectuals, see for instance Gustavo Gutiérrez's classic *A Theology of Liberation: History,*

Politics and Salvation, tr. and ed., Sister Caridad Inda and John Eagleson (Maryknoll, 1973).

SECTION THREE

Culture and Ideology

1. Autonomy, Community, Women's Rights

Johanna Brenner and Nancy Holmstrom

In recent years, some of the theoretical precepts and political demands heretofore taken as fundamental to feminism have come under attack on the left and within the feminist movement itself: 1) a struggle for women's rights to control her own body; 2) critique and rejection of the nuclear family in favor of full integration of women into the public domain; 3) assertion of sexual liberation as fundamental to women's liberation. Ranging from Jean Bethke Elshtain and Christopher Lasch on the right, to Betty Friedan and 'Friends of the Family' on the left, these critics, despite their differences, have a common thrust which we will call 'left' conservative feminism.[1] While meeting fairly consistent opposition, they have also pushed socialist-feminists onto the defensive. This is especially the case for Elshtain, who uses the idiom of feminism and calls upon understandings that socialist- and radical-feminists share.

If rather cavalier about the subordination of women, Elshtain is thoroughgoing in her indictment of liberal feminism for its hyper-valuation of male-defined success, its acceptance of the competitive and hierarchical structures of capitalist society, and its elitist commitment to the technocratic welfare state. Elshtain's affirmation of the traditional family and critique of state services and childcare pays homage to 'woman's sphere' and traditional feminine values of nurturance, intimacy, and commitment, thereby appealing to a strong strain within feminism itself.[2]

While few socialist-feminists accept Elshtain's celebration of the traditional family, we find a deepening skepticism about the possibility of non-familial (non-kin, non-household) forms of solidarity, adult relationships, and child-raising. We see a retreat from that side of feminism that has emphasized women's need for fulfilling work, intellectual challenge, and sexual exploration, as well as a growing unease about the demand for women's rights.

This reevaluation of feminist politics occurs in the midst of a larger public debate and struggle. The combination of social changes of the 60s, employment recomposition, and economic crises have undermined the traditional family. The political response has been contradictory, but at present momentum is with conservatives. Fundamentalist organizations like the Moral Majority and the anti-abortion movement may be most visible, but pro-family politics and familial ideology have more sophisticated and more important sources and constituencies. While the Democrats ran the first woman vice-presidential candidate, and while more women are working for pay outside their homes, weddings are big again, family is celebrated in the media, and most Americans surveyed agree that strengthening the family is an important goal of social policy. A new ideal of a two-earner family and more consensual marriage is replacing the old male-breadwinner female-housewife form. The effort to resuscitate the family is understandable. It remains the primary institution for caring for children. And as public life becomes more competitive and brutal, the family becomes an even more important source of emotional and economic survival at the same time as its capacity to provide them diminishes.

Feminists have not been exempt from these pressures. Given the decline of the left and women's movements, given also the tremendous difficulty of building collective and communal forms for sharing economic resources and providing for our social/emotional needs, most have returned to couple-based households (both heterosexual and lesbian) and motherhood (many with a live-in coparent). While this is partly the 60s generation coming up against the biological clock, these choices, however positive, make women more open to a critique of feminism which denigrates the rewards of public life — work, political organizing, etc.

Though seductive, this critique is intellectually barren, resting on a series of false counter-positions. In each area — family, sexuality, rights, abortion — the critique insists that we choose between bourgeois individualism and traditional forms. If we value commitment, then we need give up feminist demands for autonomy. If we seek the rewards of raising children, then so much for full social participation. If we want security, then we can't hope for full self-development. While conflicts between autonomy and community and between private and public life are quite real under capitalism, and some trade-offs may be required in any society, these are not universally counterposed. Moreover, even within the limits capitalism imposes, we can win reforms that increase the social space for resistance and allow us, at least partly, to transcend these conflicts in our own lives.

The struggle for women's rights — that is, the language of rights and the goal of autonomy — is neither individualistic nor male-identified. While neither rights nor reforms constitute a full program for women's liberation, the struggle for rights is necessary to the woman's movement and can be integrated into a politics of socialist transformation. Furthermore, the concept of rights will remain pertinent to any socialist society.

Equality and Commitment

In the manichean world of 'left' conservative feminism, we have two choices. We can live in the traditional family, based on long-term commitment, an ethic of obligation and sharing, a recognition of others' needs and their claims on us. Or we can choose partnerships of 'freely contracting' individuals, negotiating the terms of their 'non-binding commitment,' obligated only to satisfy their own needs in a life of aimless striving. Over against the social contract ideology of a capitalist society based on possessive individualism, Elshtain poses the social compact of traditional family and community.[3]

Elshtain does not mention the patriarchal character of this traditional family and its consequences — wife battering, exploitation, women's forced self-sacrifice, compulsory heterosexuality and the denial of women's sexual pleasure — nor does she recognize the advantages to women of the social and economic changes (expanded access to paid work, the welfare state, the sexual revolution, etc.) that have brought the traditional family into question and allowed women to change the terms of their personal relationships with men.

Admittedly the demise of traditional marriage (in which male economic support is exchanged for female domestic and sexual services) has been two-edged: while increasing women's freedom, it has left women in some ways more vulnerable to sexual and economic exploitation. But it is impossible to return to the traditional family, and most women don't want to. Many women who work — even in blue collar and clerical jobs, generally out of economic necessity — want to keep their jobs. They appreciate the friendships and expanded sense of their own efficacy that working outside the home brings. They also want shorter hours, more time off, and an end to their double day — but they don't want to become housewives.[4] They recognize the value of their work lives to their personal relationships — daughters of working mothers are far more likely than daughters of housewives to mention their mothers as among the women they most admire.[5] The way to appeal to these women is not to celebrate the traditional family, but to show how women's supposedly 'selfish' need for individuality actually builds relationships and long-term commitment.

Instead of simply invoking community, we have to determine the conditions under which women can give and expect commitment without sacrificing their own needs. We contend that despite the distortion effected by capitalist society on this concept, the liberal-feminist demand for full participation of women in the public domain of work and politics is essential. The object is not to 'free' ourselves from commitment and obligation, but to enter these compacts from a position of equality. The fact that liberal feminists speak the language of contracts and limited liability does not justify ignoring the 'material basis' of mutuality. No one is or ever can be truly independent, so there is nothing categorically wrong with dependence, which is simply a condition of human existence. But for relationships to be equally fulfilling, dependence has to be equal, and that requires women's having equal access with men to economic survival and political power.

Ultimately, mutually rewarding relationships between men and women require broad social changes — control over reproduction, quality childcare, equal work, the socialization of the so-called private responsibilities of women in the family. Anthropological data support this point. Relationships are more egalitarian in societies where women are more equally empowered in the public domain.[6] In capitalist social formations, women gain power by earning income; the closer the spouses' incomes, the more equal their roles in decision-making.[7] People of equal power surely have a better chance of creating relationships that combine commitment and unity with autonomy.

Individuality and Solidarity

In opposition to the contemporary 'obsession with self' and the bourgeois conception of 'self-actualization' as occurring only when the self is free from obligations to others, 'left' conservative feminism proposes the traditional community in which self-identity is always constructed in relational terms. The 'I' is always defined as part of a 'we' that preexisted it and will continue to exist beyond it in the future. Against the rootless superficial individualism of an increasingly atomized society, left conservative feminism counterposes the grounded identities of participants in a dense web of social ties.[8]

Left conservative feminism forgets that with all its defects, bourgeois individualism represented an advance over feudalism in which social ties were based on force, on necessity, and on the suppression of everyone, women most brutally. But there are alternatives to the either/or of the identity, obligation, and support provided by oppressive community, and the insecurity of 'free market' individuality. The ahistorical, atomistic individualism based on market values that defines the self in bourgeois thought is not the only way to define autonomy. In our view, the value of non-traditional communities consists in their being freely chosen but also premised on mutual obligations and individuals' right to expect group support.

The women's movement ideally, and to a certain extent in practice, represents a community in which the conflicts between individuality and community can be transcended. The group is expected to support and encourage each woman's individual development. Yet, each member is also understood to share important interests with other women — not because of biology primarily, but because of the history and society we unfortunately share. Through the recognition of mutual interests and a collective struggle around them, a sense of 'we,' not just 'I,' emerges. But this sense of collectivity is not based on obedience and conformity, does not require unconditional subordination. No one is forced to belong to the group, so people cannot be constrained in the same way as in the traditional family and community where one's daily survival depends on participation. Moreover, the group's long-term goals (equality, self-determination) and daily activity (political action) support structures and interactions (education, discussion, decision) that help each member become a critical and self-confident thinker, capable of preserving an independent point of view.

The group persists only so long as it continues to meet individual needs. But, as individuals participate, their needs also change — they develop commitments and ties to the group. This kind of solidarity is found in other movements as well — workers' movements, socialist movements, Black liberation — although it may be called by different names — sisterhood, brotherhood, comradeship.

Constructing a group life that preserves this balance between individuality and collectivity is not simple. People fail in their commitments, dissent is treated as disloyalty. The women's movement has had plenty of failures along with notable successes. But the lessons of both provide the basis for new commitments. With all the failures, our experience still validates the possibility of reconciling autonomy and community.

Sexual Freedom and Intimacy

The counterposition between self-expression and commitment, autonomy and community permeates feminist debate over sexuality. Elshtain's critique is echoed by Irene Diamond and Lee Quinby when they argue, in a *Sign* symposium, that the demand for control over our bodies slips too readily into a language of domination and that instead of demanding 'sexuated pleasure,' feminists should seek to foster 'the pleasure of intimacy, citizenry, cooperation, community, and communion.'[9]

The feminist challenge to a heterosexual ideal based on dominance/submission and the double standard has cut in two directions. On the one hand, the hyper-individualism of the dominant ideology within which sexual freedom and consent are defined constructs sexual equality in terms of a bourgeois contract. Men and women are to be equally consumers and providers of sex. Women can take the same predatory stance toward men that men have taken toward women. In reality, the gross economic and social inequalities between men and women ensure that women end up the losers in such bargains. On the other hand, the recognition of women's right to demand sexual pleasure, to initiate sexual interactions, to be lustful, to be lesbian, has crucially improved many women's lives.

Those who see in the sexual revolution only new forms of domination (Marcuse's repressive desublimation, Foucault's deployment of sexuality) and sexual exploitation of women are forced to retreat into a narrow ideal that excludes the pleasures of sexual experimentation and play. To emphasize 'intimacy and communion' *rather than* 'sexuated pleasure' is to deny our potential for a wide variety of sexual/affectional relationships which range from casual sexual encounters to sexual friendships to deeply felt, long-term sexual intimacy. On the other hand, those who ignore the dangers of sexual freedom in the context of a male-dominated society simply open the door to the right-wing critique. In this society, long-term commitments do offer protection, however tenuous, for many women in heterosexual unions. Rather than allowing conservatives to force us into a choice between the protection and repressiveness of traditional heterosexual relationships (or of coupling modeled after them) and the freedom and danger of life lived outside them, we need to define a more historicized approach. This approach would hold onto a vision of sexual liberation while criticizing its degraded and manipulative versions in (capitalist) pornography, advertising, 'swinging' life-styles, etc. It would require us to identify with the ideals of consensual sexual pleasure and experimentation as we organize for changes in the social, economic, and political context within which we engage in sexual practices and which inevitably define their meaning.[10]

Who Cares for the Children?

While socialist-feminists, until recently, regarded the privatized world of the family as fundamentally anti-social and a prison for women, left conservative feminism centers on the family as the locus of nurturance, as the source for personalities capable of loyalty and commitment, and as one point of resistance to the imperatives of bureaucratic, technocratic state power.[11] On this view, private and public are treated as universal, counterposed entities, rather than historically created and thus potentially merged ways of organizing human interaction and social life.

It is easy enough for feminists to reject Lasch's claim that responsible and independent adults can only be produced by a successful resolution of the Oedipal drama, since that necessitates the subordination of women to the authority of men within the family and outside it.[12] It may be more difficult to reject Elshtain's claim that it is only within the bonds and loyalties of the family, the intense ties to particular others (especially our mothers) that we develop the capacity to make other commitments.[13]

In the evolution of feminist thinking from the early 70s to the present, motherhood and mothering have moved from the periphery to the center, perhaps even replacing sexuality as the primary issue for analyzing women's oppression. Many feminists share in Elshtain's derision of the liberal feminist ideal of the career-woman and her co-parenting husband, spending 'quality time' with their child, produced in her 30s when her career is well-established. This is a 'life-style' that few can achieve in capitalism; moreover, it leaves in place both the heterosexual, marriage-based household and the capitalist workplace as the primary institutions for organizing reproduction and production. Elshtain's attack on 'collective childcare' as children cared for by no one in particular strikes a responsive chord.[14] Daycare is often understaffed and chaotic, with high turnover and inadequate space. Many women have too little time for themselves or their children.[15] But perhaps more important, the pleasure of parenting and the value of the work mothers do, as well as the 'nurturant' values associated with mothering, to all of which Elshtain appeals, are significant elements in feminist visions of a good society.

Insofar as socialist-feminism defines nurturance as it arises in the intense relationship between mothers (or parents) and children within the nuclear family, we remain vulnerable to Elshtain's critique. Left conservative feminism imbues 'good' childrearing with the characteristics of motherhood institutionalized in this society. There is no appreciation here for the need to liberate women and children from each other — to liberate parents not only from the continuous responsibility which depresses and impoverishes their lives, but also from the excessive investment in their own children that privatized families encourage. Ignored entirely is the need to liberate children from excessive dependence, emotional and physical, on one or two adults in order to enable their more extensive participation in social life. Public experience teaches children to share, work together, appreciate the claims of others and the limits of individual autonomy, to develop a capacity for decision and leadership.

Children need security, attention, and guidance in relationships with loving adults — but no one has proven their absolute need for exclusive relationships mandated by nuclear family households. Children may require continuity in their lives — but we already know that something is very wrong in the often over-protected and smothered childhoods of children with stay-home mothers (nor is there any reason to assume that things would improve with stay-home fathers).

The data thusfar overwhelmingly support the conclusion that in most areas children in daycare do as well as, in many areas do better than, children raised at home. Alice Clarke-Stewart argues that children in preschool daycare are more precocious intellectually and socially, less compliant and more assertive than children raised at home.[16] Rather than looking to preserve the privatized isolation of the nuclear family, why not favor the open and fluid network of adults and children cooperating across households that Stack found in her study of poor Black families?[17] Indeed, why not envision such networks based on friendship rather than kinship ties?[18]

The most radically collective modern childrearing system that we know much about are the left kibbutzim. Children live in communal settings from several days after birth, though mothers breastfeed on demand for the first five to six months. Parents visit daily throughout childhood and retain close relationships with their children. The major care-giver is the 'metaplot.' The child grows up in a dense web of caring personal relationships; mothering is described as 'multiple.'[19] Two early and quite limited studies (small groups and 'observational' methods) by researchers committed to traditional forms reported some strengths but stressed deficiencies in kibbutz children.[20] Recent work, much of it large-scale, empirical, and longitudinal, has found kibbutz children and kibbutz-raised adults to be very effective in terms of motivation, independence, psychological health, and worldly success.[21] There is no persuasive evidence that kibbutz child-rearing disables children, and much reason to believe it enhances human development. At the very least, such collective experiments deserve our whole-hearted support. They could hardly do worse than the present system.

No Haven, No Heartless World

Even expressed in its weaker form as 'the place you come home to,' the image and idiom of the family privileges ties of solidarity based on 'personal life' and denigrates those based on other kinds of relationships. If we envision, for example, a radically democratized organization of production which allows individuals to 'be themselves' at work, which breaks down the division between work and play, which makes work self-affirming instead of soul-destroying and allows individuals to build a sense of community and collegiality on the basis of the common purposes and shared decisions of their efforts, can we not then envision work as a place where we are 'at home'? If we define the family, or some sort of 'private life,' through stark contrast with the rest of social life (work, community, politics, etc.), we give up the ground that connects desire for a rich and rewarding life with socialism. For we then accept the contemporary bourgeois worldview that human meaning and fulfillment can, indeed must, be centered on personal life, that public life is necessarily impoverished. Instead, we need to argue for the possibility of radically changing the competitive, individualistic, and hierarchical organization of work and community life. Extension of the values now located exclusively in family life — solidarity, respect, and a commitment to others' development — across a society requires the elimination of 'the family' in its meaning as a special place for those values.

Kinship, love, and 'good things to eat' tend go together in our society; but they are tendentially connected.[22] How then do we want to 'deconstruct' the family? Should households take responsibility for children and the daily needs of adults, or should we meet more of our needs outside the place where we sleep and enjoy privacy? What kinds of spaces will we live in? What kinds of bonds will connect the people who share living spaces? Where will children live and how will they be cared for? In a brief for radical 'deconstruction,' Michèle Barrett and Mary McIntosh argue the benefits of a society where most emotional and physical needs are met outside of households.[23] In her generally positive review of their book, Judith Stacey asserts that households formed by people whose economic and emotional needs are guaranteed elsewhere have little concern for commitment and stability. 'Whatever view one takes about the desirability of long-term emotional commitments among adults, it seems cavalier to ignore the possibility that relational and residential decisions we make might conflict with the needs and interests of children.'[24]

We would argue the virtues of separating the pooling of resources for day-to-day support from questions of intimacy and parenting. The fear that without emotional or economic necessity people will have no patience for 'working at' their relationships assumes the bourgeois ideology of fundamentally antisocial human nature and the Smithian world of the invisible hand. The weight of the psychological evidence in this regard points in the direction of relationships impossibly distorted by lack of alternatives, rather than made more rewarding by them. This is not to say that after the advent of socialism no one ever be jealous or hurt by lost love, or that the demands of a parent's life (e.g. to relocate) will never conflict with the interests of a child (e.g., in staying put). But why not assume that in a society where men and women lead rich and rewarding lives, the decision to have a child will be made far more freely than it is in our society (for women especially)? Those who choose to be parents will do so only if they are willing to accept the necessary trade-offs, which in any case will be far less stark than they now are. Moreover, when relationships break up, or someone moves, the pain of loss must surely be much less for children (and adults for that matter) who have many loving relationships and their own place in the world.[25]

The Family vs. the State

For left conservative feminism, the family and private life preserve a private sphere of individual choice and a defense against overweening collective power. Elshtain, for example, claims that women's 'maternal thinking' is a source of pacifist resistance to militarism; the family and traditional solidarities (ethnic, religious) are protectors of democracy, of the individual against domination.[26]

Elshtain's invocation of 'maternal thinking' draws upon a significant body of work in feminist theory asserting distinct male and female worldviews (either biologically or socially determined, or both). The work of Carol Gilligan and Sarah Ruddick is best known.[27] In contrast to male morality organized around abstract rights, female morality is based on concrete human need. In contrast to a male drive for mastery stands the female commitment to nurturance and protection of human life. Elshtain simply ignores the conservative and destructive side of women's traditional family roles.[28] There is nothing automatically oppositional in women's involvement with and care for their own children. The considerations that may lead women to peace movements — the interest in preserving the lives of their children — may also lead them to support military build-up and a strong defense. Concern for one's family can lead to a willing ignorance about public issues and a disregard for the people belonging to other families (e.g., women in neighborhood-based anti-busing movements).

But even if our goal is to generalize 'maternal thinking' to society, it won't be done by maintaining the family as a launching pad for maternal campaigns for peace and justice. Only radical democratization of public life can integrate care and nurturance into social decisions. The problem with public life is not so much that it is dominated by 'male thinking,' but that there are no institutions for active participation of individuals in making the decisions which affect their lives. The preservation of the family as a sphere supposedly protective of individual needs over against a public sphere organized for social needs simply guarantees that public decisions will continue to reflect the private interests and public purposes of dominant groups. The issue is not one of values but of power and decision-making. Even a public power more 'attuned' to needs could not function to meet them without this. Needs are not obvious, not all needs can be met, nor are all needs compatible. The full participation of all in decision-making is crucial. In making women in the family no longer solely or even primarily responsible for caring, we will not lose nurture but rather ensure that public actions more fully reflect individual needs.

On the same grounds, we reject left conservative feminism's critique of demands for expanded public services in which they argue that feminism has accelerated individuals' reliance on social engineering experts, increasing vulnerability to technocratic control.[29] Again, their argument ignores the other side of the process. While women may become dependent on the welfare state (as workers in it, as well as clients), they are less dependent on individual men and thus in a better position to engage in political activity and public life, including organizing together to improve the quality and extent of public services. We do not have to defend, indeed we should not defend, the elitist and bureaucratic character of the existing welfare state. The appeal of socialist compared to liberal reforms lies in our demand for public services that are worker- and client-controlled, democratic, and integrated into the communities they serve.

Socialist-feminists are understandably hesitant to embrace a vision of democratic and collective life which reconciles needs of individuals and the group. The failure of 20th-century revolutions to maintain individual freedom has produced considerable scepticism about the possibility of reconciling individual autonomy with collectivity. In this context, Judith Stacey points to the 'potential hazards in an excessively collectivized existence,' preferring instead an approach which acknowledges 'the dangers of intolerance and social pressures to conform' and creates 'more space for privacy, even anonymity,' providing 'relief from the onerous aspects of community.'[30] This is a timely warning. But in our view, it cannot be implemented by stripping the family of its 'patriarchal and anti-social elements' while preserving it as a place to come home to.

To defend 'family' as a realm of privacy protected from societal interference or obligation replicates the bourgeois division between state and civil society in which individual autonomy is only guaranteed negatively — i.e., as the right to be left alone to act without interference — rather than positively — i.e., as the right to have certain kinds of choices made available. Rather than counterposing private to public life, we would argue that individual autonomy can only be guaranteed by a radical democratization of the social order. We need not assume that with socialism the obligations of the individual to the collective will disappear, nor that the interests of individuals and the group will automatically be similar. We need only claim that decision-making in all areas of life — schools, neighborhoods, workplaces, broader economic decisions, management of resources, uses of wealth, military questions, etc. — will be organized so that individuals and groups who have different ideas can argue for and defend them, that political minorities are guaranteed the opportunities and resources necessary to organize. In addition, democratization requires structures through which the obligations of the individual to the community can be negotiated; it further requires that compulsory action be limited as far as possible, that available choices be maximized.

Family as a Source of Resistance

Family ties can and have contributed to the self-organization of oppressed groups. In general, however, familial ties cut in the opposite direction — toward fragmentation and away from building political organization and collective struggle. This is especially the case today with extended family networks attenuated and not constituent of broader communities (as was previously the case, say, in the ethnic communities around mills and factories). While the family based on a monogamous bond between two adults who undertake to care for themselves and their own children is not a contractual relationship, it fits well into an atomized society of contracting individuals. Families change the war of each against all into a war of twos against twos. Commitment to one person does not automatically exclude solidarity with others. Yet, because other kinds of solidarity normally appear so much more tenuous (and they are), building and protecting family resources — emotional and economic — appears a reasonable strategy for survival. Under normal conditions of life in capitalist society — competition on a labor market, insecurity, political atomization — familial ties become a substitute for wider networks and communities. Without those broader networks, people have no way or hope for changing the rules of the game. Playing within the rules means surviving on one's own, often at the expense of others. Thus, for example, it is not surprising that married people are far less sympathetic to expanding social services than single people. In the 1984 election the marriage gap exceeded the gender gap.[31]

Family and other more traditional ties (ethnicity) have fueled and supported collective political organization only when inserted into oppositional movements.[32] These movements define solidarity in terms which, unlike that of the family, do not fit into an individualistic worldview. Oppositional movements are premissed on the need for broader long-term commitments (beyond purely personal connections) and on collective struggle. In the context of these other solidarities, family ties of kinship and marriage may contribute to building collectively. But it is the non-familial connections which make possible transformed consciousness. Struggle opens people to social and cultural innovations which break through the fundamental individualism of the family. Collective and communal forms of societal organization appear as logical extensions of the relationships individuals construct in social movement — they do not flow directly from the practices of family life.[33]

Abortion and Women's Rights

Feminists have often posed their demands as demands for women's rights, focusing most attention in recent years on the right to abortion. Not only has this particular demand been attacked, but the whole notion of women's rights has been criticized by left conservative feminists as individualistic and presupposing a bourgeois political framework. For example, Betty Friedan's 'discovery' that feminists were mistaken to focus on abortion when the 'real issue' is the right to have children (as if the two can be separated) is echoed by Wendy Brown in an article critical of the politics of the reproductive rights movement.[34] For socialists, she argues, the abortion issue should be approached from communitarian, collective values, not the values of bourgeois society. Rather than minimizing the pain and grief of abortion, as Brown claims many feminists do, we should cease to focus on the inherently limited concept of women's rights and concentrate instead on the social changes that will allow women to enjoy fully their capacity for nurturance. Although we agree that liberal feminists define the issue too narrowly,[35] we will argue, against left conservative feminists, that posing feminist demands as women's rights is perfectly valid, and, specifically, that women's right to abortion is and always will be fundamental to a good society.

Although talk of rights often reflects a liberal perspective, it need not. Most philosophers agree that to say people have a right — for example, a basic human right to food — is just to say that they ought to have food and that no one ought to prevent them from having it; or, more coercively, that others ought to do what they can to enable them to have the food they need. Thus, 'rights' can be understood as moral claims and moral judgements understood as claims about rights.

As socialists, we think that workers do have — in the moral sense — and should have — in the legal sense—the right to control collectively the means of production, their labor and the product of their labor. One way of describing socialism is to say that under socialism the working class has this right, whereas under capitalism, capitalists do and workers do not. Workers' right to control the means of production is a right that they can have as a group, but not as individuals. Since they can't individually control the means of production, this is a right the class possesses *as a class*, not as individuals.

However, rights can also be individual, which is how liberals exclusively define rights. For example, the right to self-development would be a claim that all members would have on the group. In both capitalist and socialist societies, rights are meaningful and important, not inherently individualistic in a bad sense of a liberal concept of right. This latter is true of abortion rights.

Women have a right to abortion because it is essential to their self-determination — individually and collectively. Partly this is due to the biological fact that they bear children. But it is also due to mutable social and historical conditions: viz., that women are expected — indeed forced — to assume primary responsibility for children they bear. In a sexist society like our own, women need to assert their rights to control their reproduction, since others would unilaterally deprive them of this control and thus compel women to be sexual and domestic servants. If present social/historical conditions changed so that women no longer had primary responsibility for rearing children — imagine a non-sexist, truly democratic society — would each individual woman still have the right to abortion? In other words, is the right to abortion an individual right in a non-sexist society as well as in sexist ones? Since having children or not having children has implications for society as a whole, even for future generations, if society would assume responsibility for caring for children, then should each individual woman have the exclusive right to decide whether or not to have children, as we believe she does now?

In such a society, which would entail genuine community and collective decision-making, the issue of obligation to the collective to which our critics like to appeal has more validity. Nevertheless, it is still the individual woman who would have to bear a child or to undergo an unwanted abortion. That seems to keep the right to abortion an individual right. On the other hand, one could argue, such a democratic socialist society would have the right to expect various commitments from individuals; individuals could not simply do what they want all the time no matter how it affected the rest of the society. Is bearing a child or refraining from having a child so much different from the labor of defense such a society might democratically require of its members (and which could involve risks equal to pregnancy or abortion)? If there is no fundamental difference, then should society have the right to make reproductive decisions, in the way that decisions about production or defense are made. But that means abortion would no longer be women's right.

We find it difficult to resolve this dilemma. We might be willing to say that in such a society abortion would not be an individual right. However, we think it would still remain a right of women collectively. That is, there ought to be democratic structures by which women collectively could decide important matters that particularly affect women and would still particularly affect them even in these changed social conditions. Even in the best of societies women would still need rights over their reproduction. Marx said that rights are limited because they are the application of an equal standard to individuals who are necessarily unequal, i.e. not the same.[36] In the case of reproduction, the fact that, despite individual differences among them, women are equal to each other while being unequal to, i.e. different from, men, determines that they (and not men) have these rights. Only women would be in a position to appreciate both the needs of the society as a whole and what reproductive rights would mean to the individual woman.

In fact, however, we think there would be very few circumstances in which women as a group would be justified in intruding on an individual's reproductive choices. If women's real interest as to whether or not to have children were not in conflict with the interests of the rest of the society, then their desires, or at least actions, would probably be in accord as well — or could be brought into accord by social pressure, moral persuasion, and material incentives. The cases where these would not work would be too insignificant to do much damage. More problematic would be the situation where there is a genuine conflict of individual and group interest, where, say, individuals want more children than there are resources to support.[37] However, this situation would be decidedly rare in a socialist society, and a variety of noncoercive measures would most likely be effective. If not, it would still be worse on the whole to coerce women to have children or abortions than it would for society to have too many or too few children.

Socialist-Feminist Strategy

In conclusion, we reject the counterposition of a 'politics of rights' to a 'politics of human needs.' The crux of the issue is not whether to be for women's rights but how we define rights, how we argue for them, and how we organize around them. A socialist-feminist approach can be distinguished from a liberal feminist strategy precisely by focusing on that counterposition between autonomy and community which liberal feminism ignores and which lies at the heart of the anti-feminist backlash. Today women (and men) are forced to sacrifice one human need in order to fulfill another. Our politics ought to center on concrete reforms which allow people to get beyond these dilemmas. Further, the reforms we demand and the way we organize for them (the kinds of movements we build) ought to prefigure the social/personal relationships and reordered priorities we want to achieve through socialist revolution.

We can reappropriate 'control' and 'choice' if we locate them in a political framework emphasizing the social and economic changes necessary to provide women with real choice and real control. For example, liberal feminism defends abortion as a woman's 'right to choose,' in terms of her right to make the decision by herself, her 'right to privacy.' A socialist-feminist strategy locates abortion on demand within a broader constellation of 'reproductive rights' which create the conditions for women to choose *to be* or *not to be* mothers. Real choice depends on 'having money, a room, a job, some help, and also the ability to reflect, to analyze.'[38] The conditions for choice include, in addition to abortion, safe, effective contraception; an end to sterilization abuse (especially prevalent against women of color and poor women); quality medical care and childcare; adequate housing; a living wage; adequate maternity/paternity leave; shorter workdays for parents with no loss in pay; freedom to express sexual preference.[39]

'Reproductive rights' are claims women have on the society. The reproductive rights program includes reforms which increase women's capacity to have and raise children outside of the traditional family — by themselves, with another woman — as well as creating the work environments and social services necessary to support men's more equal involvement in childrearing and women's more equal involvement in public life. Finally, by forcefully including the right to have children, reproductive rights politics allow us to defend more effectively women's decision not to have children. This is crucial if feminists are to resist a pro-natalism that implicitly denigrates women without children and capitulates to compulsory motherhood.[40]

A similar argument can be made for a socialist-feminist approach to the family. The question is not are we for or against the family, but how can we address the complex of issues raised by 'family politics' in a way that strengthens the alternatives to the family/household as a privileged source of support and nurturance. In general we agree with Barrett and McIntosh's proposal for a political strategy which: 1) works for immediate changes to increase the range of available choices; 2) works towards collective institutions for accomplishing the tasks at present allocated to private family life — especially income maintenance, the work of making meals, cleaning and housekeeping, and the work of caring for children, the old, and the sick or disabled. Maternity leave, higher wages, and child-care subsidies, for example, will begin to increase women's independence, access to public life, and choices about our living arrangements. Caring in a lively and sociable setting not shut away in isolated flats and houses, meals available at school and work, neighborhood cooperatives for adults to share child-care, dinnertime, and socializing — all help to undercut the special attraction of privatized family life.[41]

In the end, though, no particular set of reforms will automatically reconcile our need for autonomy *and* community. The key lies in using the fight for reforms to shape a socialist-feminist politics and movement around women's participation in a public life that is both challenging and supportive, democratic and nurturant. We cannot allow the difficult personal choices we are all forced to make or the conservative environment we face to rob us of our capacity to envision a different world, to insist that our vision is, finally, the only way out of the contradiction between autonomy and community, and to use our vision to explain and motivate the reform struggles in which we engage. To lose our nerve at this point is to regress to subordination.

Notes

1.   Lasch is more anti-capitalist than feminist, and Friedan more feminist than anti-capitalist. We are here addressing as 'Left' conservative feminism that

260

subset of all these writers' propositions which are troubling to socialist-feminists. For an excellent summary and critique of the whole literature, see Judith Stacey, 'The New Conservative Feminism,' *Feminist Studies*, 9, 3 (Fall, 1983). See also, Michèle Barrett and Mary McIntosh, 'Narcissism and the Family: A Critique of Lasch,' *New Left Review* 135 (September-October, 1982), pp. 35-48.

2.　See, e.g., 'Feminism, Family, and Community,' *Dissent* (Fall 1982), pp. 442-49.

3.　'Feminism, Family and Community,' pp. 445-46.

4.　See Myra Marx Ferree, 'Working Class Jobs: Paid Work and Housework as Sources of Satisfaction,' *Social Problems* 23, 4 (April 1976), pp. 431-41; and Judith Baker Agassi, *Comparing the Work Attitudes of Women and Men* (Lexington, MA, 1982), p. 219.

5.　Lois Wladis Hoffman, 'Effects on Child,' in *Working Mothers*, Lois Wladis Hoffman and F. Ivan Nye, eds. (San Francisco, 1974), pp. 132-33.

6.　See, e.g., Peggy Reeves Sanday, *Female Power and Male Dominance* (Cambridge, 1981), Chapter 6.

7.　Philip Blumstein and Pepper Schwartz, *American Couples*, (New York, 1983), pp. 53-54. Working-class women gain more power from going to work than do middle-class wives, in part because they bring in a higher percentage of total family income when they work; see Stephan J. Bahr, 'Effects on Power and Division of Labor in the Family,' in Hoffman and Nye, pp. 178-85.

8.　See Jean Bethke Elshtain 'Antigone's Daughters: Reflection's on Female Identity and the State,' in *Families, Politics, and Public Policy: A Feminist Dialogue on Women and the State*, Irene Diamond, ed. (New York 1983), p. 445.

9.　'American Feminism in the Age of the Body,' *Signs* 10, 1 (Autumn 1984), pp. 119-125.

10.　For a critique of the 'sex debate' which begins to define a middle ground, see, in the same volume, Ann Ferguson, 'Sex War: The Debate Between Radical and Libertarian Feminists,' pp. 106-112 and Ilene Philipson, 'The Repression of History and Gender: A Critical Perspective on the Feminist Sexuality Debate,' pp. 113-118. For further specification of a strategic approach to these issues, see Ann Ferguson, 'The Sex Debate in the Women's Movement: A Socialist-Feminist Approach,' *Against the Current* (September-October 1983), pp. 10-16.

11.　Elshtain, pp. 300-311; and Christopher Lasch, *The Culture of Narcissism: American Life in an Age of Diminishing Expectations*, (New York, 1978), pp. 224-32.

12.　Lasch, *Haven in a Heartless World: The Family Beseiged*, (New York, 1977), pp. 174-83.

13.　'Antigone's Daughters,' p. 307.

14.　'Feminism, Family, and Community,' p. 448.

15.　In addition to quality day-care, reducing the amount of time parents must work is essential to alleviating these hardships.

16.　*New York Times* (4 September 1984), p. 12. See also, Alice Clarke-Stewart, *Daycare* (Cambridge, MA, 1982), pp. 63-67. The quality of care, especially the ratio of adults to children, makes an important difference. Kagan, et al., for example, argue that three children to one adult is an upper limit for the care of children under three years old. They find in general that 'a child's attendance at daycare staffed by conscientious and nurturant adults during the first two and one-half years of life does not seem to produce a psychological profile very much different from rearing totally in the home.' Jerome Kagan, Richard B. Kearsley, Philip R. Zelazo, *Infancy: Its Place in Human Development*, (Cambridge, MA, 1978), pp. 260-66.

17. Carol B. Stack, *All Our Kin: Strategies for Survival in a Black Community,* (New York, 1974). On Childrearing, see Chapter 5.

18. While the domestic networks Stack studied included non-relatives, they were organized primarily around kinship relationships. For a discussion of this point, see Martha A. Ackelsberg, ' "Sisters" or "Comrades"? The Politics of Friends and Families,' in Diamond, ed., *Families, Politics, and Public Policy,* pp. 339-56, esp. 348-49.

19. There are actually a variety of kibbutzim whose practices have changed over time. The most thoroughly studied group have done childrearing as described. See A. I. Rabin and Benjamin Beit-Hallahmi, *Twenty Years Later: Kibbutz Children Grown Up,* (New York 1982). One major deficiency from a feminist perspective is that women, the mother and (female) metaplot appear to be major caregivers for the first year.

20. Bruno Bettelheim, *The Children of the Dream,* (New York, 1969), and M.E. Spiro, *Children of the Kibbutz,* (Cambridge, MA, 1958).

21. See Rubin and Beit-Hallahmi; and Uri Leviatan and Elliette Orchan, 'Kibbutz Ex-members and Their Adjustment to Life Outside the Kibbutz,' *Interchange* 13, 1 (1982), pp. 16-28

22. Michèle Barrett and Mary McIntosh, *The Anti-Social Family,* (London, 1982), p. 159. See also, Jane Collier, Michelle Z. Rosaldo, and Sylvia Yanagisako, 'Is There a Family? New Anthropological Views', and Rayna Rapp, 'Family and Class in Contemporary America: Notes Toward An Understanding of Ideology,' in *Rethinking the Family: Some Feminist Questions,* Barrie Thorne, ed. with Marily Yalom (New York, 1982), pp. 25-39 and pp. 168-187, respectively.

23. *The Anti-Social Family,* passim.

24. 'Should the Family Perish?' *Socialist Review,* 14, 2 (March–April 1984), p. 121.

25. Kagan et al, for example, argue that even children who suffer extreme maternal deprivation or disruption in early years (e.g., orphans) recover when placed in a benevolent and supportive environment; *Infancy,* pp. 141-44.

26. 'Antigone's Daughters,' pp. 307-310.

27. Carol Gilligan, *In a Different Voice,* (Cambridge, MA, 1982); and Sarah Ruddick, 'Maternal Thinking,' *Feminist Studies,* 6, 2 (Summer 1980), pp. 342-67. See also, Nancy C. M. Hartsock, *Money, Sex and Power: Toward a Feminist Historical Materialism,* (New York, 1983), esp. Chapter 10, and Sandra Harding, 'What Is the Real Material Base of Patriarchy and Capital?' in *Women and Revolution: A Discussion of the Unhappy Marriage of Marxism and Feminism,* Lydia Sargent, ed. (Boston, 1981), pp. 135-63.

28. Ruddick, on the other hand, does recognize this other side of mothering.

29. This is the assertion of Lasch, *Haven in a Heartless World,* pp. xiv-xvi, and Elshtain, 'Antigone's Daughters,' p. 303, and 'Feminism, Family, and Community,' p. 447. See also Betty Friedan, *The Second Stage,* (New York, 1981), pp. 241, 306-7.

30. Stacey, 'Should the Family Perish?' p. 123.

31. Reagan voters: 61% of men, 57% of women, 65% of married men, 60% of married women, 53% of unmarried men, 50% of unmarried women. *New York Times* (8 November 1984), p. 11.

32. For example, Herb Mills has described the relationship between waterfront, neighborhood, family, and union which built the Longshoreman's Union in San Francisco. In Harry C. Boyte and Sara M. Evans, 'Strategies in Search of America: Cultural Radicalism, Populism and Democratic Culture,' *Socialist*

Review 14, 3-4 (May-August 1984), pp. 73-100; esp. p. 87, the authors emphasize the process of working together in constructing collectivity out of grass-roots organizing. We would put equal weight on the purposes and political objectives around which people struggle. Transformed consciousness arises from a process of politicization within the context of collective action, but it does not arise automatically from collective action itself.

33. This is not to deny that the impetus for participation may come out of family needs or the defense of family resources: for example, the entry of the coal miners' wives into the 1984-85 British coal strike which changed the women's relationship to politics, to the union, (perhaps, to their husbands). See Angela Weir and Elizabeth Wilson, 'The British Women's Movement,' *New Left Review* 148 (November-December 1984), pp. 74-103; esp. p. 101.

34. Friedan, *The Second Stage*, pp. 258-9; Wendy Brown, 'Reproductive Freedom and the Right to Privacy: A Paradox for Feminists,' in Diamond, ed., *Families, Politics, and Public Policy*, pp. 322-38.

35. For a nice discussion of the limitations of the liberal approach, see Rosalind Pollack Petchesky, 'Reproductive Freedom: Beyond a "Woman's Right to Choose," ' *Signs* 5, 4 (1980), and the further development of these arguments in her *Abortion and Woman's Choice* (New York, 1984).

36. In a society where everyone got what s/he needed, hence where there would be no conflict of interest, the concept of rights would not apply. Marx makes this point in the *Critique of the Gotha Programme* as a means of clarifying the inherently limited nature of rights — but not in order to dismiss the need for rights short of 'pure communism.'

37. The conflict in China between the government's effort to keep down population and the peasants' efforts to have more children would seem a case in point. In our view it is not. However, the Chinese case raises a host of complex issues beyond the scope of this paper, including the problem of building social-ism in an underdeveloped country, whether reproductive, or indeed any, decisions are democratically made in China, whether China is a socialist society, as well as the more general difficulty of how to handle conflicts of interests between present and future generations.

38. Denise Riley, 'The Serious Burdens of Love?: Some Questions on Child-care, Feminism and Socialism,' in Lynne Segal, ed. *What Is To Be Done About the Family?* (London, 1983), p. 133.

39. See, Committee for Abortion Rights and Against Sterilization Abuse (CARASA), *Women Under Attack: Abortion, Sterilization Abuse, and Reproductive Freedom* (New York, 1979), For a discussion of reproductive rights politics and feminist theory on sex, reproduction, and the family, see Linda Gordon, 'Why Nineteenth-Century Feminists Did Not Support "Birth Control" and Twentieth-Century Feminists Do: Feminism, Reproduction, and the Family,' in Thorne, *Rethinking the Family*, pp. 40-53, esp, pp. 49-52.

40. 'Reproductive rights' also breaks from Friedan's attempt to excise 'sexual politics' — lesbianism and abortion — from feminism as the condition for alliances with all those 'including anti-abortion Catholics, who want to fight for our right to have children.' *The Second Stage*, pp. 103-111.

41. *The Anti-Social Family*, Chapter IV. For a discussion of the contradictions in welfare state policy and how feminists might deal with them, see Fran Bennett, 'The State, Welfare, and Women's Dependence,' in Segal, *What Is To Be Done About the Family?*, pp. 190-214.

2. Makin' Flippy-Floppy:
Postmodernism and the Baby-Boom PMC

Fred Pfeil

Fredric Jameson's 'Postmodernism, or the Cultural Logic of Late Capitalism' seems to be the last word on the subject of postmodernism, and/or on the postmodern subject.[1] Ranging magisterially over a wide array of aesthetic practices and terrains from Pop art to poetry, from contemporary 'retro' films to L A's new Bonaventure Hotel, Jameson provides us with a stunning phenomenology of the postmodern: what, he asks, is it like to be in the presence of this object, to watch this sort of film or read this book, to stand or move in this peculiar architectural 'hyper-space'? His answers are a *tour de force* of existential description, which in turn underwrites the credibility of his larger claim that the common characteristics he has discovered in these works — their depthlessness, ahistoricity, and the centerlessness in particular, with all their associated effects — together compose what he calls the 'cultural dominant' of late capitalism *tout court*. For Jameson, then, the postmodern sensibility is essentially the effect or reflection of the deep structure of the capitalist mode of production, which, now having reconstituted itself on a new, even more multinationalized and penetrative basis, is seen to be all ready to catch the next Kondratieff wave.

Jameson's Postmodernism thus takes its place alongside Luckács's Realism: the former stands in relation to multinational or late capitalism in the same way the latter stands to the 'golden age' of industrial capital, as an aesthetic expression of the mode of production as totality, and as a part of that totality itself. It is not necessarily my purpose in the present essay to dispute this claim, or to enter the long lists of those engaged with the totality question, that philosopher's stone (along with ideology) of Marxist theory. What I want to argue instead is simply that the totalizing power of such a Lukacsian depiction, in its bid to offer itself to us not only as final word but as full story, ought to be resisted. For underneath the apparent naturalness and inevitability of 'postmodernism' and 'late capitalism' as what Gramsci calls 'organic movements' lies another level of unnatural, willed and contingent reality — the reality of the 'conjuncture.'[2] And such a distinction is crucial for us as cultural and political agents; for the 'organic' in all its achieved naturalness is always the effect of innumerable conjunctural struggles won or lost, on the cultural, political, and economic levels alike. The organic, the totality, may set its limits above us, demarcate our moving space; but it is only on the level of the conjunctural that we in turn can act and move to change the space's shape and trajectory.

What follows is an analysis of postmodernism not as the inevitable effusion of an entire mode of production but as a cultural-aesthetic set of pleasures and practices created by and for a particular social group at a determinate moment in its collective history. Specifically, I will be arguing that postmodernism is preeminently the 'expressive form' of the 'social and material life-experience' of my own generation and class,[3] respectively designated as the 'baby boom' and the 'professional-managerial class,' or PMC.[4] To make this argument, I will need to describe that 'life-experience,' or at least its main determinants, at some length, if still too sketchily to qualify as a full treatment; only then will we make a full return to postmodernist works themselves, at which point some of their most distinctive features may become legible in new, and newly salient ways. This essay's main value will stand or fall on the extent to which it states the obvious — beginning with the obvious fact that most postmodern culture is first and foremost a production of and for a uniquely large and privileged generation, the majority of whom are placed in a uniquely ambivalent relationship to, that is to say, on the very hinge of, the capital-labor contradiction which both underwrites and undermines capitalism as much as ever, albeit in new, more complex and elaborate ways.

Before proceeding to this task, however, it is probably necessary to establish quite firmly a fact which stands behind and enables all that will follow here: namely, that the generation of the baby boom is also generally describable as a class. For if it be accepted that what Stanley Aronowitz has called the 'technical intelligentsia,' the Ehrenreichs the 'PMC,' Albert and Hahnel the 'coordinators,'[5] is by any or all of these names a class — or class fraction, if you will — we must also come to grips with the reality that the overwhelming majority of those United States citizens who, in 1980, were between 25 and 35 years of age were members of that class, at least occupationally. Of the 37.4 million citizens between those ages, 22.2 million were employed in 1980 in managerial and professional specialty occupations; professional specialty occupations (i.e., engineers, architects, computer scientists, systems analysts); health diagnosing occupations (primarily dentists and doctors); in health assessment and treating (licensed nurses and therapists); as teachers, librarians and counselors; and in technical, sales, and administrative support occupations (lower-level managerial — not including salesclerks in stores).[6] That's 59% of all 25-35 year olds, 82% of all those employed.[7] Clearly, such amazing statistics are rife with implications, chief among which must be their effects on our reading of the recent history of class struggle in the U.S. On the one hand, they lend credence to theories of the *embourgeoisement* and massification of the U.S. working class, whose children, we may well surmise, have been groomed and encouraged to fly the coop outward and upward, at the expense of old class traditions, networks and ties. Yet they also suggest a degree of successful class struggle as well, insofar as upward mobility for the next generation in terms of work status, if not actual remuneration, was an implicit but very real political demand of the 50s and 60s — a demand which had already brought up to 'a quarter of the sons of skilled blue-collar workers and close to a fifth of the sons of semi-skilled workers . . . into the PMC' by the mid-sixties, according to one study noted by the Ehrenreichs,[8] and which emerged explicitly in the 'open university' and 'open admission' struggles of the 60s and early 70s. The statistics attest to a striking convergence of middle- and working-class trajectories in the post-war period as, through the 50s, 60s, and 70s, the bulk of the baby boom was funneled into the professional-managerial class by pressures from above and below. It is this common experience we must now examine, albeit necessarily in schematic and abstracted form — for it is this specific experiential matrix from which postmodernism draws its life.

I. From Baby Boom to PMC: A Social History

The Private Sphere

And you may find yourself
in a beautiful house
with a beautiful wife,
And you may ask yourself—
Well . . . how did I
get here?
—Talking Heads, 'Once in a
Lifetime,'
Remain in Light (1980)

So hold me, Mom, in your long
arms.
In your automatic arms. Your
electronic arms. In your long
arms.
—Laurie Anderson, 'O
Superman,'
Big Science (1982)

By the private sphere, I mean those spaces and experiences set off and against the public realms of economy and the State — chiefly, in other words, those networks of kinship and collectivity which we call friends and family, those experiences we group together as our private or personal lives.[9] Yet the most striking transformation in this private sphere for both middle and working classes in post-World War II America is precisely the invasion and colonization of its hitherto sacrosanct territory by new economic and political exigencies and concerns. Here I am referring first and foremost to that network of politico-economic strategies and decisions that underlay the mass movement out of the cities and into the suburbs in the 1940s and 1950s.[10] Suburbanization, not affordable urban public housing, was the combined reply of business and state interests to the potentially dangerous popular demand for affordable space in the post-war years; and it proved a most effective solution. All those Levittowns and census tracts, loosely tied together by federally funded expressways and beltways, those interminable circuits of 'living units' splayed out around the cities' decaying cores, not only made a fine living for whole hosts of speculators and developers — much of it, of course, on federally guaranteed low-interest mortgages and loans — by literally distancing both blue- and white-collar workers from their place of work, by snapping the nuclear family out and away from wider networks of neighborhood, kin and clan, they also boosted consumption while simultaneously shrinking both the private and public sphere. Workplace and neighborhood cultures effectively dried up and disappeared; now the attenuated family 'unit' stayed home in its own private living room and watched tv.

By breaking up these old communal networks and cultures, suburbanization thus paved the way for the commodification of daily life on a newly expanded scale. For wives and mothers in particular, as Ehrenreich and English have made stunningly clear, hordes of commodities and experts offered themselves in exchange for those cheaper, friendlier, more socialized functions and services of the past — and offered dire prophecies of what would come if the whites weren't white enough, the car not new enough, the house not kept pretty and picked up.[11] The official goal of all this spending and striving was a level of privatized consumption and attainment exaggerated even by previous middle-class standards; yet it was, to a very real extent, the only goal or life-model in town. And one consequence of these new quantitatively higher standards of consumption was, paradoxically enough, that more and more women sneaked out of their gilded cages, found paying jobs, and went (back) to waged work in the public sphere.

Yet this movement in turn coexisted uneasily with a whole different set of expectations, also brilliantly evoked in *For Her Own Good,* for childrearing.[12] Even as the state took over more responsibility for the child's formal socialization through increased public schooling, even as the television, that most effective and anonymous of all informal socializers, reached more greedily and precisely for the child's attention span, mothers were saddled with increasingly exclusive responsibility for the proper scientifically-guided and tested formation of the infant self. Insofar as the child is seen as a possible candidate for PMC status, and PMC status as the nearest thing to a guarantee of the good life, the importance of proper childrearing becomes paramount; for if this status is viewed as attainable through individual merit, rather than by inheritance, and it is further agreed that 'a child's future achievement is determined by the nuances of its early upbringing,'[13] then the science of childraising is everything. It is, in fact, far too important to be left to women themselves, who must be cautioned and advised at every turn, lest they either suffocate the child in too much love, stunt it permanently with maternal deprivation, or ruin its chances in yet some other way.

For Her Own Good pausibly locates one source of contemporary 'second-wave' feminism in the impossible double-bind dilemmas suburbanized and/or middle-class mothers and housewives were forced to live during these Cold War years of the Great Barbecue: confined to a space simultaneously more privatized and more colonized than ever before, simultaneously pushed out towards the (waged) workworld for that oh-so-useful second income, and pressed back into the atomized home to fulfill her rightful role as full-time mother under the watchful eye of distant experts from Dr. Gesell to Benjamin Spock.[14] For our purposes, however, it is more important to sum up all the transformations described so far within the private sphere in terms of their cumulative effect on the traditional oedipal 'family romance' of engenderment and individuation. The extreme separation of working life from hearth and home, production from leisure time, and, indeed, the withering of the entire public sphere effected by suburbanization and the spread of tv, transform the hitherto socially-backed authority of the Father into an increasingly diminished and abstract principle. It is symptomatic, not coincidental, that at no time in its ten-year-plus run on tv did *Ozzie and Harriet* ever disclose where, or even if, the affable, bemused Ozzie worked. At the same time, however, Mother was implicitly invested with a new if always dubious authority, by being saddled with the exclusive responsibility for the primary socialization of the child. Such transformations, together with the entrance of increasing numbers of women into the paid workforce, serve to erode (but not, as yet, wholly dissolve) the socially-constructed polarities around which gendered identifies had formerly been constructed: e.g., male = authority/autonomy/freedom/power/public sphere, female = nurturance/identification/connectedness/love/private sphere. And the result of these partial dissolutions is in turn a partial dissolution, decentering and devaluation of the autonomous ego (together, of course, with its fully inflatable, completely internalized super-ego) — which in turn is variously deplored as the road to a narcissistic, spectacularized hell and cautiously celebrated and encouraged as a first step toward a 'true differentiation' in which 'mutuality and autonomy, nurturance and freedom, identification and separation' would be united in 'creative tension' with one another within the single self.[15]

The Public Sphere

I see the states
  across this big nation
I see the laws
  made in Washington D C
I think of the ones
  I consider my favorites
I think of the people who are
  working for me
—Talking Heads, 'Don't Worry
About the Government,'
Talking Heads 1977 (1977)

When TV signals are sent out,
they don't stop. They keep
going. They pick up speed as
they leave the solar system.
By now, the first TV programs
ever made have been traveling
for over thirty years. They
are well beyond our solar system now. All those characters
from cowboy serials, variety
hours and quiz shows are sail-
ing out. They are the first
true voyagers into deep space.
And they sail farther and farther out, intact, still talking.
—Laurie Anderson, *United
States*, Parts I-IV (1979-1983)

Rather than linger over these substantive debates about the decline of oedipality, however, let us move on to consider the configurations of the public world which confront the post-World War II PMC-bound subject. In this archetypal story of the socialization of our typical baby-boom PMCer, be he/she working- or middle-class in background, acquaintance with the actual world of production comes last. (Indeed, for at least some of those from middle-class backgrounds, it is an hour that hardly strikes at all.) Here a personal anecdote may serve in lieu of fuller explanation and development to come. I come from a small factory town and vividly remember, from somewhere in the late 50s, in the middle of my elementary school years, a day when the teacher asked us what our fathers (just fathers, of course) actually did for a living. Most of us, middle-class and working-class alike, realized—with some trepidation and anxiety, I seem to remember—that we had no idea, not a clue; and my guess is that our ignorance was typical of the times.

If the realm of production appeared to us, though, only as an absent or misty shape, it was no more veiled than the shape of the State, no more obscure than the notion of political struggle. Politics for most of us found no place in the privatized house-hold; while at school, from primary to college, American politics and history were at best delivered up to us in a narrative as a series of 'social problems' addressed and eventually resolved by a happily coincident series of great men, who thus rose to the top.[16] These were, of course, until late in the 1960s, the golden years of the 'American Century,' in which our country happily and profitably served as the 'policeman of the world,' and of the joyously proclaimed 'end of ideology,' years when organized labor was largely bought off and incorporated, thanks to the induced consumerist hunger of its rank and file from below and state coercion from above, and when U.S. foreign investment and military might lived on a seemingly perpetual round-the-world honeymoon with one another, virtually undisturbed by any rivals. The formative notion of our politics, which still remains alive behind subsequent shocks and revaluations, was a bizarre combination of meritocratic-professionalist and consumerist ideologies whose most perfect expression is probably still the image of JFK (unless and until replaced with that of Reagan or Gary Hart), as the ultimate in snappy looks (a good image, an attractive commodity) and problem-solving pragmatism (from 'The Freeze' to any number of 'new ideas' candidacies).

The inculcation of meritocratic-professionalist ideology is, of course, the special mission of our educational system, with all its up-to-date methods of testing, tracking, and evaluation.[17] Most notable for our purposes, however, at least in state-supported post-secondary education, is the profound diversification and specialization during this period of what we may accurately describe as the 'knowledge industry,' now rationalized into a new set of class-divided and dividing 'layers' or 'tiers' — vo-tech schools and community colleges, public and private universities — each of which is itself further fragmented from within by new subdisciplines and specialized areas with their own jargons or idiolects.[18] We need to understand this development dialectically: it is not merely the result of state-industrial imperatives, or some *zeitgeist* of specialization, but of pressure from below as well, not least from the desire of corporatized working-class parents both to send their children to college and to secure for them a specific, marketable set of techniques and skills. The consequence of such rationalization and fragmentation, however, as Terry Eagleton has recently noted, has been the virtual dissolution of the university as an autonomous public sphere and its reconstitution as meritocratically-legitimated sorting mechanism for the market in labor power.[19] The baby boom PMCers witnessed and embodied (and, occasionally, rebelled against) this transition, briefly standing to speak at campus rallies and demonstrations for 'free speech' on behalf of an ephemeral public sphere of which their own presence signalled the demise.

Nothing, finally, epitomizes the utter subsumption and fragmentation of the public sphere at the hands of the market more succinctly, or conveys the ideology of consumerism more effectively, than the television we grew up watching. For most of us, in fact, television was all the public sphere we had: it brought us the world in the comfort, safety, and privacy of our living rooms; it told us what was happening, what the new looks, the new products were, what was news, kept us in touch; it came from a space or realm beyond discussion, not only in the sense that we had (and have) no control over what's on, but in its overwhelming physical-visual credibility; and it landed in a space which at the time at least was beneath discussion — the realm of hearth and home, where, as Todd Gitlin says, 'our guard is down when we watch.'[20] Such a trajectory gave television enormous power — power to scoop up our attention and sell it to advertisers, to socialize us into uniformly depoliticized citizens, to negotiate and promote on a national level the very definitions of what is legitimate and desirable. Television is thus, as we shall see, on even the deepest levels of aesthetic-dramatic rhythm and form, the *lingua franca* of this generation and class; at the same time, its deployment constitutes the *sine qua non* of what John Brenkman has called the 'mass-mediated public sphere' at work, a sphere, or pseudo-sphere (in the sense in which it is finally only an uninhabitable mirage), which 'is formed only as it continually appropriates, dismantles, and reassembles the signifying practices of social groups.'[21]

Production and the PMC

So think about this little scene
Apply it to your life
If your work isn't what you love
Then something isn't right

Just think of Bob and Judy

They grow it in those farmlands
Then they bring it to the store
They put it in their car trunks
Then they bring it back home

And I say

They're happy as can be
Inventing situations
  Putting them on TV
  —Talkings Heads, 'Found a
    job,'
    *More Songs About
    Buildings and Food* (1978)

I wouldn't live there
  if you paid me
  —Talking Heads, 'The Big
  Country,'

    *More Songs About
    Buildings and Food* (1978)

The classic definition of the PMC's place in the relations of production of contemporary capitalism is, of course, the Ehren-reichs': situated 'between labor and capital,' the PMC consists of 'salaried mental workers who do not own the means of production and whose major function in the social division of labor may be described broadly as the reproduction of capitalist culture and capitalist class relations.'[22]

Such a site has no clear borderlines on either side. Those placed in the top income brackets of what the U.S. Bureau of the Census calls 'managerial and professional specialty occupations,' for example, may be politically as fully recuperated by capital as nurses or elementary and secondary teachers, at the bottom of this salariat, are recuperable by labor. Yet it includes all those responsible for administrating, rehabilitating, ameliorating, mediating—in short, of reproducing the capital/labor relation, from the point of production, where the industrial engineer is deployed, to the dizzy, whirling realms of distribution and realization, where the admen and marketing people live with all their retinues, from the provinces of social service workers, those colorless halls in which the 'safety nets' are spread out for those qualified to be caught up in them, to those most apparently abstracted and autonomous realms of 'cultural production' from MGM in LA to Mary Boone in Soho to New Haven's Yale.

What binds these obviously gelatinous and heterogeneous 'middle strata' together as a class, though, is more than this external, functional description; it is also constituted by a class ethos which includes as one of its leading elements an internal set of norms, values, and attitudes towards work — both the work we do, and the work of our parents and peers in the old middle and working class. This 'mind-set' towards work is over-determined and accentuated by generational difference, but is nonetheless fundamentally enabled by the peculiar nature of PMC work processes themselves, dependent as they are for their proper functioning on some combination of the internalization of bureaucratized norms (academic and/or legal regulations, company policy, etc.) specialized discourses and behaviors ('being a professional'), and, not least, an almost guildlike sense of individual autonomy and ability within the more or less horizontally-perceived company of one's peers, with whom one not only works but 'networks' for the final satisfaction of each and all.[23] Such requirements and values (for which the way is laid, as we have seen, by education) differ markedly both from those of traditional middle-class and/or petit-bourgeois sectors (i.e., from both the 'organization man' and the small-scale entrepeneur), and from traditional working-class notions of solidarity and cohesion in the face of direct pressures and controls applied from above. For the PMC, by contrast, Foucault's otherwise rather dubious ontology of power is experientially true. His view that power, 'permanent, repetitious, inert, and self-reproducing,' has no definable or limitable sources, 'comes from everywhere,'[24] has been met with such acclaim by PMC intellectuals here precisely because the mixture of canniness and befuddlement it contains and effects expresses the perspective of an entire class, an entire way of life.

On the one hand the particular *durée* of PMC working life, with its historically strange concatenations of contingent work assignment or project, bureaucratized procedure, and internalized norms of professional conduct; on the other hand, the sense of self as a member of a profession, with all that entails, from possession of specialized skills and training to vocational pride and identification. If, looking up from this vantage point and with these values, up through the layers they themselves compose, the PMC finds it hard to fix on the ruling class, it can likewise only look back and down at the working class across an enormous gulf of differing meanings, values and experiences constituted first and foremost by differences in work. Yet we should not forget that this gulf is often enough a literal, physical fact as well: much PMC working life is utterly different and separate from any large-scale organized industrial production of material things; such production, in any case, is truly disappearing from our national landscape. As Mike Davis notes in 'The Political Economy of Late-Imperial America,' an article whose argument we shall have occasion to examine in more detail below, in the 1980-82 recessionary period alone, while blue-collar employment fell by 12%, the number of managers and administrators grew by 9%.[25] Similar transformations characterize the entire post-war period; their sharper pace and greater visibility at present are merely one more symptom that the benefits of the post-war accords between organized labor, big business and the federal government have been derived and used up by all — those in the upper brackets of labor who gave up control over the shop floor and investment policy in exchange for wage increases for themselves and social mobility for their children; those corporations who poured the profits from post-war consumerism and productivity gains to U.S. military-backed investment in new plant and production abroad with low slave-labor wage inputs, or into purely speculative enterprise; and the government which, in this new situation, now finds it necessary to switch the focus of its already truncated Keynesianiam from consumerism and the social wage to military spending (the military remaining as vanguard of what is left of the domestic economy and as guarantor of U.S. capital's newly-expanded, multinationalized accords.')[26] In their childhood and adolescence, they were major beneficiaries, unwitting dupes and target audiences of and for the old post-war capital-labor-government accords, but today's baby-boom PMC finds itself a critical stake in the formation of this new regime—though, so far at least, hardly a fully knowing or mobilized agent in its construction.

II. Postmodernism, Culture of the PMC

Having thus limned the overall constituent features of PMC construction in the postwar period, we are now finally in a position to analyze postmodernism — or at least a sector of it, a postmodernism within the Postmodernism Jameson has described — specifically as the culture of this same PMC, a re-working into aesthetic form of its central experiences, preoccupations, and themes. Such constitutive elements, of course, do not neatly sort themselves out in any one-to-one way as delimitable causes, sources or origins of postmodernist work, but rather appear within the works we shall examine as the more or less mediated social aspects of an overdetermined aesthetic-cultural field. As Brecht once said, our problem lies not with the concept of determination itself, but with the fact that there are always so many of them — and this fact holds no less true for cultural than for any other kind of human endeavour. Inevitably, in the analysis that follows, we will be dividing up the terrain of post-modernism into categorial aspects whose separateness is provisional and heuristic at best, and mapping the same ground on a number of overlapping grids. Searching out the level of the concrete through such tracings and retracings is, finally, the only way to do justice to the social object under study — by which here I mean both the PMC and its cultural universe — and avoid the pernicious temptation of first fixing on, then projecting, totalizing and judging, that object's single origin or end.

One example of such premature and relatively unhelpful totalization is a common thesis (among both Marxists and non-Marxists) about the nature of contemporary culture which I myself once embraced: that there has been, in contemporary American society and culture as a whole 'a decisive breakdown in the hitherto antagonistic yet mutually dependent categories of high culture on the one hand, mass or "popular" culture on the other.'[27] To such a statement, it is quite easy to staple any number of equally global assertions concerning, say, the collapse of culture as a zone of relative autonomy, the infiltration of the Symbolic through all other categories, the divorce and free-floating release of the Signifier from the Signified—assertions which I object to now not on the grounds that they are false, but rather that they are incompletely and unevenly true. To return to our opening example, we may ask for whom is the 'breakdown' of the mass/high culture distinction more real, the American working class or the PMC? The answer is as salutary as it is obvious, insofar as it brings us back to the concrete question of what constellation of specific social practices and experiences enables such a breakdown to take place, and is affected in its turn by it — back to, among other factors, the concatenated effects of a long and deep acquaintance with consumer culture on and off the tube and the acquired taste for high culture which it is the business of the liberal arts 'component' of a college education to transmit.

Thanks to these and other class-specific experiences, then, our PMC subject typically finds him/herself an extraordinarily well-rounded, complete cultural consumer and connoisseur, eminently capable of taking pleasure in a spectrum of choices (all within postmodernist territory, as we shall see) ranging from just a step ahead of mass culture (the low, stoned funkiness of *Saturday Night Live*) to just a foot short of high (the Glass/Wilson 'opera' *Einstein on the Beach*). We can, in fact, quite easily construct the array of postmodernist works from which we shall be drawing our examples in what follow along just such a spectrum, from general accessibility and relatively low mediation to limited access and its associated formalist highs:

Saturday Night Live	*Ghost-busters*	*Repo Man*	Talking Heads	Laurie Anderson	*Einstein on the Beach*
mass culture					high culture

What common aspects of these works — a popular television show, a blockbuster film and an independent feature, an art-rock bank, a performance artist, and an avant-garde spectacle of new music, dramaturgy and dance — reproduce the social experience and constitution of the present-day PMC and, in doing so, enable us to describe them as postmodernist? We are now prepared to provide some partial descriptions and tentative reconstructions in answer to this question.

I. Deindividualization and the Déjà Lu

Bud: Hey, Look at that. Look
   at those assholes . . .
   Ordinary fuckin' people
   I hate 'em.
—*Repo Man* (Alex Cox,
   1984)

Home . . . is where I want
      to be
But I guess I'm already there

—Talking Heads, 'This Must
   Be the Place (Naive Melody),'
   Speaking in Tongues (1982)

You're walking. And you don't
      always realize it,
but you're always falling.
With each step, you fall forward
slightly.
And then catch yourself from
falling.
Over and over you're falling
And then catching yourself
from falling
And this is how you can be
walking and falling
at the same time.
—Laurie Anderson
'Walking and Falling,'
Big Science (1982)

This is the time.
And this is the record of the
time.
— Laurie Anderson, 'From the Air,'
Big Science (1982)

Like all the constitutive features of postmodernism I will be discussing here, deindividualization emerges both through form and as content. In works near the mass culture 'pole' of our spectrum, of course, its presence is so obvious as to be virtually beneath comment: all the characters in the quick sketches that compose a *Saturday Night Live* program are obviously, deliberately two-dimensional piles of mass media stereotypes and PMC 'life-style' clichés (e.g., two PMC 'singles' out on a date). Similarly, on the high culture end of our scale, in *Einstein on the Beach* there is no question of identifying (with) any speaker or *actant* on the stage as an individualized character, given both the assemblages of discontinuous slogans, pop culture quotations, and stray verbal junk that comprise the opera's spoken utterances—e.g.,

I feel the earth move under my feet, I feel tumbling down tumbling down. I feel it Some ostriches are a like into a satchel. Some like them . . .

One of the most beautiful streets of Paris is called 'Les Champs Elysee,' which means: 'The Elysian Fields,' It is very broad, bordered with trees, and very pleasant to look at.

| SWEARING TO GOD | WHO LOVES YOU |
| FRANKIE VALLI | THE FOUR SEASONS[28] |

— and the utterly depersonalized (hieratically intoned or recited dead-pan; drawn out or repeated ad nauseam) mode of their utterance. So, too, David Byrne, the singer/composer of the art-rock band Talking Heads, 'sings' the tag-end, often slightly askew common language clichés and phrases which make up the lyrics of his songs in rigid enunciations punctuated by atonal swoops and squawks; in live concert he alternatively stands tensely at the mike, eyes staring straight forward, bugging and glazed, and twitches spastically and/or mechanically about the stage. Laurie Anderson blocks what we might call the 'expressivity effect' that simultaneously renders the performer a distinct, unique individual and, in enfolding us within that expressivity, confirms our own sense of unique 'personhood' as well. By alternately recycling her voice through a variety of distorting electrical filters (through which it may emerge, for example, as either that of an electrified child or a playback of a white businessman's voice at a slightly dragging speed) and assuming a breathy affectlessness inflected only by a tinge of boredom and a *soupçon* of religious awe — like the tone of the recorded operator on the phone as it tells you just what time it is about to become —she gives her voice a 'duplicity' which, as Janet Kardon has said, 're-peoples an absent self, or more accurately, a self that is turned down almost to zero.'[29]

We may thus view this thematic of deindividualization along our mass-high culture spectrum as running from the utterly stereotypical and clichéd (*Saturday Night Live*), through meretricious or merely shallow emptiness (*Ghostbusters*') Bill Murray character, Dr. Peter Venkman, or *Repo Man*'s Otto) to nearly total effacement and dispersal (Talking Heads, Laurie Anderson, *Einstein on the Beach*). And such a continuum in turn supplies us with an important clue to the whole thematic's rootedness in that dialectric of colonization and privatization we have already described in our discussion of the 'private sphere' above. It mimes the ceaseless process of the consumerized self's construction, fragmentation, and dissolution at the hands of a relentless invasive world of products. As William Leiss has it, within what he overly tactfully refers to as the 'high-intensity market setting,' the privatized subject learns 'to identify states of feeling systematically with appropriate types of commodities:

> The vast number and variety of material objects enjoins the person to break down states of feeling into progressively smaller components and instructs him in the delicate art of recombining the pieces fittingly. The 'wholeness,' the integration of the components, tends to become a property of the commodities themselves . . . [The] fragmentation of needs requires on the individual's part a steadily more intensive effort to hold together his identity and personal integrity. In concrete terms this amounts to spending more and more time in consumption activities.[30]

Postmodernist work may recode this perpetual vicious cycle of constructing oneself and dispersing into heaps of *de trop* rubble — of 'walking and falling' as Laurie Anderson has it — in a variety of ways, and strike a variety of attitudes towards it. One attitude might be the instantly self-cancelling nostalgia for the authenticity of the non-coded non-commodified 'real' expressed in the Talking Heads line quoted at the beginning of this section. Something like the same reluctance to part with the concept of the non-commodified self may play its part in *Repo Man*'s depiction of its main character. Otto (Emilio Estevez) is at first pointedly distinguished from all those who, like his friend Kevin (shown singing a 7-Up jingle in a mindless trance as he stocks the supermarket shelves) or his zonked-out parents (in late-hippie costume, slack eyes glued to the born-again evangelist shilling on the screen), live only under the sign of the commodity; yet, lacking any other means of characterization outside of or beyond just such signifying systems, the film can only recode him as a numbly reactive vacuity throughout most of the rest of its length. Similarly, the central guarantee of Bill Murray's Peter Venkman in *Ghostbusters* as 'our hero' is a level of crass self-interest so low as to be resistant to any of the stereotypical roles that ensnare, delude and trivialize the film's secondary characters, from the EPA zealot to the techno-twit PMCer, Venkman's dialectical Other, whom the film systematically lampoons and derides.

One attitude, then, towards the commodification and fragmentation of the self is horror and disgust towards those trapped in and defined by the endlessly proliferating codes, clichés and slogans of everyday life: a horror whose underlying anxiety that even the subject him/herself feeling it is not 'free' emerges in the mumbled choruses of Talking Heads' 'Once in a Lifetime' ('Same as it ever was . . . same as it ever was . . . '), and which, in both this and other Talking Heads' songs, as well as in Bud's casually savage, off-the-cuff remark to Otto ('Ordinary fucking people, I hate 'em') is tied in turn to a specific *class* anxiety. For the life with car and home and wife threateningly conjured up in 'Once in a Lifetime,' the lives of the kids playing out in the streets of L A out beyond Bud's windshield, are images which conjoin unself-conscious immersion with middle- and (urbanized, ghettoized) working-class life. The flip side for the baby-boom PMC of the attentuated, contradictory desire for 'home' will be the bliss of escaping from codification and definition altogether, by dispersing and scattering oneself through the codes and clichés— what I would call, borrowing yet another line from Talking Heads, the pleasure of 'Burning Down the House,' And this pleasure will be a feature attraction of performances and works on the high culture end of our spectrum: the Heads themselves, Laurie Anderson, *Einstein on the Beach*.

To these already quite complex readings and ramifications of the deindividualization 'thematic' we must then introduce another, more directly psychoanalytic level of complication as well. However much the decline of oedipality and the erosion of the autonomous male ego as both actuality and as cultural ideal may be results of the deep structural workings, struggles, and necessities of the post-war system, they retain an important specificity and dynamic of their own. In that light, we can return to read Anderson's 'Walking and Falling' not only as a description of the individual self stumbling from one commodified, fragmented signification to another, but as a cunning metaphorical exposé, from a point on the other side of oedipality — a backward glance, as it were, on the autonomous, unified, and efficacious ego as a half-truth at best. Similarly, through and beyond all the motifs of shallowness, vacuity, and dispersal we have already described, especially in their problematizing effects on narrativity itself, we may discern the problems and possibilities inscribed within the concept of the post- or non-oedipal self—just as we may usefully (mis)read 'Deconstruction' in the Eagleton quote that follows as both a narrative/dramatic and a social process, whose problematic implications for both the aesthetic activity of plotting and the political activity of strategizing and organizing he well (if not entirely intentionally) describes:

> In a curious historical irony, the death of the free subject is now an essential condition for the preservation of that freedom in transformed style. Deconstruction rescues the heterogeneity of the subject from its hypostatization, but only at the cost of liquidating the subjective agency which might engage, politically rather than textually, with the very ideological systems which necessitated this strategy in the first place. It is for this reason that it reproduces a blending of bleakness and euphoria, affirmation and resignation, characteristic of the liberal humanist position[31]

We will return to the question of the political valence of the PMC, including and especially the problem of political agency written into both its internal 'character' and its pivotal position within the structure of the U.S.-dominated world capitalist system, in the closing pages of this essay. Here, let us instead linger for one final moment over the obverse of deindividualization — the 'déjà lu' or 'always-already-read'[32] on the other side of its coin, as it were, whose constitutive omnipresence in these postmodern works we have not yet attempted to read as typically multivalent and overdetermined responses to and reworkings of the experiences of the baby-boom PMC within both the public sphere and the realm of production. One way of recovering those experiences is to analyze the pleasures offered us by and through the presence of the *déjà lu* in these works. Who gets the joke of Don Pardo's (resurrected seemingly unaltered from the days of that infamous quiz show of the 50s, *The Price is Right*) announcing 'Live from New York — it's Saturday Night!'? What potential delights spring from the foregrounded *bricolage* of past films and film genres in *Repo 4an* and *Ghostbusters* (in the former, just for starters, *Rebel Without a Cause,* sci-fi B-films of the Cold War 50s, and *Close Encounters of the Third Kind;* in the latter, those same 50s B-films with their small teams of heroic scientists, occult films of the 60s and 70s, and old Andy Hardy re-runs)? In whose cultural universe are both the Einstein and the Patty Hearst figures of *Einstein on the Beach* fully resonant? Who smiles with the hippest satisfaction at the simultaneously slightly wrenched and *recherché* character of Laurie Anderson's and/or David Byrne's lines? The answer is, of course, the baby-boom PMC, but not only or simply because of its uniquely thorough and comfortable familiarity with both the mass and high branches of the culture industry. What Janet Kardon admits of Anderson's performances is generally true of all postmodernist work, even *Saturday Night Live:* 'the most ingenious and educated "get the most out of it."' [33] Nor is there anything particularly new (or innocent) within class society about this pleasure of simple cultural recognition, of identifying oneself as a member of a small, broadly literate elect. For the PMC these simple pleasures are compounded and problematized by the lived experience, in both the public sphere and the realm of production, of what Anderson herself (following William Burroughs) describes as the 'virus' of language: language devolved, that is, from medium of communication to fragmented materiality which in turn is consumed and internalized as so many fragmented discourses, political, professional, consumerist, etc., etc. The PMC pleasure of recognition is thus nicely complicated and extended by the gnawing, teasing sense that the sign or convention, even when correctly read, recognized, and comprehended, makes no real or necessary sense, supplies no true social significance. As

Sigourney Weaver says to the smirking Bill Murray of *Ghost-busters*, 'You don't look like a scientist, You look like a game show host.' His Dr. Peter Venkman thus stands for us as an icon both of the sleaze and absence which are the end of the line for the old, unitary, unassimilated self, and of the fallen materiality of language within the fragmented ruins of the public sphere and the mystified, bureaucratized, abstracted work-world of the PMC.

II. *Kenosis and Apocalypse*

Miller: A lot of people don't really realize what's going on. They view life as a bunch of unconnected incidences and things. Suppose you're thinking about a plate of shrimp. Suddenly somebody'll say something like 'plate' or 'plate of shrimp,' out of the blue, no explanation. No point in looking for one either. It's all part of the cosmic unconsciousness.
— *Repo Man* (Alex Cox, 1984)

It's hard to imagine
How nothing at all
Could be so exciting
Could be so much fun.
—Talking Heads, 'Heaven,'
Fear of Music (1979)

We have already established that acts of cultural recognition are especially characteristic of the baby-boom PMC, given its unique familiarity with the whole terrain of cultural production from mass to high; now we need to ask more specifically what such actions feel like to us, how and how much experientially, existentially, they mean. Bear in mind that what is recognized, especially if it comes from or through the pseudo-discourse of mass media, is apt to be already estranged, pried loose from its point of origin in any genuinely social discourse or personal experience, distorted and crystallized into an infinitely manipulable, reproduceable fragment which, in this new stereotypical form, may be rubbed up and recombined with any other and then returned, as intrusively and insidiously as possible, to the consciousness of the privatized viewer/consumer to be recognized and chosen as 'my program,' 'my perfume,' 'my song.' Thus the serialized logic of the 'life-style' and the 'taste-group' simultaneously feeds on and undermines any genuinely social discourse or collectivity; it substitutes the always-shifting pseudo-collectivity of 'life-style' and 'taste-group' for the public realm lost. Recall, too, the obvious fact that for years now the baby-boom PMC has been the primary target of many, if not most, of the commodified messages, from M&M ads to *Masterpiece Theatre*, beamed out by the U.S. culture industry to the world, due to the unique combination of our numbers and our overall share of disposable income. These facts then translate, in terms of the experience of cultural recognition or 'tagging' on the part of the baby-boom PMC, into an extraordinarily steep and foreshortened 'half-life' or abrupt decay from the pleasure traditionally attendant on cultural recognition as a confirmation of one's membership in a genuine collectivity (class-based or otherwise) sharply downward to weariness, indifference, or even disgust.

Postmodernist form takes its distracted bearings and stumbling pulse from such constant manic swings from exhiliration to contempt. The quick fade — in pleasure, in confirmation, in the possibility of meaning itself — is built into the nature of *Saturday Night Live*, whose sketches and bits are almost entirely about other tv shows, films, and ads and their standard formats. There is, of course, sound business reasoning behind the marked brevity of most of these discontinuous comic sketches, which seem to become both briefer and more discontinuous as the evening wears on and the number of real commercials per comic sketch begins to climb. But I would suggest also that behind that brevity and discontinuity also lies the problematic dynamic we have just described: one each sketch has gotten its share of initial laughs from its own playfully distorted reference to mass culture (e.g., a dull Sunday afternoon or late-night interview format, a ridiculous ad for a useless or bizarre product), there is nowhere to go comically or dramatically but down — or on to the next bit.

Much the same aesthetic-dramatic impulse informs Laurie Anderson's work: the basic unit of her massive six-hour-plus *United States* Parts I-IV, for example, is a verbal/visual/musical 'bit' less than two minutes long. Potentially dramatic material is sketched out but never developed; instead, it is typically interrupted and/or brought to a halt by abrupt *non sequitur*. The sound and feel of the work as a whole bears a more than accidental resemblance to the experience of moving your radio dial across the bands, pausing to listen a few seconds to what's on each station, or to flipping through the channels on the tube in the typically yearning, loathing project of 'seeing what's on.' Shorten each bit still more, to a single scrap of common language, slightly wrenched or verbatim, and we are once again near the territory of the Talking Heads song, and a new understanding of lead singer David Byrne's behavior—alternatively enthusiastic, even vehement, and estranged—towards lyrics that in obvious ways both are and are not 'his own':

NO VISIBLE MEANS OF
SUPPORT   AND YOU HAVE NOT SEEN
    EVERYTHING'S STUCK   NUTHIN' YET
    TOGETHER
I DON'T KNOW WHAT YOU   STARING INTO THE TV SET
EXPECT
    FIGHTING FIRE WITH FIRE
('Burning Down the House,' *Speaking in Tongues* [1982])

Imagine these lyrics sung in such a way atop a thick, intricate musical texture of minimalist rock 'n roll chops, synthesizer tracings and doodlings, and heavy African polyrhythms, and one has captured the Talking Heads sound itself as a distilled expression of the privatized, channel-flipping self riding the waves of a serialized collectivity he/she can finally neither take nor leave.

Similarly, of what is now one of her best-known single 'bits' or pieces, 'Let $X=X$,' Anderson says that it 'was saying let this code alone, this code is self-reflexive.'[34] Yet the message that all signs, including those of language, are codes, and should not (and/or can not—for this is both warning and prohibition) be broken, derives not only from PMC immersion in the pseudo-universe of round-the-clock entertainment and consumption, but from the PMC's relations of and to production as well. Divorced from both the site and the experience of material production, separated by virtue of the mystified opacity of our own professional codes from the real systemic function of the reproductive functions we serve, what appears around us in our lives as administrators, social service workers, teachers, etc., is apt to look like a welter of random codes to be administered and observed. Insofar as the code succeeds in passing itself off to us as 'self-reflexive,' the resultant view taken towards one's work will inevitably be both frustrating, depressing, self-contemptuous—and blissfully self-exonerative.

The result of these impulses and experiences on the level of aesthetic and/or dramatic form are those larger structurations of repetition and discontinuity which promote the quite distinctive effect of *kenosis* — evacuation of content, numbing-out of feeling and sense — associated with so much postmodernist work. If in the public world signification is always a ruse or a shuck, in the world of the professions an auto-referential result at best, on the cultural terrain the PMC prepares for its own delectation the draining-off of sense and referentiality will become an aesthetic principle. Think, for example, of how the figures of Albert Einstein and Patty Heart are processed in *Einstein on the Beach*, how virtually all sense of their former significance (Einstein as socialist-pacifist, author of relativity theory, 'father' of the atom bomb; Patty Hearst as wealthy young heiress turned bank-robbing terrorist) is worn away and used up through literal replication of the figures, repetition of *non sequiturs* and inexpressive, unreadable actions — and, not least, by the immersion of their mystified and multiplied presences within a music whose hypnotically rapturous, obsessional, claustrophobic and/or infinitely expansive repetitiousness is from time to time without warning starkly cut off, only to be replaced by another seemingly endless block of sound. Or, moving back down our spectrum, think of the extent to which *Repo Man* reproduces in its own tone and tempo that very relation between the bone-numbing vacuity and circularity of daily life and work (driving around those blank, uncharacterizable, rundown spaces of L A) and sudden jolts of sensationalized, idiotic violence and spectacularity (flight from government agents; mad scientist with dead aliens in the trunk) which it is thematically about.

My principal claim concerning the form of postmodern works is identical to a speculation of Todd Gitlin's on the formal dynamics and structurations of commercial tv: in both, 'regularity and discontinuity, superficially discrepant, may be linked at a deep level of [social] meaning.'[35] By way of conclusion to this section, let me concede that all these peculiar amalgams of disjunct successions without transition and long *durées* also derive some of their power and possibility from the dynamics of 'deoedipalization' in the private sphere of PMC life. The collapse of the public/private distinction, the erosion of the division of labor, psyche, and affirmed value on which the construction of both the reality and the ideal of the oedipalized ego depend, also help the PMC subject to construct and enjoy works proferring ambiguous pleasures of immersion and circulation quite different from the more traditional (and even more ambivalent) narrativized dramas of oedipal desire and its always frustrated or ionized fulfillment. I have already suggested that there are indeed some distinct political difficulties as well as opportunities posed us by this dynamic of deoedipalization, both of which might be drawn out here from consideration of the full implications of supplanting dramatic forms pitting the heroic, oedipalized self against the world of postmodern work where selfhood is portrayed as at best the most liminal possibility on the veriest edge of dispersion in a maelstrom of fragmented, ceaselessly circulating codes. Here, though, we may rather content ourselves for the moment with some brief consideration of the more restricted question of the nature and possibility of climaxes and conclusions within postmodern work. Given the combinations of senselessness, dispersion and *durée* it effects, given its aesthetics of numbness and kenosis, how can such works end? How may they themselves take up the question of ending in any meaningful way?

Let us start with what is obvious from even the most casual acquaintance with *Saturday Night Live,* the music of Talking Heads, Laurie Anderson's performance work, and/or *Einstein on the Beach:* neither climaxes nor significant endings are strictly necessary; winding down, dribbling away, or simply coming to an arbitrary halt are perfectly okay. Yet the impulse towards dramatic shape and conclusive ending often stages its own return of the repressed within these works in explicitly apocalyptic figurations and motifs. Of course there are also other and more external reasons in the Reagan 80s why such motifs are popping up; but the bomb that drops with such, at first agonizing, then finally numbing slowness in *Einstein,* the Statue of Liberty that turns into a missile taking off in *United States* Part IV, *Repo Man*'s alien visitations, and *Ghostbuster's* Armageddon also suggest the simultaneous desire for and dread of some ultimate, externally-imposed moment of truth which might once and for all put an end to the endless, senseless repetitions and switching operations of which these works and our lives seem to be made.

This possibility is simultaneously called up and mockingly cancelled: the take-off of the Statue of Liberty is just another bit in the middle of a pointedly shapeless show; *Einstein's* bombe, like Einstein or Patty Hearst, finally doesn't mean or matter all that much; Otto's final ascension with the aliens is merely one more brief occasion for him to feel 'intense.' But the most extraordinary, laceratingly hilarious and terrifying spectre of this doom — one whose appearance and psychic function both sum up and depend on all the social processes we have described here, from privatized consumption to deoedipalization — is surely that of the monstrous Sta-Puff marshmallow man helplessly conjured up by Dan Ackroyd in *Ghostbusters,* in response to the devil's offer and command for Ackroyd and his pals to choose the image in which their doom will be sealed. Under the shadow of this image-spectre and its scandalous, delicious fusion of endless circularity, uninterrupted maternal nurturance (Ackroyd explains to his shocked friends that the marshmallow man was the one being he knew would never hurt him, who would always be there), and threat/promise of a final end, we must now try to draw from this discussion of the PMC and its culture some conclusions concerning the valence, and indeed the very possibility, of a PMC politics.

Conclusion: From Impasse to Opening

Duke: I know a life of crime led me to this sorry fate. And yet I blame society. Society made me what I am.

Otto: That's bullshit. You're a white suburban punk, just like me

Duke: But it still hurts. (*Dies.*)
—*Repo Man* (Alex Cox, 1984)

I'm tired of travelling
I want to be somewhere
—Talking Heads, 'The Big Country,' *More Songs About Buildings and Food* (1978)

Where you're going, you've always known it
Where you're going, it's Michelob.
—jingle from beer commercial broadcast during program hours for *Saturday Night Live,* January 1985

Recall this essay's opening premiss: that the value of a conjunctural analysis of postmodernism must lie in the usefulness and specificity of the strategic questions that analysis puts before us and the projects it suggests, I will now try to sketch out, very briefly, what some of those questions and projects are; but first let me say something about what they will not be. It seems to me useless to make any recommendations, predictions or suggestions concerning the aesthetico-political future of post-modernist cultural works. If a good deal of postmodernism is a cultural expression and crystallization of the life-experience of the baby-boom PMC, that future obviously turns on the political future of the PMC — on what it ends up doing, and who it does it with, from here on in.

To see this point more clearly still, and to begin to strategize that future, it will help to touch on a point we have not yet mentioned concerning the internal lineage of postmodernist cultural work: to look, that is, to its historical position as successor to and supplanter of the 'counter-culture' of the 60s. The social-historical origins of this latter, officially-dubbed 'counter-culture,' with its often quite addled mixture of consumerist, alternative, and oppositional themes, have been recovered by John Clarke and others in *Resistance Through Rituals* as a result and expression of a wide-ranging mutation within the dominant culture attendant on the formation of the new class position of the PMC. In this new, strange social space, Clarke and his co-authors argue, and in some measure against it, the baby-boom PMC constructed a ' "negating" of a dominant culture' which yet emerged 'from within that culture.'[36] This contradiction, they maintain, 'may account for the continual oscillation' or ' "negative dialectic" ' of 60s counter-culture 'between two extremes: total critique and — its reverse — substantial incorporation.' Thus,

> by extending and developing their 'practical critique' of the dominant culture from a privileged position inside it, they have come to inhabit, embody and express many of the contradictions of the system itself. Naturally, society cannot be 'imaginarily' reconstructed from that point. But that does not exhaust their emergent potential. For they also prefigure, anticipate, foreshadow — though in truncated, diagrammatic and 'Utopian' forms — emergent social forms. These new forms are rooted in the productive base of the system itself, though when they arise at the level of the 'counterculture' only, we are correct to estimate that their maturing within the womb of society is as yet incomplete . . . These larger meanings of the rise of the counter-culture cannot be settled here — if only because, historically, their trajectory is unfinished. What they did was to put these questions on the political agenda. Answers lie elsewhere.[37]

We should not overlook the more than temporal distance that

lies between (for example) the old *East Village Other* and the present-day *Village Voice;* and yet the applicability of these words to contemporary postmodernist work still seems to me significant. Postmodernism — or at least those aspects and examples of it we have here examined — remains a counter-culture in the terms set and described by Clarke as a 'diffuse . . . milieu' which is 'divergent with respect to both traditional middle-class and working-class values and strategies.'[38] Indeed, as we have seen, that diffuseness is foregrounded as an obvious and enabling feature of postmodernist work; that disaffiliation, its most basic formal principle. And what seems most worth noting here by way of an update to Clarke, circa the early 80s, is the extent to which what is left of the older, traditional working and middle classes has formed into a culturally and politically reactive and reactionary core that has proved highly susceptible to the material and ideological blandishments offered by Reagan and the New Right.

This latter point is, it seems to me, obvious; but it requires further elaboration here, if only because it directly contradicts the rather widely-held notion on the Left that it is the PMC, not the working class, which together with the traditional middle class has supplied the indispensable support the ruling class needs to complete its replacement of the post-war 'Fordist' consensus by the new Raw Deal of the 'Reaganist' regime. This is the view taken, for example, by Mike Davis in the article cited earlier. Davis sees and explores, often with great insight and intelligence, the same political-economic dynamics we have described here: the erosion of the post-war consensus; the emergence of the PMC, described by him as a 'sub-bourgeois mass layer of managers, professionals, new entrepeneurs and rentiers';[39] the development of Reaganism as both a new politics and a new economic regime. Yet for all his local and specific criticism of big labor's collusive partnership in the corporatist-consumerist consensus of the post-war years, and subsequent refusal, in the heat of the 60s, to join with the civil rights, anti-poverty, and anti-war movements in what might then have been 'a genuinely hegemonic reform force,'[40] Davis turns away from any larger acknowledgement of either the effects of the always uneven and contradictory working-class struggle in the 50s and 60s to liquidate itself by launching its sons and daughters through college and into the PMC, or of its subsequent equally corporatist and deeply racist reaction against those classes and class fractions immediately above and below it in the 70s and 80s.[41]

The point here is not to demonize the U.S. working class as a whole, not even its most corporatized, reactionary, and racist sectors. Indeed, it seems to me not at all hard to understand why a white workforce stung by both inflation and unemployment, socked by a grossly disproportionate share of the cost of all social welfare programs, both proud and resentful of the degree of its children's access to education, white-collar jobs, 'alternative' politics and life-styles, should turn ugly and join that petit-bourgeois-ruling-class coven which conjures up Reagan. Here, the argument Stuart Hall has made with reference to wide sectors of the British working class is equally applicable: 'it has to be acknowledged that sexist and racist and jingoist ideas have deeply penetrated and naturalised themselves . . . drawing exactly on 'immediate experience,' and simply mirroring it.'[42] Similarly we must give suburbanization and the tv their due credit in account of the debasement and destruction of any potentially counter-hegemonic working-class public sphere. But the argument that it is the 'new *haute bourgeoisie*,' that is, the baby-boom PMC, whose relentless 'overconsumptionism' fueled the overall 'strategy of cost-displacement towards the working and unwaged poor' from the tax revolts of the mid-70s to the present is simply and seriously wrong. It was not primarily PMC 'overconsumptionism' which, together with ruling-class interests, gave rise to the right-wing populism that brought us Reagan; it was also white working- and middle-class *ressentiment*.

Having made this point, however, I hasten to make equally clear what I am not claiming of the baby-boom PMC. It is not untouched by Reaganism and the 'overconsumptionist' demiurge; it is not, in and of itself, a potentially revolutionary class. Rather, as the culture it makes for itself implies, and despite fractional consolidations and tendencies both left and right,[43] it is still to date most accurately characterized by its resistance to incorporation — a resistance which, as I have argued, coexists uneasily and inevitably with a concomitant desire for home. Today, every attempt is being made to recuperate the baby-boom PMC *in toto* under the very sign of 'overconsumptionism' under which Davis seeks to pillory it. To see such an attempt in full swing, one has only to read the Michelob jingle quoted at the beginning of this section; or, better still, to see the full commercial itself, with its sleek young professionals networking and laughing away as they unwind; or to slide through the slick, dishonest prose of the recent cover story on 'The Year of the Yuppie' in *Newsweek*[44] — an issue which, fortuitously, also triumphantly predicts of *Einstein on the Beach* that, on the basis of recent revival performances, 'With its status as a masterpiece assured, *'Einstein'* will endure.'[45]

Yet the flip side of such attempted consolidations is the possibility that sections of the baby-boom PMC may still be assimilable to a new counter-hegemonic bloc. This hope — admittedly, a slim one at best — is based on experiences and aspects of PMC existence which do not so much belie 'overconsumptionist' preoccupations with 'lifestyle' as walk paradoxically along with them. From the PMC's ambiguous coign of vantage, for example — though probably not above lower and middle managerial and professional levels at best — may come a relatively full awareness of the international division of labor in mutinational capitalism, which in turn may breed an informed, global anti-imperialist solidarity with struggling peasants and workers from the Philippines to South Africa and El Salvador. From its numbers in the health and social services sectors comes a vivid and immediate knowledge of what the abandonment of traditional manufacturing industries, the slashing of social welfare budgets, and the new 'top-down' race war against blacks and all other minorities have meant in human terms. And out of the dynamic of its own still incomplete 'deoedipalization' come new sensitivities to and critiques of militarism, the wholesale destruction of nature, and the full panoply of depredations wrought by authorized, masculinist Power, as well as struggles to develop new forms of non-hierarchical, non-vanguardist social organization on both the micro- and macro-level in and through which a sense of unity in difference, differentiation through mutual recognition may be extended and evolved.

It would be sheer fantasy to suggest that such tendencies and possibilities can be much further developed or extended over many factions of the PMC in the absence of inter-class, multiracial, and multi-national alliances with large sectors of the international working class, including and probably beginning with those members of that giant 'reserve army' who live within our boundaries without ever yet having been incorporated within any 'Fordist' or 'Reaganist' deal; it would be worse than fantasy to suggest that these necessary alliances will be quick or easy to construct. But the possibility that much of what we now call postmodernism might be turned and engaged in more progressive political directions is finally a function of the extent to which such alliances are constructed, such a political bloc, with its concomitant new public sphere, evolved. Let us conclude, then, by noting that in addition to all the other elements, themes and subthemes we have attempted to read in the postmodernist works examined here, we may also find traces and occasional figurations of just such an alliance — or, if you will, of the 'Utopian' desire which pre-figures and projects its possibility — in the inter-racial, cross-class relationships lamely and lately portrayed in *Ghostbusters,* offered as pure sensationalist adventure in the climactic chase scenes of *Repo Man*, served up as a complexly-layered sound and group performance dynamics by Talking Heads, and coolly sublimated into something like a design motif in the selectively black-and-white choreography of *Einstein on the Beach*. In each case, we can easily see ways in which the portrayal is vaingloriously delusory, even downright politically offensive; what has to be emphasized again, moreover, is that all such figurations are at present no more than trace elements of a dream whose concrete realization would require on all sides enormous amounts of hard work and painful struggle. Yet the dream of such an unprecedented collectivity, *qua* dream, does exist, and is as much a product of the routines and rhythms of life for many within the baby-boom PMC as that far more widely vaunted privatized, consumerized cynicism attributed to it as its single essence and ethos. One final word concerning the relationship between these dreams and desires in postmodernist culture, and the possibility of their realization during our actual social and political lives. I yield the floor to Gramsci, still our foremost expert and best guide to such dfficult projects as the one whose liminal possibility I have suggested: 'But this reduction to economics and to politics means precisely a reduction of the highest superstructures to the level of those which adhere more closely to the structure itself — in other words, the possibility and necessity of creating a new culture.'[46] The future of postmodernist cultural production — and, of course, of a good deal more than that — rides precisely on whether, when, and how this 'reduction' will be made.

Notes

1.   *New Left Review* (July-August 1984), pp.53-92. This essay is also in effect a 'totalization' of several earlier addresses and essays on the same subject, specifically: 'Theories of Postmodernism,' delivered at the Conference on Marxism and the Interpretation of Culture,' University of Illinois at Champaign-Urbana, July 1983; and 'Postmodernism and Consumer Society,' in *The Anti-Aesthetic*, ed. Hal Foster (Port Townsend, Washington, 1983), pp. 119-134.

2.   See 'The Modern Prince,' in Antonio Gramsci, *Selections from the Prison Notebooks*, ed. Quintin Hoare and Geoffrey Nowell-Smith (London, 1971), especially pp. 177-78.

3.   The specific quotations are from John Clarke, Stuart Hall, et al., 'Subcultures, Cultures and Class,' in Hall et al., *Resistance Through Rituals* (London, 1976), p. 10. I acknowledge my indebtedness throughout this essay to the groundbreaking theoretical work of Stuart Hall and his former colleagues and students at the Birmingham Center for Contemporary Cultural Studies.

4.   Barbara Ehrenreich and John Ehrenreich, 'The Professional-Managerial Class,' in Pat Walker, ed., *Between Labor and Capital* (Boston, 1979), pp. 5-45.

5.   Aronowitz's term appears in 'Cracks in the Historical Bloc: American Labor's Historic Compromise and the Present Crisis,' in *Social Text* 5 (Spring 1982), pp. 22-52; Albert and Hanel's in 'A Ticket to Ride: More Locations on the Class Map,' in Walker, *Between Labor and Capital*, pp. 243-78.

6.   U.S. Bureau of the Census, *1980 Census of Population* (Washington, D C, 1984), Vol. I, Part I, Section, Table 280, pp. 232-37.

7.   Figures for all 25-35 year-olds in the population are taken from U.S. Bureau of the Census, *Nta istical Abstract of the United States 1984*, 104th edition (Washington, D C, 1984), p. 34.

8.   'The Professional-Managerial Class,' p. 31.

9.   The conception of the 'public sphere' from which the 'private sphere' is derived, both by implication and through the actual historical development of bourgeois society, comes originally from Jürgen Habermas, *Strukturwandel der Öffentlichkeit* (Neuwied, 1962).

10.   For an incisive account of post-war suburbanization, see Gwendolyn Wright, *Building the Dream: A Social History of Housing in America* (New York, 1981), pp. 240-61.

11.   Barbara Ehrenreich and Deirdre English, *For Her Own Good: 150 Years of Experts' Advice to Women* (New York, 1978), pp. 283 ff.

12.   Ehrenreich and English, pp. 211-265.

13.   Ehrenreich and Ehrenreich, p. 29.

14.   Ehrenreich and English, pp. 269-324.

15.   The literature on the erosion of oedipality, both feminist and anti-feminist, is extensive. For an example of the anti-feminist depiction and analysis of this 'problem,' see Jon R. Schiller's 'The new "family romance," ' in *Triquarterly* 52 (Fall 1981), pp. 67-84; and for a dismantling of Schiller's (and Christopher Lasch's) position, see Jessica Benjamin, 'The Oedipal Riddle: Authority, Autonomy, and the New Narcissism,' in Mark Kamm et al., *The Problem of Authority in America* (Philadelphia, 1981), pp. 195-224.

16.   The 'great man' ideology of history as progress and its depoliticizing effects are vividly described in Jonathan Kozol, *The Night Is Dark and I Am Far from Home* (New York, 1976), pp. 43-47.

17.   See Samuel Bowles and Herbert Gintis, *Schooling in Capitalist America*

(New York, 1976), pp. 18-49, 102-148.

18.   Bowles and Gintis, pp. 201-223.

19.   Terry Eagleton, *The Function of Criticism* (London, 1984), p. 87.

20.   Todd Gitlin, *Inside Prime Time* (New York, 1983), p. 333. My discussion of the cultural and political effects of television here and throughout owes much to Gitlin's work.

21.   John Brenkman, 'Mass Media: From Collective Experience to the Culture of Privatization,' *Social Text* 1 (Winter 1979), p. 108.

22.   Ehrenreich and Ehrenreich, p. 12.

23.   This description of the work ethos of the PMC both draws on and differs from that of the Ehrenreichs; cf. 'The Professional-Managerial Class,' p. 26.

24.   Michel Foucault, *The History of Sexuality*, vol. I, trans. Robert Hurley (New York, 1978), p. 93.

25.   *New Left Review* 143 (January-February 1984), p. 23.

26.   For four distinct but overlapping accounts of this shift in the political economy of U.S. capitalism, see the article by Mike Davis cited in n. 25 above, pp. 6-38; Aronowitz, 'Cracks in the Bloc'; Samuel Bowles, David Gordon, and Thomas Weisskopf, *Beyond the Waste Land* (New York, 1983), pp. 62-94; and Alan Wolfe, *America's Impasse* (New York, 1981), pp. 13-48.

27.   The phrase is quoted from my own 'Postmodernism as a "Structure of Feeling," ' in *Marxism and the Interpretation of Culture: Limits, Frontiers, Boundaries*, ed. Cary Nelson and Larry Grossberg (Urbana, Illinois, 1985). It now seems to me that this earlier essay is seriously flawed by an urge to subsume and explain all features of postmodernist cultural work under the concept of the deoedipalization of the American middle-class home, and project a revised radical project exclusively from it.

28.   Texts quoted from the booklet accompanying the original recording of Robert Wilson and Philip Glass's *Einstein on the Beach* (Tomato Records,TOM-4-2901, 1979). First and third excerpt by Christopher Knowles, second by Samuel Johnson.

29.   Janet Kardon, 'Laurie Anderson: A Synesthetic Journey,' in Kardon, ed., *Laurie Anderson: Works from 1969 to 1983* (Philadelphia, 1983), p. 29.

30.   William Leiss, *The Limits of Satisfaction* (Toronto, 1976), p. 19.

31.   Eagleton, p. 99.

32.   The term is Roland Barthes' in *S/Z*, trans, Richard Howard (New York, 1974); see especially pp. 18-21.

33.   Kardon, p. 30.

34.   Laurie Anderson, '*United States*: A Talk with John Howell,' *Live Art* 5 (1981), p. 7.

35.   Todd Gitlin, 'Prime-Time Ideology: The Hegemonic Process in Television Entertainment,' in *Social Problems* 26, 3 (February 1979), p. 255.

36.   Clarke, et al., 'Subcultures, Cultures and Class,' p. 63.

37.   Clarke, et al., pp. 70-71.

38.   Clarke, et al., p. 60

39.   Davis, 'Political Economy of Late-Imperial America,' p. 21.

40.   Davis, p. 21.

41.   Though both processes are noted: the first on p. 12; the second on p. 34.

42.   Stuart Hall, 'The Battle for Socialist Ideas in the 1980s,' in *The Socialist Register 1982*, ed M. Eve and D. Musson (London, 1982), p. 5.

43.   While Davis is correct to label and condemn the 'overconsumptionism' of those sectors of the PMC (located, be it noted, towards its upper reaches) which

call for 'accelerated depreciation allowances, unfettered speculative real-estate markets and rampant condominiumization, sub-contracting of public services,' etc., is it not equally obvious that other PMC sectors, chiefly 'professionals and licenced technicians,' supply the core of both the feminist movement and the white American Left?

44.   See the 31 December 1984 issue, pp. 14-31, in which *Newsweek's* staff writers make the same move as Davis, only far more crudely and blatantly: having conceded that, of the voting bloc of 20 million it finds among the baby-boom PMC, only 4 million make $40,000 or above per year, *Newsweek* proceeds to construct its 'Yuppie' image (the equivalent of Davis's 'overconsumptionist') entirely from examples of the lives and values of this latter elite of the PMC.

45.   Alan Rich, 'Once More Onto the Beach,' *Newswee ⁻*(31 December 1984), p. 67.

46.   'State and Civil Society,' in *Prison Notebooks*, p. 276.

3.   The Big Chill

John Higgins

'Will you marry me?—Both of you!' (Meg)

'It is the belief that kinship, love and having nice things to eat are naturally
and inevitably bound up together that makes it hard to imagine a world in
which 'family' plays little part. This mythologized unity must be picked
apart, strand by strand, so that we can understand its power and meet the
needs of each of its seperate elements more fully.' (*The Anti-Social Family* p.
159)

I first saw Lawrence Kasdan's film, *The Big Chill*, in Boston in
December 1983. I went to see it with a group of friends, some of
whom had seen it already but who had liked it so much they
didn't mind seeing it again. I was told that the title of the film
referred in part to the current political climate — that freezing of
progressive social movements which had culminated in the election (now re-election) of Ronald Reagan. I enjoyed seeing the
film; it provided the usual scopophilic pleasures of mainstream
Hollywood cinema, an unusually witty script and — best of
all — a soundtrack composed mainly of Tamla Motown hits of
the late sixties. My analysis here of the film is in part simply a
recognition of that pleasure, an acceptance, but also an inter-
rogation of it. For in the discussion and analysis of the film
which followed its projection and our passive spectatorship, I
discovered that I deeply disliked the film and what I called at the
time its appeal to an ideology of 'socially repressive biological
and physical familialism.' It is the awkwardness and necessity of
that phrase which I want to work on here, an awkwardness and a
necessity produced by mapping onto the forms of common
speech and conversation the concepts and difficulties associated
with reading and academic labour. This essay is, then, in part a
continuation of that argument with friends, but also, with a
conscious emphasis, an extension of that argument beyond
them, in precisely the kind of movement which the film denies: a

movement from society in the limited sense of the company of one's fellows, to its larger sense as the system of common life.[1] The film closes with a wish to remain in that closed circle of friends — 'We're going to stay here forever,' as Michael puts it — to stay in that comfortable and secure household where the action of the film largely takes place. This essay is produced precisely from a desire to address the issues of the film beyond that closed circle, to make their discussion public rather than private.

Such a desire can in fact be seen as the founding impulse of film studies — the desire in the first instance to make film the object of a scientific analysis, a necessarily public object, an object defined by a particular analytic discourse. It is one of the central paradoxes of cinema that it occupies both a public and a private space: public, in that the conditions for the projection of films remain concentrated in public cinemas; and private, in that the organization of that projection is usually around a notion of the spectator as a private individual, as a passive consumer who, once that moment of consumption is achieved, will want to leave the cinema. It is the particular economic logic of mainstream cinema that it should address itself to public and everyday questions in order to maintain a public; and it is the peculiar logic of capitalist cinema that it should only ever address those public issues to private individuals as passive consumers.[2]

It is the fact of that address which is contested by the analysis of film which takes as its starting-point the terms of the construction of that address, the terms of the construction of public meanings for the spectator. *The Big Chill* calls particularly for such analysis, for one level of the terms of its narrative image is 'popular memory' as described by the late Michel Foucault: 'There's a battle for and around history going on . . . The intention is to re-program, to stifle what I've called 'popular memory'; and also to propose and impose on people a framework in which to interpret the present.'[3] *The Big Chill* is, as we shall see, precisely such an attempt to stifle or to repress a certain history and at the same time to impose a certain view of the present on its audience.

The history which the film wishes to repress is the history represented by the figure of Alex: the history of the active radicalism of the late sixties and early seventies. And the framework which the film wishes to impose as a way of articulating the present is a certain familialism, in the sense given to the word by

Michele Barrett and Mary McIntosh as 'those ideologies modelled on what are thought to be family values and the rendering of other social phenomena like families,' familialism as that dominant though often self-contradictory set of social meanings.[4] I shall examine two major themes of the film, and their interaction. The first will be that of the recovery of lost hope, and the ways in which that recovery necessitates the replacement of Alex with Nick in such a way as to suggest that the wounds of American society are healing over (equivalent to being forgotten, in the logic of the film); and secondly, the ways in which this replacement also helps to support and to sustain the ideology of familialism, despite the strains it suffers throughout the film.

At first sight, the disturbance or violence which opens the film seems to be Alex's death. We see in the opening sequence the response of the main characters — Alex's oldest and dearest friends — to the news of his death, first of all on the level of griefstricken looks (Sarah and Karen), and secondly in the pre-parations and travelling towards the funeral (Michael, Sam, Meg and Nick), Only one character seems strangely unmoved and unmoving — Alex's girlfriend Chloe, who is shown practicing Yoga with an expressionless face. Alex, it turns out, has committed suicide (we see the scars on his wrist in the opening sequence of the film, where shots of the preparation of Alex's body for the funeral divide the sequences showing his friends). It might seem a 'rationally grounded expectation'[5] that an important element of the film's diegesis and narrative completion might be to discover an explanation for Alex's suicide. Certainly the film does make a puzzle out of Alex's death. 'I don't know why this happened,' says Harold at the funeral service, and the characters pause from time to time to wonder why he did it. One element of the title of the film may refer to that puzzling disturbance which makes Nick suggest, while jogging with Sam and Harold, that perhaps they are just angry with Alex for not leaving them with any explanation of his suicide (which Sam goes so far as to deny, in a typically self-deceiving gesture). And in fact we are offered, towards the end of the film, some solution to this puzzle, a resolution of the enigma.

Nick says he has found the explanation in Alex's coatpocket (Chloe had given Alex's jacket to Nick), and hands Michael a document. The document is a newspaper cutting, an article Michael had written years before, celebrating Alex's refusal to accept the Richmond fellowship — an article written in a radical style — 'Just the right amount of fanaticism,' quips Michael. But the only link made to Alex's suicide is Nick's remark that Alex had kept his induction papers, too. As a solution to the central enigma of the film, these hints are hardly very strong. All that they do suggest — and this would be in keeping with my general reading of the film, and is indeed informed by that — is that in some way Alex's refusal to accept the Richmond fellowship was the turning-point in his life which led him into the blind alley culminating in his suicide.

Nick was therefore right when he said to Meg, in a gesture of ironic comfort, that maybe Alex had committed suicide because Meg had told him she thought he was wasting his life. Alex was finally trapped by his own identification of himself as a radical — the celebratory article by Michael thus being precisely a kind of induction paper. This reading may seem strained but a more important point lies in the fact of that strain. The film really pays little attention to the causes or motives of Alex's suicide; rather, it is primarily concerned with the consequences of the suicide, not its motives.

Alex is presented in the film as a central figure, admired by all his friends for his ideals. But we can also see a certain ambivalence towards Alex and towards the apparent radicalism he represents. Harold emphasizes Alex's centrality to the group in his speech at the funeral:

'I knew Alex and I loved him . . . I know a lot of us haven't seen each other for a long time, but I know that neither time nor distance can break the bonds that we feel. Alex drew us together from the beginning and now he brings us together again. I don't know why this happened but I do know that there was always something about Alex that was too good for this world. I only hope that wherever he is now . . . '

Harold breaks down. I want to emphasize Harold's notion that Alex 'was too good for this world.' Alex didn't (doesn't) quite fit in; and one element of that not fitting in is the fact of his suicide — a dramatic acknowledgement of that lack. That Alex should be seen as lacking in something is also apparent from the preacher's speech, another statement of that ambivalence. The preacher admits that he didn't know Alex personally (Richard will echo this in his denunciation of Alex), and he goes on to give the details of his career — or, rather, his lack of career: 'A brilliant student at the University of Michigan, Alex gave up . . .and chose to follow a seemingly random series of occupations.' The preacher is clearly puzzled by Alex's 'dropping out' (as it used to be called), and some of that puzzlement informs his next remarks, which also display a certain ambivalence towards Alex: 'When a man like Alex chooses to leave us, there's got to be something wrong in this world. It makes me angry and I don't know what to do with my anger. Are not the satisfactions of being a good man amongst other common men enough to sustain us any more? Where did Alex's hope go? Maybe that is the small comfort we can each take with us today — to try and regain that hope. It must have eluded Alex.' On the one hand, there is a certain sympathy for Alex — if Alex has killed himself, he must have had good reason. But on the other hand, the preacher's anger is relatively undefined — Alex's suicide makes him angry, but it may be because it demonstrates a lack he cannot see: the question of what will sustain us. In that case, Alex's loss of hope makes the preacher angry, for Alex can then be seen as responsible for losing that hope. In any case, the task of the auditors (including the spectators of the film) is to regain the hope which had 'eluded' Alex. 'Eluded' is the crucial verb. It suggests that hope was there to be found, only Alex didn't look hard enough for it. A similar reproach is made by Richard as he explains his own philosophy of life to Sam and Nick, a view grounded in the family and justified by the need to provide for his children: 'You set your priorities and try to be the best person you can . . . I wonder if your friend Alex knew that. One thing for sure, he certainly couldn't live with it. Nobody said it was going to be easy out there. At least nobody said that to me.' Once again, the film offers us a view of Alex from outside the circle of his friends, and that view is hardly an uncritical one. Crucially, Sam and Nick are unable to respond to Richard's criticisms (though it can be argued that Sam and Nick take Richard's speech simply as revenge for overhearing them speak about him in a disparaging way before they came into the kitchen. Nick's impish look at Sam certainly suggests that they both simply shrug off Richard's remarks). But the main point stands: in the diegesis of the film as a total address, Richard's remarks remain unanswered.

Beyond this ambivalence, Alex's death poses the problem of regaining that lost hope to which the preacher refers. Indeed, the preacher's reference is repeated a few scenes later when the journalist Michael phones his boss to ask for permission to spend the weekend with his friends. His reason: it will make a good story. As he explains to his boss: 'It's about everything — suicide, depression, where did our hope go? Yeah, that's it. Lost hope . . . Yeah, well you think everything's boring. You wouldn't say that if it was the lost hope diet!' Michael acts as the potential narrator, given within the narration. At the end of the film, he declares that he will go off and write a book about the weekend he has just spent. At various crucial points in the film, the scene is presented from his physical point of view.

It is this taking up and generalizing of Alex's specific tragedy into a social analysis that makes it possible for the film as a whole to move away from the terms of that specific tragedy to the veneral theme of lost hope. And it is on this level that Nick's replacement of Alex is crucial to the logic of the film, allowing the film to close, in Karen's words, with a 'certain symmetry.' The symmetry is provided precisely by Nick's replacing Alex, being different from Alex in such a way that the ambivalence which Alex produced is dissolved — and in a sense forgotten. For, as Nick says in the final group discussion, 'Alex died for all of us a long time ago.' The condition for Nick to make that statement is precisely that he has taken over Alex's position in the group (the position seems largely to be that of conscience or super-ego). In order to grasp that condition and that sense, let us now examine the developing identification in the film between Nick and Alex, as well as the terms of their difference.

The opening sequence shows each of the main characters in some physical detail, except Nick. We only see the back of Nick's body in the seat of his Porsche, the hand reaching for drugs in the dashboard, and a portion of his face reflected in the rearview mirror — and even then, he is wearing sunglasses. In fact, the sequence showing Nick comes immediately after we have been shown the brushing of Alex's hair — though crucially without seeing his face (we only have a shot of the hair and forehead). The faces of each are hidden; both are enigmatic, and the sharing of that enigma is the first element of their joint identification.

Nick makes his next appearance in the film at the moment when the preacher is talking about Alex. We leave the scene of the chapel as the preacher begins discussing what happened to Alex after university, and we see Nick's Porsche driving up to the church. As Nick enters, we hear the preacher saying 'a random series of occupations.' As if to underline the instability of Nick's own occupational identity, at that moment he introduces himself to the funeral assistant as a pallbearer — an essentially temporary identification. Nick's lateness also introduces another theme: his lawlessness. As his dependence on drugs has already revealed, Nick lives outside of social regulations. Neither married nor settled in a proper profession or career, his uprootedness seems to match that of Alex. In his self-interview, he acknowledges his own movement through random occupations leading to his current status as a 'Yankee drug-dealer' (as the law calls him). The problem for the film is to bring Nick into society — and one element of that is finding him an occupation. This Harold begins to do by telling him (just as he had told Alex) about the sale of his little company to a big company which will result in a tripling of the price of the shares. The transformation can be understood in two shots of Nick: the first, when he sits crosslegged on the porch of the house, gazing into space, and greets Harold and Sarah as they come back to the house with a 'Hi guys' — obviously stoned; the second, in which Nick is sitting on the porch of the house Alex was repairing, fully alert to the sounds of nature around him. The contrast is between responsiveness and unresponsiveness, and responsibility and irresponsibility. But the main feature of Nick's own change (note that he insists all along he is 'evolving') involves Chloe, his pairing off with her, which both makes him a stand-in for Alex, and also ensures, on a certain level, that he too will not commit suicide. But in order to understand this, we need to understand Chloe's role more thoroughly.

Chloe is presented to us in the opening sequence as an expressionless body, the epitome of what Laura Mulvey has described as the figure of woman in cinema: 'Traditionally, the woman displayed has functioned on two levels: as erotic object for the characters within the screen story, and as erotic object for the spectator within the auditoriums.'[6] Her body is displayed as she practices yoga in that opening sequence, and again later, in a repetition of this image, when Nick asks her about Alex and her relation to Alex. Her position as erotic object is underlined by Michael's reactions to her after he has been introduced to her at the funeral. After dinner, Harold, in an important shot, asks Michael to 'look after' Chloe. Her position at the funeral is an uncertain one. Michael asks who she is and Harold replies: 'Alex's girlfriend' — clearly an awkward position. Now that Alex is dead, the possessive apostrophe can hardly function.

Chloe is unable to sit at the front of the church, as Alex's parents object (or would object), so that she is unplaced. (In the drive to the reception, she expresses a desire to be in the limousine rather than in the car with Sam and Michael. They read this as a natural feeling of embarrassment about her position rather than what she says it is: 'I've always wanted to ride in a limo.') Unplaced, or rather, difficult to place, an excess. As Harold speaks to Michael, Chloe turns her head towards him, straining to look backwards, an object of their gaze. Michael says: 'Sure, I'll look after her,' as his gaze now becomes an aggressively sexual one — almost parodied as such in the sequence which follows, where he stares determinedly at her for most of the ceremony. The problem of 'looking after' Chloe is also the problem of looking at Chloe. As the erotic object of the film's gaze, the problem is how to satisfy that gaze, how to frame it. It is no accident that the repetition of Chloe's yoga exercises before the film's camera should also be before the video-camera held by Nick as he interrogates her about Alex. Chloe refuses Michael's gaze, refuses to be appropriated by it. She sits self-possessed as Michael stares at her throughout the ceremony; and, leaving it, she refuses to enter the car through the door he opens for her. After the reception, when Michael goes to her room to ask her how she is, she replies, once again scantily clad, that she is 'fine.' Michael does not have the right qualifications to take her over from the dead Alex, despite her insecure and tangential position within the group. (Karen asks her what she will do next. Chloe replies that she will stay on at the house until Sarah throws her out — she is under no illusions as to her tangential position.) What are the right qualifications? As Michael makes another attempt to ingratiate himself with Chloe, Karen and Harold look on. 'It's not right,' says Karen. 'We can't blame it on Chloe,' Harold responds, 'she's just a kid.' And as a kid, she needs someone who will be a father figure for her — precisely the basis for her relations with Nick.

In order to grasp the dynamics of that relation, we need to examine Nick's 'confessional' self-interview with the video, conducted with self-mockery as he projects two characters (interviewer and interviewed) in different, equally unnatural and stilted voices. Nick poses and responds to several questions about his life over the past ten years:

'So you came back from Vietnam a changed man?'

'Well, why don't you just tell everybody!'
'Then, in 1972, you went back to Michigan to enter the doctoral
program in psychology, but you just couldn't seem to get that thesis
finished.'
'I chose not to. I'm not hung up on this completion thing. I was
evolving.'
'Then you went to work for KTFO in San Francisco.'
'Where I had a small, but deeply disturbed following.'

At this point, Chloe, who has been sitting on the staircase
outside of Nick's range of vision, pricks up her ears. Two points
need emphasizing here: first, Nick resembles Alex in his vagabondage, his shifting of careers; but second, Nick has reasons, or
at least a defense, for that vagabondage — his 'evolution.'

Nick's account of himself closes with a reference to his current
drug-dealing, which he refuses to acknowledge explicitly:

'And what are you evolving into?'
'I'm in sales.'
'What kind of sales?'
'I don't have to answer that.'

He then joins Harold, Michael and Chloe for a drive out to the
'place' which Alex had been fixing up: a Thoreauesque cottage in
the woods (the cottage is never referred to as a home, only a
'place,' as it has yet to become a home, i.e., a family residence).
As far as Chloe is concerned, the crucial point is Nick's position
as a radio psychologist — as she explains to him later, she waI
one of his 'deeply disturbed following'; moreover, his advice
really helped her: 'I thought I was a pervert or something, but
you told me I would be all right if I did my homework and went to
bed at a reasonable hour.' Nick groans at this, but she assures
him that the advice was helpful.

Chloe's assurances here help to heal a split which occurs many
times in the film: the split between saying and meaning,
between truth and role-playing. Nick confesses to Chloe that he
gave up his post at KFTO after hearing a tape of one of his own
shows and being unable to bear the superficial advice he was
giving to desperate people. Chloe's insistence — 'You really
helped me' — validates Nick's speech, unifying role and
speaker in a way which eludes most of the other characters.
'Sometimes I can't believe what I hear myself saying,' says Sarah
after talking to her daughter on the phone (her admission is

made doubly significant as she is also at that point smoking a joint with Meg — after she had criticized Chloe at the funeral for being stoned in front of Meg who, of course, was equally drugged, unbeknownst to Sarah). Richard makes the same avowal in his confessional speech, and even Michael acknowledges a certain hypocrisy in his own speech, but one which he qualifies as being more straightforwardly honest than that of people who have illusions about what they are doing. Chloe shares with Nick a straightforwardly truthful speech (in opposition, for example, to Karen, who distinguishes between two registers of truth and falsehood in her very first conversation with Sam; and Sam himself, an actor who can remember his scripts but not shopping lists, but who seems to carry his role as actor into his social relations — take for instance his obvious lie to Karen about remembering her youthful writings.) Chloe is not afraid of offending and neither is Nick. Thus, she can say to Nick at the cottage: 'You remind me of Alex,' and he can reply: 'I ain't him.' The stakes are those of resemblance, not identity. It is the possibility that Nick can resemble Alex in some respects but be unlike him in others, which is crucial for his eventually replacing Alex for Chloe, and for the group as a whole.

A further marker of Nick's identification with Alex comes during the dinner on Saturday evening, when Nick is asked to step in to solve a dispute in much the same away as Alex (we imagine) would have done: 'Nick, help me with these bleeding hearts?' begs Harold, as the group discusses whether they have improved morally, or grown worse since their student days. Nick replies precisely as Alex's stand-in: 'I know what Alex would have said,' and, after a slight pause, 'What's for dessert. At least I'm not cynical about dessert.' In this way, the unity of the group is maintained by not discussing any further the issues which threaten that unity — precisely the terms of that social hope which Alex's suicide is seen to threaten. In the final discussion, the conversation turns again to the mystery of Alex's suicide. Nick now fully occupies the position of authority which we can see as having previously belonged to Alex (respected by all, paternal almost), so that Nick can lay Alex to rest (as one would speak of laying a ghost to rest, of placating a spirit): 'Alex was no different from us. He didn't know what to do. Wise up folks. We're all alone out here. I'm so sick of people selling their psyches in exchange for a little attention. Alex died for all of us a long time ago.' For Nick, the crucial question is not why Alex committed suicide: 'For some of us, it's a question of why not.' And this is the crucial identification. Here Nick fully identifies with the most difficult aspect of Alex — his socially disturbing suicide — but at the same time he maintains a distance from Alex — Alex is dead, as he points out.

What makes it possible for Nick to identify with Alex's suicide is his own cause for depression — the injuries he sustained in Vietnam. The film is not entirely specific about what these are: Nick may be literally castrated; he is certainly incapable of sexual intercourse (when Meg asks him to make love with her, he replies: 'Did I ever tell you what happened to me in Vietnam?' We never hear what did happen to him in Vietnam as the scene changes, we only hear Meg's horrified scream, and her later remark that Nick is no longer a candidate for impregnating her. Nick says of himself: 'I can't jerk off,' and 'Now the equipment doesn't work at all.') What takes Nick beyond Alex's position is the fact that his acknowledged wound can be — healed, forgotten, overcome? — the crucial point is that Chloe takes him off with her despite his protestation: 'You know I can't do anything, don't you?' Nick's wound in a sense represents the same thing as Alex's suicide: a wound on the body politic, the sign of some disturbance — Vietnam/social disturbances/radicalism/dropping out — *bref*, the sixties. That Chloe can forget the wound is related to her position as a member of the younger generation (the generation of America's new or to be regained hope): 'I'm not so hung up about the past as you people are,' as she puts it. She, we can say, represents precisely that 'popular memory' which the film would like to construct — which forgets the past, doesn't see its relevance.

Nick's replacement of Alex then works on several levels. By replacing Alex, Nick solves the film's problem of what to do with Chloe's excess — excess as 'Alex's girlfriend,' excess as main erotic object of the film's vision. She becomes 'Nick's girlfriend,' and thus no longer a trouble to the erotic eye. By appropriating Chloe (it's hard to think of a suitable term for the function of this film's offensive patriarchal system), Nick is effectively healed of his physical cum psychic scars, his 'equipment' and his speech. The consequence of Nick's healing is that he can take Alex's place without the danger of a further disruption from that place: Nick is not Alex, he is still evolving. Nick will move from being an outlaw to being a rentier (we presume he will follow Harold's advice and buy shares so that he will be able to change from his profession of drug dealer).

I hope to have shown how the ways in which Nick replaces Alex in the logic of the film corresponds to a certain desire to regain that hope which eluded Alex; and some of the connotations of that elusive hope. I now wish briefly to discuss the dominant familialism of the film, the general framework in which that particular replacement is made and which makes it possible.

The title of the film, 'The Big Chill,' seems at odds with the image of a group of cheerful-looking people together in a living room. This puzzle is one of the components of the narrative image of the film, one of the enigmas it promises to solve. In fact, the 'big chill' is precisely outside that group, in the larger society beyond their household society. Meg makes the first of several references to that world outside when she says: 'It's a cold world out there. Sometimes I think I've gotten a little frosty myself.' She tells an exemplary tale from her practice as a lawyer: 'Two of my clients broke into a house, tied up the husband, raped the wife, blew the whole place up and ran away.' The danger lurks precisely outside, from outside the homestead. Harold emphasizes that the police have twice saved his own home from burglary when Nick asks him how long he's been friendly with cops. The answer is: since he's owned property — which is to say, since property no longer is a crime, as Michael puts it. The group of friends celebrate their bonds of friendship and affection as they come together for the weekend 'at the home of Mr and Mrs Cooper.'

The opening sequence can help us specify the particular sense of home which dominates the film. It begins with a child's voice trying to articulate a song (Three Dog Night's 'Joy to the World'), the very song that will serve to close the film as musical accompaniment. The beginning then presents us with a family situation in the sense of the biological family — the father bathing the child, and at the same time, introducing him to language ('What's this?' 'A towel.' 'Supertowel!' 'Boy's gonna get superclean for his supermum!'). Children represent in the film a large part of adult motivation, as Richard and Sam emphasize in particular. The telephone call which brings news of Alex's suicide interrupts this family scene, and the film ends by restoring it — but not with the same family scene. For the end of the film has all the adults together, and all the children elsewhere. What can this mean?

The opposition between the social, external world and the secure home of the household is an artificial one. Michael's closing words, 'We're never going to leave,' express exactly that artificiality. It is an artificiality Nick had called attention to the previous evening, when he had asked what were the real bonds between any of them, how many of them had really known Alex when none of them had known him well enough to be able to prevent his suicide? All of them will have to return to that wider and colder world; and the depth of the group's ties are questioned. The work of the film is to deny these problems. On the simplest level, we never do see them leave the Cooper house. For the spectator, they remain in that household. More important, Nick's assertion of individual isolation was countered by Sarah: 'Yes, I do believe you can help other people.' And her words are yransformed into deeds immediately. She goes into the kitchen, calls her husband, and asks him to make love with their friend Meg.

Paradoxically, this breaking of the marriage vows is used to affirm the strength of those 'familial' ties, the bonds that link the group of friends together. But the paradox is dissolved by the fact that Harold's sleeping with Meg in some sense balances out Sarah's adultery with Alex. It is a part of the 'symmetry' of the film's closure. The terms used to negotiate this exchange are their marriage. Sarah asks Harold if he will do something for her, and he replies he'd do anything, 'I'd even marry you!' This declaration recalls Nick's observation, when Harold admitted how hurt he felt when Alex and Sarah made love. Nick responds: 'But she didn't marry Alex.'

Marriage is the affirmative and certain social bond, even when it is used as here, to condone adultery. The spectator has been prepared for this event in several previous scenes. Sarah had in fact suggested it the first time Meg began to talk about her desire to have a child. Harold once remarks that Meg is wearing a dressing-gown like his wife's, and adds: 'I always want to jump her when she's wearing that.' Nick's denial of the bonds that unite the group is not only denied on the level of his own experience (when it came to it, even Sam helped Nick get away from the law, and injured himself in doing so, playing his television identity in public), but by Sarah's selfless action towards Meg ('Greater love hath no woman — but to lay down another woman before her husband'); even Karen and Sam's long-awaited fling only results in Karen's going back to her husband Richard, probably all the more aware of the responsibilities — and securities — of marriage due to Sam's advice (there is certainly no sign of her going off alone to join Sam in Los Angeles, as he at one moment suggested). Only Michael remains outside this celebration of the (extended) familial — but then, he will write its story.

Conclusion

In *Towards 2000*, Raymond Williams writes: 'It is clear that if people are to defend and promote their real interests, on the basis of lived and worked and placeable social identifies, a large part of now alienated and centralized powers and resources must be actively regained, by new actual societies which in their own terms, and nobody else's, define themselves. All effective socialist policies, over the coming generations, must be directed towards this practice, for it is only in the re-emphasis or formation of these full active social identities that socialism itself — which depends absolutely on authentic ideas of a society — can develop.' Re-emphasis or formation: it is worth considering precisely the role of the family and the familial in this. Williams has his characteristic emphasis: 'In intellectual analysis it is often forgotten that the most widespread and most practical thinking about the future is rooted in human and local continuities. We can feel the continuity of life to a child or a grandchild . . . We are born into relationships, and we live and grow through relationships.'[8] The problem can be seen, in a sense, in *The Big Chill:* the ways in which the function of the familial is precisely to create a limit, an area of privacy outside the public and social world which is somehow casually attached to it. The human and local continuities of the family seem to be both a resource and a hindrance for thinking about society. Thinking in terms of the family seems to block thought about the whole society, precisely because it always tries to represent society's bonds as familial bonds.

Notes

1. See the entry in Raymond Williams, *Keywords* (London, 1983), for *Society*:

'Society is now clear in two main senses: as our most general term for the body of institutions and relationships within which a relatively large group of people live; and as our most abstract term for the condition in which such institutions and relationships are formed' (p. 291). But the history of the word, as Williams shows, is bound up with its etymological sense as companion and company of fellows.

2. The work of Christian Metz is exemplary in this regard. For an appreciation of Metz's rigorous 'scientific' approach to the study of film and the pedagogic and democratic desire which informed it, see Roland Barthes's essay 'Apprendre et Enseigner,' in his *Essais Critiques IV : Le Bruissement de la Langue* (Paris, 1984), where he writes: 'When Metz teaches some subject, some classification, some synthesis . . . he always shows . . . that *he is teaching himself at the same time* whatever he is supposed to be communicating to others. His discourse — and this is its proper idiolectic virtue — manages to confound two moments: that of assimilation, and that of exposition' (p. 206). For an excellent introduction to film studies, see John Ellis, *Visible Fictions* (London, 1982). For an interesting history of film theory in the past fifteen years, see Raymond Bellour, *L'Analyse du Film* (Paris, 1979).

3. 'Michel Foucault: Interview' in *Edinburgh '77 Magazine No.2: History/Production Memory* (p. 24). For a critical discussion of Foucault's arguments concerning 'popular memory,' see the essay by Stephen Heath in that same issue, 'Contexts.' This has been in part reprinted in *Questions of Cinema* (Bloomington, 1981).

4. See Michele Barrett and Mary McIntosh, *The Anti-Social Family* (London, 1982), p. 26, and also the following: 'The structures and values of family life play a very important part in the organization and ethos of institutions rightly thought of as 'social' but wrongly contrasted with the family as an exclusively 'private' affair. No such opposition between family and society exists. Just as the family has been socially constructed, so society has been familialized. Indeed it can be argued that in contemporary capitalist society one dominant set of social meanings is precisely an ideology of familialism' (p. 31).

5. The phrase is Noel Carroll's from his review of *Questions of Cinema* in *October* No. 23 (Winter 1982). In this review, Carroll states his disagreement with the Lacanian approach to the study of film narrative but, as far as I can see, offers no reasoned explanation of the grounds of that disagreement. I cite the footnote from page 132: 'My own approach to the analysis of coherence reception in film begins by assuming spectators with relatively stable cognitive processes and with knowledge of the film medium and its conventions. The combination of these factors provides us with spectators who at any moment in the film have a range of *rationally grounded expectations,* which allows them, through processes of tacit reasoning, to derive meaning from cinematic stimuli. I think that if we build knowledge and cognition into our model of the film-spectator — hardly frivolous presuppositions — we simply do not need to talk about suture (emphasis added). Carroll is quite right to point out that knowledge and cognition are 'hardly frivolous suppositions.' Presumably, he means that they are givens for his theory; but of course, once knowledge and cognition are treated as givens, as presuppositions, the whole possibility of analysis is pre-determined: the 'rationally grounded expectations' will always fit the narrative logic, the meaning will always be transparently clear for the spectator by virtue of his or her innate logic or tacit reason. I try to show in my analysis that the work of representation is in excess of any such model of rationally grounded expec-

tations. We do not need to talk about suture so long as we resist talking about representations and ideology, which Carroll also rejects: 'There will be no point in extracting ourselves from ideology if we do so only at the price of entering a new ideology, especially where the new ideology engages in the same "tyrannical" process of subject construction' (p. 96).

6. Laura Mulvey, 'Visual Pleasure and Narrative Cinema,' in *Popular Television and Film*, Tony Bennett et al., eds. (London, 1981), p. 210.

7. Narrative image: 'The narrative image of a film is a complex phenomenon that occurs in a number of media: it is the film's circulation outside its performace in cinemas . . . The narrative image proposes a certain area of investigation which the film will carry out; it states the thematic of the film, but refuses to do more than that. The narrative image is an enigma, an offer; the film is offered as the resolution of the narrative image.' John Ellis, *Visual Fictions*, pp. 31-33. For a more sophisticated account, see Chapter Four of *Questions of Cinema*, 'Film Performance,' by Stephen Heath.

8. Raymond Williams, *Towards 2000*, (London, 1983), pp. 197, 5, 179.

SECTION FOUR

Review

Recent Historiography of the Communist Party U.S.A.

Michael Goldfield

Section 1. Introduction

The key to an understanding of the mainsprings of U.S. politics is a recognition of the historic weakness of broad forms of class organization among U.S. workers. This weakness is accentuated by the inability of radical tendencies to sustain significant roots in working class organizations. The absence of even a reformist labor or socialist pole distinguishes American politics from the politics of all other economically developed countries.[1]

Many writers have argued that the weakness of working class radicalism is an inherent feature of American society. Thus, an investigation into its causes might reveal something about the unique nature of U.S. politics. For Marxists, however, who believe that this exceptional character of U.S. politics is neither pre-ordained nor permanent, its existence poses additional serious questions: it is not only important to understand the structural and conjunctural reasons for this so-called 'backwardness' of the working class and radical movements in this most economically developed capitalist country. One must also ask: under what conditions might a mass radical labor upsurge come about? What might those who desire such a movement do to hasten its emergence?

One approach to these questions quite naturally leads to a consideration of the last major era of mass-based, left-led labor politics. This period is the 1930s and 1940s when the Communist Party, with its tens of thousands of members, had broad influence within the working class and other segments of U.S. society. What caused communism to grow as a trend in the United States? What caused it to decline so rapidly, leaving hardly a trace, virtually breaking the six-decades tradition of American working-class radicalism? Perhaps the answers to these questions will throw some small light on both the questions posed for Marxists, and the ones about the nature of American politics itself.

In pursuing this historical approach, it would appear that we are exceedingly fortunate. In the past decade there has been a huge outpouring of new scholarship on the history of the U.S. Communist Party.[2] There have been dozens of theses, a number of frank autobiographies, and many general works and narrow case studies. Much of this material is rich and descriptive, the product of lengthy labors by the authors. Thus, one might expect that a careful study of this new work would readily yield answers to the important questions concerning the rise and fall of the Communist Party. Yet such a harvest is not readily reaped. Different authors find differing reasons for the periods of success and the periods of failure of the CP. Often they even differ over which period was its most successful and when the decline actually began. Most of the authors have views which are themselves not consistent.

Thus, despite vast amounts of new research, the history of the Communist Party is far from 'settled.' There are several reasons why this might be the case. First, there may be legitimate ground for differences in evaluating a complicated social phenomenon. A deeper reason, however, is suggested by Maurice Isserman in his preface to *Which Side Were You on?:* 'The history of communism in America is bitterly contested terrain . . . one seldom has to dig far to uncover the writer's underlying political assumptions' (p. vii). How one analyzes the Communist Party, what one thinks was the essence of its problems (its subservience to Moscow, its sectarianism towards other groups, the massiveness of the repression against it in the late 1940s and early 1950s, its hiding of its socialist views, its tailing of Roosevelt), even how one dates its rises and fall — these define a position on the current political landscape.

There may, however, be a more comprehensive framework for looking at the history of the Communist Party in the United States, a point of view from which the differences between authors and the contradictions between the general analyses and the empirical descriptions of each can all be explained. In this essay, I will try to suggest such a framework. My strategy for getting there, however, will by necessity be somewhat roundabout. I will examine in detail a diverse offering of recent scholarship on the Communist Party, commenting on its strengths and weaknesses. The initial focus will be on a series of vexed issues that preoccupy several authors. One central theme will be the inability of many of the current writers to deal intelligibly with the relation of CP work in the 1920s to its later growth. I will try to show contradictions and inconsistencies that emerge in the writings of these authors, tracing the problems to their modes of analysis. The threads will then be pulled together and some conclusions drawn.

In this essay, I will be looking at a diverse range of offerings. Consideration will be given to Philip Jaffe's *The Rise and Fall of American Communism* (1975), a little-mentioned, virulently anti-communist piece, which summarizes important material from CP leader Earl Browder's oral history tapes and previously unavailable private papers.[3] Some attention will also be given to Harvey Klehr's *The Heyday of American Communism* (1984), a recent anti-communist treatment that has received many favorable reviews. Other works range from a contemporary defense of CP policies in Roger Keeran's *The Communist Party and the Auto Workers Unions* (1980), to two sympathetic 'New Left' historical treatments: Mark Naison's *Communists in Harlem During the Depression* (1983), which finds many positive features of the CP work in Harlem during the 1930s; and Maurice Isserman's *Which Side Were You On?* (1982), which provides a contemporary defense of the policies of Earl Browder, viewing the World War II period as the highpoint of Communist mass-based radicalism.

In addition to these five recent authors, I will also be drawing on the writing of James Cannon, the founder of American Trotskyism and former leader of the Socialist Workers Party. In a more limited way, use will be made of two other books: left-wing critic Martin Glaberman's *Wartime Strikes* (1982), and New Left historian Nelson Lichtenstein's *Labor's War at Home* (1982). These latter are particularly helpful in understanding the CP's role within the trade union movement during World War II. To the credit of all the more recent writers, they are joined by one common feature that distinguishes them from the vast majority of the earlier writings, be they academic anti-communists, party supporters, or government informers. All the recent writings are fundamentally honest, reporting many facts which do not always enhance their own general arguments.

Finally, I will occasionally refer to a number of other important works, including Draper 1966 and 1968, Cochran 1967, Foster 1952, and Starobin 1972.

Section 2. Was The CP a Genuine Reflection of U.S. Radicalism?

This question, at first sight, has a peculiar flavor to it. It is posed initially by those conservative anti-communists who regard the CP as little more than a foreign-controlled fifth column, a transplanted group, subservient to a foreign power, subsidized with Russian money, who under uniquely favorable circumstances, using trickery, deception, and manipulation, gained a temporary foothold in American life. On this view, the CP was not even a product of U.S. radicalism like other groups.

It is tempting to dismiss such caricatures without a moment's consideration as merely the product of Cold War historiography.[4] Yet, versions of such characterizations continue to be put forward today and treated respectfully. Harvey Klehr's *The Heyday of American Communism*, a disorganized and uninformed study, perhaps comes closest to this caricature.[5] Klehr sees the CP as largely a foreign-born, irrelevant and unheeded group of rootless individuals, a clown show controlled by Moscow. Unable to succeed as radicals, they gained momentary success by disguising themselves as liberals. In Klehr's own words: 'After years in the political wilderness [the CP] won respectability after 1935 by blending into the liberal mainstream' (p. xi). The CP also gained hegemony on the left in 1935 only as the Socialist Party (SP) began to tear itself apart (p. 117).

We must recognize, of course, that one strand of the questioning of the 'authenticity' of the CP as a representative of 'American' radicalism is a traditional anti-radical, conservative theme, prominent at many times in diverse cultures. The British, for example, undoubtedly overplayed the French responsibility for the American Revolution. The eight U.S. anarchists tried for the 1886 Haymarket bomb in Chicago were all regarded as foreigners, products of alien ideologies. The Industrial Workers of the World (IWW, or Wobblies), now regarded as so authentically American, were once considered dangerous 'outside agitators.' The echoes of the 1960s from Southern racists who complained about the 'outside agitators' from the civil rights groups, or those in high places who accused anti-war demonstrations as being controlled or manipulated from Moscow, still ring loud.

Certainly Lewis Coser's and Irving Howe's description of the CP in their 1957 anti-communist classic, *The American Communist*

Party, as the adherent of an 'alien' ideology must be placed in this category:

> But what is remarkable — and perhaps helps prepare one for the later history of American Communism — is the thoughtless assumption that the 'dictatorship of the proletariat' could be a relevant and desirable concept in a country like the United States with its long democratic and parliamentary tradition . . . The simple truth is that the left wing did not derive its talk about 'soviets' and 'proletarian dictatorship' from an examination of the actualities of American life. (pp. 29-30)

Is not this attempt to brand the CP as 'alien' or 'un American' in its ideology merely an attempt by conservatives (even if they are the bearers of a 'radical' past like Coser and Howe) to deny the validity of radical ideas? Certainly the proof that concepts have a foreign origin is not sufficient to deny their legitimacy. Is the idea of soviets any more alien than Socratic dialogues, liberty, equality, and fraternity, or religious intrusions on the state?

The question, however, does not easily go away. It is interwoven with all sorts of other themes put forth by critics of the party. Jaffe, for example, ties it not only to the question of the party's relation to Moscow, but to its line changes, its sectarianism, and many other issues:

> The answer to the question of whether the American Communist Party was a political party in the American tradition is without doubt the key to a better understanding of the role that Communist parties played not only in the United States, but throughout the world. How independent was the American Party? Why did it find it necessary to change its political line every few years? To what extent was it what its enemies termed 'subversive'? (p. 178).

To these questions Jaffe has ready answers. He does not think that it became the dominant force on the left by any attractive powers of its own. Rather,

> from 1920-1946 it witchhunted every opposing political group and personality until almost nothing of importance was left of the radical movement but the hard-bitten, dogmatic Communist Party. (p. 52)

> I concluded that the very years in which the Party reached its greatest popularity represented the 'dark age' of American radicalism. (p.13)

The CPUSA, in its unrelenting drive to convert its Party into a duplicate of the Party Stalin and Lenin had built in Russia, ran roughshod over every left opposition political group, concentrating particularly on the Socialist Party which even in 1932 polled more then 900,000 votes for its Presidential candidate . . . Thus, whatever chance the American left had of building a democratic socialist movement into a meaningful political party was destroyed. (pp. 13-14)

The concerns about the 'authenticity' of the Communist Party are not the province of the hard anti-communists alone. All these questions about the so-called alien character of the CP are dealt with at length by many of those who are somewhat sympathetic to the Communist Party. In opposition to the anti-communist characterizations, a number of young historians with political backgrounds in the student movement of the 1960s, portray the CP as developing into the thirties (or even into the 1940s) as a partially independent movement, responding to its milieus and constituencies in the tradition of earlier American radicalism. Thus, Maurice Isserman concedes that the 1920s were Moscow-inspired, but argues that later years were different:

Draper made a strong case for the decisive effect Russian influence had in shaping American communism in the 1920s.

But Draper's generalization cannot stand as the whole story of American communism in the decades that followed the 1920s, years in which tens of thousands of Americans joined the party and hundreds of thousands came under its influence. (p. viii)

What developed, according to Isserman, was an authentic American radicalism, or rather an approach that had the potential to become that:

'Browderism' held the potential for leading to something other than itself — sheltering and lending legitimacy to the efforts of those American Communists who had the capacity for and commitment to finding what would later be described as the 'American Road to Socialism' . . .

Browderism was not the American Road to Socialism. But the Communists faced a more prosaic task in 1945: finding the road to a stable, ongoing genuinely democratic socialist movement. When they stepped back from Browderism they took a fatal detour off that road. (pp. 242-43)

Mark Naison, in *Communists in Harlem during the Depression*, similarly wants to challenge the traditional anti-communist view, which he characterizes as 'a tendency, quite powerful during the Cold War years, to view Communist activity largely through the dynamics of manipulation, disillusionment, and betrayal . . . ' He rejects those authors who 'view the Party as the arm of an international conspiracy, an alien tendency within black protest which used the legitimate grievances of blacks as a "front for the expansion of world communism." ' (p. xv). He examines the development of the CP from a radical fringe group into the mainstream of community activity in Harlem, attempting to look at both the role of the Soviet Union in shaping its work, and the independent development of the lines and activities by black Communists.

Finally, we have the opinion expressed by Roger Keeran in *The Communist Party and the Auto Workers Union*. Keeran, in contrast to most other writers, does not see any of these questions as a problem at all: 'The party's membership in the Communist International and support of the Soviet Union did not keep it from being the main expression of native, working class radicalism during the 30 years after 1919 . . . It was a blend of national and international radicalism.' (p. 3) Many issues lie buried in these various statements. I will attempt at first to isolate them, treating first the question of the degree to which the Communist Party was an 'authentic' U.S. radical group. As convoluted as it appears in the presentations of many authors, this question is no diversion. The issue of 'authenticity' pushes us to examine the formation and early work of the CP. To understand the party's strengths and weaknesses, its rise and fall, its course of development, one must first of all comprehend its origin. The errors in analysis in many writers begin with their failures properly to characterize the CP's roots and early growth.

Indigenous Roots of the Communist Party

Those writers who fail to see the indigenous roots of the U.S. CP in the most radical elements of the U.S. working class movement are blinded to the process by which the CP grew and developed. Even many who recognize these roots, however, impose preconceptions on the development of the CP which deny the early hegemony that it established among left groups in this country, well before the onset of the depression.

The CP was formed in 1919, after the Socialist Party minority right-wing leadership refused to allow the left wing to take over the organization democratically. The SP and its leadership were largely discredited at this time by their failure to follow the democratic will of the organization, their unwillingness to support the Bolshevik Revolution, and their former support for or half-hearted opposition to World War I. The drop in SP membership from 100,000 to 12,000 between 1919 and 1923 probably vastly understates the degree of decline in party activists.[6] The SP, despite its periodic high electoral showings and a membership increase in the 1930s, never recovered as an organization from the 1919 split. It retained neither its élan, a numerous devoted cadre, or any number of the prestigious leaders — after Eugene Debs's health failed in 1922 — who gave it their primary allegiance. The most dynamic activists and leaders of the SP in 1919 left to form the core of the new Communist Party. Within a few years of its formation, the Communist movement, its chaotic and often unrealistic romantic expectations notwithstanding, attracted and absorbed many of the more radical elements of the IWW, the small black socialist milieu, and the bulk of left-wing trade union activists. That this process was in good part stimulated by the CP's existence as the U.S. representative of Bolshevism should not prevent our understanding its status as the heir to U.S. radical traditions.

Virtually every author one reads gives examples of how previously unsympathetic or antagonistic activists joined the CP throughout the 1920s and 1930s. Klehr, with his penchant for identifying CP members from released FBI files, cites dozens of formerly anti-communist leaders of farm organizations and unions, public officials and intellectuals. Even at the height of CP sectarianism between 1928 and 1933, this process went on. Naison describes how the CP in Harlem, despite its bitter attacks on Marcus Garvey's United Negro Improvement Assocation (UNIA) was able to attract streetwise UNIA leaders, including Steve Kingston, Louis Campbell, and William Fitzgerald, into its organization in 1930. This 'alien' organization attracted ministers (like Adam Clayton Powell, Jr.), and Congressmen (like Vito Marcantonio and John Bernard — both of whom receive unflattering descriptions in Klehr, p. 291). In another little-known, but highly representative incident, the CP secretly drew into its orbit in 1936 Gerald Fielde, the humble, mild-mannered, obsequious, pro-company representative to the McCormick Works, International Harvester company-controlled Works Council. Fielde, who was to become the leader of the CP-dominated Farm Equipment Workers Union (FE), developed such a record of militancy and radicalism that one of the conditions of the 1955 United Auto Workers–FE merger, in which the UAW absorbed all former FE staff members and local officers, was that Fielde not be included.[7]

The Communist Party had powers of attraction based on its roots, its work, and its politics during the 1920s and early 1930s which far exceeded those of all other radical groups. It was identified with the Bolshevik Revolution and was the most serious, dedicated, revolutionary group in the country. Those who merely look at its declining membership (before the 1930s) or its small electoral support in 1932 and 1936 compared to the SP miss totally what contemporaries understood. As James Cannon, one of its most hostile critics, states in his *History of American Trotskyism:* 'the CP entered the thirties — the period of the great radical revival — as the dominating center of American radicalism. It had no serious contenders.' (1979, p. 93) Both the hard anti-communists and the New Left historians tend to downplay the strong indigenous roots of the CP at its origin and throughout the 1920s. Thus, they fail to take into account the importance of work in this early period to the party's subsequent growth.

Section 3. What Led The CP to Grow?

Many authors tend to distort the process by which radical groups gain adherents, looking only at the particular times that these groups actually grow numerically or increase their electoral support. While such figures should not be excluded from the balance sheet, it is important, particularly when studying a small group, to study the periods when it gained sympathy, increased its respect, or made important breakthroughs. Study of these conditions may provide the causal links that best explain future growth. I will argue that virtually all modern commentators on the CP, with few exceptions, distort the process by which the Party grew, often overemphasizing certain quantitative indicators. That this distortion is often in the service of erroneous preconceptions about what caused CP growth makes it difficult for them to explain other aspects of the party's activity.

I have already suggested, however, that those, like Isserman, who want to see the late 1930s and the 1940s as the period when the CP was closest to 'authentic' American radicalism, must downplay the 'authenticity' of the CP in the 1920s and early 1930s. The most extreme attempt to belittle this earlier period of work may be found in Klehr. Thus, it is instructive to start with him.

By attributing all CP growth to the post-1935 period, when the CP 'merged into the liberal mainstream,' Klehr fundamentally distorts the actual success of the CP in the earlier periods. Some examples, using information presented by Klehr himself, readily make the point. Virtually all those who remark the CP influence in the formation of the CIO recognize the degree to which John L. Lewis and the CIO leaders needed the Communists. In auto, e.g., the Communists were the leaders of many of the pre-CIO strikes and attempted organization of unions. They were in on the ground floor in CIO organizing. A clear indication of their pre-CIO strength in the labor movement is available in a description by Bert Cochran, a former leader in the UAW, and at the time the labor director for the Socialist Workers Party (SWP):

> The Stalinists entered the CIO with the best disciplined, the most experienced and largest political cadre in the labor movement. They were able to participate actively and effectively in practically all the original major organizing campaigns and strike struggles. When the immense national union structures were set up, the Stalinists were in possession of an organizational machine not too inferior to the Lewis combination. (quoted from the introduction to Cannon 1973a)

Klehr dismisses all this. He tells us that in 1932, there were 'only' about 800 Communists in the Detroit area. The CP-led Auto Workers Union 'was not a force to be reckoned with' (p 58). But 800 Communist cadre, a large number of whom were working in plants in the auto industry, organized in nuclei of 10-15 members in a dozen plants, each with a circle of sympathizers, many units publishing popular in-plant newspapers (as Keeran notes in impressive detail), hardly betokens an organization to be sneered at.

Keeran, in his valuable, well-researched book, sensibly describes how the unemployed organizing laid the basis for CIO organizing and CP influence, particularly in auto. Klehr, describing the CP-led unemployed marches, involving hundreds of thousands in 1931, chooses to stress the unstable character of the CP-led unemployed organizations.[8]

Klehr's utter insensitivity to the issues surrounding party growth is nowhere better exemplified than in his many comments on its membership size. In denigrating the CP's size in 1933, he says: 'After several years of Depression, 26,000 members, while better than the 7,000 of 1930, was little to boast of' (p. 158). And, in one moment of supreme obtuseness, he declares: 'No CIO union had a majority or even a substantial minority of Communist members' (p. 240). Nor registered Democrats, practising Protestants, or even union activists one hastens to add. It is, of course, no wonder that preoccupations about the 'authenticity' of U.S. communism and the hostility of U.S. life to radicalism lead most fervent anti-communists to provide us with little meaningful explanation about how and why the CP grew.[9]

While Klehr is by far the most crude in his distortions of CP growth, he is not alone. More subtly Isserman tends to confuse the causes of party growth during World War II with policies the party was carrying out at the time. I will argue later that the seeds of CP decline, the loss of its moral authority, were quite pronounced during this period. More fruitful than proceeding to an analysis of each author, however, will be a description of the early work of the CP, which laid the basis for its later growth. Recent CP historiography, while it slights this period in its analysis, presents rich and useful details which allow us to understand it better. To facilitate this examination, I shall temporarily switch to a chronological exposition, commenting on key points and the merits of various authors in passing.

CP Work in the 1920s.

Most investigators agree that the Communist Party alone among radical groups was in the right position at the right time to take part fully in the forming and organizing of the CIO in 1935 and 1936. It is also generally agreed that their proper positioning is in part responsible for the tremendous influence they had after the formation of the CIO. How did they arrive there?

The story goes back at least to 1921. It was in that year that the Communist Party, under the influence of the Moscow-based Communist International (referred to as the Commintern or CI) developed a clear orientation in their trade union work. Rejecting the revolutionary dual union approach of their first two years, they oriented their work toward building left-wing trade union centers within the American Federation of Labor. They successfully agitated across the country around three principle demands: defense of the Soviet union, organizing the unorganized into industrial unions, and the formation of a (farmer-) labor party. Their vehicle for this agitation was obtained with the recruitment in 1921 of William Z. Foster and his associates, who led the Trade Union Education League (T.U.E.L.), the most prominent U.S. left-wing labor group at the time.

The attraction of the Russian Revolution and the quick success of the T.U.E.L. work, led by the organizationally talented Foster, attracted new radicals to the CP's trade union work. On this basis, the CP placed a top priority for getting many of its active working class cadre involved in this sphere of activity. Keeran's highly informative book describes the work in the automobile industry in detail. In early 1922, for example, Keeran tells us that although the overwhelming majority of Detroit Communists were wage earners, only 5% were trade union members. He describes how the CP who, unlike the SP, based its organization primarily on the workplace, began to change this condition.[10] Keeran also describes how the CP carefully began in 1922 to develop fruitful working relationships with the anti-communist SP leadership of the Auto Workers Union. They started building the union, taking responsibility for issuing the union newspaper that reached thousands of auto workers. Between 1924 and 1930, the CP established stable party organizations and shop papers in a dozen auto plants.[11]

Similar work was carried on by the CP in a large number of industries. Party groups gained members and pursued significant activities in mining, electric, steel, and maritime among others. The greatest organizational success of the party trade unions work came, however, in the fur and leather industries, centered primarily in New York City, and secondarily in Chicago. An open Communist leadership drove the gangsters out of the fur workers' union, revitalizing its organization throughout the late 1920s. The eventually organized Fur and Leather Workers Union, with its highly politicized membership, stood firm during the McCarthy period, refusing to disavow its elected CP leadership.[12]

The result of this CP activity is summarized by James Cannon, one of its leaders until his 1928 expulsion for Trotskyism:

> The Communist Party held the line of class struggle and revolutionary doctrine in that long ten-year period of boom, prosperity and conservatism before the crash of 1929. It was in that period —fighting for revolutionary ideas against a conservative environment as we are trying to do today, refusing to compromise the principle of class independence — that the CP gathered and prepared its cadres for the great upsurge of the thirties (1979, p. 93)

One thing must be made clear about this period. Although there were individual radicals here and there, some members of the SP, and some remaining active Wobblies, the only organization with large numbers of working class members willing to risk their jobs and even their lives, willing to sustain their faith for long periods of time in tranquil periods, was the Communist Party. Isserman, as well as Klehr, by downplaying the importance of this period in building the Communist Party, misses the key to understanding its rapid growth in the 1930s, as well as its equally rapid decline later. Even Naison, who describes many cases where the integrated trade union work of the CP was important to party work in Harlem, neglects a discussion of this early period of organization.

The Third Period in the U.S.

In 1928, the Sixth World Congress of the Comintern declared the existence of the third period in the growing crisis of world capitalism. The first period was after World War I, where revolutionary struggles were breaking out, beginning with the Bolshevik Revolution. The second period, one of capitalist stabilization, supposedly began sometime after 1923, with the defeat of the last German workers' uprising. The third period was the one which the CI declared was to see the final capitalist crisis, the rapid growth of Communist organizations, the disintegration of reformist workers' groups, and the revolutionary overthrow of capitalism. The policies following from this analysis nowhere had more disastrous impact than in Germany, where the Communist Party predicted 'After Hitler, Us,' continuing to attack the Social Democrats as 'social fascists' even after the Nazis had seized power.[13]

In general, past commentators on the Third Period activities of the U.S. CP have described it both as highly sectarian and as detrimental to Communist mass work and organizational growth. Although the present generation of New Left historians tends to concur with this assessment (preferring the Popular Front period), all of them describe highly important gains during these years.[14] Even Klehr's book is full of details about Third Period party activities. He describes, for example, a funeral attended by 50,000 people in January 1930, for Steve Katoris, a party activist killed by New York City police at a demonstration (pp. 32-33). A similar funeral in Detroit in 1932 for four party activists killed by police in a protest march on Ford's River Rouge plant was attended by '20,000 to 40,000 people.' 'Above the coffin was a large red banner with Lenin's picture' (p. 59). At the initiative of the Comintern, the CP took the lead in unemployed work by leading demonstrations on International Unemployment Day, 6 March 1930. It is estimated that over one million demonstrated across the country (p. 34). Characteristically, Klehr belittles these activities as ephemeral.

Membership increased from 7,000 to 26,000 between 1929 and 1933. Most of this increase occurred in 1932 and 1933. Recruitment of workers was especially low during 1929 and 1930 (Keeran says that no workers were recruited to CP in-plant auto nuclei during these years). Recruitment from the unemployed was uneven. Perhaps the highpoint was achieved in Chicago. Klehr describes one incident[15] in 1931 in which 500 people in a Chicago southside black neighbourhood returned furniture to the home of a recently evicted widow. The police returned, opened fire, killing three people. The coffins were viewed, again under an enormous portrait of Lenin. The funeral procession with 60,000 participants and 50,000 cheering onlookers was led by workers carrying Communist banners. 'Within days, 2,500 applications for the Unemployed Councils and 500 for the Party were filled out'. (pp. 332-33) Sectarian and militant —admittedly; ineffective — hardly.[16]

The CP and the Black Question

The real distinguishing positive feature of the Third Period, however, what made the party unique among U.S. radical groups, was its line on and commitment to the fight against black oppression. Largely because of this position, the Party's work in the Third Period in the U.S., in contrast to Communist work in many other countries, did reap many positive results.

No previous largely white U.S. radical group had focused attention on the plight of blacks. While the IWW organized black workers, since it stood for the militant unity of all workers in one big revolutionary union, it had no program for fighting discrimination. The SP policy ranged from the benign neglect of Debs, who said 'We have nothing special to offer the Negro and we cannot make separate appeals to all races,'[17] to the undisguised chauvinism of SP leader Victor Berger. What the SP line permitted in practice can be seen from the publication of racist jokes in the Auto Workers Union newspaper when the union was under SP leadership (Keeran, p. 54).

Even during the early 1920s, the CP was rhetorically quite outspoken in its opposition to racial discrimination and in its demands for black equality. The Sixth Congress of the CI, however, placed the 'Negro Question' at the center of the U.S. CP's strategy. The CI resolution argued that blacks were an oppressed nation, with a territory in the blackbelt region of the South, so called because of its dark soil in which cotton flourished. Blacks were entitled to the democratic right of territorial secession if they so desired. The Negro question was revolutionary in two other senses. First, the demands against black oppression were viewed as posing a fundamental challenge to the whole capitalist system. Second, the winning of whites to the fight for these demands was seen as a prerequisite for winning them to revolutionary positions in general, and hence for the revolutionary unification of the working class.[18]

The CP began to change fundamentally on the basis of the 1928 and the subsequent 1930 resolutions. Their largely successful efforts — not without a great deal of prodding by black members — to involve white members in fighting discrimination duly impressed a wide range of people in the black community.[19] The Party's efforts even penetrated to its extensive immigrant membership. As Naison notes: 'Not only Jews felt moved by the Party's position: Finnish, Polish, Hungarian, Irish, Italian, and Slavic Communists became passionate exponents of the Party's position on the Negro question' (p. 49). Another key result of the CP's new position was to put special emphasis on organizing blacks in the South. It gave an impetus to CP work among black workers, centered in Birmingham,

Alabama. The CP orientation also led to the highly dangerous organization of black sharecroppers, initially in Alabama, and eventually throughout the whole South. By 1935, the Share-cropper's Union claimed to have 12,000 members. This effort, potentially a key lever to the future unionization of the whole South, was liquidated by the CP in 1936 (see Goldfield 1980a; Klehr, p. 335).

The Party's position on the South also led it to publicize and fight against the lynching of blacks in that region. In 1931, in the heart of the Third Period, the CP took the initiative in a case that was to gain for it major political leadership among blacks throughout the country. This was the case of the Scottsboro boys, nine black youths seized on a freight train in rural Alabama and accused of raping two white girls who had been riding with them. The Scottsboro defense laid the basis for large-scale influence and recruitment of blacks of every strata throughout the United States. Defense activities involving significant numbers of whites as well as many blacks were numerous, widely attended, broadly supported, and well publicized. Naison comments:

> The campaign to free the Scottsboro boys, more than any single event, marked the Communist Party's emergence as a force in Harlem's life. The Party's role in the case, and its conflicts with the NAACP, were front-page news for years, and its protest rallies gave it entry to churches, fraternal organizations, and political clubs that were previously closed to it. (p. 57).

The diverse and highly successful work of the CP among blacks during the early 1930s underscores the need to get beyond the limited stereotypes of most writers about the Third Period. Customarily, CP work during this time is characterized as sectarian, isolated and quite limited. Gains made are attributed to the depression. Yet, the CP's audacity and revolutionary approach, sectarian as it might have been, gained for it masses of supporters, not only among a wide range of political moderates, but *more importantly*, among thousands of potentially revolutionary working-class people. The moderates respected the CP and allied with it, whether in Harlem or in the CIO, because they recognized the value of its committed cadre and its ability to mobilize mass support. These abilities were based on the CP's growing strength among new layers of emerging militants throughout the population.

Problems of the Third Period

While the CP won new support among the unemployed, blacks, and intellectuals during the Third Period, the CI approach was not without its problems. Sectarianism, the refusal to form united fronts with reformists and with other radicals, and the virtual abandonment of the AFL — all policies carried out under CI 'guidance' — destroyed some of their trade union bases and weakened most of the rest.

One of the areas of TUEL strength, for example, had been in mining. A combination of tyrannical rule by John L. Lewis, the United Mine Workers (UMW) president, and a continuing mine owners offensive had decimated the union. The CP, with major strength in southern Illinois and pockets of support in West Virginia, Pennsylvania, Alabama, and Kentucky, had become an important influence among miners in the 1920s. By early 1928, their struggle against Lewis, organized in the 'Save the Union' movement, was gaining ground. They were united in this struggle with John Brophy, the leader of the Progressive Miners' group and other dissidents. With the coming of the 6th CI Congress, they attacked their erstwhile allies as 'social fascists,' pulled their forces out of the UMW, and attempted to build a revolutionary dual union, the National Miners Union (NMU). Needless to say, these activities virtually destroyed years of patient work in the UMW. Though the NMU was to lead many militant strikes, its sectarian behavior led it to squander much of its resources. By 1932, with Lewis's UMW leading the major miners' strikes and growing rapidly, the NMU was reduced to a mere shell.

Keeran initially argues that a similar strategy in auto did not hurt the CP there (p. 64), but this seems unlikely.[20] The party undoubtedly missed winning important influence among those large numbers of workers who rejected the small AWU and desired affiliation with the AFL. Keeran is somewhat ingenuous at key junctions when he argues that 'Even the mistaken aspects of the Third Period had a positive side.' (p. 120) In this respect, he mentions the exposure by the CP of New Deal labor legislation, especially the ineffectual National Industrial Recovery Act (NIRA), the criticisms of Roosevelt, and the skepticism with which they treated AFL leaders. But, it was precisely these policies — which the CP was soon to abandon — that gained the party political support among militant workers.[21] This policy of forthright political criticism is not to be confused with those truly 'mistaken aspects,' including dual unionism and the refusal to work with other forces.

A stronger indictment of the effect of Third Period policy on CP work is given by James Cannon:

> Now you may want to know why Lewis rather than the radicals is leading the fight for industrial unionism. The answer is that in the five years of the crisis, the most radical, the Communists (Stalinists), left the AFL. They went out of the AFL and pulled many others out with themselves. That's why when all this upsurge from the ranks is taking place, there have been no militants ready to spring into a place of leadership.
>
> 'The AFL and the Start of the CIO,' (26 November 1935; rpt. in Cannon 1971, p. 81).

Despite the problems of the Third Period, the CP emerged with increased cadre in most industries. The party membership as a whole had grown many times; its influence was extended and deepened in many sectors of the population.

The Seventh Congress and the Popular Front

The period between the 13th plenum in late 1933 and the 7th CI Congress in 1935 marks a transition period from the Third Period to that of the Popular Front.[22] After the 7th Congress, in an almost complete reversal of its Third Period stance, the CP allied itself with anti-fascist, 'democratic' forces, dropped its revolutionary slogans, and subordinated itself in many cases to moderate leaders, refraining from criticizing them. These later constraints even extended to President Franklin Delano Roosevelt, previously described as a fascist. The Popular Front period, from 1935-1939, is the one that many sympathetic writers today prefer.[23]

The successes of the CP in the Popular Front era were, of course, legion. The beginning of this period coincided with mass ferment in many sectors of U.S. society. Communists became the acknowledged leaders among students, farmers, and 'anti-fascist' intellectuals. Their work in the prior period gave them a dominating influence among blacks, allowing them to form and provide *de facto* leadership for the National Negro

Congress, which became the main organizational vehicle for protest activity among blacks. As is well-known, they gained substantial leadership in the new CIO unions. Even in Washington, as anti-communists were later to charge, CP members (hardly subversive) filled many New Deal agencies.[24] It is, at the very least, debatable whether the Communist Party in the United States could have grown as much with a left line as it did with the Popular Front.

The Popular Front period, however, had its weaknesses, which few commentators discuss in detail. Some of these weaknesses were inherent in the strategy of the Popular Front.[25] Other weaknesses were due to the unquestioning nature of support for Soviet foreign and domestic policy.

The Popular Front orientation, with its emphasis on broad, temporary coalitions, required the dropping of more radical forms of organization. Among the first to go was the League of Struggle for Negro Rights, the party auxiliary that agitated against lynching and gave the full party analysis of the roots of black oppression; its publication, the *Liberator*, was also discontinued. Perhaps more significant, however, was the quiet abandonment in 1936 of the militant Sharecroppers' Union in the South. Overwhelmingly black, striking concrete blows at the most heinous forms of Jim Crow, it was considered an embarrassment to the CP's less radical work in largely white farmers' organizations.

The CP did much during the Popular Front period to hide (or give up) its independent radical identity. This was especially evident in the trade unions. During the 1920s and early 1930s, party shop units planned party tactics, recruited rank and file workers, and educated their members. Most units had newspapers which projected the Communist viewpoint on the plant, industry, union, and the world, as well as exposing shop conditions. Even where the CP led the union, as in the Fur and Leather Workers or the Auto Workers Union, or worked in coalition with other groups, the units represented the independent activity and politics of the party, unconstrained by coalitions or broader leadership responsibilities. When CP trade unionists occupied trade union leadership positions, they also met in fractions to plan and coordinate tactics. These principles of organization were employed by Communists around the world. They distinguished a revolutionary working class party at the organizational level from reformist electoral parties like the Social Democrats or SP, whose members were loosely organized by election districts.

The abolition of party shop units, newspapers, and union fractions in 1939 was another casualty of the Popular Front period. The dissolution of shop units and papers deprived the CP of an important organizational vehicle for recruiting and for strengthening its political support among workers for its full political line. The wide support of its trade union leaders, based on their militant leadership during the 1930s, was to prove insufficient at a later time, when their winter political views were to come under heavy attack. Those writers who defend the Popular Front strategy tend to approve of the dissolution of these party centers for the purpose of expediency in trade union leadership politics. Isserman, for example, says approvingly: 'The Communists' strength in the leadership of many of the new CIO unions made such relics of the 1920s and early 1930s unnecessary' (p. 8).

In the name of unity, the CP on occasion refused leadership even when it was offered, in favor of supporting more moderate forces. This orientation, formally referred to as building the center-left coalition, was nowhere more prevalent than in the UAW. At the first UAW convention in 1936, CP leader Wyndham Mortimer's Progessive Caucus dominated the elections and carried its entire program. Though the caucus delegates originally wanted Mortimer for president of the union, he withdrew his name from nomination (Keeran, p. 149).

At the 1939 UAW Convention, the CP and their allies again gained control. Under pressure from the national CP, pressure which had been called for by Sidney Hillman and Phillip Murray of the CIO leadership, the left caucus not only failed to run the still popular Mortimer, but withdrew the candidacy of their left ally for president, George Addes. They further agreed to abolish Mortimer's vice-presidential post. Finally, all in the name of unity, Mortimer and other Communists declined nomination to the union executive board. 'Thus, for the first time since the founding of the UAW, no officer or Executive Board member was a Communist' (Keeran, p. 200). Such conciliation hardly seems fitting for a self-proclaimed vanguard party of the working class.

The CP made capitulations in political principle which further undermined its credibility. Keeran, like most current defenders of the CP, approves of their support, without debate, at the 1936 UAW convention for 'an Innocuous committee resolution that expressed "unalterable opposition to Fascism, Nazism and Communism and all other movements, intended to distract the attention of the membership of the Labor Movement from the primary objectives of unionism" ' (p. 146). The CP was to support even stronger attacks on their positions without doing battle. At the 1940 CIO convention, a CP supporter, CIO general counsel Lee Pressman, introduced the strongly worded resolution equating communism and fascism, damning the influence of both in the labor movement. CP member Len DeCaux in his book *Labor Radical* describes this maneuver as a 'smart move.' As Bert Cochran notes, 'It was an accumulation of such "smart" moves that helped in time to bury the Communists. By voting hypocritically for resolutions that denounced them, they appeared as unprincipled tricksters whose dubious associations and ideas could not stand the light of day.'[26] (Cochran 1977, pp. 145-146) Problems of other kinds were also to appear. Naison provides a convincing account of the way the CP gained strength in Harlem during the early 1930s; they did so on the basis of mass mobilizations and militant tactics. The CP during the Popular Front period was to 'come off the street corners of Harlem.' Instead, its influence was to rest more and more on its institutional power in the new American Labor Party (dominated by moderate CIO leaders led by Sidney Hillman), in the welfare system, and in the city trade unions. Rather than attempting to combine its previous activities with these new arenas of strength, it simply abandoned the former. Naison, who intends no criticism, describes CP leaders in Harlem in this period as 'wheeling and dealing like Tammany stalwarts' (Naison, p. 172).

Though willing to compromise many of its principles on domestic issues, the CP gave little ground in its attacks on critics of Soviet domestic or foreign policy.[27] This was particularly true of their vituperative tirades against those who questioned one of the greatest of Stalin's crimes — the preposterously staged 1936-1938 Moscow trials and the execution of numerous party members, including virtually all the old Bolshevik leaders. The CP lost much moral authority in its total failure to make substantive replies to its critics, although in the case of the trials, there was perhaps little to be said.[28]

Thus, the period of party history called 'the height of Communist influence in the United States' (Naison, p. 170), and the 'Heyday of American Communism' (Klehr), was not without its Achilles heel.

The Molotov – Ribbentrop Pact

There are many who regard the signing of the pact between Nazi Germany and the Soviet Union on 22 August 1939, and the subsequent invasion of Poland, as its greatest calumny, a recognition of moral bankruptcy, the end of its period of broad support and respect among liberals.[29] Certainly this view is shared by all fervent anti-communists (Klehr, p. 409; Jaffe, p. xxx). Jaffe explains CP growth during 1942-1945 as a type of fools paradise, in which the U.S. CP temporarily 'basked in the reflected glow cast upon it by the Soviet Union's phenomenal military achievements against Hitler's armies' (p. 53). It is clear that the CP weakened its moral authority by the nature of its political somersaults. The lack of internal debate, the suddenness of the turns, the absence of self-criticism, qualifications, or even reasoned political explanations put its behavior in stark contrast to the political traditions it wanted to appropriate for itself.[30] Naturally, the CP lost much support and credibility with its swift change of line after the signing of the pact. This was especially true among intellectuals. Also interesting is the degree to which the CP gained support in some sectors by a return to more militant tactics and left-wing programs. This additional support was evident in certain areas of its work among blacks and workers.

Naison first describes the loss of support for the CP in Harlem in the latter phases of the Popular Front period:

> Preoccupied with the international crisis, concerned with expanding their electoral influence and their power base in the CIO, Communists, in 1939, failed to give voice to the growing fears of blacks that they were being locked out of the mainstream of the economy . . .

> Even before the Nazi-Soviet Pact, therefore, Harlem Communists found themselves on the defensive in confronting Harlem's economic problems. Weakened by defections of rank-and-file organizers, challenged by nationalists for leadership of the poor, the Party experienced a narrowing of its local power base and growing skepticism of its political outlook. (pp. 272-73)

The signing of the Molotov-Ribbentrop pact marked the end of the Popular Front. With the U.S. no longer the potential ally of the USSR against Hitler, attacks on Roosevelt and more militant class perspectives reappeared. The change to more aggressive tactics and a renewal of many of its more left-wing positions allowed the CP to recoup certain of its lost respect. The party maintained strong support among unionized black workers, according to Naison. It used its trade union base to 'reassert its claim to leadership in the struggle to end discrimination in employment.' Left-wing unions, pressed by the party leadership, 'began to act more aggressively to challenge discriminatory practices in their industries: 'By the spring of 1941, several unions in New York had initiated actions to break open white-only shops and the [CP-led] Transport Workers Union — long an embarrassment to Harlem organizers — had thrown its support behind a Harlem-wide movement to end discrimination in employment on city buses.' (p. 288) By similarly aggressive initiatives, the CP gained support among other workers. It played a key role in the organization of Ford by the UAW in 1941, assuming leadership in the key strike. By its renewed militancy in defense of workers' interests, it gained 'increased prestige and strength at the local level' in the UAW (Keeran, p. 225).

This is not to say that the CP gained in general from its policies during the pact period. On the contrary, its lack of integrity not only undermined its long-term moral stance, but left it open for bitter attacks by leaders in the black community and in the labor movement, all of which took their toll.

CP Growth During World War II

The biggest divergence of opinion, however, exists in evaluating CP strength during World War II. Not that commentators have serious disagreements on membership figures or leadership positions. Rather, there is the question of the degree to which strength and renewed growth were substantive or merely a fragile illusion. Isserman sees the period during World War II as the highpoint of CP strength and influence. Like Jaffe (who is occasionally ambiguous about how he sees the CP), he regards the policies followed under Browder from 1935-1945 as responsible for the party's successes.[31] Others, however, regard CP policies during World War II, especially in the trade unions, as providing the immediate cause for the swift post-World War II demise.[32]

It is well-known that the CP's line of going all-out to win the war against Germany led it to follow many extreme policies. This was particularly true in the trade unions, where it opposed any tactics that might interfere with production. The CP was the strongest supporter of the no-strike pledge, showing no shame at crushing wildcats, denouncing strike leaders, breaking legal strikes (e.g. at Wards), and even, reputedly, fingering militants to the FBI. Much to the dismay of many workers, it pushed for speedup in the form of an incentive pay scheme designed to raise wartime productivity. The CP opposed many protests which it feared might jeopardize war production, including struggles against company-imposed racial and sexual discrimination patterns.

Isserman, while not completely denying these facts, attempts to recast some of them in a more favorable light. In particular, he argues that the Communists did not 'abandon' the fight against racial discrimination, but 'forced that struggle into narrow channels' (p. 141). He emphasizes CP policies against racial discrimination in the National Maritime Union (NMU), where recent scholarship has shown that the CP (perhaps due to their extensive Negro cadre there and strong black support) did not capitulate as it did in other places. Much of Isserman's argument seems to hinge on his claim that the policy may have been inadequate and limited but did not constitute 'the "abandonment" so often alleged' (p. 143), something of a backhanded defense.[33] In the end, however, Isserman resorts to an unconvincing method of proof. He attempts to refute the charges against the CP by pointing to the election of black party leader Ben Davis to the New York City council (under the sponsorship of the Reverend Adam Clayton Powell, Jr.) and membership gains among blacks.[34] In terms of party strength in general, Isserman relies almost completely on membership growth after the 1943 Teheran agreement, which heralded glowing U.S.-Soviet friendship. He attempts to cast doubt on the party's growing weakness among workers by the following argument:

> The fact that relatively large numbers of industrial workers were joining at a time when the Communists were vigorously denouncing all strikes and edging toward the idea of extending the no-strike pledge into the postwar era suggests that the connection between

shop-floor militancy and workers' political judgments is not as simple and direct as some left-wing labor historians would like to believe. (pp. 205-206)

Keeran, no critic of CP policies, proves to be a much more reliable observer. He is anxious to defend the CP, but makes clear that in the UAW (despite party recruitment!) there was a sharp decline in CP influence. He does not deny the CP 'advocacy of incentive pay and the no-strike pledge' contributed to this decline. Rather, he wants to add two additional factors outside the union: these include the decline in 'labor and left-wing influence generally in the country during the war, and the internal crisis in the Communist party over Browder's policies' (p. 227). He provides little proof or argument for the importance of these two factors. As Jaffe shows convincingly, there was no crisis in the CP over Browder, until the word came from Moscow in mid-1945, well after the effects of CP wartime policies had done their damage. To cite the decline of left-wing influence in general is somewhat circular, since, as I have argued earlier, the CP was, for the most part, the left. Thus, the decline of the CP is being explained in large part by the decline of the CP. Moreover, the decline in prestige of the labor leadership of the CIO, who shared the CP's views about productivity and the no-strike pledge, again takes us back to the CP policies. The clear disproof that it was labor or leadership in general is shown in the impressive unity of the miners who followed (or pressed) John L. Lewis, when in 1943 they repeatedly defied the no-strike pledge. Tremendous support for Lewis, in opposition to their own leaders, was shown in all unions, particularly in the UAW (Glaberman, pp. 92-97; Lichtenstein, p. xxx); needless to say, Lewis was denounced by the CP in terms formerly reserved only for the Trotskyists.[35]

Keeran, in presenting much of the information which undermines many of his more general statements, notes how CP influence in the UAW declined particularly sharply in the last year of the war. With the opening of the second front against the Germans in 1944, and allied victories over Germany and Japan, the war seemed to be approaching its end. Layoffs and increased labor discipline began in many war-related industries. 'The dogmatic adherence to a policy of labor sacrifice at a time when neither domestic nor international conditions clearly warranted it, inevitably eroded the influence of the Communists and CIO leaders as well. In the UAW this became evident in the controversies around both incentive pay and the no-strike pledge.' (p. 237) This situation, so clear to all careful observers, is not changed by Isserman's appeals to membership growth of the CP in the party in general or in auto in particular.

Section 4. The Soviet and Comintern Connection

This issue is the major sticking point for all the recent commentators. Most of the anti-communist writers feel that proof of the connection is sufficient to damn the CP, and constitutes an explanation of its essential nature. Most of those who argue that there were some positive aspects of CP work feel they have to prove a certain amount of independence for the U.S. party. Virtually none examines the policies of the Comintern, how they were developed, and the relation between Russian events and the guidelines set for member parties.

Contrary to the tendency of most contemporary commentators to hold national party independence or an 'American' approach as a supreme principle, those attracted to the early Communist movement had no such desire. To millions of workers around the world, the Bolshevik Revolution was an inspiration and a guideline for their own work. The leaders of Soviet Russia declared the international character of their revolution and asked for worldwide support. The path of nationally independent parties had been followed by the 2nd International; its major parties, led by its German affiliate, had supported their own governments in waging war against other countries. Despite pledges by all parties at Stuttgart (1907) and other international congresses not to slaughter fellow workers in other countries, all major parties except the Bolsheviks had capitulated in World War I. The Comintern was established, supposedly embodying the internationalist principles and discipline which would prevent such traitorous activity.

The Russian Revolution coincided with, stimulated, and gave great authority to the pre-1918 anti-war left which had emerged in the U.S. and other countries around the world. Any number of incidents indicate the tremendous power of Bolshevism. One amusing circumstance is described by Draper (1966, p. 159). The Russian language federation, of the SP, and later of the U.S. CP, prior to 1918, was of modest size and in its 'great majority' was 'pro-Menshevik.' After the October Revolution, this federation grew to many times its former size, with hardly a member to be found who did not proclaim his long-standing Bolshevism. Within this context, for good or for ill, the international movement, formally organized in the CI, dominated at first merely by the moral authority of its Soviet leaders, had a decisive ability to influence and shape its member parties.

I would argue, however, contrary to the views of many of the recent commentators, that the early influence, particularly on the U.S. party, was largely positive. Despite the assertions of Draper (explicitly accepted, e.g., by Isserman), this control was not always easily exercised, nor was it reflected in the abject forms of submission which it would later embody. A number of facts in early party history serve to underscore both these points.

CP–CI Relations in the 1920s

In 1919, upon its formation, party adherents in the labor movement adhered to the revolutionary syndicalist approach of the traditional left wing in this country. Carried away by their own romanticism, they even went so far as occasionally to call for soviets as a demand in their strikes, with predictably disastrous consequences. Under Lenin's influence at the 1920 2nd Congress of the Third International, the U.S. delegates were convinced of the problems with their revolutionary dual union approach. As Keeran's work indicates, however, it took several years and much prodding before the majority of Communist workers were to begin the more patient work within reformist trade unions. The highly positive results of its work have already been described.

The early CP was also deeply faction-ridden, having formed itself into two separate parties. These two groups, with virtually no real principled differences, refused to merge, even after numerous instructions from the CI to do so. Finally, they were forced to merge in 1921, upon threat of expulsion from the CI, thus ending the diversion of a large percentage of their mutual energies from internecine warfare.

By all accounts, the SP had been historically weak on the question of black equality. Thus, there was little in even the left SP heritage to force the new CP to address this question. The Soviets; with much more experience with questions of national and ethnic oppression, attempted to press the issue of black oppression from the beginning with their American comrades. Harry Haywood describes how CI representatives began to raise the question of black self-determination in the black-belt South in 1924, more than four years before the position was eventually adopted by the CI. This pressure by the Soviets did much to strengthen the CP's work both among blacks and in winning large numbers of whites to the struggle for black equality. In contrast to the bureacratic domination that would come later, this hardly represents the 'orders from Moscow' assumed by most commentators, following Draper, that supposedly characterized CP-CI relations in the 1920s.

The bureacratic screws were tightened after the expulsion of the Trotskyists in 1928, and of the elected Lovestone leadership in 1929, all under Moscow's direction. While all parties were shaped by the policies of the CI and the politically degenerate Soviet state, the U.S. CP was to become more heavily dominated than many other parties. It was not isolated like the Chinese and Yugoslav parties, with their great difficulties in always maintaining close contact with the CI. Unlike the British, Canadian, or Italian parties, with their traditions of strong, recognized leadership, it was highly factional. Finally, the weak U.S. party was often a pawn of Soviet diplomacy in its dealings with the U.S. government.

Klehr and Jaffe, however, overplay the Soviet connection to such a degree as to make no sense of it. For Klehr, the CP is something of a cross between a fifth column and a clown show, always striving 'to provide what the Comintern wanted, no more, no less . . . ' By failing to understand its link to traditional native American radicalism, Klehr cannot account for the attractive power of the CP, how it grew, and why it commanded such respect, even in high places. He also leaves us unable to explain how CP activists organized movements, often mixing so well with their milieus, developing innovative, effective tactics of protest (things described vividly by Naison and Keeran). The logic of extreme anti-communism forces its proponents to oscillate between denouncing the Soviet Union and proving the CP's ties to it. Jaffe, so much sharper than Klehr when he concentrates on the latter, frequently gets himself in trouble when moves to the former. For example, with all the real crimes of Stalin, Jaffe unconvincingly blames him for the start of the Cold War (p. 85), puts the total blame for the Hitler takeover on the CI, absolving the Social Democrats completely.[36] Finally, Jaffe's denunciation of Stalin for describing Roosevelt and Churchill as two different kinds of pickpockets merely exposes his own patriotic soul. (p. 229)

As one-dimensional as are the analyses of Jaffe and Klehr and other anti-communists, they are undoubtedly a useful counterweight for certain of the more whimsical remarks about the actual or potential independence of the CP from the CI. Isserman, for example, while paying frequent critical homage to all sorts of servile behavior toward Moscow and various forms of venality on the part of the CP, ultimately holds to a quite romantic view of their independent struggle. He describes the CP, beginning in the 1930s and throughout World War II, as an organization of thousands of dedicated souls, struggling for an American road to socialism. Thus, he takes great pains to find independence where hardly any existed. He describes the activities of the German immigrant Gerhardt Eisler, who some have, probably erroneously, speculated was a high level CI representative to the U.S. CP. Isserman states: 'But by the mid-1930s that post retained less of the aura of mystery and authority that earlier Commintern representatives had wielded with such disastrous consequences for American Communists.' (p. 170) Yet, as Isserman well knows, such a representative was not necessary in order to get instructions from the CI in the mid-1930s. There were frequent trips by Browder and others to get direct instructions from Georgi Dimitrov, the head of the CI, and other top level officials. In 1938, as Jaffe describes in great detail, Dimitrov set up a secret radio link with Browder which was monitored every night for instructions from the CI. This link was still operating seven years later!

Naison and Keeran, while attempting to stress the CP's independence in ways similar to Isserman, are both more subtle in their descriptions of the independent initiatives of the CP, thus giving those willing to read between the lines a realistic appraisal of how CI directives were implemented and occasionally circumvented. Naison describes a broad fund-raising affair for the CP-led Scottsboro defense case:

> The tone of this event — so divergent from what Communist critics were writing about black music, and from the Party line in general — dramatized the degree of autonomy which Harlem Communists exercised in planning local tactics . . . Their actions confound the image of the black Communist as puppet or automaton, unwilling to take

initiatives without direct orders from the top. Obedient in the last instance to Central Committee directives, they were also influenced by popular feelings in the community they worked in. (p. 72)

Naison later tells how in July of 1933, the top CP leadership decided to put an end to the 'free-wheeling' style of its Harlem branch. Their concerns were in response to CI criticism of their work. The CP put James Ford, their top black leader, in charge of Harlem (Naison, p. 95). He eliminated much of the independent initiatives of the Harlem branch, as well as their careless organizational practices, which had resulted in little membership growth. Within a year and a half, the black membership under Ford, who stressed recruiting, had more than tripled (p. 134). In this incident, we glimpse both the reality and the limits of independence in the early 1930s.

Keeran, in an otherwise carefully researched and highly informative book, goes through the greatest contortions to defend the integrity of the CP. This feature of his otherwise impressive manuscript has not gone unnoticed by some commentators. Keeran provides us with invaluable descriptions of the Communist work in auto trying to build the independent Auto Workers Union (AWU) from the early 1920s until the organization was dissolved in 1934. He also describes other work in MESA (Mechanics Educational Society of America) and in AFL affiliates in 1933. He takes pains, though, to inform us: 'It is important to note, however, that two years before the Seventh Congress of the Comintern changed from the Third Period to the Popular Front, John Anderson and other Communists had already joined MESA, and Mortimer had led the union at White Motors into the AFL' (p. 120). First, it should be emphasized that the CP, even during its most sectarian phases, did not always refuse to enter broader organizations or to work with others when the tactical situation forced them to do so. Moreover, it is ingenuous, for those familiar with the history of the CI, to argue that the tactical line did not change until the 1935 Seventh Congress. Hitler took power in Germany in the beginning of 1933. Several months later the rigid sectarian policies were already being reconsidered. The first public sign of change came with the announcements from the 13th plenum of the Executive Committee of the CI in late 1933. This was a period during which there was considerable tactical flexibility, although the guidelines were far from clear. By 1934, a united front in France with the formerly 'social fascist' Socialist

Party was ordered. Thus, Keeran's documentation of some tactical flexibility during the sectarian Third Period would demonstrate at most the limited independence which Naison points out. Such flexibility in late 1933 and in 1934, however, was not at all discordant with the thinking of Moscow.

Despite variations between parties and a certain amount of domestic flexibility, the Communist Parties outside the Soviet Union were, by the late 1920s, treated as mere tools of Soviet policy. Contrary to wishful thinking by Isserman and others, the situation gew worse, not better. The most important question, however, that determined the fortunes and character of the American party was not the fact of subordination to Moscow, but the content of Moscow's wishes.

A clear understanding of the evolution of the U.S. Communist Party must be based on a recognition of its gradual evolution from a revolutionary working class party at its formation to being mainly a 'border guard' for the Soviet state. By the late 1920s, with Stalin at the helm, the bureacratic degeneration of the Soviet party and state was far advanced. With the failure of the British general strike in 1926 and the bloody defeat of the Chinese uprising in 1927, the Soviet leadership no longer saw the possibilities for their own country's survival linked to revolutionary successes abroad. Rather, they saw their best defense now to be located in diplomatic maneuvering, supported by the CPs in capitalist countries. This was to be their strategy for buying time for the economic and military development of Soviet society.

Trotsky argued that the Soviet leadership during the 1930s squandered many revolutionary opportunities. According to Trotsky, Stalin engineered crushing defeats, most dramatically in Germany in 1933, and in Spain during 1936-1939.[37] Thus, the traditional Communist goals of organizing the working class and its allies for the revolutionary struggle for socialism became subordinated to supporting and complementing Soviet foreign policy and to the unqualified defense of heinous crimes against the population inside the Soviet Union. Despite its policies at home and its debilitating effect on foreign Communist Parties, the Soviet Union remained a contradictory social formation, a society in which capitalism remained overthrown, but had stalled in its attempt to build socialism.[38] The goals of the Soviet Union towards the CI affiliate parties were reflected in the ideology of building 'socialism in one country.'[39]

The traditional Marxist view, of course, was that socialism could not be built in one country. The successful transition required the joint efforts of at least several economically developed countries. Thus, stimulating and aiding revolutions was a high priority. If, however, socialism could be successfully built in the Soviet Union alone, facilitating the ultimate triumph of socialism on a world scale, further revolutions were not necessary. Foreign parties could be reduced to the role of 'border guards.'

That the role of border guard often required the organization of broad liberal pressure groups or occasional self-effacement was part of the bargain. The contradictory nature of the U.S. CP devolves from the fact that it was not merely a foreign policy office or an unregistered lobbyist. Its role as border guard was superimposed over its historical *and* continuing role as a mass-based militant working class party. The two roles often were in conflict, occasionally in diametric opposition. In such cases, it never was in doubt which was master. And, in the end, the one played a large role in destroying the other.

Section 5. Why The CP Failed

Why it Declined so Drastically

How strong was the Communist Party before it declined? According to Bert Cochran:

> They had decisive influence over half the auto union, hegemony in the electrical union, the mine, mill, and smelter workers, the office and government workers, a voice in the rubber and the steel union. They were in effective control of the most important central bodies, including New York, Cleveland, Detroit, Chicago, Los Angeles. (*New International*, March 1949; quoted in Cannon 1973a)

Virtually all this was lost by 1950.

The question remains: what led to the decline of the CP? As James Cannon asks: 'Why did it collapse so miserably in the fifties?' (1971, p. 93). Most writers in this country accept that subordination to Moscow was primary. Not only Klehr, Jaffe, and traditional anti-communists, but most liberals and left reformists also take this to be the key. I have argued, however, that this is at best only part of the answer. Thus, it is worth looking at some of the alternative explanations, before drawing out a fuller explanation from the discussion so far.

Objective Conditions

Roger Keeran articulately puts forward the traditional explanation of those who defend the general policies of the CP. The explanation hinges on at least five factors: the backwardness of U.S. workers, the tenuousness of CP leadership among them, post-war affluence, the intensity of the Cold War, and the extent of the repression faced by the party. These objective conditions need little elaboration. Any radical movement in the post-World War II period would have been on the defensive and facing a difficult situation. Were it not for the conjuncture of all these unfavorable conditions, the CP might well have maintained its strong toehold in U.S. politics. An analysis of the role played by these conditions is usually absent from the explanations of more conservative writers.

It is also clear to some students of the CP, including myself, that tz ‚' had done much to prepare its own grave. The CP hung on and hardened itself during the lengthy boom of the 1920s, under much fiercer repression. Yet, starting with more cadre and resources in 1945, they reached a state of collapse and total isolation little more than a decade later. What were the reasons?

Browderism

The argument of Isserman, which echoes earlier claims by Gates, Dennis, and Starobin, is that the CP could have been successful if they had not only been more independent from Moscow, but had continued their stance of progressivism, as the left wing of the New Deal. In the eyes of these critics (which oddly enough sometimes includes the anti-communist Jaffe), it was the break with 'Browderism,' the return in 1945 to sectarian, 'un-American' policies, that hurt the CP fatally.

Such a line of argument, however, has many weaknesses. It refuses to recognize the policies of the CP from which it developed strength, attracted militants, gained moral authority, and came to be the dominant force on the left. Its ties to the Soviet Union, its militant position on the Negro question, its general program of class struggle played no small part in this. Isserman and other writers make the unwarranted assumption that only popular front coalitions attract people. But sometimes, even if only sometimes, the more radical positions attract; they particularly attract, at such times, the most militant members of the working class.

Contrary to the claims of certain of these critics that the CP had greater independence under Browder, its policies of support for Roosevelt as well as support for the Moscow trials, its patriotism as well as its hiding of its socialist views under liberal democratic 'American' traditions, were all dictated by Moscow. To the extent that the U.S. CP had any independence, it was during the earlier, revolutionary period of the 1920s, so disliked by the pro-Browder authors. Further, the CP's general acceptance during World War II was not merely based on its political subordination to the New Deal coalition. It was also due to the coincidence of the CP's pro-Soviet orientation with the wartime aims of U.S. capitalism and its politicians. When the wartime alliance broke down, either the CP's relation to the liberal Democrats or its relation to the Soviet Union had to go. The only way this alliance with the politicians and moderate CIO officials could have continued after the onset of the Cold War would have been for the CP to have abandoned its support of the Soviet Union. To have done so would have been to reject what the CP stood for; few of the pro-Browder supporters have quite gone this far.

The idea that Browderism was a phenomenon somehow different, more 'American' than the role of border guards demanded of all Stalinist parties is a myth. To hold this view is to fail to understand the nature of the political relations between the CI and Soviet Union and its subordinate parties. A similar error, of course, is made by those left critics of the CP who see its problems in its failure to break sufficiently with Browderism.[40]

The view I find most plausible about the Communist Party's demise is put forward in the writings of James Cannon, founder and former leader of the SWP:

> The decline of the American Stalinists began before the witch-hunt started against them. It got well under way in the latter period of the Second World War when they were still basking in the favor of the government and doing all their dirty work of supporting the war and the no-strike pledge, promoting incentive pay, backing speedup schemes, fingering militants for the FBI, cheering for the imprisonment of the leaders of the Socialist Workers Party. (1973, p. 129)[41]

The fundamental cause of the CP's demise, according to Cannon, was its moral bankruptcy, a characteristic that became more and more apparent, not only to liberal and left critics, but to militant workers as well.[42] The accumulation of perfidy, unprincipled behavior, and outright treachery from the 1930s on eventually caught up with the Communist Party. Much of the moral corruption of the CP is exposed in its support of the federal government's prosecution of the SWP Trotskyist leadership under the Smith Act, later to be used against the CP itself in the late 1940s. But in 1940, the CP, as Jaffe demonstrates, supplied briefs on the SWP to the government. They branded the SWP as enemy agents, sometimes as imperialist agents (during the pact period), at other times as Nazi agents. Some of the CP 'exposures' were used by the national Teamster leadership when they broke the militant SWP-led Minneapolis truckers' local (Glaberman, p. 140).

The culmination of these activities may well have been the summary way the CP, on orders from Moscow, first attacked Earl Browder, their longtime general secretary, then removed him from the leadership, and finally expelled him. In 1944, Browder, who had been called the world's greatest English-speaking Marxist and 'the American Stalin,' had led the dissolution of the CP and the formation of the Communist Political Association. In this activity, he had the unanimous support in May 1944, of the whole CP leadership. In July 1945, after indirect criticism from the Soviets, Browder was denounced as a 'revisionist,' getting not a single vote from his former supporters. Cannon refers to such behavior by the whole CP leadership as degrading, exposing to all that they were no more than the 'trained seals of the Communist apparatus' (Cannon 1977, p. 119).

While their moral bankruptcy was the underlying cause for their rapid, almost total demise, the immediate cause was their policies in the labor movement during World War II. The CP, unlike the left groups and labor leaders who opposed the no-strike pledge, lost leadership of the increasingly militant workers in the CIO. This was reflected in day-to-day shop activities, in many local union elections, and in some convention meetings. This growing isolation from rank-and-file workers they shared with other labor leaders. The resulting bureacratization of the labor movement during World War II is described in much detail by Nelson Lichtenstein in *Labor's War at Home*. Their activities also separated and placed them in opposition to all other forces on the left, many of whom were gaining support based on their association with the anti-no-strike pledge movement. The CP came more and more to depend on its bureacratic relations with other union officials to maintain its position.

When the tide turned and the Cold War began, moderate labor leaders, whose alliance with the CP had only been based upon a coincidence of wartime interests, turned on the CP. These labor leaders had corporate and government support in their attacks. What the CP lacked was the backing of militants, in whose eyes they had become discredited, and other left forces, whom they had denounced and betrayed to the government during the war. With few friends and unable to generate much credibility, the CP, unlike previous radical groupings under attack, was easily blown away with nary a trace.

Was the CP Decline Inevitable?

I have tried to suggest that the CP did not sink its most important roots by subordinating itself to liberal politicians and moderate labor leaders. There is some evidence that the CP gained its most reliable support when it followed left-wing policies based on a class struggle approach, when it took forthright stands in struggling against black oppression, when it engaged in uncompromising exposure of liberal politicians and reformist labor leaders. They often gained the most credibility when they forthrightly put forward and defended their own views. Such an argument in no way condones the sectarian idiocy of the Third Period, nor the Stalinist treachery which pervades most of the Party's history. But this framework not only takes issue with those commentators who highlight the 1935-1945 period, it also suggests why their analysis of the first decade of party history (1919-1929) and the Third Period is so inadequate.

The reason most commentators give short shrift to this early period is that they 'prefer' the later, less radical periods. If the CP gained strength, successfully prepared itself in its revolutionary periods, then perhaps its more moderate periods were not the *key* to its growth then.[43] The New Left historians and present CP defenders are advocates of these later periods. They achieve an uneasy marriage with the conservative interpreters, whose preference is to show that the United States is inhospitable to radicalism; for the latter, the CP only grew when it rejected radicalism.[44] It should be clear that all their capitulations and conciliations, from hiding their politics, failing to defend their own views at conventions, and disbanding their shop groups, to refraining from criticism of Roosevelt or CIO leaders, all did the CP little good in the end. Moreover, there is evidence that where their organizing was based on the building of solid political support, it did not desert them when the Cold War began. One, among many examples, is their base in the Fur and Leather Workers Unions, formed not only through building a militant union, but on the basis of winning people to their then revolutionary politics in the 1920s. This political support did not readily elude them when the Cold War began.

The Tragedy of the Communist Party Demise

In what lies the tragedy of the demise and isolation of the Communist Party in the U. S.? Its elimination as a political force in the labor movement and in the political life of this country meant a crippling of the left. Cannon argues that they themselves, having sown the seeds of their own destruction, are neither tragic nor worthy of tears from those who would see the U.S.'s exceptional character ended. Rather, Cannon argues that the CP was

> directly responsible for the demoralization and disorientation of the richly promising movement. The Roosevelt social program was the decisive factor in heading off the *the mass movement* and diverting it into reformist channels. But the Stalinists, who supported Roosevelt for reasons of Kremlin foreign policy, miseducated, betrayed, corrupted, and demoralized *the vanguard* of this movement — a vanguard which numbered tens of thousands of the best and most courageous young militants — and thus destroyed the first great prospects to build a genuine revolutionary party in America on a mass basis. (1973a, p. 127)

The tragedy of the party is what the CP did to its victims and the possibilities which it destroyed:

> The chief victim of Stalinism in this country was the magnificent left-wing movement, which arose on the yeast of the economic crisis in the early Thirties and eventually took form in the CIO through a series of veritable labor uprisings. Such a movement, instinctively aimed at American capitalism, was bound to find political leader-

ship. Conditioned by their frightful experiences, the workers in the vanguard of the great mass movement were ready for the most radical solutions. The Stalinists, who appeared to represent the Russian Revolution and the Soviet Union, almost automatically gained the dominating position in the movement; while thousands of young militants — not the worst, but in many cases the very best — were recruited into the Communist Party.

The tragedy lies ultimately in how the CP betrayed the confidence of the tens of thousands of militants it attracted:

> By their whole policy and conduct; by their unprincipled opportunism, their unscrupulous demagoguery, systematic lying and calculated treachery — the Stalinists demoralized the left-wing labor movement. They squandered its militancy and robbed it of the moral resources to resist the reactionary witch-hunt instituted in the unions with the beginning of the 'cold war.' Murray and Reuther only appear to be the conquerors of the left-wing workers. It was really the Stalinists who beat them. (1973b, pp. 295-96)

This view of the demise of the Communist Party of the United States, a view which I believe most fits the facts reported by all the other investigators, finds little echo in their writings. It helps explain the differences among various authors, and why each has such difficulties explaining certain facts that are uncongenial to their political perspectives. The perspective presented here also suggests, not only that the exceptional character of U.S. politics is not inevitable, but that broad class alternatives to labor reformism and popular front politics are not, at certain conjunctures, incongruous with U.S. society.

Notes

1. This feature has been highlighted by many non-radical writers, in the so-called American exceptionalism literature. See, e.g., Sombart 1976, Perlman 1949, Hartz 1955, Lipset 1960, and Bell 1960. Foster 1952, p. 33, notes that the problem of the lack of class-consciousness of U.S. workers was apparent to U.S. Marxists in the 1850s.

2. During its first ten years, from 1919 to 1929, the party went through a series of name changes. In 1929, it adopted its present name, Communist Party, USA. In this essay, I generally refer simply to the Communist Party (CP), rather than reflect its changing names at different times. For a detailed description of these changes and their circumstances, with references, see Goldfield 1980a.

3. Jaffe, once a supporter of the CP, was for many years a close confidant of Browder's. Much of the more interesting material in his book first appeared in

articles published in the early 1970s in *Survey*.

4.   Perhaps the classic in this genre is Max Kempelman's *The Communist Party vs. the CIO* (New York, 1957). See Goldfield 1980a, for a detailed discussion of this work.

5.   Klehr's book is among the most unevenly documented and politically obtuse of all recent books on the CP. More often than the others, he makes broad, unsupported statements (for example, on p. 339, he talks of bitter and divisive black-white relations in the CP in Harlem in 1934; just the opposite is shown by Naison, whom Klehr gives little evidence of having read). In spite of its many deficiencies (a small number of which will be noted in the course of this essay), Klehr's book has been treated with extreme kindness and respect by reviewers. See, for typical examples, Hal Draper's praise on the book's jacket; Ronald Radosh's review in the *New Republic* 190 (March 1984), pp. 29-34; and Lewis Coser in *Contemporary Sociology* 13 (1984). This first-class treatment afforded Klehr's shoddy goods is further evidence for what Andrew Kopkind has aptly described as the 'return of Cold War liberalism.'

6.   See Goldfield 1980a, for a more detailed discussion and fuller references.

7.   See Ozanne, pp. 154, 220.

8.   An invaluable corrective in understanding both the volatility and instability of all unemployed organizing may be found in Cannon 1979, p. 206.

9.   This is true even of Draper, whose detailed research is impressive, and, in view of his former CP membership, shows sensitivity on certain other issues.

10.   See p. 37.

11.   While Keeran's book provides many rich details of the CP's practical trade union work, he tells us little about how the particular party line was carried out. He gives us no information about the relation of day-to-day work in the AWU to the national workplace and union campaigns organized under the umbrella of the TUEL. Knowledge of these activities must be gleaned from party publications and the writings of Foster, among others.

12.   The dramatic story of this union is given in detail in Foner 1950. Unfortunately, we learn very little about the functioning of the CP because, unlike Keeran, Foner hardly mentions the party at all.

13.   Trotsky analyzed the theoretical problems of the program of the Sixth Congress in *The Third International After Lenin*. He specifically analyzed the discordance between the Third Period turn and tactics with the defeats in Britain (1926) and China (1927), and the loss in CP membership around the world in the previous years in his 'The Turn in the Communist International and the Situation in Germany' (26 September 1930); rpt. in Trotsky 1971. Another useful source is Claudin 1975, Part One.

14.   In 1933, Hitler took power in Germany. The largest Communist Party outside the Soviet Union was totally destroyed, virtually all its cadre murdered during the next two years. The CI began, at first gingerly, to reassess the question of fascism, including how best to unite with Social-Democratic workers. The line of the CI began to show public evidence of change after the 13th plenum of the Executive Committee in 1933. By 1935, at the 7th World Congress, the new official position was declared. Thus, the end of the Third Period, anywhere between 1933 and 1935, is ambiguous. Few of the many writers who take strong positions against the Third Period take account of the 1933-1935 transition period.

15.   The facts reported here, as in many other cases reported by Klehr, may be exaggerated. Surprisingly, despite his otherwise hostile attitude toward the CP, he uncritically takes this incident, as well as much other material, without

additional confirmation or any qualification from the party's newpaper. In this respect, he is less circumspect about his source material than other writers.

16.   Klehr also describes the flood of intellectuals into the CP during the Third Period, while virtually none joined the SP: 'Homeless and confused intellectuals barely favored Thomas with a glance. "Becoming a Socialist right now," John Dos Passos explained in 1932, "would have just about the same effect on anybody as drinking a bottle of near-beer" ' (p. 78).

17.   I.M. Rubinow, 'The Negro and Socialism' *The New York Call* (19 May 1912); quoted from Spero and Harris, p. 405.

18.   See Goldfield 1980a for a more complete discussion. One important weakness of Naison is that he fails to discuss, except in passing, the 1928 and 1930 CI resolutions on the Negro question. There is almost nothing concerning the role of the Soviets in the adoption of the resolution nor on their role in monitoring the U.S. CP's implementation, although the resolutions were clearly central to CP work. On the other hand, one of Naison's strengths is to give large amounts of detail about Party activities in Harlem during the period from 1930-1933.

19.   Naison mentions this throughout, beginning on p. 46.

20.   Later he does admit that the 'party's reliance on revolutionary unions proved ill-conceived' (p. 120). Keeran has the habit, which has disturbed many of his reviewers, of talking quite positively about CP line changes when they are first introduced, then criticizing them just before they are changed again.

21.   For instance, the CP began to attack the NRA when it was passed in 1933. At this time labor leaders were either quite positive (e.g., Lewiş and Hillman) or non-commital. By mid-1934, not only militant workers, but many moderate labor leaders were referring to the act as the National Run Around. It was, of course, clear to many who spoke this truth from the outset. See Fraser 1984.

22.   There is also some indication that there was a difference between the first year and one-half or so and the rest of the Popular Front period. For a description of this former time, see Staughton Lynd, 'The Possibility of Radicalism in the Early 1930s: The Case of Steel,' *Radical America* 6, 6 (November-December 1972).

23.   This not only includes Naison and Isserman, but Starobin, Dennis, and others as well.

24.   James Gross's study of the National Labor Relations Board gives a balanced appreciation of their influence there.

25.   This was merely the first stage in many of the two-stage theories of revolution then guiding all CPs in economically developed capitalist countries. All these theories had certain things in common: There is a first stage, in which a broad coalition, including liberal capitalists, is formed to struggle for the establishment of complete democracy; the second stage, which begins only after the completion of the democratic stage, involves a peaceful transition to socialism — peaceful, since the violent antagonists (right-wing capitalists, racist politicians, anti-communists, etc.) have been eliminated during the previous stage. The classical criticism of this notion is simply this. In order to establish the alliances necessary to complete the first stage, the goals of the second stage must be abandoned. On the other hand, adhering to and preparing for the second stage at an early time would entail the destruction of the coalition. Marxists have traditionally criticized such notions as a disguise for non-revolutionary politics.

26.   For those who believe that such political spinelessness was merely a result of policies under Earl Browder's leadership, it is well to recall the CP sponsorship of the frontal attack against them at the 1946 CIO convention. See Cochran 1977, p. 267 for details.

27. The CP's unqualified defense of Soviet foreign policy created obstacles among ordinary people in Harlem earlier than it did in most places. The support for Ethiopian resistance to the invasion of Mussolini's troops in 1935 was a popular cause in Negro communities around the country. The Soviet Union neither stopped its trade with Italy, nor at first did it publicly condemn the aggression. Never good at distinguishing between Soviet foreign policy and the proper actions for Communists, the CP was unable to combat successfully attacks in the press and by nationalist street speakers. As a result, according to Naison (p. 174), they lost many members, rapid growth in Harlem coming to a complete halt.

28. For those with doubts on this issue, Roy Medvedev's *Let History Judge* and Robert Conquest's *The Great Terror* should be consulted.

29. For an account that minimizes the importance of the pact in determining the Soviet Union's character, see James Cannon's 15 October 1939 speech; rpt. in Cannon 1970, p. 211.

30. Though it is rarely acknowledged by their antagonistic critics, both Marx and Lenin were insistent about not sparing any criticism of their respective parties. The CP's perfidy was even more extreme when it reversed itself again after the invasion of the Soviet Union by Germany on 22 June 1941. Keeran apologizes: 'For those who believed in the necessity of defending the world's only socialist nation from outside attack, the CP's policy changes had eminent justification' (p. 207). It was, however, not merely the substance of its changes which discredited the party. As Martin Glaberman documents extensively in *Wartime Strikes*, one day Britain, the U.S., and China (then led by Chiang Kai-shek) were 'imperialist powers,' the next day, without further explanation, they were 'great democracies.' See Glaberman, pp. 65-67 for references and discussion.

31. Jaffe considers the CP's precipitous decline to have resulted from its abandonment of these policies in 1947-1948; see p. 99.

32. This is the position taken explicitly by James Cannon; see Cannon 1973a, p. 129.

33. Isserman does, however, offer numerous insights and interesting materials. He is one of the few commentators to mention the party's role in relation to women. He marshalls evidence to show that the CIP did struggle, successfully in many instances, to open up employment opportunities for women in the defense industries during World War II. He is a poignant critic of certain of the more hypocritical practices of the Workers Party on the question of blacks. He observes (note 53, p. 278) that the Workers Party, a splinter group from the SWP, while criticizing CP anti-discrimination policy in the NMU, was working within the Seafarers International Union (SIU), without challenging its 'rigidly Jim Crow' policies. This lack of attention to the question of blacks and the fight against discrimination is also a serious weakness in James Cannon's writings.

34. Glaberman, himself a member at the time of the Workers Party, attempts to explain this contradiction in part by arguing that, despite national CP policies, 'on a personal level and on the shop floor, CP members were the most consistent and principled element in the labor movement in fighting for the rights of black workers' (p. 73). Thus, the CP heritage, implanted deeply in its cadre, was not easily erased by the new line.

35. Keeran's ingenuous remarks are often quite annoying, detracting from his generally fine scholarship. He asserts, for example: 'Naturally, a tension existed between labor's traditional commitment to improve wages and working

conditions and its new commitment to avoid strikes and provide increased production for the war effort. The Communists recognized this tension' (p. 228). On the contrary, the CP acted as if it recognized none of this.

36. See p. 35. While this is not the place for a detailed analysis of the culpability of the left in the rise of Hitler, it is clear that the Social Democrats shared the tragic underestimate of the Nazis with the Communists. It is enough to read Paul Sweezy's description of German Social Democratic leader Rudolph Hilferding, who wrote in January of 1933, that the 'primary aim of the socialists was to fight the communists' (p. xviii). Hilferding repeated these sentiments only days before fleeing from Gestapo arrest.

37. See Trotsky 1971 and 1973. Fernando Claudin, somewhat critical of Trotsky, takes a similar view of Germany and Spain.

38. See Goldfied 1980b for more detailed discussion of these issues.

39. For further discussion, see Trotsky 1957, Claudin, and the new collection by Tariq Ali 1984.

40. See Goldfield 1980a for an extended analysis of this position.

41. The SWP today should not be confused with the organization that existed at the time of Cannon's writings. The Socialist Workers Party, although at a later date than the CP, began moving to the right. By the 1960s, it was no longer one of the more radical groups on the left. In the past several years, it has substantially disavowed its Trotskyist heritage.

42. Such an analysis, of course, must explain why other pro-Soviet parties were not equally decimated at the same time. A comparison, for example, with the mass strength of the postwar Italian and French Communist Parties would undoubtedly look at the following points: 1) The French and especially the Italian parties inherited a much more extensive left tradition; they had sunk deep roots and gained much prestige within their respective working classes in the 1920s. 2) Perhaps most important, their moral credibility was refurbished by their courageous leadership of the resistance movements against fascism. 3) Thus, they had little chance to capitulate to the ruling classes in their countries, who had either collaborated with or were themselves fascists. 4) Secondarily, the exposure of Stalin's crimes and of the CP in general was greater in the U.S., in part due to the existence of the largest Trotskyist movement in the West here.

43. Isserman, in particular, attacks those whom he accuses of the 'pick and choose' approach to which period of CP history they prefer. He, of course, 'picks and chooses' the 1935-1945 period, by arguing that he is looking at a 'generation' of Communists.

44. Even the question of numerical growth is not always the right one to focus on, particularly when looking at a party whose goal is to gain the leadership of a class. The Bolsheviks, arguably, solidified their hold on the more radical sections of the Russian working class by opposing World War I in 1914 and by refusing support to the 1917 Provisional Revolutionary Government, two acts which initially lost them members. In less dramatic fashion, one must consider the likelihood that there are lags between the gaining of prestige by a left-wing party for its principled activities, and actual gains in size through new recruitments. Similarly, there may also be lags between declining prestige and actual losses in membership.

Bibliography

Ali, Tariq, ed. 1984. *The Stalinist Legacy*. New York: Penguin Books.

Bell, Daniel. 1960. *The End of Ideology*. New York: The Free Press.

Cannon, James. 1962. *The First Ten Years of American Communism*. New York: Pathfinder.

—. 1973a. *Speeches to the Party*. New York: Pathfinder.

—. 1973b, *Notebook of an Agitator*. New York: Pathfinder.

—. 1971. *Speeches for Socialism*. New York: Pathfinder.

—. 1979. *The History of American Trotskyism*. New York: Pathfinder.

—. 1975. *The Socialist Workers Party in World War II*. New York: Pathfinder.

—. 1977. *The Struggle for Socialism in the 'American Century.'* New York: Pathfinder.

—. 1970. *The Struggle for a Proletarian Party*. New York: Pathfinder.

Charney, George. 1968. *A Long Journey*. Chicago: Quadrangle Books.

Claudin, Fernando. 1975. *The Communist Movement*. Part One and Part Two. New York: Monthly Review Press.

Cochran, Bert. 1977. *Labor and Communism*. Princeton: Princeton University Press.

—. ed. 1959. *American Labor in Midpassage*. New York: Monthly Review.

Conquest, Robert. 1973. *The Great Terror*. New York: Collier.

Dennis, Peggy. 1977. *The Autobiography of an American Communist*. Westport, Conn.: Lawrence Hill.

Draper, Theodore. 1966. *The Roots of American Communism*. New York: Viking.

—. 1968. *American Communism and Soviet Russia*. New York: Viking.

Foner, Philip. 1950. *The Fur and Leather Workers Union*. Newark, New Jersey: Nordan Press.

Foster, William. 1952. *The History of the Communist Party of the United States*. New York: International Publishers.

Fraser, Steve. 1984. 'From the "New Unionism" to the New Deal,' *Labor History*. Vol. 25:3 (Summer, 1984).

Gates, John. 1958. *The Story of an American Communist*. New York: Thomas Nelson.

Glaberman, Martin. 1980. *Wartime Strikes*. Detroit: Bewdick/Ed.

Goldfield, Michael. 1980a. 'The Decline of the Communist Party and the Black Question in the U.S.: Harry Haywood's *Black Bolshevik.*' *Review of Radical Political Economy*. 12:1 (Spring, 1980).

Goldfield, Michael and Rothenberg, Melvin. 1980b. *The Myth of Capitalism*

358

Reborn. San Francisco: Soviet Union Study Project.

Gross, James. 1981. *The Reshaping of the National Labor Relations Board.* Albany: State University of New York Press.

Hartz, Louis. 1955. *The Liberal Tradition in America.* New York: Harcourt, Brace, and World.

Haywood, Harry. 1978. *Black Bolshevik.* Chicago: Liberator Press.

Howe, Irving and Coser, Lewis. 1957. *The American Communist Party.* New York: Praeger.

Isserman, Maurice. 1982. *Which Side Were You On?* Middletown, Conn.: Wesleyan University Press.

Jaffe, Philip. 1975. *The Rise and Fall of American Communism.* New York: Horizon Press.

Keeran, Roger. 1980. *The Communist Party and the Auto Workers Union.* Bloomington, Indiana: Indiana University Press.

Klehr, Harvey. 1984 *The Heydey of American Communism.* New York: Basic Books.

Lichtenstein, Nelson. 1982. *Labor's War at Home.* London: Cambridge University Press.

Lipset, Seymour M. 1960. *Political Man.* New York: Doubleday.

Medvedev, Roy. 1971. *Let History Judge.* New York: Vintage.

Naison, Mark. 1983. *Communists in Harlem During the Depression.* Chicago: University of Illinois Press.

Ozanne, Robert. 1967. *A Century of Labor-Management Relations at McCormick and International Harvester.* Madison, Wisconsin: University of Wisconsin Press.

Perlman, Selig. 1949. *The Theory of the Labor Movement.* New York: Augustus M. Kelly.

Record, Wilson. 1971. *The Negro and the Communist Party.* New York: Atheneum.

Sombart, Werner. 1976. *Why is there no Socialism in the United States?* White Plains, NY: M.E. Sharp.

Spero, Sterling and Harris, Abram. 1931. *The Black Worker.* New York: Columbia University Press.

Starobin, Joseph. 1972. *American Communism in Crisis, 1943-1957.* Berkeley: University of California Press.

Sweezy, Paul, ed. 1975. Boehm-Bawerk's *Karl Marx and the Close of His System.* London: Merlin Press.

Trotsky, Leon. 1957. *The Third International After Lenin.* New York: Pioneer.

—. 1971. *The Struggle Against Fascism in Germany.* New York: Pathfinder.

—. 1973. *The Spanish Revolution (1936-1939).* New York: Pathfinder.